Risk Management
and
Financial Institutions

Also by John Hull:

Options, Futures, and Other Derivatives
Fundamentals of Futures and Options Markets

Risk Management
and
Financial Institutions

John Hull

Maple Financial Chair in Derivatives and Risk Management
Joseph L. Rotman School of Management
University of Toronto

PEARSON
Prentice
Hall

UPPER SADDLE RIVER, NJ 07458

Library of Congress Cataloging-in-Publication Data is on file

AVP/Executive Editor: David Alexander
Editorial Director: Jeff Shelstad
Editorial Assistant: Michael Dittamo
Media Project Manager: Nancy Welcher
AVP/ Executive Marketing Manager: Sharon Koch
Marketing Assistant: Patrick Barbera
Managing Editor (Production): Cynthia Regan
Production Editor: Melissa Feimer
Permissions Supervisor: Charles Morris
Manufacturing Buyer: Diane Peirano
Cover Design: Bruce Kenselaar
Cover Illustration/Photo: Getty Images Inc. – Photodisc
Composition: The Geometric Press

Credits and acknowledgments borrowed from other sources and reproduced, with permission, in this textbook appear on appropriate page within text.

Pearson Education LTD.
Pearson Education Singapore, Pte. Ltd
Pearson Education, Canada, Ltd
Pearson Education–Japan

Pearson Education Australia PTY, Limited
Pearson Education North Asia Ltd
Pearson Educacien de Mexico, S.A. de C.V.
Pearson Education Malaysia, Pte. Ltd

10 9 8 7 6 5 4 3 2
ISBN 0-13-239790-0

To
Michelle, Peter, and David

CONTENTS IN BRIEF

Contents

BUSINESS SNAPSHOTS

Preface

This book is based on an elective course entitled Financial Risk Management I have taught at University of Toronto for many years. The main focus of the book is on the risks faced by banks and other financial institutions, but much of the material presented is equally important to nonfinancial institutions. Like my popular text *Options, Futures, and Other Derivatives*, this book is designed to be useful to practitioners as well as college students.

The book is appropriate for elective courses in either risk management or the management of financial institutions. It is not necessary for students to take a course on options and futures markets prior to taking a course based on this book, but if they have taken such a course much of the material in the first four chapters will not need to be covered. Chapter 13 on credit derivatives and Chapter 17 on weather, energy, and insurance derivatives can be skipped if this material is covered elsewhere or is not considered appropriate. Chapter 18 on big losses and what we can learn from them is a great chapter for the last class of a course because it draws together many of the points made in earlier chapters.

The level of mathematical sophistication in the way material is presented has been managed carefully so that the book is accessible to as wide an audience as possible. For example, when covering copulas in Chapter 6, I present the intuition followed by a detailed numerical example; when covering maximum-likelihood methods in Chapter 5 and extreme value theory in Chapter 9, I provide numerical examples and enough details for readers to develop their own Excel spreadsheets. This is a book about risk management and so there is very relatively little material on the valuation of derivatives contracts. (This is the main focus of my other two books *Options, Futures, and Other Derivatives* and *Fundamentals of Futures and Options Markets*.) For reference, I have included at the end of the book appendices that summarize some of the key derivatives pricing formulas that are important to risk managers.

Slides

Several hundred PowerPoint slides can be downloaded from my website. Instructors who adopt the text are welcome to adapt the slides to meet their own needs.

Questions and Problems

End-of-chapter problems are divided into two groups: "Questions and Problems" and "Assignment Questions". Solutions to Questions and Problems are at the end of the book, while solutions to Assignment Questions are made available by the publishers to adopting instructors in the Instructors' Manual.

Acknowledgments

Many people have played a part in the production of this book. I have benefited from interactions with many academics and risk managers. I would like to thank the students in my MBA Financial Risk Management elective course who have made many suggestions as to how successive drafts of the material could be improved. I am particularly grateful to Ateet Agarwal, Ashok Rao, and Yoshit Rastogi who provided valuable research assistance as the book neared completion. Eddie Mizzi from The Geometric Press did an excellent job editing the final manuscript and handling the page composition.

Alan White, a colleague at the University of Toronto, deserves a special acknowledgment. Alan and I have been carrying out joint research and consulting in the area of derivatives and risk management for over twenty years. During that time we have spent countless hours discussing key issues. Many of the new ideas in this book, and many of the new ways used to explain old ideas, are as much Alan's as mine.

Special thanks are due to many people at Prentice Hall, particularly my editor David Alexander, for their enthusiasm, advice, and encouragement.

I welcome comments on the book from readers. My e-mail address is:

hull@rotman.utoronto.ca

John Hull
Joseph L. Rotman School of Management
University of Toronto

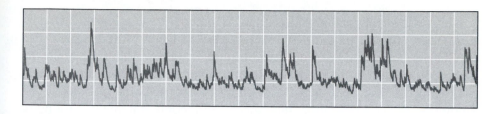

Introduction

1

Imagine you are the Chief Risk Officer of a major corporation. The CEO wants your views on a major new venture. You have been inundated with reports showing that the new venture has a positive net present value and will enhance shareholder value. What sort of analysis and ideas is the CEO looking for from you?

As Chief Risk Officer it is your job to consider how the new venture fits into the company's portfolio. What is the correlation of the performance of the new venture with the rest of the company's business? When the rest of the business is experiencing difficulties, will the new venture also provide poor returns—or will it have the effect of dampening the ups and downs in the rest of the business?

Companies must take risks if they are to survive and prosper. The risk management function's primary responsibility is to understand the portfolio of risks that the company is currently taking and the risks it plans to take in the future. It must decide whether the risks are acceptable and, if they are not acceptable, what action should be taken.

Most of this book is concerned with the ways risks are managed by banks and other financial institutions, but many of the ideas and approaches we will discuss are equally applicable to other types of corporations. Risk management is now recognized as a key activity for all corporations. Many of the disastrous losses of the 1990s, such as those at Orange County in 1994 and Barings Bank in 1995, would have been avoided if good risk management practices had been in place.

This opening chapter sets the scene. It starts by reviewing the classical arguments concerning the risk/return trade-offs faced by an investor who is choosing a portfolio of stocks and bonds. It then considers whether the same arguments can be used by a company in choosing new projects and managing its risk exposure. After that the focus shifts to banks. The chapter looks at a typical balance sheet and income statement for a bank and examines the key role of capital in cushioning the bank from adverse events. It takes a first look at the main approaches used by a bank in managing its risks and explains how a bank avoids fluctuations in net interest income.

1.1 RISK vs. RETURN FOR INVESTORS

As all fund managers know, there is a trade-off between risk and return when money is invested. The greater the risks taken, the higher the return that can be realized. The trade-off is actually between risk and *expected return*, not between risk and actual return. The term "expected return" sometimes causes confusion. In everyday language an outcome that is "expected" is considered likely to occur. However, statisticians define the expected value of a variable as its mean value. Expected return is therefore a weighted average of the possible returns where the weight applied to a particular return equals the probability of that return occurring.

Suppose, for example, that you have $100,000 to invest for one year. One alternative is to buy Treasury bills yielding 5% per annum. There is then no risk and the expected return is 5%. Another alternative is to invest the $100,000 in a stock. To simplify things a little, we suppose that the possible outcomes from this investment are as shown in Table 1.1. There is a 0.05 probability that the return will be +50%; there is a 0.25 probability that the return will be +30%; and so on. Expressing the

Table 1.1 Return in one year from investing $100,000 in equities.

Probability	Return
0.05	+50%
0.25	+30%
0.40	+10%
0.25	−10%
0.05	−30%

returns in decimal form, the expected return per year is

$$0.05 \times 0.50 + 0.25 \times 0.30 + 0.40 \times 0.10$$
$$+ 0.25 \times (-0.10) + 0.05 \times (-0.30) = 0.10$$

This shows that in return for taking some risk you are able to increase your expected return per annum from the 5% offered by Treasury bills to 10%. If things work out well, your return per annum could be as high as 50%. However, the worst-case outcome is a -30% return, or a loss of \$30,000.

One of the first attempts to understand the trade-off between risk and expected return was by Markowitz (1952). Later Sharpe (1964) and others carried the Markowitz analysis a stage further by developing what is known as the capital asset pricing model. This is a relationship between expected return and what is termed systematic risk. In 1976 Ross developed arbitrage pricing theory—an extension of the capital asset pricing model to the situation where there are several sources of systematic risk. The key insights of these researchers have had a profound effect on the way portfolio managers think about and analyze the risk/return trade-offs that they face. In this section we review these insights.

Quantifying Risk

How do you quantify the risk you take when choosing an investment? A convenient measure that is often used is the standard deviation of return over one year. This is

$$\sqrt{E(R^2) - [E(R)]^2}$$

where R is the return per annum. The symbol E denotes expected value, so that $E(R)$ is expected return per annum. In Table 1.1, as we have shown, $E(R) = 0.10$. To calculate $E(R^2)$, we must weight the alternative squared returns by their probabilities:

$$E(R^2) = 0.05 \times 0.50^2 + 0.25 \times 0.30^2 + 0.40 \times 0.10^2$$
$$+ 0.25 \times (-0.10)^2 + 0.05 \times (-0.30)^2 = 0.046$$

The standard deviation of returns is therefore $\sqrt{0.046 - 0.1^2} = 0.1897$, or 18.97%.

Investment Opportunities

Suppose we choose to characterize every investment opportunity by its expected return and standard deviation of return. We can plot available

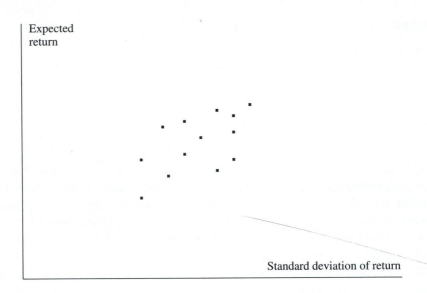

Figure 1.1   Alternative risky investments.

risky investments on a chart such as Figure 1.1, where the horizontal axis is the standard deviation of return and the vertical axis is the expected return.

Once we have identified the expected return and the standard deviation of return for individual investments, it is natural to think about what happens when we combine investments to form a portfolio. Consider two investments with returns R_1 and R_2. The return from putting a proportion w_1 of your money in the first investment and a proportion $w_2 = 1 - w_1$ in the second investment is

$$w_1 R_1 + w_2 R_2$$

The expected return of the portfolio is

$$\mu_P = w_1 \mu_1 + w_2 \mu_2 \tag{1.1}$$

where μ_1 is the expected return from the first investment and μ_2 is the expected return from the second investment. The standard deviation of the portfolio return is given by

$$\sigma_P = \sqrt{w_1^2 \sigma_1^2 + w_2^2 \sigma_2^2 + 2\rho w_1 w_2 \sigma_1 \sigma_2} \tag{1.2}$$

Table 1.2 Expected return, μ_P, and standard deviation of return, σ_P, from a portfolio consisting of two investments. The expected returns from the investments are 10% and 15%, the standard deviation of the returns are 16% and 24%, and the correlation between the returns is 0.2.

w_1	w_2	μ_P	σ_P
0.0	1.0	15%	24.00%
0.2	0.8	14%	20.09%
0.4	0.6	13%	16.89%
0.6	0.4	12%	14.87%
0.8	0.2	11%	14.54%
1.0	0.0	10%	16.00%

where σ_1 and σ_2 are the standard deviations of R_1 and R_2, and ρ is the coefficient of correlation between the two.

Suppose that μ_1 is 10% per annum and σ_1 is 16% per annum, while μ_2 is 15% per annum and σ_2 is 24% per annum. Suppose also that the coefficient of correlation, ρ, between the returns is 0.2 or 20%. Table 1.2

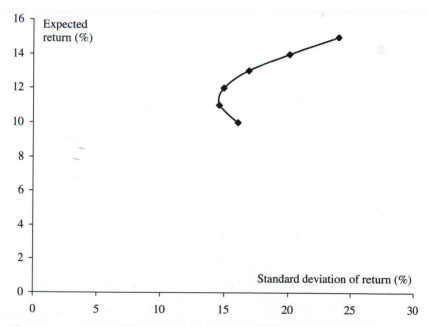

Figure 1.2 Alternative risk/return combinations from two investments as calculated in Table 1.2.

shows the values of μ_P and σ_P for a number of different values of w_1 and w_2. The calculations show that by putting part of your money in the first investment and part in the second investment a wide range of risk/return combinations can be achieved. These are plotted in Figure 1.2.

Most investors are risk-averse. They want to increase expected return while reducing the standard deviation of return. This means that they want to move as far as they can in a "north-west" direction in Figures 1.1 and 1.2. As we saw in Figure 1.2, forming a portfolio of the two investments that we considered helps them do this. For example, by putting 60% in the first investment and 40% in the second, a portfolio with an expected return of 12% and a standard deviation of return equal to 14.87% is obtained. This is an improvement over the risk/return trade-off for the first investment. (The expected return is 2% higher and the standard deviation of the return is 1.13% lower.)

Efficient Frontier

Let us now bring a third investment into our analysis. The third investment can be combined with any combination of the first two investments to produce new risk/return trade-offs. This enables us to move further in the north-west direction. We can then add a fourth investment. This can be combined with any combination of the first three investments to produce yet more investment opportunities. As we continue this process,

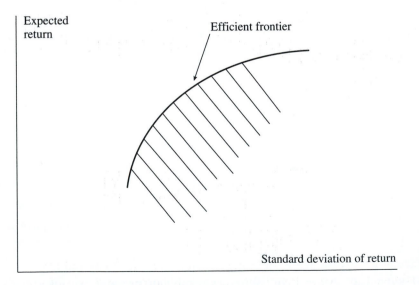

Figure 1.3   The efficient frontier of risky investments.

considering every possible portfolio of the available risky investments in Figure 1.1, we obtain what is known as an *efficient frontier*. This represents the limit of how far we can move in a north-west direction and is illustrated in Figure 1.3. There is no investment that dominates a point on the efficient frontier in the sense that it has both a higher expected return and a lower standard deviation of return. The shaded area in Figure 1.3 represents the set of all investments that are possible. For any point in the shaded area, we can find a point on the efficient frontier that has a better (or equally good) risk/return trade-off.

In Figure 1.3 we have considered only risky investments. What does the efficient frontier of all possible investments look like? To consider this, we first note that one available investment is the risk-free investment. Suppose that the risk-free investment yields a return of R_F. In Figure 1.4 we have denoted the risk-free investment by point F and drawn a tangent

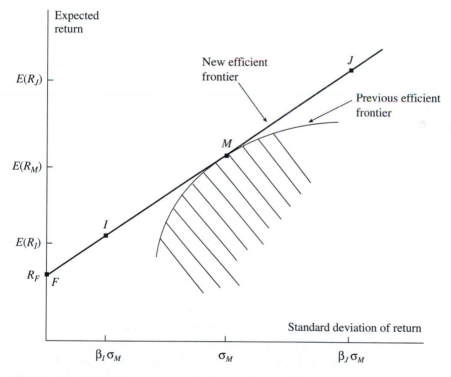

Figure 1.4 The efficient frontier of all investments. Point I is achieved by investing a percentage β_I of available funds in portfolio M and the rest in a risk-free investment. Point J is achieved by borrowing $\beta_J - 1$ of available funds at the risk-free rate and investing everything in portfolio M.

from point F to the efficient frontier of risky investments. M is the point of tangency. As we will now show, the line FM is our new efficient frontier.

Consider what happens when we form an investment I by putting β_I $(0 < \beta_I < 1)$ of the funds we have available for investment in the risky portfolio, M, and $1 - \beta_I$ in the risk-free investment, F. From equation (1.1) the expected return from the investment, $E(R_I)$, is given by

$$E(R_I) = (1 - \beta_I)R_F + \beta_I E(R_M)$$

and from equation (1.2) the standard deviation of this return is $\beta_I \sigma_M$, where σ_M is the standard deviation of returns for portfolio M. This risk/return combination corresponds to point labeled I in Figure 1.4. From the perspective of both expected return and standard deviation of return, point I is β_I of the way from F to M.

All points on the line FM can be obtained by choosing a suitable combination of the investment represented by point F and the investment represented by point M. The points on this line dominate all the points on the previous efficient frontier because they give a better risk/return trade-off. The straight line FM is therefore the new efficient frontier.

If we make the simplifying assumption that we can borrow at the risk-free rate of R_F as well as invest at that rate, we can create investments that are on the line from F to M but beyond M. Suppose, for example, that we want to create the investment represented by the point J in Figure 1.4, where the distance of J from F is β_J $(\beta_J > 1)$ times the distance of M from F. We borrow $\beta_J - 1$ of the amount that we have available for investment at rate R_F and then invest everything (the original funds and the borrowed funds) in the investment represented by point M. After allowing for the interest paid, the new investment has an expected return, $E(R_J)$, given by

$$E(R_J) = \beta_J E(R_M) - (\beta_J - 1)R_F$$

and the standard deviation of the return is $\beta_J \sigma_M$. This shows that the risk and expected return combination corresponds to point J.

The argument that we have presented shows that, when the risk-free investment is considered, the efficient frontier must be a straight line. To put this another way, there should be a linear trade-off between the expected return and the standard deviation of returns, as indicated in Figure 1.4. All investors should choose the same portfolio of risky assets. This is the portfolio represented by M. They should then reflect their appetite for risk by combining this risky investment with borrowing or lending at the risk-free rate.

It is a short step from here to argue that the portfolio of risky investments represented by M must be the portfolio of all risky investments. How else could it be possible that all investors hold the portfolio? The amount of a particular risky investment in portfolio M must be proportional to the amount of that investment available in the economy. The investment M is usually referred to as the *market portfolio*.

Systematic vs. Nonsystematic Risk

How do investors decide on the expected returns they require for individual investments? Based on the analysis we have presented, the market portfolio should play a key role. The expected return required on an investment should reflect the extent to which the investment contributes to the risks of the market portfolio.

A common procedure is to use historical data to determine a best-fit linear relationship between returns from an investment and returns from the market portfolio. This relationship has the form

$$R = \alpha + \beta R_M + \epsilon \tag{1.3}$$

where R is the return from the investment, R_M is the return from the market portfolio, α and β are constants, and ϵ is a random variable equal to the regression error.

Equation (1.3) shows that there are two components to the risk in the investment's return:

1. A component βR_M, which is a multiple of the return from the market portfolio

2. A component ϵ, which is unrelated to the return from the market portfolio

The first component is referred to as *systematic risk*; the second component is referred to as *nonsystematic risk*.

Consider first the nonsystematic risk. If we assume that the ϵ's for different investments are independent of each other, the nonsystematic risk is almost completely diversified away in a large portfolio. An investor should not therefore be concerned about nonsystematic risk and should not require an extra return above the risk-free rate for bearing nonsystematic risk.

The systematic risk component is what should matter to an investor.

When a large well-diversified portfolio is held, the systematic risk represented by βR_M does not disappear. An investor should require an
expected return to compensate for this systematic risk.

We know how investors trade off systematic risk and expected return
from Figure 1.4. When $\beta = 0$, there is no systematic risk and the expected
return is R_F. When $\beta = 1$, we have the same systematic risk as point M
and the expected return should be $E(R_M)$. In general,

$$E(R) = R_F + \beta[E(R_M) - R_F] \qquad (1.4)$$

This is the capital asset pricing model. The excess expected return over the
risk-free rate required on the investment is β times the excess expected
return on the market portfolio. This relationship is plotted in Figure 1.5.
Suppose that the risk-free rate is 5% and the return on the market portfolio
is 10%. An investment with a β of 0 should have an expected return of 5%;
an investment with a β of 0.5 should have an expected return of 7.5%; an
investment with a β of 1.0 should have an expected return of 10%;
and so on.

The variable β is the *beta* of the investment. It is equal to $\rho\sigma/\sigma_M$, where
ρ is the correlation between the return from the investment and the return
from the market portfolio, σ is the standard deviation of the return from
the investment, and σ_M is the standard deviation of the return from the

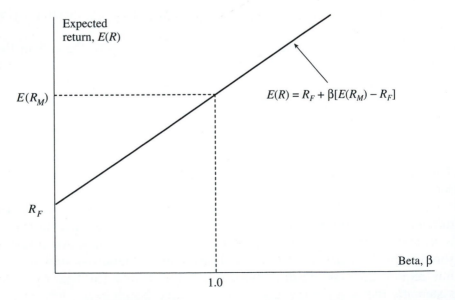

Figure 1.5   The capital asset pricing model.

market portfolio. Beta measures the sensitivity of the return from the investment to the return from the market portfolio. We can define the beta of any investment portfolio in a similar way to equation (1.3). The capital asset pricing model in equation (1.4) should then apply with the return R defined as the return from the portfolio.

In Figure 1.4 the market portfolio represented by M has a beta of 1.0 and the riskless portfolio represented by F has a beta of zero. The portfolios represented by the points I and J have betas equal to β_I and β_J, respectively.

Assumptions

The analysis we have presented makes a number of simplifying assumptions. In particular, it assumes:

1. Investors care only about the expected return and the standard deviation of return
2. The ϵ's for different investments in equation (1.3) are independent
3. Investors focus on returns over just one period and the length of this period is the same for all investors
4. Investors can borrow and lend at the same risk-free rate
5. There are no tax considerations
6. All investors make the same estimates of expected returns, standard deviations of returns, and correlations for available investments

These assumptions are of course not exactly true. Investors have complex sets of risk preferences that involve more than just the first two moments of the return distribution. The one-factor model in equation (1.3) assumes that the correlation between the returns from two investments arises only from their correlations with the market portfolio. This is clearly not true for two investments in the same sector of the economy. Investors have different time horizons. They cannot borrow and lend at the same rate. Taxes do influence the portfolios that investors choose and investors do not have homogeneous expectations. (Indeed, if the assumptions of the capital asset pricing model held exactly, there would be very little trading.)

In spite of all this, the capital asset pricing model has proved to be a useful tool for portfolio managers. Estimates of the betas of stocks are readily available and the expected return on a portfolio estimated by the capital asset pricing model is a commonly used benchmark for assessing the performance of the portfolio manager.

Arbitrage Pricing Theory

A more general analysis that moves us away from the first two assumptions listed above is *arbitrage pricing theory*. The return from an investment is assumed to depend on several factors. By exploring ways in which investors can form portfolios that eliminate their exposure to the factors, arbitrage pricing theory shows that the expected return from an investment is linearly dependent on the factors.

The assumption that the ϵ's for different investments are independent in equation (1.3) ensures that there is just one factor driving expected returns (and therefore one source of systematic risk) in the capital asset pricing model. This is the return from the market portfolio. In arbitrage pricing theory there are several factors affecting investment returns. Each factor is a separate source of systematic risk. Unsystematic risk is the risk that is unrelated to all the factors and can be diversified away.

1.2 RISK vs. RETURN FOR COMPANIES

We now move on to consider the trade-offs between risk and return made by a company. How should a company decide whether the expected return on a new investment project is sufficient compensation for its risks?

The ultimate owners of a company are its shareholders and a company should be managed in the best interests of its shareholders. It is therefore natural to argue that a new project undertaken by the company should be viewed as an addition to its shareholder's portfolio. The company should calculate the beta of the investment project and its expected return. If the expected return is greater than that given by the capital asset pricing model, it is a good deal for shareholders and the investment should be accepted. Otherwise it should be rejected. The argument suggests that nonsystematic risks should not be considered in the accept/reject decision.

In practice, companies are concerned about nonsystematic as well as systematic risks. For example, most companies insure themselves against the risk of their buildings being burned down—even though this risk is entirely nonsystematic and can be diversified away by their shareholders. They try to avoid taking high risks and often hedge their exposures to exchange rates, interest rates, commodity prices, and other market variables. Earnings stability and the survival of the company are important managerial objectives. Companies do try and ensure that the expected returns on new ventures are consistent with the risk/return trade-offs of their shareholders. But there is an overriding constraint that the risks taken should not be allowed to get too large.

Most investors are also concerned about the overall risk of the companies they invest in. They do not like surprises and prefer to invest in companies that show solid growth and meet earnings forecasts. They like companies to manage risks carefully and limit the overall amount of risk—both systematic and nonsystematic—they are taking.

The theoretical arguments we presented in Section 1.1 suggest that investors should not behave in this way. They should encourage companies to make high-risk investments when the trade-off between expected return and systematic risk is favorable. Some of the companies in a shareholder's portfolio will go bankrupt, but others will do very well. The result should be an overall return to the shareholder that is satisfactory.

Are investors behaving suboptimally? Would their interests be better served if companies took more nonsystematic risks because investors are in a position to diversify away these risks? There is an important argument to suggest that this is not necessarily the case. This argument is usually referred to as the "bankruptcy costs" argument. It is often used to explain why a company should restrict the amount of debt it takes on, but it can be extended to apply to all risks.

Bankruptcy Costs

In a perfect world, bankruptcy would be a fast affair where the company's assets (tangible and intangible) are sold at their fair market value and the proceeds distributed to bondholders, shareholders, and other stakeholders using well-defined rules. If we lived in such a perfect world, the bankruptcy process itself would not destroy value for shareholders. Unfortunately the real world is far from perfect. The bankruptcy process leads to what are known as bankruptcy costs.

What is the nature of bankruptcy costs? Once a bankruptcy has been announced, customers and suppliers become less inclined to do business with the company; assets sometimes have to be sold quickly at prices well below those that would be realized in an orderly sale; the value of important intangible assets such as the company's brand name and its reputation in the market are often destroyed; the company is no longer run in the best interests of shareholders; large fees are often paid to accountants and lawyers; and so on. Business Snapshot 1.1 is a fictitious story, but all too representative of what happens in practice. It illustrates

---

Business Snapshot 1.1   The Hidden Costs of Bankruptcy

Several years ago a company had a market capitalization of $2 billion and $500 million of debt. The CEO decided to acquire a company in a related industry for $1 billion in cash. The cash was raised using a mixture of bank debt and bond issues. The price paid for the company was close to its market value and therefore presumably reflected the market's assessment of the company's expected return and its systematic risk at the time of the acquisition.

Many of the anticipated synergies used to justify the acquisition were not realized. Furthermore the company that was acquired was not profitable. After three years the CEO resigned. The new CEO sold the acquisition for $100 million (10% of the price paid) and announced the company would focus on its original core business. However, by then the company was highly levered. A temporary economic downturn made it impossible for the company to service its debt and it declared bankruptcy.

The offices of the company were soon filled with accountants and lawyers representing the interests of the various parties (banks, different categories of bondholders, equity holders, the company, and the board of directors). These people directly or indirectly billed the company about $10 million per month in fees. The company lost sales that it would normally have made because nobody wanted to do business with a bankrupt company. Key senior executives left. The company experienced a dramatic reduction in its market share.

After two years and three reorganization attempts, an agreement was reached between the various parties and a new company with a market capitalization of $700,000 was incorporated to continue the remaining profitable parts of the business. The shares in the new company were entirely owned by the banks and the bondholders. The shareholders got nothing.

---

how, when a high-risk decision works out badly, there can be disastrous bankruptcy costs.

We mentioned earlier that corporate survival is an important managerial objective and that shareholders like companies to avoid excessive risks. We now understand why this is so. Bankruptcy laws vary widely from country to country, but they all have the effect of destroying value as lenders and other creditors vie with each other to get paid. This value has often been painstakingly built up by the company over many years. It makes sense for a company that is operating in the best interests of its shareholders to limit the probability of this value destruction occurring. It does this by limiting the total risk (systematic and nonsystematic) that it takes.

When a major new investment is being contemplated, it is important to consider how well it fits in with other risks taken by the company. Relatively small investments can often have the effect of reducing the overall risks taken by a company. However, a large investment can dramatically increase these risks. Many spectacular corporate failures (such as the one in Business Snapshot 1.1) can be traced to CEOs who made large acquisitions (often highly levered) that did not work out.

1.3 BANK CAPITAL

We now switch our attention to banks. Banks face the same types of bankruptcy costs as other companies and have an incentive to manage their risks (systematic and nonsystematic) prudently so that the probability of bankruptcy is minimal. Indeed, as we shall see in Chapter 7, governments regulate banks in an attempt to ensure that they do exactly this. In this section we take a first look at the nature of the risks faced by a bank and discuss the amount of capital banks need.

Consider a hypothetical bank DLC (Deposits and Loans Corporation). DLC is primarily engaged in the traditional banking activities of taking deposits and making loans. A summary balance sheet for DLC at the end of 2006 is shown in Table 1.3 and a summary income statement for 2006 is shown in Table 1.4.

Table 1.3 shows that the bank has $100 billion of assets. Most of the assets (80% of the total) are loans made by the bank to private individuals and corporations. Cash and marketable securities account for a further 15% of the assets. The remaining 5% of the assets are fixed assets (i.e., buildings, equipment, etc.). A total of 90% of the funding for the assets comes from deposits of one sort or another from the bank's customers and counterparties. A further 5% is financed by subordinated long-term debt

Table 1.3 Summary balance sheet for DLC at end of 2006 ($ billions).

Assets		Liabilities and net worth	
Cash	5	Deposits	90
Marketable securities	10	Subordinated long-term debt	5
Loans	80	Equity capital	5
Fixed assets	5		
Total	100	Total	100

Table 1.4   Summary income statement for DLC in 2006 ($ billions).

Net interest income	3.00
Loan losses	(0.80)
Noninterest income	0.90
Noninterest expense	(2.50)
Pre-tax operating income	0.60

(i.e., bonds issued by the bank to investors that rank below deposits in the event of a liquidation) and the remaining 5% is financed by the bank's shareholders in the form of equity capital. The equity capital consists of the original cash investment of the shareholders and earnings retained in the bank.

Consider next the income statement for 2006 shown in Table 1.4. The first item on the income statement is net interest income. This is the excess of the interest earned over the interest paid and is 3% of assets in our example. It is important for the bank to be managed so that net interest income remains roughly constant regardless of the level of interest rates. We will discuss this in more detail in Section 1.5.

The next item is loan losses. This is 0.8% of assets for the year in question. Even if a bank maintains a tight control over its lending policies, this will tend to fluctuate from year to year. In some years default rates in the economy are high; in others they are quite low.[1] The management and quantification of the credit risks it takes is clearly of critical importance to a bank. This will be discussed in Chapters 11, 12, and 13.

The next item, noninterest income, consists of income from all the activities of a bank other than lending money. This includes trading activities, fees for arranging debt or equity financing for corporations, and fees for the many other services the bank provides for its retail and corporate clients. In the case of DLC, noninterest income is 0.9% of assets. This must be managed carefully. In particular, the market risks associated with trading activities must be quantified and controlled. Market risk management procedures are discussed in Chapters 3, 8, 9, and 10.

The final item is noninterest expense and is 2.5% of assets in our

---

[1] Evidence for this can be found by looking at Moody's statistics on the default rates on bonds between 1970 and 2003. This ranged from a low of 0.09% in 1979 to a high of 3.81% in 2001.

example. This consists of all expenses other than interest paid. It includes salaries, technology-related costs, and other overheads. As in the case of all large businesses, these have a tendency to increase over time unless they are managed carefully. Banks must try and avoid large losses from litigation, business disruption, employee fraud, etc. The risk associated with these types of losses is known as *operational risk* and will be discussed in Chapter 14.

Capital Adequacy

Is the equity capital of 5% of assets in Table 1.3 adequate? One way of answering this is to consider an extreme scenario and determine whether the bank will survive. Suppose that there is a severe recession and as a result the bank's loan losses rise to 4% next year. We assume that other items on the income statement are unaffected. The result will be a pre-tax net operating loss of 2.6% of assets. Assuming a tax rate of 30%, this would result in an after-tax loss of about 1.8% of assets.

In Table 1.3 equity capital is 5% of assets and so an after-tax loss equal to 1.8% of assets, although not at all welcome, can be absorbed. It would result in a reduction of the equity capital to 3.2% of assets. Even a second bad year similar to the first would not totally wipe out the equity.

Suppose now that the bank has the more aggressive capital structure shown in Table 1.5. Everything is the same as Table 1.3 except that equity capital is 1% (rather than 5%) of assets and deposits are 94% (rather than 90%) of assets. In this case one year where the loan losses are 4% of assets would totally wipe out equity capital and the bank would find itself in serious financial difficulties. It would no doubt try to raise additional equity capital, but it is likely to find this almost impossible in such a weak financial position.

Table 1.5 Alternative balance sheet for DLC at end of 2006 with equity only 1% of assets (billions).

Assets		Liabilities and net worth	
Cash	5	Deposits	94
Marketable securities	10	Subordinated long-term debt	5
Loans	80	Equity capital	1
Fixed assets	5		
Total	100	Total	100

It is quite likely that there would be a run on deposits and the bank would be forced into liquidation. If all assets could be liquidated for book value (a big assumption), the long-term debtholders would likely receive about $4.2 billion rather than $5 billion (they would in effect absorb the negative equity) and the depositors would be repaid in full.

Note that equity and subordinated long-term debt are both sources of capital. Equity provides the best protection against adverse events. (In our example, when the bank has $5 billion of equity capital rather than $1 billion, it stays solvent and is unlikely to be liquidated.) Subordinated long-term debt holders rank below depositors in the event of a default. However, subordinated long-term debt does not provide as good a cushion for the bank as equity. As our example shows, it does not necessarily prevent the bank's liquidation.

As we shall see in Chapter 7, bank regulators have been active in ensuring that the capital a bank keeps is sufficient to cover the risks it takes. Regulators consider the market risks from trading activities as well as the credit risks from lending activities. They are moving toward an explicit consideration of operational risks. Regulators define different types of capital and prescribe levels for them. In our example DLC's equity capital is Tier 1 capital; subordinated long-term debt is Tier 2 capital.

1.4 APPROACHES TO MANAGING RISKS

Since a bank's equity capital is typically very low in relation to the assets on the balance sheet, a bank must manage its affairs conservatively to avoid large fluctuations in its earnings. There are two broad risk management strategies open to the bank (or any other organization). One approach is to identify risks one by one and handle each one separately. This is sometimes referred to as *risk decomposition*. The other is to reduce risks by being well diversified. This is sometimes referred to as *risk aggregation*. In practice, banks use both approaches when they manage market and credit risks as we will now explain.

Market Risks

Market risks arise primarily from the bank's trading activities. A bank has exposure to interest rates, exchange rates, equity prices, commodity prices, and the market variables. These risks are in the first instance managed by the traders. For example, there is likely to be one trader (or a group of traders) working for a US bank who is responsible for the dollar/yen exchange rate risk. At the end of each day the trader is required to ensure that risk limits specified by the bank are not exceeded. If the end of the day is approached and one or more of the risk limits is exceeded, the trader must execute new hedging trades so that the limits are adhered to.

The risk managers working for the bank then aggregate the residual market risks from the activities of all traders to determine the total risk faced by the bank from movements in market variables. Hopefully the bank is well diversified, so that its overall exposure to market movements is fairly small. If risks are unacceptably high, the reasons must be determined and corrective action taken.

Credit Risks

Credit risks are traditionally managed by ensuring that the credit portfolio is well diversified (risk aggregation). If a bank lends all its available funds to a single borrower, then it is totally undiversified and subject to huge risks. If the borrowing entity runs into financial difficulties and is unable to make its interest and principal payments, the bank will become insolvent.

If the bank adopts a more diversified strategy of lending 0.01% of its available funds to each of 10,000 different borrowers, then it is in a much safer position. Suppose that in a typical year the probability of any one borrower defaulting is 1%. We can expect that close to 100 borrowers will default in the year and the losses on these borrowers will be more than offset by the profits earned on the 99% of loans that perform well.

Diversification reduces nonsystematic risk. It does not eliminate systematic risk. The bank faces the risk that there will be an economic downturn and a resulting increase in the probability of default by borrowers. To maximize the benefits of diversification, borrowers should be in different geographical regions and different industries. A large international bank with different types of borrowers all over the world is likely to be much better diversified than a small bank in Texas that lends entirely to oil companies. However, there will always be some systematic risks that cannot be diversified away. For example, diversification does not protect a bank against world economic downturns.

Since the late 1990s we have seen the emergence of an active market for credit derivatives. Credit derivatives allow banks to handle credit risks one by one (risk decomposition) rather than relying solely on risk diversification. They also allow banks to buy protection against the overall level of defaults in the economy. We discuss credit derivatives in Chapter 13.

1.5 THE MANAGEMENT OF NET INTEREST INCOME

As mentioned earlier net interest income is the excess of interest received over interest paid. It is the role of the asset/liability management function to ensure that fluctuations in net interest income are minimal. In this section we explain how it does this.

To illustrate how fluctuations in net interest income could occur, consider a simple situation where a bank offers consumers a one-year and a five-year deposit rate as well as a one-year and five-year mortgage rate. The rates are shown in Table 1.6. We make the simplifying assumption that market participants expect the one-year interest rate for future time periods to equal the one-year rates prevailing in the market today. Loosely speaking, this means that the market considers interest rate increases to be just as likely as interest rate decreases. As a result the rates in Table 1.6 are "fair", in that they reflect the market's expectations. Investing money for one year and reinvesting for four further one-year periods gives the same expected overall return as a single five-year investment. Similarly, borrowing money for one year and refinancing each year for the next four years leads to the same expected financing costs as a single five-year loan.

Now suppose you have money to deposit and agree with the prevailing view that interest rate increases are just as likely as interest rate decreases. Would you choose to deposit your money for one year at 3% per annum or for five years at 3% per annum? The chances are that you would choose one year because this gives you more financial flexibility. It ties up your funds for a shorter period of time.

Table 1.6   Example of rates offered by a bank to its customers.

Maturity (years)	Deposit rate	Mortgage rate
1	3%	6%
5	3%	6%

Now suppose that you want a mortgage. Again you agree with the prevailing view that interest rate increases are just as likely as interest rate decreases. Would you choose a one-year mortgage at 6% or a five-year mortgage at 6%? The chances are that you would choose a five-year mortgage because it fixes your borrowing rate for the next five years and subjects you to less refinancing risk.

When the bank posts the rates shown in Table 1.6, it is likely to find that the majority of its depositors opt for one-year maturities and the majority of its customers seeking mortgages opt for five-year maturities. This creates an asset/liability mismatch for the bank and subjects its net interest income to risks. There is no problem if interest rates fall. The bank will find itself financing the five-year 6% mortgages with deposits that cost less than 3% and net interest income will increase. However, if rates rise, the deposits that are financing these 6% mortgages will cost more than 3% and net interest income will decline. A 3% rise in interest rates would reduce the net interest income to zero.

It is the job of the asset/liability management group to ensure that the maturities of the assets on which interest is earned and the maturities of the liabilities on which interest is paid are matched. One way to do this in our example is to increase the five-year rate on both deposits and mortgages. For example, we could move to the situation in Table 1.7 where the five-year deposit rate is 4% and the five-year mortgage rate 7%. This would make five-year deposits relatively more attractive and one-year mortgages relatively more attractive. Some customers who chose one-year deposits when the rates were as in Table 1.6 will switch to five-year deposits when rates are as in Table 1.7. Some customers who chose five-year mortgages when the rates were as in Table 1.6 will choose one-year mortgages. This may lead to the maturities of assets and liabilities being matched. If there is still an imbalance with depositors tending to choose a one-year maturity and borrowers a five-year maturity, five-year deposit and mortgage rates could be increased even further. Eventually the imbalance will disappear.

The net result of all banks behaving in the way we have just described is

Table 1.7   Five-year rates are increased in an attempt to match maturities of assets and liabilities.

Maturity (years)	Deposit rate	Mortgage rate
1	3%	6%
5	4%	7%

Business Snapshot 1.2   Expensive Failures of Financial Institutions in the US

Throughout the 1960s, 1970s, and 1980s, Savings and Loans (S&Ls) in the United States failed to manage interest rate risk well. They tended to take short-term deposits and make long-term fixed-rate mortgages. As a result they were seriously hurt by interest rate increases in 1966, 1969–70, 1974, and the killer in 1979–82. S&Ls were protected by government guarantees. Over 1,700 failed in the 1980s. A major reason for the failures was their inadequate interest rate risk management. The total cost to the US taxpayer of the failures has been estimated to be between $100 and $500 billion.

The largest bank failure in the US, Contintental Illinois, can also be attributed to a failure to manage interest rate risks well. During the period 1980 to 1983 its assets (i.e., loans) with maturities over a year totaled between $7 billion and $8 billion, whereas its liabilities (i.e., deposits) with maturities over a year were between $1.4 billion and $2.5 billion. Continental failed in 1984 and was the subject of an expensive government bailout.

---

that long-term rates tend to be higher than those predicted by expected future short-term rates. This phenomenon is referred to as *liquidity preference theory*. It leads to long-term rates being higher than short-term rates most of the time. Even when the market expects a small decline in short-term rates, liquidity preference theory is likely to cause long-term rates to be higher than short-term rates.

Many banks now have sophisticated systems for monitoring the decisions being made by customers so that, when they detect small differences between the maturities of the assets and liabilities being chosen, they can fine-tune the rates they offer. Sometimes derivatives such as interest rate swaps are also used to manage their exposure. The result is that net interest income is very stable and does not lead to significant risks. However, as indicated in Business Snapshot 1.2, this has not always been the case.

SUMMARY

An important general principle in finance is that there is a trade-off between risk and return. Higher expected returns can usually be achieved only by taking higher risks. Investors should not, in theory, be concerned with risks they can diversify away. The extra return they demand should be for the amount of nondiversifiable systematic risk they are bearing.

For companies, investment decisions are more complicated. Companies are not in general as well diversified as investors and survival is an important and legitimate objective. Both financing and investment decisions should be taken so that the possibility of financial distress is low.

This is because financial distress leads to what are known as bankruptcy costs. These costs arise from the nature of the bankruptcy process and almost invariably lead to a reduction in shareholder value over and above the reduction that took place as a result of the adverse events leading to bankruptcy.

Banks must manage the risks they face carefully. Equity capital is typically about 5% of assets and profit before taxes is often less than 1% of assets. Large trading losses, an economic downturn leading to a sharp rise in loan losses, or other unexpected events can lead to an erosion of equity capital and put the bank in a precarious position. Regulators have become increasingly active in ensuring that the capital a bank keeps is commensurate with the risks it takes.

Two general approaches to risk management are risk decomposition and risk aggregation. Risk decomposition involves managing risks one by one. Risk aggregation involves relying on the power of diversification to reduce risks. Banks use both approaches to manage market risks. Credit risks have traditionally been managed using risk aggregation, but with the advent of credit derivatives the risk decomposition approach can be used.

A bank's net interest income is the excess of the interest earned over the interest paid. There are now well established asset/liability management procedures to ensure that this remains roughly constant from year to year. These involve adjusting the rates offered to customers to ensure that the maturities of assets and liabilities are matched.

FURTHER READING

Markowitz, H. "Portfolio Selection," *Journal of Finance*, 7, 1 (March 1952), 77–91.

Ross, S. "The Arbitrage Theory of Capital Asset Pricing," *Journal of Economic Theory*, 13 (December 1976), 343–362.

Sharpe, W. "Capital Asset Prices: A Theory of Market Equilibrium," *Journal of Finance*, September 1964, 425–442.

Smith, C. W., and R. M. Stulz, "The Determinants of a Firm's Hedging Policy," *Journal of Financial and Quantitative Analysis*, 20 (1985), 391–406.

Stulz, R. M., *Risk Management and Derivatives*. Southwestern, 2003.

QUESTIONS AND PROBLEMS (Answers at End of Book)

1.1. An investment has probabilities 0.1, 0.2, 0.35, 0.25, and 0.1 of giving returns equal to 40%, 30%, 15%, −5% and −15%. What is the expected return and the standard deviation of returns?

1.2. Suppose that there are two investments with the same probability distribution of returns as in Problem 1.1. The correlation between the returns is 0.15. What is the expected return and standard deviation of return from a portfolio where money is divided equally between the investments.

1.3. For the two investments considered in Figure 1.2 and Table 1.2, what are the alternative risk/return combinations if the correlation is (a) 0.3, (b) 1.0, and (c) −1.0.

1.4. What is the difference between systematic and nonsystematic risk? Which is more important to an equity investor? Which can lead to the bankruptcy of a corporation?

1.5. Outline the arguments leading to the conclusion that all investors should choose the same portfolio of risky investments. What are the key assumptions?

1.6. The expected return on the market portfolio is 12% and the risk-free rate is 6%. What is the expected return on an investment with a beta of (a) 0.2, (b) 0.5, and (c) 1.4?

1.7. "Arbitrage pricing theory is an extension of the capital asset pricing model." Explain this statement.

1.8. "The capital structure decision of a company is a trade-off between bankruptcy costs and the tax advantages of debt." Explain this statement.

1.9. A bank's operational risk is the risk of large losses because of employee fraud, natural disasters, litigation, etc. It will be discussed in Chapter 14. Is operational risk best handled by risk decomposition or risk aggregation.

1.10. A bank's profit next year will be normally distributed with a mean of 0.6% of assets and a standard deviation of 1.5% of assets. The bank's equity is 4% of assets. What is the probability that the bank will have a positive equity at the end of the year? Ignore taxes.

1.11. Why do you think that banks are regulated to ensure that they do not take too much risk but most other companies (e.g., those in manufacturing and retailing) are not?

1.12. Explain carefully the risks faced by Continental Illinois in the 1980 to 1983 period based on the data in Business Snapshot 1.2.

1.13. Explain carefully why interest rate risks contributed to the expensive S&L failures in the United States.

1.14. Suppose that a bank has $5 billion of one-year loans and $20 billion of five-year loans. These are financed by $15 billion of one-year deposits and $10 billion of five-year deposits. Explain the impact on the bank's net interest income of interest rates increasing by 1% every year for the next three years.

1.15. List the bankruptcy costs incurred by the company in Business Snapshot 1.1.

ASSIGNMENT QUESTIONS

1.16. Suppose that one investment has a mean return of 8% and a standard deviation of return of 14%. Another investment has a mean return of 12% and a standard deviation of return of 20%. The correlation between the returns is 0.3. Produce a chart similar to Figure 1.2 showing alternative risk/return combinations from the two investments.

1.17. Which items on a DLC's income statement in Table 1.4 are most likely to be affected by (a) credit risk, (b) market risk, and (c) operational risk.

1.18. A bank estimates that its profit next year is normally distributed with a mean of 0.8% of assets and the standard deviation of 2% of assets. How much equity (as a percent of assets) does the company need to be (a) 99% and (b) 99.9% sure that it will have positive equity at the end of the year. Ignore taxes.

1.19. Suppose that a bank has $10 billion of one-year loans and $30 billion of five-year loans. These are financed by $35 billion of one-year deposits and $5 billion of five-year deposits. The bank has equity totaling $2 billion and its return on equity is currently 12%. Estimate what change in the interest rates next year would lead to the bank's return on equity being reduced to zero. Assume that the bank is subject to a tax rate of 30%.

1.20. Explain why long-term rates are higher than short-term rates most of the time. Under what circumstances would you expect long-term rates to be lower than short-term rates?

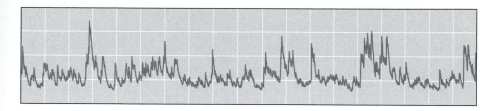

CHAPTER **2** **Financial Products and How They Are Used for Hedging**

Companies trade a variety of financial instruments to manage their risks. Some of these instruments are referred to as standard or "plain vanilla" products. Most forward contracts, futures contracts, swaps, and options fall into this category. Others are designed to meet the particular needs of a corporate treasurer. These are referred to as "exotics" or structured products. This chapter describes the instruments and how they trade. It discusses the circumstances when a company should hedge, how much hedging it should do, and what instruments should be used.

2.1 THE MARKETS

There are two types of markets in which financial instruments trade. These are known as the *exchange-traded* market and the *over-the-counter* (or OTC) market.

Exchange-Traded Markets

Exchanges have been used to trade financial products for many years. Some exchanges such as the New York Stock Exchange (NYSE) focus on the trading of stocks. Others such as the Chicago Board of Trade (CBOT) and the Chicago Board Options Exchange (CBOE) are concerned with the trading of derivatives such as futures and options.

The role of the exchange is to define the contracts that trade and organize trading so that market participants can be sure that the trades they agree to will be honored. Traditionally individuals have met at the exchange and agreed on the prices for trades, often by using an elaborate system of hand signals. Exchanges are increasingly moving to *electronic trading*. This involves traders entering their desired trades at a keyboard and a computer being used to match buyers and sellers. Not everyone agrees that the shift to electronic trading is desirable. Electronic trading is less physically demanding than traditional floor trading. However, traders do not have the opportunity to attempt to predict short-term market trends from the behavior and body language of other traders.

Sometimes trading is facilitated with market makers. These are individuals who are always prepared to quote both a bid price (the price at which they are prepared to buy) and an offer price (the price at which they are prepared to sell). Typically the exchange will specify an upper bound for the spread between a market maker's bid and offer prices.

Over-the-Counter Markets

The over-the-counter market is an important alternative to exchanges. It is a telephone- and computer-linked network of traders who work for financial institutions, large corporations, or fund managers. Financial institutions often act as market makers for the more commonly traded instruments.

Telephone conversations in the over-the-counter market are usually taped. If there is a dispute over what was agreed, the tapes are replayed to resolve the issue. Trades in the over-the-counter market are typically much larger than trades in the exchange-traded market. A key advantage of the over-the-counter market is that the terms of a contract do not have to be those specified by an exchange. Market participants are free to negotiate any mutually attractive deal. A disadvantage is that there is usually some credit risk in an over-the-counter trade (i.e., there is a small risk that the contract will not be honored). Exchanges have organized themselves to eliminate virtually all credit risk.

2.2 WHEN TO HEDGE

Most nonfinancial companies have no particular skills or expertise in predicting variables such as interest rates, exchange rates, and commodity prices. It makes sense for them to hedge the risks associated with these variables as they arise. The companies can then focus on their main activities. By hedging, they avoid unpleasant surprises such as a foreign exchange loss or a sharp rise in the price of a commodity that has to be purchased.

It can be argued that companies need not hedge because the company's shareholders can implement their own hedging programs, deciding which of the company's risks to keep and which to get rid of. However this assumes—unrealistically—that a company's shareholders have as much information about the risks faced by the company as the company's management. It also ignores the bankruptcy costs arguments in Section 1.2.

Hedging and Competitors

It is not always correct for a company to choose to hedge. If hedging is not the norm in a certain industry, it can be dangerous for one company to choose to be different from all others. Competitive pressures within the industry may be such that the prices of the goods and services produced by the industry fluctuate to reflect raw material costs, interest rates, exchange rates, and so on. A company that does not hedge can expect its profit margins to be roughly constant. However, a company that does hedge can expect its profit margins to fluctuate!

To illustrate this point, consider two manufacturers of gold jewelry, SafeandSure Company and TakeaChance Company. We assume that most companies in the industry do not hedge against movements in the price of gold and that TakeaChance Company is no exception. However, SafeandSure Company has decided to be different from its competitors and to use futures contracts to lock in the price it will pay for gold over the next 18 months.

If the price of gold goes up, economic pressures will tend to lead to a corresponding increase in the wholesale price of the jewelry, so that TakeaChance Company's profit margin is unaffected. By contrast, SafeandSure Company's profit margin will increase after the effects of the hedge have been taken into account. If the price of gold goes down, economic pressures will tend to lead to a corresponding decrease in the wholesale price of the jewelry. Again, TakeaChance Company's profit margin is unaffected. However, SafeandSure Company's profit margin goes down. In extreme conditions, SafeandSure Company's profit margin could become negative as a result of the "hedging" carried out! This example is summarized in Table 2.1.

Table 2.1   Danger in hedging when competitors do not.

Change in gold price	Effect on price of gold jewelry	Effect on profits of TakeaChance Co.	Effect on profits of SafeandSure Co.
Increase	Increase	None	Increase
Decrease	Decrease	None	Decrease

The example emphasizes the importance of looking at the big picture when hedging. All the implications of changes in commodity prices, interest rates, and exchange rates on a company's profitability should be taken into account in the design of a hedging strategy.

2.3 THE "PLAIN VANILLA" PRODUCTS

In this section we review the products that most commonly trade in financial markets. We focus on those that involve stocks, currencies, commodities, and interest rates. Less traditional products such as credit derivatives, weather derivatives, energy derivatives, and insurance derivatives are covered in later chapters.

Long and Short Positions in Assets

The simplest type of trade is the purchase or sale of an asset. Examples of such trades are:

1. The purchase of 100 IBM shares
2. The sale of 1 million British pounds
3. The purchase of 1000 ounces of gold
4. The sale of $1 million worth of bonds issued by General Motors

The first of these trades would typically be done on an exchange; the other three would be done in the over-the-counter market. The trades are sometimes referred to as *spot contracts* because they lead to almost immediate "on the spot" delivery of the asset.

Short Sales

In some markets it is possible to sell an asset that you do not own with the intention of buying it back later. This is referred to as shorting the asset. We will illustrate how it works by considering a short sale of shares of a stock.

Suppose an investor instructs a broker to short 500 IBM shares. The broker will carry out the instructions by borrowing the shares from another client and selling them on an exchange in the usual way. The investor can maintain the short position for as long as desired, provided there are always shares available for the broker to borrow. At some stage, however, the investor will close out the position by purchasing 500 IBM shares. These are then replaced in the account of the client from which the shares were borrowed. The investor takes a profit if the stock price has declined and a loss if it has risen. If, at any time while the contract is open, the broker runs out of shares to borrow, the investor is *short-squeezed* and is forced to close out the position immediately, even if not ready to do so.

An investor with a short position must pay to the broker any income, such as dividends or interest, that would normally be received on the securities that have been shorted. The broker will transfer this to the client account from which the securities have been borrowed. Consider the position of an investor who shorts 500 shares in April when the price per share is $120 and closes out the position by buying them back in July when the price per share is $100. Suppose that a dividend of $1 per share is paid in May. The investor receives $500 \times \$120 = \$60,000$ in April when the short position is initiated. The dividend leads to a payment by the investor of $500 \times \$1 = \$500$ in May. The investor also pays $500 \times \$100 = \$50,000$ for shares when the position is closed out in July. The net gain is, therefore,

$$\$60,000 - \$500 - \$50,000 = \$9,500$$

Table 2.2 illustrates this example and shows that the cash flows from the short sale are the mirror image of the cash flows from purchasing the shares in April and selling them in July.

An investor entering into a short position is required to maintain a *margin account* with the broker. The margin account consists of cash or marketable securities deposited by the investor with the broker to guarantee that the investor will not walk away from the short position if the share price increases. An initial margin is deposited and, if there are adverse movements (i.e., increases) in the price of the asset that is being shorted, additional margin may be required. The margin account does not represent a cost to the investor. This is because interest is usually paid on the balance in margin accounts and, if the interest rate offered is unacceptable, marketable securities such as Treasury bills can be used to

Table 2.2 Cash flows from short sale and purchase of shares.

	Purchase of Shares	
April:	Purchase 500 shares for $120	−$60,000
May:	Receive dividend	+$500
July:	Sell 500 shares for $100 per share	+$50,000
Net profit = −$9, 500		
	Short Sale of Shares	
April:	Borrow 500 shares and sell them for $120	+$60,000
May:	Pay dividend	−$500
July:	Buy 500 shares for $100 per share	−$50,000
	Replace borrowed shares to close short position	
Net profit = +$9, 500		

meet margin requirements. The proceeds of the sale of the asset belong to the investor and normally form part of the initial margin.

Forward Contracts

A forward contract is an agreement to buy an asset in the future for a certain price. Forward contracts trade in the over-the-counter market. One of the parties to a forward contract assumes a *long position* and agrees to buy the underlying asset on a certain specified future date for a certain specified price. The other party assumes a *short position* and agrees to sell the asset on the same date for the same price.

Forward contracts on foreign exchange are very popular. Table 2.3 provides quotes on the exchange rate between the British pound (GBP) and the US dollar (USD) that might be provided by a large international

Table 2.3 Spot and forward quotes for the USD/GBP exchange rate, August 5, 2005 (GBP = British pound; USD = US dollar; quote is number of USD per GBP).

	Bid	*Offer*
Spot	1.7794	1.7798
1-month forward	1.7780	1.7785
3-month forward	1.7761	1.7766
6-month forward	1.7749	1.7755

bank on August 5, 2005. The quotes are for the number of USD per GBP. The first row indicates that the bank is prepared to buy GBP (also known as sterling) in the spot market (i.e., for virtually immediate delivery) at the rate of $1.7794 per GBP and sell sterling in the spot market at $1.7798 per GBP; the second row indicates that the bank is prepared to buy sterling in one month's time at $1.7780 per GBP and sell sterling in one month at $1.7785 per GBP; and so on.

Forward contracts can be used to hedge foreign currency risk. Suppose that on August 5, 2005, the treasurer of a US corporation knows that the corporation will pay £1 million in six months (on February 5, 2006) and wants to hedge against exchange rate moves. The treasurer can agree to buy £1 million six months forward at an exchange rate of 1.7755 by trading with the bank providing the quotes in Table 2.3. The corporation then has a long forward contract on GBP. It has agreed that on February 5, 2006, it will buy £1 million from the bank for $1.7755 million. The bank has a short forward contract on GBP. It has agreed that on February 5, 2006, it will sell £1 million for $1.7755 million. Both the corporation and the bank have made a binding commitment.

What are the possible outcomes in the trade we have just described? The forward contract obligates the corporation to buy £1 million for $1,775,500 and the bank to sell £1 million for this amount. If the spot exchange rate rose to, say, 1.8000 at the end of the six months the forward contract would be worth +$24,500 (= $1,800,000 − $1,775,500) to the corporation and −$24,500 to the bank. It would enable 1 million pounds to be purchased at 1.7755 rather than 1.8000. Similarly, if the spot exchange rate fell to 1.6000 at the end of the six months, the forward contract would have a value of −$175,500 to the corporation and a value of +$175,500 to the bank because it would lead to the corporation paying $175,500 more than the market price for the sterling.

In general, the payoff from a long position in a forward contract on one unit of an asset is

$$S_T - K$$

where K is the delivery price and S_T is the spot price of the asset at maturity of the contract. This is because the holder of the contract is obligated to buy an asset worth S_T for K. Similarly, the payoff from a short position in a forward contract on one unit of an asset is

$$K - S_T$$

These payoffs can be positive or negative. They are illustrated in Figure 2.1.

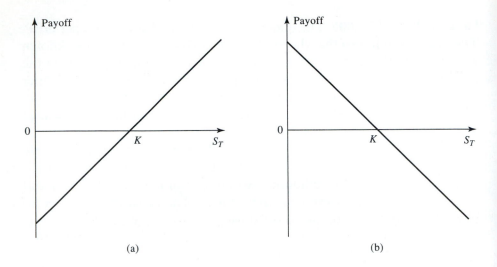

Figure 2.1   Payoffs from forward contracts: (a) long position and (b) short position. Delivery price $= K$; price of asset at contract maturity $= S_T$.

Because it costs nothing to enter into a forward contract, the payoff from the contract is also the trader's total gain or loss from the contract.

Futures Contracts

Futures contracts like forward contracts are agreements to buy an asset at a future time. Unlike forward contracts, futures are traded on an exchange. This means that the contracts that trade are standardized. The exchange defines the amount of the asset underlying one contract, when delivery can be made, exactly what can be delivered, and so on. Contracts are referred to by their delivery month. For example the September 2007 gold futures is a contract where delivery is made in September 2007. (The precise times, delivery locations, etc., are defined by the exchange.)

   One of the attractive features of futures contracts is that it is easy to close out a position. If you buy (i.e., take a long position in) a September gold futures contract in March you can exit in June by selling (i.e., taking a short position in) the same contract. In forward contracts final delivery of the underlying asset is usually made. Futures contracts by contrast are usually closed out before the delivery month is reached. Business Snapshot 2.1 is an amusing story indicating a potential pitfall in closing out contracts.

   Futures contracts are different from forward contracts in that they are settled daily. If the futures price moves in your favor during a day, you make an immediate gain. If it moves in the opposite direction, you make

---

Business Snapshot 2.1   The Unanticipated Delivery of a Futures Contract

This story (which may well be apocryphal) was told to the author of this book by a senior executive of a financial institution. It concerns a new employee of the financial institution who had not previously worked in the financial sector. One of the clients of the financial institution regularly entered into a long futures contract on live cattle for hedging purposes and issued instructions to close out the position on the last day of trading. (Live cattle futures contracts trade on the Chicago Mercantile Exchange and each contract is on 40,000 pounds of cattle.) The new employee was given responsibility for handling the account.

When the time came to close out a contract, the employee noted that the client was long one contract and instructed a trader at the exchange to go long (not short) one contract. The result of this mistake was that the financial institution ended up with a long position in two live cattle futures contracts. By the time the mistake was spotted, trading in the contract had ceased.

The financial institution (not the client) was responsible for the mistake. As a result, it started to look into the details of the delivery arrangements for live cattle futures contracts—something it had never done before. Under the terms of the contract, cattle could be delivered by the party with the short position to a number of different locations in the United States during the delivery month. Because it was long the financial institution could do nothing but wait for a party with a short position to issue a *notice of intention to deliver* to the exchange and for the exchange to assign that notice to the financial institution.

It eventually received a notice from the exchange and found that it would receive live cattle at a location 2,000 miles away the following Tuesday. The new employee was dispatched to the location to handle things. It turned out that the location had a cattle auction every Tuesday. The party with the short position that was making delivery bought cattle at the auction and then immediately delivered them. Unfortunately, the cattle could not be resold until the next cattle auction the following Tuesday. The employee was therefore faced with the problem of making arrangements for the cattle to be housed and fed for a week. This was a great start to a first job in the financial sector!

---

an immediate loss. Consider what happens when you buy one September gold futures contract on the Chicago Board of Trade when the futures price is $580 per ounce. The contract is on 100 ounces of gold. You must maintain a margin account with your broker. As in the case of a short sale, this consists of cash or marketable securities and is to ensure that you will honor your commitments under the contract. The rules for determining the initial amount that must be deposited in a margin account, when it must be topped up, and so on, are set by the exchange.

Suppose that the initial margin requirement on your gold trade is $2000. If, by close of trading on the first day you hold the contract, the September gold futures price has dropped from $580 to $578, then you lose 2×100 or $200. This is because you agreed to buy gold in September for $580 and the going price for September gold is now $578. The balance in your margin account would be reduced from $2,000 to $1,800. If, at close of trading the next day, the September futures price is $577, then you lose a further $100 from your margin account. If the decline continues, you will at some stage be asked to add cash to your margin account. If you do not do so, your broker will close out your position.

In the example we have just considered, the price of gold moved against you. If instead it moved in your favor, funds would be added to your margin account. The Exchange Clearinghouse is responsible for managing the flow of funds from investors with short positions to investors with long positions when the futures price increases and the flow of funds in the opposite direction when the futures price declines.

The relationship between futures or forward prices and spot prices is given in Appendix A at the end of the book.

Swaps

The first swap contracts were negotiated in the early 1980s. Since then the market has seen phenomenal growth. Swaps now occupy a position of central importance in the over-the-counter derivatives market.

A swap is an agreement between two companies to exchange cash flows in the future. The agreement defines the dates when the cash flows are to be paid and the way in which they are to be calculated. Usually the calculation of the cash flows involves the future values of interest rates, exchange rates, or other market variables.

A forward contract can be viewed as a simple example of a swap. Suppose it is March 1, 2007, and a company enters into a forward contract to buy 100 ounces of gold for $600 per ounce in one year. The company can sell the gold in one year as soon as it is received. The forward contract is therefore equivalent to a swap where the company agrees that on March 1, 2008, it will pay $60,000 and receive $100S$, where S is the market price of one ounce of gold on that date.

Whereas a forward contract is equivalent to the exchange of cash flows on just one future date, swaps typically lead to cash flow exchanges taking place on several future dates. The most common swap is a "plain

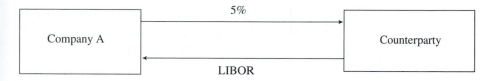

Figure 2.2 A plain vanilla interest rate swap.

vanilla" interest rate swap where a fixed rate of interest is exchanged for LIBOR.[1] Both interest rates are applied to the same notional principal. A swap where company A pays a fixed rate of interest of 5% and receives LIBOR is shown in Figure 2.2. Suppose that in this contract interest rates are reset every six months, the notional principal is $100 million, and the swap lasts for three years. Table 2.4 shows the cash flows to company A when six-month LIBOR interest rates prove to be those shown in the second column of the table. The swap is entered into on March 5, 2007. The six-month interest rate on that date is 4.2% per year or 2.1% per six months. As a result, the floating-rate cash flow received six months later on September 5, 2007, is 0.021 × 100 or $2.1 million. Similarly, the six month interest rate of 4.8% per annum (or 2.4% per six months) on September 5, 2007, leads to the floating cash flow received six months later (on March 5, 2008) being $2.4 million, and so on. The fixed-rate cash flow paid is always $2.5 million (5% of $100 million

Table 2.4 Cash flows (millions of dollars) to company A in swap in Figure 2.2. The swap lasts three years and has a principal of $100 million.

Date	6-month LIBOR rate (%)	Floating cash flow received	Fixed cash flow paid	Net cash flow
Mar. 5, 2007	4.20			
Sept. 5, 2007	4.80	+2.10	−2.50	−0.40
Mar. 5, 2008	5.30	+2.40	−2.50	−0.10
Sept. 5, 2008	5.50	+2.65	−2.50	+0.15
Mar. 5, 2009	5.60	+2.75	−2.50	+0.25
Sept. 5, 2009	5.90	+2.80	−2.50	+0.30
Mar. 5, 2010	6.40	+2.95	−2.50	+0.45

---

[1] LIBOR is the *London Interbank Offered Rate*. It is the rate at which a bank offers to make large wholesale deposits with another bank and will be discussed in Chapter 4.

applied to a six-month period).[2] Note that the timing of cash flows corresponds to the usual way short-term interest rates such as LIBOR work. The interest is observed at the beginning of the period to which it applies and paid at the end of the period.

Plain vanilla interest rate swaps are very popular because they can be used for many purposes. For example, the swap in Figure 2.2 could be used by company A to transform borrowings at a floating rate of LIBOR plus 1% to borrowings at a fixed rate of 6%. (Pay LIBOR plus 1%, receive LIBOR, and pay 5% nets out to pay 6%.) It can also be used by company A to transform an investment earning a fixed rate of 4.5% to an investment earning LIBOR minus 0.5%. (Receive 4.5%, pay 5%, and receive LIBOR nets out to receive LIBOR minus 0.5%.)

Example 2.1

Suppose a bank has floating-rate deposits and five-year fixed-rate loans. As explained in Section 1.5, this exposes the bank to significant risks. If rates rise, then the deposits will be rolled over at high rates and the bank's net interest income will contract. The bank can hedge its risks by entering into the swap in Figure 2.2 (taking the role of Company A). The swap can be viewed as transforming the floating-rate deposits to fixed-rate deposits. (Alternatively, it can be viewed as transforming fixed-rate loans to floating-rate loans.)

Many banks are market makers in swaps. Table 2.5 shows quotes for US dollar swaps that might be posted by a bank.[3] The first row shows that the

Table 2.5   Swap quotes made by a market maker (percent per annum).

Maturity (years)	Bid	Offer	Swap rate
2	6.03	6.06	6.045
3	6.21	6.24	6.225
4	6.35	6.39	6.370
5	6.47	6.51	6.490
7	6.65	6.68	6.665
10	6.83	6.87	6.850

---

[2] Note that we have not taken account of day count conventions, holidays, calendars, etc., in Table 2.4.

[3] The standard swap in the United States is one where fixed payments made every six months are exchanged for floating LIBOR payments made every three months. In Table 2.4 we assumed that fixed and floating payments are exchanged every six months.

Business Snapshot 2.2   Procter and Gamble's Bizarre Deal

A particularly bizarre swap is the so-called "5/30" swap entered into between Bankers Trust (BT) and Procter and Gamble (P&G) on November 2, 1993. This was a five-year swap with semiannual payments. The notional principal was $200 million. BT paid P&G 5.30% per annum. P&G paid BT the average 30-day CP (commercial paper) rate minus 75 basis points plus a spread. The average commercial paper rate was calculated by taking observations on the 30-day commercial paper rate each day during the preceding accrual period and averaging them.

The spread was zero for the first payment date (May 2, 1994). For the remaining nine payment dates, it was

$$\max\left[0, \frac{98.5\left(\dfrac{\text{5-year CMT\%}}{5.78\%}\right) - (\text{30-year TSY price})}{100}\right]$$

In this, five-year CMT is the constant maturity Treasury yield (i.e., the yield on a five-year Treasury note, as reported by the US Federal Reserve). The 30-year TSY price is the midpoint of the bid and offer cash bond prices for the 6.25% Treasury bond maturing on August 2023. Note that the spread calculated from the formula is a decimal interest rate. It is not measured in basis points. If the formula gives 0.1 and the CP rate is 6%, the rate paid by P&G is 15.25%.

P&G was hoping that the spread would be zero and the deal would enable it to exchange fixed-rate funding at 5.30% for funding at 75 basis points less than the commercial paper rate. In fact, interest rates rose sharply in early 1994, bond prices fell, and the swap proved very, very expensive. (See Problem 2.30.)

---

bank is prepared to enter into a two-year swap where it pays a fixed rate of 6.03% and receives LIBOR. It is also prepared to enter into a swap where it receives 6.06% and pays LIBOR. The bid–offer spread in Table 2.5 is three or four basis points. The average of the bid and offer fixed rates is known as the *swap rate*. This is shown in the final column of the table.

The trading of swaps is facilitated by ISDA, the International Swaps and Derivatives Association. This organization has developed standard contracts that are widely used by market participants. Swaps can be designed so that the periodic cash flows depend on the future value of any well-defined variable. Swaps dependent on interest rates, exchange rates, commodity prices, and equity indices are popular. Sometimes there are embedded options in a swap. For example, one side might have the option to terminate a swap early or to choose between a number of different ways of calculating cash flows. Occasionally swaps are traded with payoffs that are calculated in quite bizarre ways. An example is a deal entered into between Procter and Gamble and Bankers Trust in 1993 (see Business Snapshot 2.2). The details of this transaction are in the public domain because it later became the subject of litigation.[4] The valuation of swaps is discussed in Appendix B at the end of the book.

Options

Options are traded both on exchanges and in the over-the-counter market. There are two basic types of options. A *call option* gives the holder the right to buy the underlying asset by a certain date for a certain price. A *put option* gives the holder the right to sell the underlying asset by a certain date for a certain price. The price in the contract is known as the *exercise price* or *strike price*; the date in the contract is known as the *expiration date* or *maturity*. *American options* can be exercised at any time up to the expiration date, but *European options* can be exercised only on the expiration date itself.[5] Most of the options that are traded on exchanges are American. In the exchange-traded equity option market, one contract is usually an agreement to buy or sell 100 shares. European options are generally easier to analyze than American options, and some of the properties of an American option are frequently deduced from those of its European counterpart.

An *at-the-money* option is an option where the strike price is close to the price of the underlying asset. An *out-of-the-money* option is a call option where the strike price is above the price of the underlying asset or a put option where the strike price is below this price. An *in-the-money* option is a call option where the strike price is below the price of the underlying asset or a put option where the strike price is above this price.

It should be emphasized that an option gives the holder the right to do something. The holder does not have to exercise this right. By contrast, in a forward or futures contract, the holder is obligated to buy or sell the underlying asset. Note that, whereas it costs nothing to enter into a forward or futures contract, there is a cost to acquiring an option.

The largest exchange in the world for trading stock options is the Chicago Board Options Exchange (CBOE; www.cboe.com). Table 2.6

---

[4] See D. J. Smith, "Aggressive Corporate Finance: A Close Look at the Procter and Gamble–Bankers Trust Leveraged Swap." *Journal of Derivatives* 4, No. 4 (Summer 1997): 67–79.

[5] Note that the terms *American* and *European* do not refer to the location of the option or the exchange. Some options trading on North American exchanges are European.

Table 2.6 Prices of options on Intel, May 29, 2003; stock price = $20.83.

Strike price ($)	Calls			Puts		
	June	*July*	*Oct.*	*June*	*July*	*Oct.*
20.00	1.25	1.60	2.40	0.45	0.85	1.50
22.50	0.20	0.45	1.15	1.85	2.20	2.85

gives the closing prices of some of the American options trading on Intel on May 29, 2003. The option strike prices are $20 and $22.50. The maturities are June 2003, July 2003, and October 2003. The June options have an expiration date of June 21, 2003; the July options have an expiration date of July 19, 2003; the October options have an expiration date of October 18, 2003. Intel's stock price at the close of trading on May 29, 2003, was $20.83.

Suppose an investor instructs a broker to buy one October call option contract on Intel with a strike price of $22.50. The broker will relay these instructions to a trader at the CBOE. This trader will then find another trader who wants to sell one October call contract on Intel with a strike price of $22.50, and a price will be agreed upon. We assume that the price is $1.15, as indicated in Table 2.6. This is the price for an option to buy one share. In the United States, one stock option contract is a contract to buy or sell 100 shares. Therefore the investor must arrange for $115 to be remitted to the exchange through the broker. The exchange will then arrange for this amount to be passed on to the party on the other side of the transaction.

In our example the investor has obtained at a cost of $115 the right to buy 100 Intel shares for $22.50 each. The party on the other side of the transaction has received $115 and has agreed to sell 100 Intel shares for $22.50 per share if the investor chooses to exercise the option. If the price of Intel does not rise above $22.50 before October 18, 2003, the option is not exercised and the investor loses $115. But if the Intel share price does well and the option is exercised when it is $30, the investor can buy 100 shares at $22.50 per share when they are worth $30 per share. This leads to a gain of $750, or $635 when the initial cost of the options is taken into account.

An alternative trade for the investor would be the purchase of one July put option contract with a strike price of $20. From Table 2.6 we see that this would cost 100 × 0.85 or $85. The investor would obtain at a cost of $85 the right to sell 100 Intel shares for $20 per share prior to July 19, 2003. If the Intel share price stays above $20 the option is not exercised and the

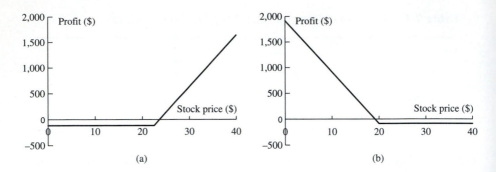

Figure 2.3   Net profit per share from (a) purchasing a contract consisting of 100 Intel October call options with a strike price of $22.50 and (b) purchasing a contract consisting of 100 Intel July put options with a strike price of $20.00.

investor loses $85. But if the investor exercises when the stock price is $15, the investor makes a gain of $500 by buying 100 Intel shares at $15 and selling them for $20. The net profit after the cost of the options is taken into account is $415.

The options trading on the CBOE are American. If we assume for simplicity that they are European so that they can be exercised only at maturity, the investor's profit as a function of the final stock price for the Intel options we have been considering is shown in Figure 2.3.

There are four types of trades in options markets:

1. Buying a call
2. Selling a call
3. Buying a put
4. Selling a put

Buyers are referred to as having *long positions*; sellers are referred to as having *short positions*. Selling an option is also known as *writing the option*.

Options trade very actively in the over-the-counter market as well as on exchanges. Indeed the over-the-counter market for options is now larger than the exchange-traded market. Whereas exchange-traded options tend to be American, options trading in the over-the-counter market are frequently European. The advantage of the over-the-counter market is that maturity dates, strike prices, and contract sizes can be tailored to meet the precise needs of a client. They do not have to correspond to those specified by the exchange. Option trades in the over-the-counter market are usually much larger than those on exchanges.

Valuation formulas and numerical procedures for options on stocks, stock indices, currencies, and futures are in Appendices C and D at the end of this book.

2.4 USING THE PRODUCTS FOR HEDGING

Futures and forward contracts provide a hedge for an exposure at one particular time. As we saw earlier the treasurer of a US company can use the quotes in Table 2.3 to buy sterling forward when it is known that the company will have to pay sterling at a certain future time. Similarly, the treasurer can use the quotes to sell sterling forward when it is known that it will receive sterling at a certain future time. Futures contracts can be used in a similar way. When a futures contract is used for hedging the plan is usually to close the contract out prior to maturity. As a result the hedge performance is reduced somewhat because there is uncertainty about the difference between the futures price and the spot price on the close-out date. This uncertainty is known as *basis risk*.

When forward and futures contracts are used for hedging the objective is to lock in the price at which an asset will be bought or sold at a certain future time. The *hedge ratio* is the ratio of the size of the futures or forward position to the size of the exposure. Up to now we have assumed that a company uses a hedge ratio of 1.0. (For example, if it has a $1 million exposure to the USD/GBP exchange rate it takes a $1 million forward or futures position.) Sometimes a company may choose to partially hedge its risks by using a hedge ratio of less than 1.0.

Even when a company wants to minimize its risks, it may not be optimal for it to use a hedge ratio of 1.0. Suppose that the standard deviation of the change in a futures or forward price during the hedging period is σ_F and the standard deviation of the change in the value of the asset being hedged is σ_S. Suppose further that the correlation between the two changes is ρ. It can be shown that the optimal hedge ratio is

$$ h = \rho \frac{\sigma_S}{\sigma_F} \tag{2.1} $$

Example 2.2

An airline expects to purchase 2.4 million gallons of jet fuel in one month's time. Because there is no futures contract on jet fuel it decides to use the futures contact on heating oil that trades on the New York Mercantile Exchange. The correlation between monthly changes in the price of jet fuel and monthly changes in heating oil futures price is 0.7. The standard deviation of monthly changes in the heating oil futures price per gallon is 0.024 and the standard deviation of the monthly changes in the price of jet oil per gallon is 0.021. The optimal hedge ratio is therefore

$$0.8 \times \frac{0.021}{0.024} = 0.7$$

Each heating oil futures contract is on 42,000 gallons of heating oil. The number of contracts the company should buy is therefore

$$0.7 \times \frac{2,400,000}{42,000} = 40$$

Example 2.3

A fund manager wants to hedge a well-diversified investment portfolio worth $2.5 million until time T using a forward contracts on the S&P 500. The index is currently 1250, so that the portfolio is worth 2000 times the index. Assume that F is the current forward rate for a contract maturing at time T. If the portfolio has a beta of 1.0, the hedge ratio should be 1.0 (see Section 1.1 for a discussion of beta). This means that the forward contract should be structured so that the payoff to the fund manager at time T is

$$2000(F - S_T)$$

where S_T is the value of the S&P 500 at time T. When $\beta = 2$, the hedge position should be doubled, so that the payoff is

$$4000(F - S_T)$$

In general, the hedge ratio should equal the beta (β) of the well-diversified portfolio, so that the payoff from the forward contract is $2000\beta(F - S_T)$. This is consistent with equation (2.1) because it is approximately true that $\sigma_S = \beta\sigma_F$ and $\rho = 1$.

As explained earlier, a swap can be regarded as a convenient way of bundling forward contracts. It can provide a hedge for cash flows that will occur on a regular basis over a period of time.

Options are a different type of hedging instrument from forwards, futures, and swaps. Whereas forward, futures, and swap contracts lock in prices for future sales or purchases of an asset, an option provides insurance. For example, the call option in Figure 2.3a could be used to guarantee that shares of Intel could be purchased for $22.50 or less in October; the put option in Figure 2.3b could be used to guarantee that a holding of shares in Intel could be sold for at least $20 in July.

A Practical Issue

It is important to realize that hedging can result in a decrease or an increase in a company's profits relative to the position it would be in with no hedging. Consider a company that decides to use a short futures position to hedge the future sale of 1 million barrels of oil. If the price of oil goes down, the company loses money on the sale of the oil and the futures position leads to an offsetting gain. The treasurer can be congratulated for having had the foresight to put the hedge in place. Clearly, the company is better off than it would be with no hedging. Other executives in the organization, it is hoped, will appreciate the contribution made by the treasurer.

If the price of oil goes up, the company gains from its sale of the oil, and the futures position leads to an offsetting loss. The company is in a worse position than it would be with no hedging. Although the hedging decision was perfectly logical, the treasurer may in practice have a difficult time justifying it. Suppose that the price of oil increases by $3, so that the company loses about $3 per barrel on the futures contract. We can imagine a conversation such as the following between the treasurer and the president:

PRESIDENT: This is terrible. We've lost $3 million in the futures market in the space of three months. How could it happen? I want a full explanation.

TREASURER: The purpose of the futures contracts was to hedge our exposure to the price of oil—not to make a profit. Don't forget that we made about $3 million from the favorable effect of the oil price increases on our business.

PRESIDENT: What's that got to do with it? That's like saying that we do not need to worry when our sales are down in California because they are up in New York.

TREASURER: If the price of oil had gone down...

PRESIDENT: I don't care what would have happened if the price of oil had gone down. The fact is that it went up. I really do not know what you were doing playing the futures markets like this. Our shareholders will expect us to have done particularly well this quarter. I'm going to have to explain to them that your actions reduced profits by $3 million. I'm afraid this is going to mean no bonus for you this year.

TREASURER: That's unfair. I was only...

PRESIDENT: Unfair! You are lucky not to be fired. You lost $3 million.

TREASURER: It all depends how you look at it...

This shows that, although hedging reduces risk for the company, it can increase risk for the treasurer if others do not fully understand what is being done. The only real solution to this problem is to ensure that all senior executives within the organization fully understand the nature of hedging before a hedging program is put in place. One of the reasons why treasurers sometimes choose to buy insurance using options rather than implementing a more straightforward hedge using forwards, futures, or swaps is that options do not lead to the problem we have just mentioned. They allow the company to benefit from favorable outcomes while being hedged against unfavorable outcomes. (Of course, this is achieved at a cost. The company has to pay the option premium.)

2.5 EXOTIC OPTIONS AND STRUCTURED DEALS

We met one exotic swap transaction in Business Snapshot 2.2. Many different types of exotic options and highly structured deals trade in the over-the-counter market. Although exotics are a relatively small part of the trading for a financial institution they are important because the profit margin on trades in exotics tends to be much higher than on plain vanilla options or swaps. Here are a few examples of exotic options:

Asian Options: Whereas regular options provide a payoff based on the final price of the underlying asset at the time of exercise, Asian options provide a payoff based on the average of the price of the underlying asset over some specified period. An example is an *average price call option* that provides a payoff in one year equal to $\max(\bar{S} - K, 0)$, where $\bar{S}$ is the average asset price during the year and K is the strike price.

Barrier Options: These options come into existence or disappear when the price of the underlying asset reaches a certain barrier. For example, a knock-out call option with a strike price of $30 and a barrier of $20 is a regular call option that ceases to exist if the asset price falls below $20.

Basket Options: These are options on a portfolio of assets rather than options on a single asset.

Binary Options: These are options that provide a fixed dollar payoff if some criterion is met. An example is an option that provides a payoff in one year of $1,000 if a stock price is greater than $20.

Compound Options: These are options on options. There are four types: a call on a call, a call on a put, a put on a call, and a put on a put. An example of a compound option is an option to buy an option on a stock currently

---

Business Snapshot 2.3 Microsoft's Hedging

Microsoft actively manages its foreign exchange exposure. In some countries (e.g., Europe, Japan, and Australia) it bills in the local currency and converts its net revenue to US dollars monthly. For these currencies there is a clear exposure to exchange rate movements. In other countries (e.g., Latin America, Eastern Europe, and Southeast Asia) it bills in US dollars. The latter appears to avoid any foreign exchange exposure—but it does not.

Suppose the US dollar strengthens against the currency of a country where Microsoft is billing in dollars. People in the country will find it more difficult to buy Microsoft products because it takes more of the local currency to buy $1. As a result Microsoft will probably find it necessary to reduce its US dollar prices or face a decline in sales. Microsoft therefore has a foreign exchange exposure—both when it bills in US dollars and when it bills in the local currency. This emphasizes the point made in Section 2.2 that it is important to consider the big picture when hedging.

Microsoft likes to use options for hedging. Suppose it uses a one-year time horizon. Microsoft recognizes that its exposure to, say, the Japanese yen is an exposure to the average exchange rate during the year because approximately the same amount of yen is converted to US dollars each month. It therefore uses Asian options rather than regular options to hedge the exposure. What is more, Microsoft's net exposure is to a weighted average of the exchange rates for all the countries in which it does business. It therefore uses basket options (i.e., options on a weighted average of exchange rates). A contract it likes to negotiate with financial institutions is therefore an Asian basket put option. This cost of this option is much less than a portfolio of put options, one for each month and each exchange rate (see Problem 2.24). But it gives Microsoft exactly the protection it requires.

Microsoft faces other financial risks. For example, it is exposed to interest rate risk on its bond portfolio. (When rates rise, the portfolio loses money.) It also has two sorts of exposure to equity prices. It is exposed to the equity prices of the companies in which it invests. It is also exposed to its own equity price because it regularly repurchases its own shares as part of its stock awards program. It likes to use sophisticated option strategies to hedge these risks.

---

worth $15. The first option expires in one year and has a strike price of $1. The second option expires in three years and has a strike price of $20.

Lookback Options: These are options that provide a payoff based on the maximum or minimum price of the underlying asset over some period. An example is an option that provides a payoff in one year equal to $S_T - S_{min}$, where S_T is the asset price at the end of the year and S_{min} is the minimum asset price during the year.

Why do companies use exotic options and structured products in preference to the plain vanilla products we looked at in Section 2.3? Sometimes the products are totally inappropriate as risk management tools. (This was certainly true in the case of the Procter and Gamble swap discussed in Business Snapshot 2.2.) But usually there are sound reasons for the contracts entered into by corporate treasurers. For example, Microsoft often uses Asian basket options in its risk management. As explained in Business Snapshot 2.3 this is the ideal product for managing its exposures.

2.6 DANGERS

Derivatives are very versatile instruments. They can be used for hedging, for speculation, and for arbitrage. (Hedging involves reducing risks; speculation involves taking risks; arbitrage involves locking in a profit by simultaneously trading in two or more markets.) It is this very versatility that can cause problems. Sometimes traders who have a mandate to hedge risks or follow an arbitrage strategy become (consciously or unconsciously) speculators. The results can be disastrous. One example of this is provided by the activities of Nick Leeson at Barings Bank (see Business Snapshot 2.4).[6]

To avoid the problems Barings encountered, it is very important for both financial and nonfinancial corporations to set up controls to ensure that derivatives are being used for their intended purpose. Risk limits should be set and the activities of traders monitored daily to ensure that the risk limits are adhered to.

SUMMARY

There are two types of markets in which financial products trade: the exchange-traded market and the over-the-counter market. In this chapter we have reviewed spot trades, forward contracts, futures contracts, swaps, and options contracts. A forward or futures contract involves an obligation to buy or sell an asset at a certain time in the future for a certain price. A swap is an agreement to exchange cash flows in the future in amounts dependent on the values of one or more market variables. There are two types of options: calls and puts. A call option gives the holder the

---

[6] The movie *Rogue Trader* provides a good dramatization of the failure of Barings Bank.

Business Snapshot 2.4   The Barings Bank Disaster

Derivatives are very versatile instruments. They can be used for hedging, speculation, and arbitrage. One of the risks faced by a company that trades derivatives is that an employee who has a mandate to hedge or to look for arbitrage opportunities may become a speculator.

Nick Leeson, an employee of Barings Bank in the Singapore office in 1995, had a mandate to look for arbitrage opportunities between the Nikkei 225 futures prices on the Singapore exchange and the Osaka exchange. Over time Leeson moved from being an arbitrageur to being a speculator without anyone in Barings head office in London fully understanding that he had changed the way he was using derivatives. He began to make losses, which he was able to hide. He then began to take bigger speculative positions in an attempt to recover the losses, but only succeeded in making the losses worse.

In the end Leeson's total loss was close to 1 billion dollars. As a result, Barings—a bank that had been in existence for 200 years—was wiped out. One of the lessons from the Barings disaster is that it is important to define unambiguous risk limits for traders and then carefully monitor their activities to make sure that the limits are adhered to.

---

right to buy an asset by a certain date for a certain price. A put option gives the holder the right to sell an asset by a certain date for a certain price. Forwards, futures, swaps, and options trade on a wide range of different underlying assets.

Forward, futures, and swap contracts have the effect of locking in the prices that will apply to future transactions. Options by contrast provide insurance. They ensure that the price applicable to a future transaction will not be worse than a certain level. Exotic options and structured products are tailored to the particular needs of corporate treasurers. For example, as we saw in Business Snapshot 2.3, Asian basket options can allow a company such as Microsoft to hedge its net exposure to several risks over a period of time.

It is important to look at the big picture when hedging. For example, a company may find that it is increasing rather than reducing its risks if it chooses to hedge when none of its competitors does so. The hedge ratio is the ratio of the size of the hedge position to the size of the exposure. It is not always optimal to use a hedge ratio of 1.0. The optimal hedge ratio depends on the variability of futures price, the variability of the price of the asset being hedged, and the correlation between the two.

FURTHER READING

Baz, J., and M. Pascutti. "Alternative Swap Contracts Analysis and Pricing," *Journal of Derivatives*, Winter 1996: 7–21.

Boyle, P., and F. Boyle, *Derivatives: The Tools That Changed Finance*. London: Risk Books, 2001

Brown, K. C. and D. J. Smith. *Interest Rate and Currency Swaps: A Tutorial*. Association for Investment Management and Research, 1996.

Brown, G. W. "Managing Foreign Exchange Risk with Derivatives." *Journal of Financial Economics*, 60 (2001): 401–448.

Flavell, R. *Swaps and Other Instruments*. Chichester: Wiley, 2002.

Geczy, C., B. A. Minton, and C. Schrand. "Why Firms Use Currency Derivatives," *Journal of Finance*, 52, No. 4 (1997): 1323–1354.

Litzenberger, R. H. "Swaps: Plain and Fanciful," *Journal of Finance*, 47, No. 3 (1992): 831–850.

Miller, M. H. "Financial Innovation: Achievements and Prospects," *Journal of Applied Corporate Finance*, 4 (Winter 1992): 4–11.

Warwick B., F. J. Jones, and R. J. Teweles. *The Futures Game*, 3rd edn. New York: McGraw-Hill, 1998.

QUESTIONS AND PROBLEMS (Answers at End of Book)

2.1. What is the difference between a long forward position and a short forward position?

2.2. Explain the difference between hedging, speculation, and arbitrage.

2.3. What is the difference between entering into a long forward contract when the forward price is $50 and taking a long position in a call option with a strike price of $50?

2.4. Explain carefully the difference between selling a call option and buying a put option.

2.5. An investor enters into a short forward contract to sell 100,000 British pounds for US dollars at an exchange rate of 1.5000 US dollars per pound. How much does the investor gain or lose if the exchange rate at the end of the contract is (a) 1.4900 and (b) 1.5200?

2.6. A trader enters into a short cotton futures contract when the futures price is 50 cents per pound. The contract is for the delivery of 50,000 pounds. How much does the trader gain or lose if the cotton price at the end of the contract is (a) 48.20 cents per pound and (b) 51.30 cents per pound?

2.7. Suppose you write a put contract with a strike price of $40 and an expiration date in three months. The current stock price is $41 and the contract is on 100 shares. What have you committed yourself to? How much could you gain or lose?

2.8. What is the difference between the over-the-counter market and the exchange-traded market? Which of the two markets do the following trade in: (a) a forward contract, (b) a futures contract, (c) an option, (d) a swap, and (e) an exotic option?

2.9. You would like to speculate on a rise in the price of a certain stock. The current stock price is $29, and a three-month call with a strike of $30 costs $2.90. You have $5,800 to invest. Identify two alternative strategies, one involving an investment in the stock and the other involving investment in the option. What are the potential gains and losses from each?

2.10. Suppose that you own 5,000 shares worth $25 each. How can put options be used to provide you with insurance against a decline in the value of your holding over the next four months?

2.11. When first issued, a stock provides funds for a company. Is the same true of a stock option? Discuss.

2.12. Suppose that a March call option to buy a share for $50 costs $2.50 and is held until March. Under what circumstances will the holder of the option make a profit? Under what circumstances will the option be exercised?

2.13. Suppose that a June put option to sell a share for $60 costs $4 and is held until June. Under what circumstances will the seller of the option (i.e., the party with the short position) make a profit? Under what circumstances will the option be exercised?

2.14. A company knows that it is due to receive a certain amount of a foreign currency in four months. What type of option contract is appropriate for hedging?

2.15. A United States company expects to have to pay 1 million Canadian dollars in six months. Explain how the exchange rate risk can be hedged using (a) a forward contract and (b) an option.

2.16. In the 1980s, Bankers Trust developed *index currency option notes* (ICONs). These are bonds in which the amount received by the holder at maturity varies with a foreign exchange rate. One example was its trade with the Long Term Credit Bank of Japan. The ICON specified that if the yen/US dollar exchange rate, S_T, is greater than 169 yen per dollar at maturity (in 1995), the holder of the bond receives $1,000. If it is less than 169 yen per dollar, the amount received by the holder of the bond is

$$1,000 - \max\left[0,\ 1,000\left(\frac{169}{S_T} - 1\right)\right]$$

When the exchange rate is below 84.5, nothing is received by the holder at maturity. Show that this ICON is a combination of a regular bond and two options.

2.17. Suppose that USD/GBP spot and forward exchange rates are as follows:

Spot	1.6080
90-day forward	1.6056
180-day forward	1.6018

What opportunities are open to an arbitrageur in the following situations: (a) a 180-day European call option to buy £1 for $1.57 costs 2 cents and (b) a 90-day European put option to sell £1 for $1.64 costs 2 cents?

2.18. A company has money invested at 5% for five years. It wishes to use the swap quotes in Table 2.5 to convert its investment to a floating-rate investment. Explain how it can do this.

2.19. A company has borrowed money for five years at 7%. Explain how it can use the quotes in Table 2.5 to convert this to a floating-rate liability.

2.20. A company has a has a floating-rate liability that costs LIBOR plus 1%. Explain how it can use the quotes in Table 2.5 to convert this to a three-year fixed-rate liability.

2.21. A corn farmer argues: "I do not use futures contracts for hedging. My real risk is not the price of corn. It is that my whole crop gets wiped out by the weather." Discuss this viewpoint. Should the farmer estimate his or her expected production of corn and hedge to try to lock in a price for expected production?

2.22. An airline executive has argued: "There is no point in our hedging the price of jet fuel. There is just as much chance that we will lose from doing this as that we will gain." Discuss the executive's viewpoint.

2.23. The standard deviation of monthly changes in the spot price of live cattle is (in cents per pound) 1.2. The standard deviation of monthly changes in the futures price of live cattle for the closest contract is 1.4. The correlation between the futures price changes and the spot price changes is 0.7. It is now October 15. A beef producer is committed to purchasing 200,000 pounds of live cattle on November 15. The producer wants to use the December live-cattle futures contracts to hedge its risk. Each contract is for the delivery of 40,000 pounds of cattle. What strategy should the beef producer follow?

2.24. Why is the cost of an Asian basket put option to Microsoft considerably less than the cost of a portfolio of put options, one for each currency and each maturity (see Business Snapshot 2.3.)?

ASSIGNMENT QUESTIONS

2.25. The current price of a stock is $94, and three-month European call options with a strike price of $95 currently sell for $4.70. An investor who feels that the price of the stock will increase is trying to decide between buying 100 shares and buying 2,000 call options ($= 20$ contracts). Both strategies involve an investment of $9,400. What advice would you give? How high does the stock price have to rise for the option strategy to be more profitable?

2.26. A bond issued by Standard Oil worked as follows. The holder received no interest. At the bond's maturity the company promised to pay $1,000 plus an additional amount based on the price of oil at that time. The additional amount was equal to the product of 170 and the excess (if any) of the price of a barrel of oil at maturity over $25. The maximum additional amount paid was $2,550 (which corresponds to a price of $40 per barrel). Show that the bond is a combination of a regular bond, a long position in call options on oil with a strike price of $25, and a short position in call options on oil with a strike price of $40.

2.27. The price of gold is currently $500 per ounce. The forward price for delivery in one year is $700. An arbitrageur can borrow money at 10% per annum. What should the arbitrageur do? Assume that the cost of storing gold is zero and that gold provides no income.

2.28. A company's investments earn LIBOR minus 0.5%. Explain how it can use the quotes in Table 2.5 to convert the investments to (a) 3-year, (b) 5-year, and (c) 10-year fixed-rate investments.

2.29. What position is equivalent to a long forward contract to buy an asset at K on a certain date and a long position in a European put option to sell it for K on that date.

2.30. Estimate the interest rate paid by P&G on the 5/30 swap in Business Snapshot 2.2 if (a) the CP rate is 6.5% and the Treasury yield curve is flat at 6% and (b) the CP rate is 7.5% and the Treasury yield curve is flat at 7% with semiannual compounding.

2.31. It is July 16. A company has a portfolio of stocks worth $100 million. The beta of the portfolio is 1.2. The company would like to use the CME December futures contract on the S&P 500 to change the beta of the portfolio to 0.5 during the period July 16 to November 16. The index is currently 1,000, and each contract is on $250 times the index. (a) What position should the company take? (b) Suppose that the company changes its mind and decides to increase the beta of the portfolio from 1.2 to 1.5. What position in futures contracts should it take?

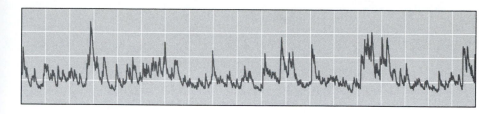

How Traders Manage Their Exposures

3

The trading function within a financial institution is referred to as the *front office*; the part of the financial institution that is concerned with the overall level of the risks being taken, capital adequacy, and regulatory compliance is referred to as the *middle office*; the record keeping function is referred to as the *back office*. As explained in Chapter 1, there are two levels within a financial institution at which trading risks are managed. First, the front office hedges risks by ensuring that exposures to individual market variables are not too great. Second, the middle office aggregates the exposures of all traders to determine whether the total risk is acceptable. In this chapter we focus on the hedging activities of the front office. In later chapters we will consider how risks are aggregated in the middle office.

This chapter explains what are termed the "Greek letters", or simply the "Greeks". Each of the Greeks measures a different aspect of the risk in a trading position. Traders calculate their Greeks at the end of each day and are required to take action if the internal risk limits of the financial institution they work for are exceeded. Failure to take this action is liable to lead to immediate dismissal.

3.1 DELTA

Imagine that you are a trader working for a US bank and responsible for all trades involving gold. The current price of gold is $500 per ounce.

Table 3.1   Summary of gold portfolio.

Position	Value ($)
Spot gold	180,000
Forward Contracts	−60,000
Futures Contracts	2,000
Swaps	80,000
Options	−110,000
Exotics	25,000
Total	117,000

Table 3.1 shows a summary of your portfolio (known as your "book"). How can you manage your risks?

The value of your portfolio is currently $117,000. One way of investigating the risks you face is to revalue the portfolio on the assumption that there is a small increase in the price of gold from $500 per ounce to $500.10 per ounce. Suppose that the new value of the portfolio is $116,900. A $0.10 increase in the price of gold decreases the value of your portfolio by $100. The sensitivity of the portfolio to the price of gold is therefore

$$\frac{-100}{0.1} = -1,000$$

This is referred to as the *delta* of the portfolio. The portfolio loses value at a rate of $1,000 per $1 increase in the price of gold. Similarly, it gains value at a rate of $1,000 per $1 decrease in the price of gold.

In general, the *delta* of a portfolio with respect to a market variable is

$$\frac{\Delta\Pi}{\Delta S}$$

where ΔS is a small change in the value of the variable and $\Delta\Pi$ is the resultant change in the value of the portfolio. Using calculus terminology, delta is the partial derivative of the portfolio value with respect to the value of the variable:

$$\text{Delta} = \frac{\partial\Pi}{\partial S}$$

In our example the trader can eliminate the delta exposure by buying 1,000 ounces of gold. This is because the delta of a position in 1,000 ounces of gold is 1,000. (The position gains value at the rate of $1,000 per $1 increase in the price of gold.) When this trade is combined with the existing portfolio, the resultant portfolio has a delta of zero. Such a portfolio is referred to as a *delta-neutral* portfolio.

Linear Products

A linear product is a product whose value at any given time is linearly dependent on the value of the underlying asset price (see Figure 3.1). Forward contracts, futures contracts, and swaps are linear products; options are not.

A linear product can be hedged relatively easily. Consider, for example, a US bank that enters into a forward contract with a corporate client where it agrees to sell the client 1 million euros at a certain exchange rate in one year. Assume that the euro interest rate is 4% with annual compounding. This means that the present value of 1 million euros in one year is 961,538 euros. The bank can hedge its risk by borrowing enough dollars to buy 961,538 euros today and then investing the euros for one year at 4%. The bank knows that it will have the 1 million euros it needs to deliver in one year and it knows what its costs will be.

When the bank enters into the opposite transaction and agrees to buy 1 million euros in one year it must hedge by shorting 961,538 euros. It

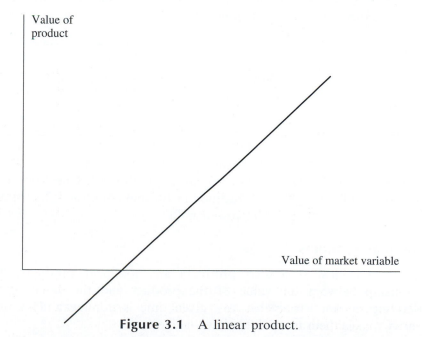

Figure 3.1 A linear product.

Business Snapshot 3.1   Hedging by Gold Mining Companies

It is natural for a gold mining company to consider hedging against changes in the price of gold. Typically it takes several years to extract all the gold from a mine. Once a gold mining company decides to go ahead with production at a particular mine, it has a big exposure to the price of gold. Indeed, a mine that looks profitable at the outset could become unprofitable if the price of gold plunges.

Gold mining companies are careful to explain their hedging strategies to potential shareholders. Some gold mining companies do not hedge. They tend to attract shareholders who buy gold stocks because they want to benefit when the price of gold increases and are prepared to accept the risk of a loss from a decrease in the price of gold. Other companies choose to hedge. They estimate the number of ounces they will produce each month for the next few years and enter into short futures or forward contracts to lock in the price that will be received.

Suppose you are Goldman Sachs and have just entered into a forward contract with a gold mining company where you agree to buy a large amount of gold at a fixed price. How do you hedge your risk? The answer is that you borrow gold from a central bank and sell it at the current market price. (The central banks of many countries hold large amounts of gold.) At the end of the life of the forward contract, you buy gold from the gold mining company under the terms of the forward contract and use it to repay the central bank. The central bank charges a fee (perhaps 1.5% per annum) known as the gold lease rate for lending its gold in this way.

---

does this by borrowing the euros today at 4% and immediately converting them to US dollars. The 1 million euros received in one year are used to repay the loan.

Shorting assets to hedge forward contracts is not always easy. Gold is an interesting case in point. Financial institutions often find that they enter into very large forward contracts to buy gold from gold producers. This means that they need to borrow large quantities of gold to create a short position for hedging. As outlined in Business Snapshot 3.1, central banks are the source of the borrowed gold.

Nonlinear Products

Options and most structured products are nonlinear products. The relationship between the value of the product and the value of the underlying market variable at any given time is nonlinear. This non-linearity makes them more difficult to hedge.

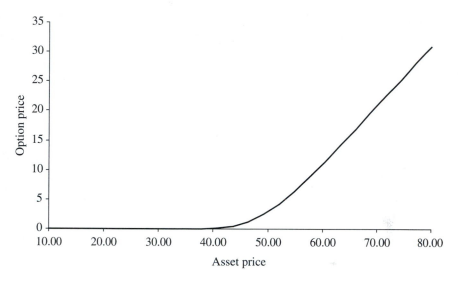

Figure 3.2 Value of option as a function of stock price.

Consider as an example a trader who sells 100,000 European call options on a non-dividend-paying stock when

1. The stock price is $49.
2. The strike price is $50.
3. The risk-free interest rate is 5%.
4. The stock price volatility is 20% per annum.
5. The time to option maturity is 20 weeks.

We suppose that the amount received for the options is $300,000 and that the trader has no other positions dependent on the stock.

The value of one option as a function of the underlying stock price is shown in Figure 3.2. The delta of one option changes with the stock price in the way shown in Figure 3.3.[1] At the time of the trade, the value of an option to buy one share of the stock is $2.40 and the delta of the option is 0.522. Because the trader is short 100,000 options, the value of the trader's portfolio is −$240,000 and the delta of the portfolio is −52,200. The trader can feel pleased that the options have been sold for $60,000 more than their theoretical value, but is faced with the problem of hedging the risk in the position.

The portfolio can be made delta neutral immediately after the trade by

---

[1] Figures 3.2 and 3.3 were produced with the DerivaGem software, which can be downloaded from the author's website. The Black–Scholes (analytic) model is used.

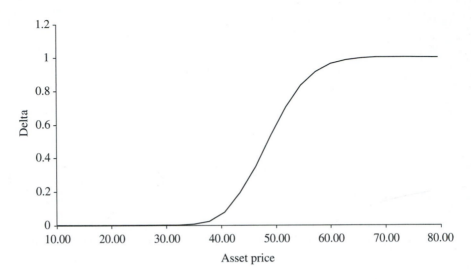

Figure 3.3   Delta of option as a function of stock price.

buying 52,200 shares of the underlying stock. If there is a small decrease (increase) in the stock price, the gain (loss) on the option position should be offset by the loss (gain) on the shares. For example, if the stock price increases from $49 to $49.10, then the value of the options will decrease by 52,200 × 0.1 = $5,220 while that of the shares will increase by this amount.

In the case of linear products, once the hedge has been set up, it does not need to be changed. This is not the case for nonlinear products. To preserve delta neutrality, the hedge has to be adjusted periodically. This is known as *rebalancing*.

Tables 3.2 and 3.3 provide two examples of how rebalancing might work in our example. Rebalancing is assumed to be done weekly. As mentioned, the initial value of delta for a single option is 0.522 and the delta of the portfolio is −52,200. This means that, as soon as the option is written, $2,557,800 must be borrowed to buy 52,200 shares at a price of $49. The rate of interest is 5%. An interest cost of approximately $2,500 is therefore incurred in the first week.

In Table 3.2 the stock price falls by the end of the first week to $48.12. The delta declines to 0.458. A long position in 45,800 shares is now required to hedge the option position. A total of 6,400 (i.e., 52,200 − 45,800) shares is therefore sold to maintain the delta neutrality of the hedge. The strategy realizes $308,000 in cash, and the cumulative borrowings at the end of Week 1 are reduced to $2,252,300. During the second week, the stock price reduces to $47.37 and delta declines again. This

Table 3.2 Simulation of delta hedging. Option closes in the money and cost of hedging is $263,300.

Week	Stock price	Delta	Shares purchased	Cost of shares purchased ($000)	Cumulative cash outflow ($000)	Interest cost ($000)
0	49.00	0.522	52,200	2,557.8	2,557.8	2.5
1	48.12	0.458	(6,400)	(308.0)	2,252.3	2.2
2	47.37	0.400	(5,800)	(274.7)	1,979.8	1.9
3	50.25	0.596	19,600	984.9	2,966.6	2.9
4	51.75	0.693	9,700	502.0	3,471.5	3.3
5	53.12	0.774	8,100	430.3	3,905.1	3.8
6	53.00	0.771	(300)	(15.9)	3,893.0	3.7
7	51.87	0.706	(6,500)	(337.2)	3,559.5	3.4
8	51.38	0.674	(3,200)	(164.4)	3,398.5	3.3
9	53.00	0.787	11,300	598.9	4,000.7	3.8
10	49.88	0.550	(23,700)	(1,182.2)	2,822.3	2.7
11	48.50	0.413	(13,700)	(664.4)	2,160.6	2.1
12	49.88	0.542	12,900	643.5	2,806.2	2.7
13	50.37	0.591	4,900	246.8	3,055.7	2.9
14	52.13	0.768	17,700	922.7	3,981.3	3.8
15	51.88	0.759	(900)	(46.7)	3,938.4	3.8
16	52.87	0.865	10,600	560.4	4,502.6	4.3
17	54.87	0.978	11,300	620.0	5,126.9	4.9
18	54.62	0.990	1,200	65.5	5,197.3	5.0
19	55.87	1.000	1,000	55.9	5,258.2	5.1
20	57.25	1.000	0	0.0	5,263.3	

leads to 5,800 shares being sold at the end of the second week. During the third week, the stock price increases to over $50 and delta increases. This leads to 19,600 shares being purchased at the end of the third week. Toward the end of the life of the option, it becomes apparent that the option will be exercised and delta approaches 1.0. By Week 20, therefore, the hedger owns 100,000 shares. The hedger receives $5 million (i.e., 100,000 × $50) for these shares when the option is exercised so that the total cost of writing the option and hedging it is $263,300.

Table 3.3 illustrates an alternative sequence of events where the option closes out of the money. As it becomes clear that the option will not be exercised, delta approaches zero. By Week 20 the hedger therefore has no position in the underlying stock. The total costs incurred are $256,600.

Table 3.3 Simulation of delta hedging. Option closes out of the money and cost of hedging is $256,600.

Week	Stock price	Delta	Shares purchased	Cost of shares purchased ($000)	Cumulative cash outflow ($000)	Interest cost ($000)
0	49.00	0.522	52,200	2,557.8	2,557.8	2.5
1	49.75	0.568	4,600	228.9	2,789.2	2.7
2	52.00	0.705	13,700	712.4	3,504.3	3.4
3	50.00	0.579	(12,600)	(630.0)	2,877.7	2.8
4	48.38	0.459	(12,000)	(580.6)	2,299.9	2.2
5	48.25	0.443	(1,600)	(77.2)	2,224.9	2.1
6	48.75	0.475	3,200	156.0	2,383.0	2.3
7	49.63	0.540	6,500	322.6	2,707.9	2.6
8	48.25	0.420	(12,000)	(579.0)	2,131.5	2.1
9	48.25	0.410	(1,000)	(48.2)	2,085.4	2.0
10	51.12	0.658	24,800	1,267.8	3,355.2	3.2
11	51.50	0.692	3,400	175.1	3,533.5	3.4
12	49.88	0.542	(15,000)	(748.2)	2,788.7	2.7
13	49.88	0.538	(400)	(20.0)	2,771.4	2.7
14	48.75	0.400	(13,800)	(672.7)	2,101.4	2.0
15	47.50	0.236	(16,400)	(779.0)	1,324.4	1.3
16	48.00	0.261	2,500	120.0	1,445.7	1.4
17	46.25	0.062	(19,900)	(920.4)	526.7	0.5
18	48.13	0.183	12,100	582.4	1,109.6	1.1
19	46.63	0.007	(17,600)	(820.7)	290.0	0.3
20	48.12	0.000	(700)	(33.7)	256.6	

In Tables 3.2 and 3.3 the costs of hedging the option, when discounted to the beginning of the period, are close to but not exactly the same as the theoretical (Black–Scholes) price of $240,000. If the hedging scheme worked perfectly, the cost of hedging would, after discounting, be exactly equal to the Black–Scholes price for every simulated stock price path. The reason for the variation in the cost of delta hedging is that the hedge is rebalanced only once a week. As rebalancing takes place more frequently, the variation in the cost of hedging is reduced. Of course, the examples in Tables 3.2 and 3.3 are idealized in that they assume the model underlying the Black–Scholes formula is exactly correct and there are no transaction costs.

Delta hedging aims to keep the value of the financial institution's position as close to unchanged as possible. Initially, the value of the written option is $240,000. In the situation depicted in Table 3.2, the value of the option can be calculated as $414,500 in Week 9. Thus, the financial institution has lost $174,500 (i.e., 414,500 − 240,000) on its short option position. Its cash position, as measured by the cumulative cost, is $1,442,900 worse in Week 9 than in Week 0. The value of the shares held has increased from $2,557,800 to $4,171,100 for a gain of $1,613,300. The net effect of all this is that the value of the financial institution's position has changed by only $4,100 during the nine-week period.

Where the Cost Comes From

The delta-hedging scheme in Tables 3.2 and 3.3 in effect creates a long position in the option synthetically to neutralize the trader's short option position. As the tables illustrate, the scheme tends to involve selling stock just after the price has gone down and buying stock just after the price has gone up. It might be termed a buy-high, sell-low scheme! The cost of $240,000 comes from the average difference between the price paid for the stock and the price realized for it.

Transaction Costs

Maintaining a delta-neutral position in a single option and the underlying asset, in the way that has just been described, is liable to be prohibitively expensive because of the transaction costs incurred on trades. Delta neutrality is more feasible for a large portfolio of derivatives dependent on a single asset. Only one trade in the underlying asset is necessary to zero out delta for the whole portfolio. The hedging transactions costs are absorbed by the profits on many different trades.

3.2 GAMMA

The *gamma*, Γ, of a portfolio of options on an underlying asset is the rate of change of the portfolio's delta with respect to the price of the underlying asset. It is the second partial derivative of the portfolio with respect to asset price:

$$\text{Gamma} = \frac{\partial^2 \Pi}{\partial S^2}$$

If gamma is small, then delta changes slowly and adjustments to keep a portfolio delta neutral only need to be made relatively infrequently.

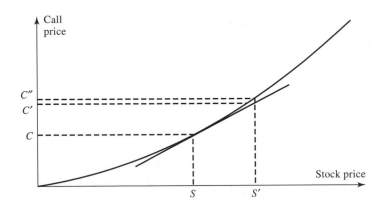

Figure 3.4   Hedging error introduced by nonlinearity.

However, if gamma is large in absolute terms, then delta is highly sensitive to the price of the underlying asset. It is then quite risky to leave a delta-neutral portfolio unchanged for any length of time. Figure 3.4 illustrates this point. When the stock price moves from S to S', delta hedging assumes that the option price moves from C to C', when in fact it moves from C to C''. The difference between C' and C'' leads to a hedging error. This error depends on the curvature of the relationship between the option price and the stock price. Gamma measures this curvature.[2]

Gamma is positive for a long position in an option. The general way in which gamma varies with the price of the underlying asset is shown in Figure 3.5. Gamma is greatest for options where the stock price is close to the strike price, K.

Making a Portfolio Gamma Neutral

A linear product has zero gamma and cannot be used to change the gamma of a portfolio. What is required is a position in an instrument, such as an option, that is not linearly dependent on the underlying asset price.

Suppose that a delta-neutral portfolio has a gamma equal to Γ, and a traded option has a gamma equal to Γ_T. If the number of traded options added to the portfolio is w_T, the gamma of the portfolio is

$$w_T \Gamma_T + \Gamma$$

Hence, the position in the traded option necessary to make the portfolio

---

[2] Indeed, the gamma of an option is sometimes referred to as its *curvature* by practitioners.

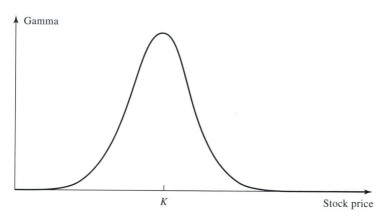

Figure 3.5 Relationship between gamma of an option and price of underlying asset. K is the option's strike price.

gamma neutral is $w_T = -\Gamma/\Gamma_T$. Including the traded option is likely to change the delta of the portfolio, so the position in the underlying asset then has to be changed to maintain delta neutrality. Note that the portfolio is gamma neutral only for a short period of time. As time passes, gamma neutrality can be maintained only if the position in the traded option is adjusted so that it is always equal to $-\Gamma/\Gamma_T$.

Making a delta-neutral portfolio gamma neutral can be regarded as a first correction for the fact that the position in the underlying asset cannot be changed continuously when delta hedging is used. Delta neutrality provides protection against relatively small stock price moves between rebalancing. Gamma neutrality provides protection against larger movements in this stock price between hedge rebalancing. Suppose that a portfolio is delta neutral and has a gamma of −3,000. The delta and gamma of a particular traded call option are 0.62 and 1.50, respectively. The portfolio can be made gamma neutral by including in the portfolio a long position of $3,000/1.5 = 2,000$ in the call option. However, the delta of the portfolio will then change from zero to $2,000 \times 0.62 = 1,240$. A quantity, 1,240, of the underlying asset must therefore be sold to keep it delta neutral.

3.3 VEGA

Another source of risk in derivatives trading is volatility. The volatility of a market variable measures our uncertainty about the future value of the variable. (It will be discussed more fully in Chapter 5.) In option valuation models, volatilities are often assumed to be constant, but in practice they do change through time. Spot positions, forwards, and swaps do not depend on the volatility of the underlying market variable, but options and most exotics do. Their values are liable to change because of movements in volatility as well as because of changes in the asset price and the passage of time.

The *vega*, $\mathcal{V}$, of a portfolio is the rate of change of the value of the portfolio with respect to the volatility of the underlying market variable.[3]

$$\mathcal{V} = \frac{\partial \Pi}{\partial \sigma}$$

If vega is high in absolute terms, the portfolio's value is very sensitive to small changes in volatility. If vega is low in absolute terms, volatility changes have relatively little impact on the value of the portfolio.

The vega of a portfolio can be changed by adding a position in a traded option. If $\mathcal{V}$ is the vega of the portfolio and $\mathcal{V}_T$ is the vega of a traded option, a position of $-\mathcal{V}/\mathcal{V}_T$ in the traded option makes the portfolio instantaneously vega neutral. Unfortunately, a portfolio that is gamma neutral will not, in general, be vega neutral, and vice versa. If a hedger requires a portfolio to be both gamma and vega neutral, then at least two traded derivatives dependent on the underlying asset must usually be used.

Example 3.1

Consider a portfolio that is delta neutral, with a gamma of $-5,000$ and a vega of $-8,000$. A traded option has a gamma of 0.5, a vega of 2.0, and a delta of 0.6. The portfolio could be made vega neutral by including a long position in 4,000 traded options. This would increase delta to 2,400 and require that 2,400 units of the asset be sold to maintain delta neutrality. The gamma of the portfolio would change from $-5,000$ to $-3,000$.

To make the portfolio gamma and vega neutral, we suppose that there is a second traded option with a gamma of 0.8, a vega of 1.2, and a delta of 0.5. If w_1 and w_2 are the quantities of the two traded options included in the portfolio, we require that

$$-5,000 + 0.5w_1 + 0.8w_2 = 0 \quad \text{and} \quad -8,000 + 2.0w_1 + 1.2w_2 = 0$$

The solution to these equations is $w_1 = 400$, $w_2 = 6,000$. The portfolio can therefore be made gamma and vega neutral by including 400 of the first traded option and 6,000 of the second traded option. The delta of the portfolio after

---

[3] Vega is the name given to one of the "Greek letters" in option pricing, but it is not one of the letters in the Greek alphabet.

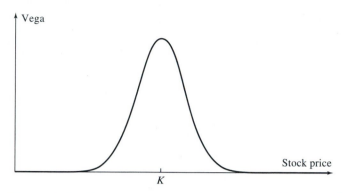

Figure 3.6 Variation of vega of an option with price of underlying asset. K is the option's strike price.

the addition of the positions in the two traded options is $400 \times 0.6 + 6,000 \times 0.5 = 3,240$. Hence, 3,240 units of the asset would have to be sold to maintain delta neutrality.

The vega of a long position in an option is positive. The variation of vega with the price of the underlying asset is similar to that of gamma and is shown in Figure 3.6. Gamma neutrality protects against large changes in the price of the underlying asset between hedge rebalancing. Vega neutrality protects against variations in volatility.

The volatilities of short-dated options tend to be more variable than the volatilities of long-dated options. The vega of a portfolio is therefore often calculated by changing the volatilities of short-dated options by more than that of long-dated options. This is discussed in Section 5.10.

3.4 THETA

The *theta*, Θ, of a portfolio is the rate of change of the value of the portfolio with respect to the passage of time with all else remaining the same. Theta is sometimes referred to as the *time decay* of the portfolio.

Theta is usually negative for an option.[4] This is because as the time to maturity decreases, with all else remaining the same, the option tends to become less valuable. The general way in which Θ varies with stock price for a call option on a stock is shown in Figure 3.7. When the stock price is very low, theta is close to zero. For an at-the-money call option, theta is

---

[4] An exception to this could be an in-the-money European put option on a non-dividend-paying stock or an in-the-money European call option on a currency with a very high interest rate.

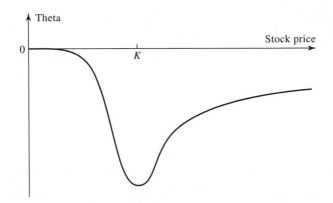

Figure 3.7 Variation of theta of a European call
option with stock price.

large and negative. Figure 3.8 shows typical patterns for the variation of
Θ with the time to maturity for in-the-money, at-the-money, and out-of-
the-money call options.

Theta is not the same type of Greek letter as delta. There is uncertainty
about the future stock price, but there is no uncertainty about the passage
of time. It makes sense to hedge against changes in the price of the

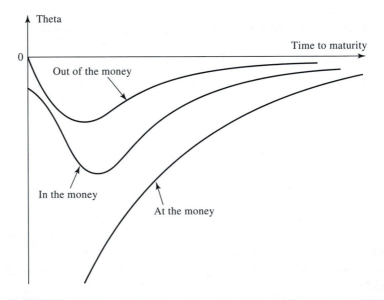

Figure 3.8 Typical patterns for variation of theta of a European
call option with time to maturity.

underlying asset, but it does not make any sense to hedge against the effect of the passage of time on an option portfolio. In spite of this, many traders regard theta as a useful descriptive statistic for a portfolio. In a delta-neutral portfolio, when theta is large and positive, gamma tends to be large and negative, and vice versa.

3.5 RHO

The final Greek letter we consider is rho. Rho is the rate of change of a portfolio with respect to the level of interest rates. Currency options have two rhos, one for the domestic interest rate and one for the foreign interest rate. When bonds and interest rate derivatives are part of a portfolio, traders usually consider carefully the ways in which the whole term structure of interest rates can change. We will discuss this in the next chapter.

3.6 CALCULATING GREEK LETTERS

The calculation of Greek letters for options is explained in Appendices C and D. The DerivaGem software, which can be downloaded from the author's website, can be used to calculate Greek letters for both regular options and exotics.

Consider again the European call option considered in Section 3.1. The stock price is $49, the strike price is $50, the risk-free rate is 5%, the stock price volatility is 20%, and the time to exercise is 20 weeks or 20/52 years. Using the Analytic (European) calculation, we see that the option price is $2.40; the delta is 0.522 (per $); the gamma is 0.066 (per $ per $); the vega is 0.121 per %; the theta is −0.012 per day; and the rho is 0.089 per %.

These numbers imply the following:

1. When there is an increase of $0.10 in the stock price with no other changes, the option price increases by about 0.522×0.1, or $0.0522.
2. When there is an increase $0.10 in the stock price with no other changes, the delta of the option increases by about 0.066×0.1, or 0.0066.
3. When there is an increase of 0.5% in volatility with no other changes, the option price increases by about 0.121×0.5, or 0.0605.

4. When one day goes by with no changes to the stock price or its volatility, the option price decreases by about 0.012.

5. When interest rates increase by 1% (or 100 basis points) with no other changes, the option price increases by 0.089.

3.7 TAYLOR SERIES EXPANSIONS

A Taylor series expansion of the change in the portfolio value in a short period of time shows the role played by different Greek letters. Consider a portfolio dependent on a single market variable, S. If the volatility of the underlying asset and interest rates are assumed to be constant, the value of the portfolio, Π, is a function of S and time t. The Taylor series expansion gives

$$\Delta\Pi = \frac{\partial\Pi}{\partial S}\,\Delta S + \frac{\partial\Pi}{\partial t}\,\Delta t + \frac{1}{2}\frac{\partial^2\Pi}{\partial S^2}\,\Delta S^2 + \frac{1}{2}\frac{\partial^2\Pi}{\partial t^2}\,\Delta t^2 + \frac{\partial^2\Pi}{\partial S\,\partial t}\,\Delta S\,\Delta t + \cdots$$

(3.1)

where $\Delta\Pi$ and ΔS are the change in Π and S, respectively, in a small time interval Δt. Delta hedging eliminates the first term on the right-hand side. The second term, which is theta times Δt, is nonstochastic. The third term can be made zero by ensuring that the portfolio is gamma neutral as well as delta neutral. Arguments from stochastic calculus show that ΔS is of order $\sqrt{\Delta t}$. This means that the third term on the right-hand side is of order Δt. Later terms in the Taylor series expansion are of higher order than Δt.

For a delta-neutral portfolio, the first term on the right-hand side of equation (3.1) is zero, so that

$$\Delta\Pi = \Theta\,\Delta t + \tfrac{1}{2}\Gamma\,\Delta S^2$$ (3.2)

when terms of higher order than Δt are ignored. The relationship between the change in the portfolio value and the change in the stock price is quadratic as shown in Figure 3.9. When gamma is positive, the holder of the portfolio gains from large movements in the market variable and loses when there is little or no movement. When gamma is negative, the reverse is true and a large positive or negative movement in the market variable leads to severe losses.

When the volatility of the underlying asset is uncertain, Π is a function

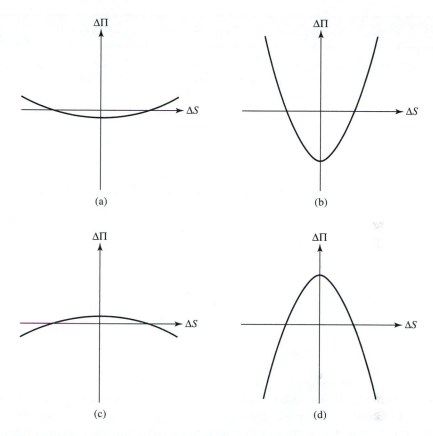

Figure 3.9 Alternative relationships between $\Delta\Pi$ and ΔS for a delta-neutral portfolio, with (a) slightly positive gamma, (b) large positive gamma, (c) slightly negative gamma, and (d) large negative gamma.

of σ, S, and t. Equation (3.1) then becomes

$$\Delta\Pi = \frac{\partial\Pi}{\partial S}\,\Delta S + \frac{\partial\Pi}{\partial\sigma}\,\Delta\sigma + \frac{\partial\Pi}{\partial t}\,\Delta t + \tfrac{1}{2}\frac{\partial^2\Pi}{\partial S^2}\,\Delta S^2 + \tfrac{1}{2}\frac{\partial^2\Pi}{\partial\sigma^2}\,\Delta\sigma^2 + \cdots$$

where $\Delta\sigma$ is the change in σ in time Δt. In this case, delta hedging eliminates the first term on the right-hand side. The second term is eliminated by making the portfolio vega neutral. The third term is nonstochastic. The fourth term is eliminated by making the portfolio gamma neutral.

Traders often define other "Greek letters" to correspond to higher-order terms in the Taylor series expansion. For example, $\partial^2\Pi/\partial\sigma^2$ is sometimes referred to as "gamma of vega".

Business Snapshot 3.2 Dynamic Hedging in Practice

In a typical arrangement at a financial institution, the responsibility for a portfolio of derivatives dependent on a particular underlying asset is assigned to one trader or to a group of traders working together. For example, one trader at Goldman Sachs might be assigned responsibility for all derivatives dependent on the value of the Australian dollar. A computer system calculates the value of the portfolio and Greek letters for the portfolio. Limits are defined for each Greek letter and special permission is required if a trader wants to exceed a limit at the end of a trading day.

The delta limit is often expressed as the equivalent maximum position in the underlying asset. For example, the delta limit of Goldman Sachs on Microsoft might be $10 million. If the Microsoft stock price is $50, this means that the absolute value of delta as we have calculated it can be no more that 200,000. The vega limit is usually expressed as a maximum dollar exposure per 1% change in the volatility.

As a matter of course, options traders make themselves delta neutral—or close to delta neutral—at the end of each day. Gamma and vega are monitored, but are not usually managed on a daily basis. Financial institutions often find that their business with clients involves writing options and that as a result they accumulate negative gamma and vega. They are then always looking out for opportunities to manage their gamma and vega risks by buying options at competitive prices.

There is one aspect of an options portfolio that mitigates problems of managing gamma and vega somewhat. Options are often close to the money when they are first sold so that they have relatively high gammas and vegas. However, after some time has elapsed, the underlying asset price has often changed sufficiently for them to become deep out of the money or deep in the money. Their gammas and vegas are then very small and of little consequence. The nightmare scenario for an options trader is where written options remain very close to the money as the maturity date is approached.

3.8 THE REALITIES OF HEDGING

In an ideal world traders working for financial institutions would be able to rebalance their portfolios very frequently in order to maintain a zero delta, a zero gamma, a zero vega, and so on. In practice, this is not possible. When managing a large portfolio dependent on a single underlying asset, traders usually make delta zero, or close to zero, at least once a day by trading the underlying asset. Unfortunately, a zero gamma and a zero vega are less easy to achieve because it is difficult to find options or

---

Business Snapshot 3.3   Is Delta Hedging Easier or More Difficult for Exotics?

We can approach the hedging of exotic options by creating a delta-neutral position and rebalancing frequently to maintain delta neutrality. When we do this, we find that some exotic options are easier to hedge than plain vanilla options and some are more difficult.

An example of an exotic option that is relatively easy to hedge is an average price call option (see Asian options in Section 2.5). As time passes, we observe more of the asset prices that will be used in calculating the final average. This means that our uncertainty about the payoff decreases with the passage of time. As a result, the option becomes progressively easier to hedge. In the final few days, the delta of the option always approaches zero because price movements during this time have very little impact on the payoff.

By contrast, barrier options (see Section 2.5) are relatively difficult to hedge. Consider a knock-out call option on a currency when the exchange rate is 0.0005 above the barrier. If the barrier is hit, the option is worth nothing. If it is not hit, the option may prove to be quite valuable. The delta of the option is discontinuous at the barrier, making conventional hedging very difficult.

---

other nonlinear derivatives that can be traded in the volume required at competitive prices (see the discussion of dynamic hedging in Business Snapshot 3.2).

There are large economies of scale in being an options trader. As noted earlier, maintaining delta neutrality for an individual option on an asset by trading the asset daily would be prohibitively expensive. But it is realistic to do this for a portfolio of several hundred options on the asset. This is because the cost of daily rebalancing is covered by the profit on many different trades.

3.9 HEDGING EXOTICS

Exotic options can often be hedged using the approach we have outlined. As explained in Business Snapshot 3.3, delta hedging is sometimes easier for exotics and sometimes more difficult. When delta hedging is not feasible for a portfolio of exotic options, an alternative approach known as *static options replication* is sometimes used. This is illustrated in Figure 3.10. Suppose that S denotes the asset price and t denotes time with the current ($t = 0$) value of S being S_0. Static options replication involves choosing a barrier in $\{S, t\}$-space that will eventually be reached

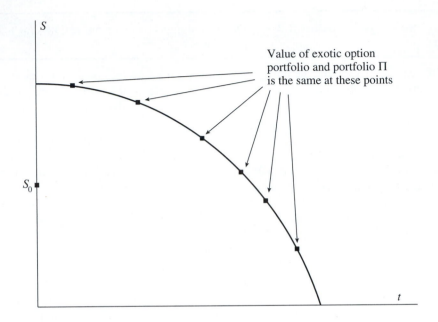

Figure 3.10   Static options replication. A replicating portfolio Π is chosen so that it has the same value as the exotic option portfolio at a number of points on a barrier.

and then finding a portfolio Π of plain vanilla options that is worth the same as the portfolio of exotic options at a number of points on the barrier. The portfolio of exotic options is hedged by shorting Π. Once the barrier is reached the hedge is unwound.

The theory underlying static options replication is that if two portfolios are worth the same at all $\{S, t\}$ points on the barrier they must be worth the same at all the $\{S, t\}$ points that can be reached prior to the barrier. In practice, values of the original portfolio and the replicating portfolio Π are matched at some, but not all, points on the barrier. The procedure therefore relies on the idea that if two portfolios have the same value at a reasonably large number of points on the barrier then their values are likely to be close at other points on the barrier.

3.10 SCENARIO ANALYSIS

In addition to monitoring risks such as delta, gamma, and vega, option traders often also carry out a scenario analysis. The analysis involves

Table 3.4 Profit or loss realized in two weeks under different scenarios ($ millions)

Volatility	Exchange rate						
	0.94	0.96	0.98	1.00	1.02	1.04	1.06
8%	+102	+55	+25	+6	−10	−34	−80
10%	+80	+40	+17	+2	−14	−38	−85
12%	+60	+25	+9	−2	−18	−42	−90

calculating the gain or loss on their portfolio over a specified period under a variety of different scenarios. The time period chosen is likely to depend on the liquidity of the instruments. The scenarios can be either chosen by management or generated by a model.

Consider a trader with a portfolio of options on a particular foreign currency. There are two main variables on which the value of the portfolio depends. These are the exchange rate and the exchange rate volatility. Suppose that the exchange rate is currently 1.0000 and its volatility is 10% per annum. The bank could calculate a table such as Table 3.4 showing the profit or loss experienced during a two-week period under different scenarios. This table considers seven different exchange rates and three different volatilities. Because a one-standard-deviation move in the exchange rate during a two-week period is usually about 0.02, the exchange rate moves considered are approximately one, two, and three standard deviations.

In Table 3.4 the greatest loss is in the lower right corner of the table. The loss corresponds to the volatility increasing to 12% and the exchange rate moving up to 1.06. Usually the greatest loss in a table such as 3.4 occurs at one of the corners, but this is not always so. For example, as we saw in Figure 3.9, when gamma is positive the greatest loss is experienced when the underlying market variable stays where it is.

SUMMARY

The individual responsible for the trades involving a particular market variable monitors a number of Greek letters and ensures that they are kept within the limits specified by his or her employer.

The delta, Δ, of a portfolio is the rate of change of its value with respect to the price of the underlying asset. Delta hedging involves creating a position with zero delta (sometimes referred to as a delta-neutral position). Since the delta of the underlying asset is 1.0, one way of hedging the portfolio is to take a position of $-\Delta$ in the underlying asset. For portfolios involving options and more complex derivatives, the position taken in the underlying asset has to be changed periodically. This is known as rebalancing.

Once a portfolio has been made delta neutral, the next stage is often to look at its gamma. The gamma of a portfolio is the rate of change of its delta with respect to the price of the underlying asset. It is a measure of the curvature of the relationship between the portfolio and the asset price. Another important hedge statistic is vega. This measures the rate of change of the value of the portfolio with respect to changes in the volatility of the underlying asset. Gamma and vega can be changed by trading options on the underlying asset.

In practice, derivatives traders usually rebalance their portfolios at least once a day to maintain delta neutrality. It is usually not feasible to maintain gamma and vega neutrality on a regular basis. Typically a trader monitors these measures. If they get too large, either corrective action is taken or trading is curtailed.

FURTHER READING

Derman, E., D. Ergener, and I. Kani, "Static Options Replication," *Journal of Derivatives*, 2, No. 4 (Summer 1995), 78–95.

Taleb, N. N., *Dynamic Hedging: Managing Vanilla and Exotic Options*. New York: Wiley, 1996.

QUESTIONS AND PROBLEMS (Answers at End of Book)

3.1. The delta of a derivatives portfolio dependent on the S&P 500 index is $-2,100$. The S&P 500 index is currently 1,000. Estimate what happens to the value of the portfolio when the index increases to 1,005.

3.2. The vega of a derivatives portfolio dependent on the USD/GBP exchange rate is 200 ($ per %). Estimate the effect on the portfolio of an increase in the volatility of the exchange rate from 12% to 14%.

3.3. The gamma of a delta-neutral portfolio is 30 (per $ per $). Estimate what happens to the value of the portfolio when the price of the underlying asset (a) suddenly increases by $2 and (b) suddenly decreases by $2.

3.4. What does it mean to assert that the delta of a call option is 0.7? How can a short position in 1,000 options be made delta neutral when the delta of a long position in each option is 0.7?

3.5. What does it mean to assert that the theta of an option position is -100 per day? If a trader feels that neither a stock price nor its implied volatility will change, what type of option position is appropriate?

3.6. What is meant by the gamma of an option position? What are the risks in the situation where the gamma of a position is large and negative and the delta is zero?

3.7. "The procedure for creating an option position synthetically is the reverse of the procedure for hedging the option position." Explain this statement.

3.8. A company uses delta hedging to hedge a portfolio of long positions in put and call options on a currency. Which of the following would lead to the most favorable result: (a) a virtually constant spot rate or (b) wild movements in the spot rate? How does your answer change if the portfolio contains short option positions?

3.9. A bank's position in options on the USD/euro exchange rate has a delta of 30,000 and a gamma of $-80,000$. Explain how these numbers can be interpreted. The exchange rate (dollars per euro) is 0.90. What position would you take to make the position delta neutral? After a short period of time, the exchange rate moves to 0.93. Estimate the new delta. What additional trade is necessary to keep the position delta neutral? Assuming the bank did set up a delta-neutral position originally, has it gained or lost money from the exchange rate movement?

3.10. "Static options replication assumes that the volatility of the underlying asset will be constant." Explain this statement.

3.11. Suppose that a trader using the static options replication technique wants to match the value of a portfolio of exotic derivatives with the value of a portfolio of regular options at 10 points on a boundary. How many regular options are likely to be needed? Explain your answer.

3.12. Why is an Asian option easier to hedge than a regular option?

3.13. Explain why there are economies of scale in hedging options.

3.14. Consider a six-month American put option on a foreign currency when the exchange rate (domestic currency per foreign currency) is 0.75, the strike price is 0.74, the domestic risk-free rate is 5%, the foreign risk-free rate is 3%, and the exchange rate volatility is 14% per annum. Use the DerivaGem software (binomial tree with 100 steps) to calculate the price, delta, gamma, vega, theta, and rho of the option. (The software can be downloaded from the author's website.) Verify that delta is correct by changing the exchange rate to 0.751 and recomputing the option price.

ASSIGNMENT QUESTIONS

3.15. The gamma and vega of a delta-neutral portfolio are 50 per $ per $ and 25 per %, respectively. Estimate what happens to the value of the portfolio when there is a shock to the market causing the underlying asset price to decrease by $3 and its volatility to increase by 4%.

3.16. Consider a one-year European call option on a stock when the stock price is $30, the strike price is $30, the risk-free rate is 5%, and the volatility is 25% per annum. Use the DerivaGem software to calculate the price, delta, gamma, vega, theta, and rho of the option. Verify that delta is correct by changing the stock price to $30.1 and recomputing the option price. Verify that gamma is correct by recomputing the delta for the situation where the stock price is $30.1. Carry out similar calculations to verify that vega, theta, and rho are correct.

3.17. A financial institution has the following portfolio of over-the-counter options on sterling:

Type	Position	Delta of option	Gamma of option	Vega of option
Call	−1000	0.50	2.2	1.8
Call	−500	0.80	0.6	0.2
Put	−2000	−0.40	1.3	0.7
Call	−500	0.70	1.8	1.4

A traded option is available with a delta of 0.6, a gamma of 1.5, and a vega of 0.8. (a) What position in the traded option and in sterling would make the portfolio both gamma neutral and delta neutral? (b) What position in the traded option and in sterling would make the portfolio both vega neutral and delta neutral?

3.18. Consider again the situation in Problem 3.17. Suppose that a second traded option with a delta of 0.1, a gamma of 0.5, and a vega of 0.6 is available. How could the portfolio be made delta, gamma, and vega neutral?

3.19. Reproduce Table 3.2. (In Table 3.2 the stock position is rounded to the nearest 100 shares.) Calculate the gamma and theta of the position each week. Calculate the change in the value of the portfolio each week (before the rebalancing at the end of the week) and check whether equation (3.2) is approximately satisfied. (*Note:* DerivaGem produces a value of theta "per calendar day". The theta in the formula in Appendix C is "per year".)

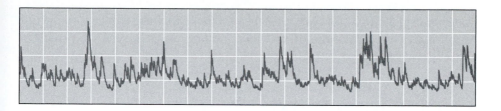

CHAPTER 4

Interest Rate Risk

Interest rate risk is more difficult to manage than the risk arising from market variables such as equity prices, exchange rates, and commodity prices. One complication is that there are many different interest rates in any given currency (Treasury rates, interbank borrowing and lending rates, mortgage rates, deposit rates, prime borrowing rates, and so on). Although these tend to move together, they are not perfectly correlated. Another complication is that, to describe an interest rate, we need more than a single number. We need a function describing the variation of the rate with maturity. This is known as the *interest rate term structure* or the *yield curve*.

Consider, for example, the situation of a US government bond trader. The trader's portfolio is likely to consist of many bonds with different maturities. The trader has an exposure to movements in the one-year rate, the two-year rate, the three-year rate, and so on. The trader's delta exposure is therefore more complicated than that of the gold trader in Table 3.1. The trader must be concerned with all the different ways in which the US Treasury yield curve can change its shape through time.

This chapter starts with some preliminary material on types of interest rates and the way interest rates are measured. It then moves on to consider the ways exposures to interest rates can be managed. Duration and convexity measures are covered first. For parallel shifts in the yield curve, these are analogous to the delta and gamma measures discussed in the previous chapter. A number of different approaches to managing the risks of nonparallel shifts are then presented. These include the use of partial durations, the calculation of multiple deltas, and the use of principal components analysis.

4.1 MEASURING INTEREST RATES

A statement by a bank that the interest rate on one-year deposits is 10% per annum sounds straightforward and unambiguous. In fact, its precise meaning depends on the way the interest rate is measured.

If the interest rate is measured with annual compounding, the bank's statement that the interest rate is 10% means that $100 grows to

$$\$100 \times 1.1 = \$110$$

at the end of one year. When the interest rate is measured with semi-annual compounding, it means that we earn 5% every six months, with the interest being reinvested. In this case, $100 grows to

$$\$100 \times 1.05 \times 1.05 = \$110.25$$

at the end of one year. When the interest rate is measured with quarterly compounding, the bank's statement means that we earn 2.5% every three months, with the interest being reinvested. The $100 then grows to

$$\$100 \times 1.025^4 = \$110.38$$

at the end of one year. Table 4.1 shows the effect of increasing the compounding frequency further.

Table 4.1   Effect of the compounding frequency on the value of $100 at the end of one year when the interest rate is 10% per annum.

Compounding frequency	Value of $100 at end of year ($)
Annually ($m = 1$)	110.00
Semiannually ($m = 2$)	110.25
Quarterly ($m = 4$)	110.38
Monthly ($m = 12$)	110.47
Weekly ($m = 52$)	110.51
Daily ($m = 365$)	110.52

The compounding frequency defines the units in which an interest rate is measured. A rate expressed with one compounding frequency can be converted into an equivalent rate with a different compounding frequency. For example, from Table 4.1 we see that 10.25% with annual compounding is equivalent to 10% with semiannual compounding. We can think of the difference between one compounding frequency and another to be analogous to the difference between kilometers and miles. They are two different units of measurement.

To generalize our results, suppose that an amount A is invested for n years at an interest rate of R per annum. If the interest is compounded once per annum, the terminal value of the investment is

$$A(1 + R)^n$$

If the interest is compounded m times per annum, the terminal value of the investment is

$$A\left(1 + \frac{R}{m}\right)^{mn} \tag{4.1}$$

When $m = 1$, the rate is sometimes referred to as the *equivalent annual interest rate*.

Continuous Compounding

The limit as the compounding frequency m tends to infinity is known as *continuous compounding*.[1] With continuous compounding, it can be shown that an amount A invested for n years at rate R grows to

$$Ae^{Rn} \tag{4.2}$$

where $e = 2.71828$. The function e^x is built into most calculators, so the computation of the expression in equation (4.2) presents no problems. In the example in Table 4.1, $A = 100$, $n = 1$, and $R = 0.1$, so that the value to which A grows in one year with continuous compounding is

$$100e^{0.1} = \$110.52$$

This is (to two decimal places) the same as the value with daily compounding. For most practical purposes, continuous compounding can be thought of as being equivalent to daily compounding. Compounding a sum of money at a continuously compounded rate R for n years involves

---

[1] Actuaries sometimes refer to a continuously compounded rate as the *force of interest*.

multiplying it by e^{Rn}. Discounting it at a continuously compounded rate R for n years involves multiplying by e^{-Rn}.

Suppose that R_c is a rate of interest with continuous compounding and R_m is the equivalent rate with compounding m times per annum. From the results in equations (4.1) and (4.2), we must have

$$Ae^{R_c n} = A\left(1 + \frac{R_m}{m}\right)^{mn}$$

or

$$e^{R_c} = \left(1 + \frac{R_m}{m}\right)^{m}$$

This means that

$$R_c = m\ln\left(1 + \frac{R_m}{m}\right) \tag{4.3}$$

and

$$R_m = m(e^{R_c/m} - 1) \tag{4.4}$$

These equations can be used to convert a rate with a compounding frequency of m times per annum to a continuously compounded rate and vice versa. The function ln is the natural logarithm function and is built into most calculators. This function is defined so that, if $y = \ln x$, then $x = e^y$.

Example 4.1

Consider an interest rate that is quoted as 10% per annum with semiannual compounding. From equation (4.3) with $m = 2$ and $R_m = 0.1$, the equivalent rate with continuous compounding is

$$2\ln\left(1 + \frac{0.1}{2}\right) = 0.09758$$

or 9.758% per annum.

Example 4.2

Suppose that a lender quotes the interest rate on loans as 8% per annum with continuous compounding and that interest is actually paid quarterly. From equation (4.4) with $m = 4$ and $R_c = 0.08$, the equivalent rate with quarterly compounding is

$$4(e^{0.08/4} - 1) = 0.0808$$

or 8.08% per annum. This means that on a $1,000 loan, interest payments of $20.20 would be required each quarter.

4.2 ZERO RATES AND FORWARD RATES

The *n*-year zero-coupon interest rate is the rate of interest earned on an investment that starts today and lasts for *n* years. All the interest and principal is realized at the end of *n* years. There are no intermediate payments. The *n*-year zero-coupon interest rate is sometimes also referred to as the *n*-year *spot rate*, the *n*-year *zero rate*, or just the *n*-year *zero*. The zero rate as a function of maturity is referred to as the *zero curve*. Suppose a five-year zero rate with continuous compounding is 5% per annum. This means that $100, if invested for five years, grows to

$$100 \times e^{0.05 \times 5} = 128.40$$

A forward rate is the future zero rate implied by today's zero rates. Consider the zero rates shown in Table 4.2. The forward rate for the period between six months and one year is 6.6%. This is because 5% for the first six months combined with 6.6% for the next six months gives an average of 5.8% for one year. Similarly, the forward rate for the period between 12 months and 18 months is 7.6% because this rate when combined with 5.8% for the first 12 months gives an average of 6.4% for 18 months. In general, the forward rate F for the period between times T_1 and T_2 is

$$F = \frac{R_2 T_2 - R_1 T_1}{T_2 - T_1} \tag{4.5}$$

where R_1 is the zero rate for maturity of T_1 and R_2 is the zero rate for maturity T_2. This formula is exactly correct when rates are measured with continuous compounding and approximately correct for other compounding frequencies. The results from using this formula on the rates in Table 4.2 are given in Table 4.3. For example, substituting $T_1 = 1.5$,

Table 4.2   Zero rates.

Maturity (years)	Zero rate (% cont. comp.)
0.5	5.0
1.0	5.8
1.5	6.4
2.0	6.8

Table 4.3   Forward rates for zero rates
in Table 4.2.

Period (years)	Forward rate (% cont. comp.)
0.5 to 1.0	6.6
1.0 to 1.5	7.6
1.5 to 2.0	8.0

$T_2 = 2.0$, $R_1 = 0.064$, and $R_2 = 0.068$, we get $F = 0.08$, showing that the forward rate for the period between 18 months and 24 months is 8.0%.

Investors who think that future interest rates will be markedly different from forward rates have no difficulty in finding trades that reflect their beliefs (see Business Snapshot 4.1).

Bond Pricing

Most bonds provide coupons periodically. The bond's principal (also known as its par value or face value) is received at the end of its life. The theoretical price of a bond can be calculated as the present value of all the cash flows that will be received by the owner of the bond. The most accurate approach is to use a different zero rate for each cash flow. To illustrate this, consider the situation where zero rates are as shown in Table 4.2. Suppose that a two-year bond with a principal of $100 provides coupons at the rate of 6% per annum semiannually. To calculate the present value of the first coupon of $3, we discount it at 5.0% for six months; to calculate the present value of the second coupon of $3, we discount it at 5.8% for one year; and so on. The theoretical price of the bond is therefore

$$3e^{-0.05 \times 0.5} + 3e^{-0.058 \times 1.0} + 3e^{-0.064 \times 1.5} + 103e^{-0.068 \times 2.0} = 98.39$$

or $98.39.

Bond Yields

A bond's yield is the discount rate that, when applied to all the bond's cash flows, equates the bond price to its market price. Suppose that the theoretical price of the bond we have been considering, $98.39, is also its market value (i.e., the market's price of the bond is in exact agreement with the data in Table 4.2). If y is the yield on the bond, expressed with

---

> **Business Snapshot 4.1**   Orange County's Yield Curve Plays
>
> Consider an investor who can borrow or lend at the rates shown in Table 4.2. Suppose the investor thinks that the six-month interest rates will not change much over the next three years. The investor can borrow six-month funds and invest for two years. The six-month borrowings can be rolled over at the end of 6, 12, and 18 months. If interest rates do stay about the same, this strategy will yield a profit of about 1.8% per year because interest will be received at 6.8% and paid at 5%. This type of trading strategy is known as a *yield curve play*. The investor is speculating that rates in the future will be quite different from the forward rates shown in Table 4.3.
>
> Robert Citron, the Treasurer at Orange County, used yield curve plays similar to the one we have just described very successfully in 1992 and 1993. The profit from Mr. Citron's trades became an important contributor to Orange County's budget and he was re-elected. (No-one listened to his opponent in the election, who said his trading strategy was too risky.)
>
> In 1994 Mr. Citron expanded his yield curve plays. He invested heavily in *inverse floaters*. These pay a rate of interest equal to a fixed rate of interest minus a floating rate. He also leveraged his position by borrowing at short-term interest rates. If short-term interest rates had remained the same or declined, he would have continued to do well. As it happened, interest rates rose sharply during 1994. On December 1, 1994, Orange County announced that its investment portfolio had lost $1.5 billion and several days later it filed for bankruptcy protection.

---

continuous compounding, we must have

$$3e^{-y\times0.5} + 3e^{-y\times1.0} + 3e^{-y\times1.5} + 103e^{-y\times2.0} = 98.39$$

This equation can be solved using Excel's Solver or in some other way to give $y = 6.76\%$.

4.3 TREASURY RATES

Treasury rates are the rates an investor earns on Treasury bills and Treasury bonds. These are the instruments used by a government to borrow in its own currency. Japanese Treasury rates are the rates at which the Japanese government borrows in yen; US Treasury rates are the rates at which the US government borrows in US dollars; and so on. It is usually assumed that there is no chance that a government will default on

an obligation denominated in its own currency.[2] Treasury rates are therefore totally risk-free rates in the sense that an investor who buys a
Treasury bill or Treasury bond is certain that interest and principal
payments will be made as promised.

Determining Treasury Zero Rates

One way of determining Treasury zero rates such as those in Table 4.2 is
to observe the yields on "strips". These are zero-coupon bonds that are
synthetically created by traders when they sell the coupons on a Treasury
bond separately from the principal.

Another way of determining Treasury zero rates is from regular Treasury bills and bonds. The most popular approach is known as the *bootstrap method*. This involves working from short maturities to successively
longer maturities and matching prices. Suppose that Table 4.2 gives the
Treasury rates determined so far and that a 2.5-year bond providing a
coupon of 8% sells for $102 per $100 of principal. We would determine
the 2.5-year zero rate as the rate R which, when used in conjunction with
the rates in Table 4.2, gives the correct price for this bond. This involves
solving

$$4e^{-0.05\times0.5} + 4e^{-0.058\times1.0} + 4e^{-0.064\times1.5} + 4e^{-0.068\times2.0} + 104e^{-R\times2.5} = 102$$

which gives $R = 7.05\%$. The complete set of zero rates is shown in
Table 4.4. The zero curve is usually assumed to be linear between the
points that are determined by the bootstrap method. (In our example, the
2.25-year zero rate would be 6.925%.) It is also assumed to be constant

Table 4.4   Rates in Table 4.2 after 2.5-year rate
has been determined using the bootstrap method.

Maturity (years)	Zero rate (% cont. comp.)
0.5	5.00
1.0	5.80
1.5	6.40
2.0	6.80
2.5	7.05

[2] The reason for this is that the government can always meet its obligation by printing
more money.

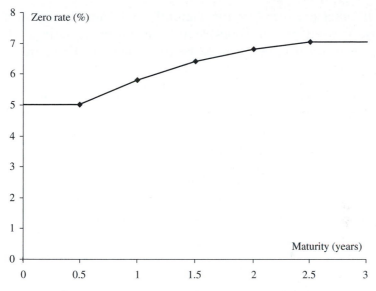

Figure 4.1 Zero curve for data in Table 4.4.

prior to the first point and beyond the last point. The zero curve for our example is shown in Figure 4.1.

4.4 LIBOR AND SWAP RATES

LIBOR is short for *London Interbank Offered Rate*. A LIBOR quote by a particular bank is the rate of interest at which the bank is prepared to make a large wholesale deposit with another bank.[3] Large banks and other financial institutions quote 1-month, 3-month, 6-month, and 12-month LIBOR in all major currencies, where 1-month LIBOR is the rate at which one-month deposits are offered, 3-month LIBOR is the rate at which three-month deposits are offered, and so on. A deposit with a bank can be regarded as a loan to that bank. A bank must therefore satisfy certain creditworthiness criteria to qualify for receiving LIBOR deposits. Typically, it must have an AA credit rating.[4]

---

[3] Banks also quote LIBID, the *London Interbank Bid Rate*. The is the rate at which a bank is prepared to accept deposits from another bank. The LIBOR quote is slightly higher than the LIBID quote.

[4] The best credit rating given to a company by the rating agency S&P is AAA. The second best is AA. The corresponding ratings from the rival rating agency Moody's are Aaa and Aa, respectively. More details on ratings are in Chapter 11.

LIBOR rates are therefore the 1-month to 12-month borrowing rates for banks (and other companies) that have AA credit ratings. How can the LIBOR yield curve be extended beyond one year? There are two ways of doing this:

1. Create a yield curve to represent the rates at which AA-rated companies can borrow for periods of time longer than one year.

2. Create a yield curve to represent the future short-term borrowing rates for AA-rated companies.

It is important to understand the difference. Suppose that the yield curve is 4% for all maturities. If the yield curve is created in the first way, this means that AA-rated companies can today lock in an interest rate of 4% regardless of how long they want to borrow. If the yield curve is created in the second way, then the forward interest rate that the market assigns to the short-term borrowing rates of AA-rated companies at future times is 4%. When the yield curve is created in the first way, it gives the forward short-term borrowing rate for a company that is AA-rated today. When it is created in the second way, it gives the forward short-term borrowing rate for a company that will be AA at the beginning of the period covered by the forward contract.

In practice, the LIBOR yield curve is extended using the second approach. The LIBOR yield curve is sometimes also called the swap yield curve or the LIBOR/swap yield curve. The LIBOR/swap zero rates out to one year are known directly from quoted LIBOR deposit rates. Swap rates (see Table 2.5) allow the yield curve to be extended beyond one year using an approach similar to the bootstrap method described for Treasuries in the previous section.[5] To understand why this is so, consider a bank that

1. Lends a certain principal for six months to an AA borrower and relends it for successive six month periods to other AA borrowers, and

2. Enters into a swap to exchange the LIBOR for the five-year swap rate

These transactions show that the effective interest rate earned from the series of short-term loans to AA borrowers is equivalent to the swap rate. This means that the swap yield curve and the LIBOR yield curve (defined using the second approach above) are the same.

---

[5] Eurodollar futures, which are contracts on the future value of LIBOR, can also be used to extend the LIBOR yield curve.

The Risk-Free Rate

The risk-free rate is important in the pricing of financial contracts. The usual practice among financial institutions is to assume that the LIBOR/swap yield curve provides the risk-free rate. Treasury rates are regarded as too low to be used as risk-free rates because:

1. Treasury bills and Treasury bonds must be purchased by financial institutions to fulfill a variety of regulatory requirements. This increases demand for these Treasury instruments driving their prices up and their yields down.

2. The amount of capital a bank is required to hold to support an investment in Treasury bills and bonds is substantially smaller than the capital required to support a similar investment in other very low-risk instruments.

3. In the United States, Treasury instruments are given a favorable tax treatment compared with most other fixed-income investments because they are not taxed at the state level.

As we have seen, the credit risk in the LIBOR/swap yield curve corresponds to the credit risk in a series of short-term loans to AA-rated borrowers. It is therefore not totally risk free. There is a small chance that an AA borrower will default during the life of a short-term loan. But the LIBOR/swap yield curve is close to risk free and is widely used by traders as a proxy for the risk-free yield curve. There is some evidence that a true risk-free yield curve, uninfluenced by the factors affecting Treasury rates that we have just mentioned, is about 10 basis points ($= 0.1\%$) below the LIBOR/swap yield curve.[6] By contrast, Treasury rates are about 50 basis points (0.5%) below LIBOR/swap rates on average.

4.5 DURATION

Duration is a widely used measure of a portfolio's exposure to yield curve movements. As its name implies, the *duration* of an instrument is a measure of how long, on average, the holder of the instrument has to wait before receiving cash payments. A zero-coupon bond that lasts n years has a duration of n years. However, a coupon-bearing bond lasting

---

[6] See J. Hull, M. Predescu, and A. White, "The Relationship Between Credit Default Swap Spreads, Bond Yields, and Credit Rating Announcements," *Journal of Banking and Finance*, 28 (November 2004), 2789–2811.

n years has a duration of less than n years, because the holder receives some of the cash payments prior to year n.

Suppose that a bond provides the holder with cash flows c_i at time t_i for $i = 1, \ldots, n$. The price B and yield y (continuously compounded) are related by

$$B = \sum_{i=1}^{n} c_i e^{-yt_i} \tag{4.6}$$

The duration D of the bond is defined as

$$D = \frac{\sum_{i=1}^{n} t_i c_i e^{-yt_i}}{B} \tag{4.7}$$

This can be written as

$$D = \sum_{i=1}^{n} t_i \left(\frac{c_i e^{-yt_i}}{B} \right) \tag{4.8}$$

The term in parentheses is the ratio of the present value of the cash flow at time t_i to the bond price. The bond price is the present value of all payments. The duration is therefore a weighted average of the times when payments are made, with the weight applied to time t_i being equal to the proportion of the bond's total present value provided by the cash flow at time t_i. The sum of the weights is 1.0.

When a small change Δy in the yield is considered, it is approximately true that

$$\Delta B = \frac{dB}{dy} \Delta y \tag{4.9}$$

From equation (4.6), this becomes

$$\Delta B = -\Delta y \sum_{i=1}^{n} c_i t_i e^{-yt_i} \tag{4.10}$$

(Note that there is an inverse relationship between B and y. When bond yields increase, bond prices decrease; and when bond yields decrease, bond prices increase.) From equations (4.7) and (4.10), we obtain the key duration relationship

$$\Delta B = -BD \Delta y \tag{4.11}$$

This can be written as

$$\frac{\Delta B}{B} = -D \Delta y \tag{4.12}$$

Table 4.5 Calculation of duration.

Time (years)	Cash flow ($)	Present value ($)	Weight	Time × Weight
0.5	5	4.709	0.050	0.025
1.0	5	4.435	0.047	0.047
1.5	5	4.176	0.044	0.066
2.0	5	3.933	0.042	0.083
2.5	5	3.704	0.039	0.098
3.0	105	73.256	0.778	2.333
Total	130	94.213	1.000	2.653

Equation (4.12) is an approximate relationship between percentage changes in a bond price and changes in its yield. The equation is easy to use and is the reason why duration, first suggested by Macaulay in 1938, has become such a popular measure.

Consider a three-year 10% coupon bond with a face value of $100. Suppose that the yield on the bond is 12% per annum with continuous compounding. This means that $y = 0.12$. Coupon payments of $5 are made every six months. Table 4.5 shows the calculations necessary to determine the bond's duration. The present values of the bond's cash flows, using the yield as the discount rate, are shown in column 3. (For example, the present value of the first cash flow is $5e^{-0.12 \times 0.5} = 4.709$.) The sum of the numbers in column 3 gives the bond's price as 94.213. The weights are calculated by dividing the numbers in column 3 by 94.213. The sum of the numbers in column 5 gives the duration as 2.653 years.

Small changes in interest rates are often measured in *basis points*. A basis point is 0.01% per annum. The following example investigates the accuracy of the duration relationship in equation (4.11).

Example 4.5

For the bond in Table 4.5, the bond price B is 94.213 and the duration D is 2.653, so that equation (4.11) gives

$$\Delta B = -94.213 \times 2.653 \Delta y$$

or

$$\Delta B = -249.95 \Delta y$$

When the yield on the bond increases by 10 basis points ($= 0.1\%$), $\Delta y = +0.001$. The duration relationship predicts that

$$\Delta B = -249.95 \times 0.001 = -0.250$$

so that the bond price goes down to $94.213 - 0.250 = 93.963$. How accurate is this? When the bond yield increases by 10 basis points to 12.1%, the bond price is

$$5e^{-0.121 \times 0.5} + 5e^{-0.121 \times 1.0} + 5e^{-0.121 \times 1.5} + 5e^{-0.121 \times 2.0}$$
$$+ 5e^{-0.121 \times 2.5} + 105e^{-0.121 \times 3.0} = 93.963$$

which is (to three decimal places) the same as that predicted by the duration relationship.

Modified Duration

The preceding analysis is based on the assumption that y is expressed with continuous compounding. If y is expressed with annual compounding, it can be shown that the approximate relationship in equation (4.11) becomes

$$\Delta B = -\frac{BD \, \Delta y}{1 + y}$$

More generally, if y is expressed with a compounding frequency of m times per year, then

$$\Delta B = -\frac{BD \, \Delta y}{1 + y/m}$$

A variable D^* defined by

$$D^* = \frac{D}{1 + y/m}$$

is sometimes referred to as the bond's *modified duration*. It allows the duration relationship to be simplified to

$$\Delta B = -BD^* \Delta y \qquad\qquad \textbf{(4.13)}$$

when y is expressed with a compounding frequency of m times per year. The following example investigates the accuracy of the modified duration relationship.

Example 4.6

The bond in Table 4.5 has a price of 94.213 and a duration of 2.653. The yield, expressed with semiannual compounding is 12.3673%. The modified duration D^* is

$$D^* = \frac{2.653}{1 + 0.123673/2} = 2.4985$$

From equation (4.13), we have

$$\Delta B = -94.213 \times 2.4985 \Delta y$$

or

$$\Delta B = -235.39 \Delta y$$

When the yield (semiannually compounded) increases by 10 basis points (= 0.1%), $\Delta y = +0.001$. The duration relationship predicts that we expect ΔB to be $-235.39 \times 0.001 = -0.235$, so that the bond price goes down to $94.213 - 0.235 = 93.978$. How accurate is this? When the bond yield (semiannually compounded) increases by 10 basis points to 12.4673% (or to 12.0941% with continuous compounding), an exact calculation similar to that in the previous example shows that the bond price becomes 93.978. This shows that the modified duration calculation is accurate for small yield changes.

4.6 CONVEXITY

The duration relationship measures exposure to small changes in yields. This is illustrated in Figure 4.2, which shows the relationship between the percentage change in value and change in yield for bonds having the same duration. The gradients of the two curves are the same at the origin. This means that both portfolios change in value by the same percentage for small yield changes, as predicted by equation (4.12). For large yield

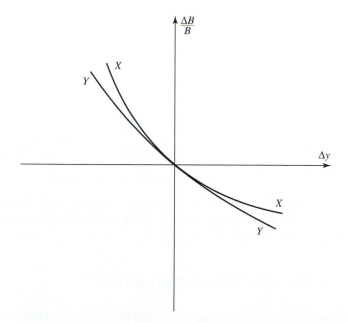

Figure 4.2 Two portfolios with the same duration.

changes, the portfolios behave differently. Portfolio X has more curvature in its relationship with yields than Portfolio Y. A factor known as *convexity* measures this curvature and can be used to improve the relationship in equation (4.12).

A measure of convexity for a bond is

$$C = \frac{1}{B}\frac{d^2B}{dy^2} = \frac{\sum_{i=1}^{n} c_i t_i^2 e^{-yt_i}}{B}$$

where y is the bond's yield. This is the weighted average of the square of the time to the receipt of cash flows. From Taylor series expansions, a more accurate expression than equation (4.9) is

$$\Delta B = \frac{dB}{dy}\Delta y + \frac{1}{2}\frac{d^2B}{dy^2}\Delta y^2$$

This leads to

$$\frac{\Delta B}{B} = -D\,\Delta y + \frac{1}{2}C(\Delta y)^2 \tag{4.14}$$

Example 4.7

Consider again the bond in Table 4.5: the bond price B is 94.213 and the duration D is 2.653. The convexity is

$$0.05 \times 0.5^2 + 0.047 \times 1.0^2 + 0.044 \times 1.5^2 + 0.042 \times 2.0^2$$
$$+ 0.039 \times 2.5^2 + 0.779 \times 3.0^2 = 7.570$$

The convexity relationship in equation (4.14) is therefore

$$\frac{\Delta B}{B} = -2.653\Delta y + \frac{1}{2} \times 7.570 \times (\Delta y)^2$$

Consider a 2% change in the bond yield from 12% to 14%. The duration relationship predicts that the dollar change in the value of the bond will be $-94.213 \times 2.653 \times 0.02 = -4.999$. The convexity relationship predicts that it will be
$$-94.213 \times 2.653 \times 0.02 + 0.5 \times 94.213 \times 7.570 \times 0.02^2 = -4.856$$

The actual change in the value of the bond is -4.859. This shows that the convexity relationship gives much more accurate results than duration for a large change in the bond yield.

4.7 APPLICATION TO PORTFOLIOS

The duration concept can be used for any portfolio of assets dependent on interest rates. Suppose that P is the value of the portfolio. We make a small parallel shift in the zero-coupon yield curve and observe the change ΔP in P. Duration is defined as

$$D = -\frac{1}{P}\frac{\Delta P}{\Delta y}$$

where Δy is size of the parallel shift. Equation (4.12) becomes

$$\frac{\Delta P}{P} = -D\,\Delta y \qquad (4.15)$$

Suppose the portfolio consists of a number of assets. The ith asset is worth X_i and has a duration D_i $(i = 1, \ldots, n)$. Define ΔX_i as the change in the value of X_i arising from the yield curve shift Δy. It follows that $P = \sum_{i=1}^{n} X_i$ and $\Delta P = \sum_{i=1}^{n} \Delta X_i$, so that the duration of the portfolio is given by

$$D = -\frac{1}{P}\sum_{i=1}^{n}\frac{\Delta X_i}{\Delta y}$$

The duration of the ith asset is

$$D_i = -\frac{1}{X_i}\frac{\Delta X_i}{\Delta y}$$

Hence,

$$D = \sum_{i=1}^{n}\frac{X_i}{P}D_i$$

This shows that the duration D of a portfolio is the weighted average of the durations of the individual assets comprising the portfolio with the weight assigned to an asset being proportional to the value of the asset.

The convexity can be generalized in the same way as the duration. For an interest-rate-dependent portfolio with value P, we define the convexity as $1/P$ times the second partial derivative of the value of the portfolio with respect to a parallel shift in the zero-coupon yield curve. Equation (4.14) is correct with B replaced by P:

$$\frac{\Delta P}{P} = -D\,\Delta y + \tfrac{1}{2}C(\Delta y)^2 \qquad (4.16)$$

The relationship between the convexity of a portfolio and the convexity of the assets comprising the portfolio is similar to that for duration: the convexity of the portfolio is the weighted average of the convexities of the assets with the weights being proportional to the value of the assets.

The convexity of a bond portfolio tends to be greatest when the portfolio provides payments evenly over a long period of time. It is least when the payments are concentrated around one particular point in time.

Portfolio Immunization

A portfolio consisting of long and short positions in interest-rate-dependent assets can be protected against relatively small parallel shifts in the yield curve by ensuring that its duration is zero. It can be protected against relatively large parallel shifts in the yield curve by ensuring that its duration and convexity are both zero or close to zero. In this respect duration and convexity are analogous to the delta and gamma Greek letters we encountered in Chapter 3.

4.8 NONPARALLEL YIELD CURVE SHIFTS

Unfortunately, the basic duration relationship in equation (4.15) only quantifies exposure to parallel yield curve shifts. The duration plus convexity relationship in equation (4.16) allows the shift to be relatively large, but it is still a parallel shift.

Some researchers have attempted to extend duration measures so that nonparallel shifts can be considered. Reitano suggests a partial duration measure where just one point on the zero-coupon yield curve is shifted and all other points remain the same.[7] Suppose that the zero curve is as shown in Table 4.6 and Figure 4.3. Shifting the five-year point involves changing the zero curve as indicated in Figure 4.4. In general, the partial duration of the portfolio for the ith point on the zero curve is

$$-\frac{1}{P}\frac{\Delta P_i}{\Delta x_i}$$

where Δx_i is the size of the small change made to the ith point on the yield curve and ΔP_i is the resultant change in the portfolio value. The sum of all the partial duration measures equals the usual duration measure.

Suppose that the partial durations for a particular portfolio are as shown in Table 4.7. The total duration of the portfolio is only 0.2. This means that the portfolio is relatively insensitive to parallel shifts in the yield curve. However, the durations for short maturities are positive while

---

[7] See R. Reitano, "Non-Parallel Yield Curve Shifts and Immunization," *Journal of Portfolio Management*, Spring 1992, 36–43.

Table 4.6   Zero-coupon yield curve (rates continuously compounded).

Maturity (years)	1	2	3	4	5	7	10
Rate (%)	4.0	4.5	4.8	5.0	5.1	5.2	5.3

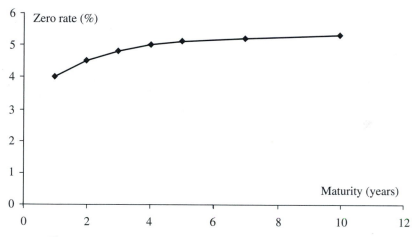

Figure 4.3   The zero-coupon yield curve in Table 4.6.

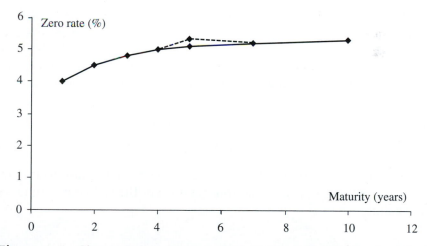

Figure 4.4   Change in zero-coupon yield curve when one point is shifted.

Table 4.7   Partial durations for a portfolio.

Maturity (years)	1	2	3	4	5	7	10	*Total*
Duration	2.0	1.6	0.6	0.2	−0.5	−1.8	−1.9	0.2

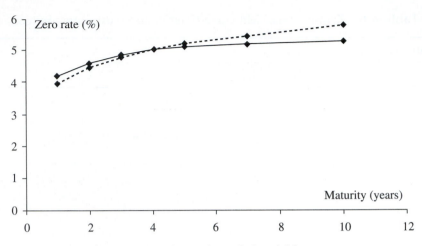

Figure 4.5   A rotation of the yield curve.

those for long maturities are negative. This means that the portfolio loses (gains) in value when short rates rise (fall). It gains (loses) in value when long rates rise (fall).

We are now in a position to go one step further and calculate the impact of nonparallel shifts. We can define any type of shift we want. Suppose that, in the case of the yield curve shown in Figure 4.3, we define a rotation where the changes to the 1-year, 2-year, 3-year, 4-year, 5-year, 7-year, and 10-year points are $-3e$, $-2e$, $-e$, 0, e, $3e$, and $6e$ for some small e. This is illustrated in Figure 4.5. From the partial durations in Table 4.7, the percentage change in the value of the portfolio arising from the rotation is

$$2.0 \times (-3e) + 1.6 \times (-2e) + 0.6 \times (-e) + 0.2 \times 0$$
$$- 0.5 \times e - 1.8 \times 3e - 1.9 \times 6e = -27.1e$$

This shows that a portfolio that gives rise to the partial durations in Table 4.7 is much more heavily exposed to a rotation of the yield curve than to a parallel shift.

4.9 INTEREST RATE DELTAS

We now move on to consider how the Greek letters discussed in Chapter 3 can be calculated for interest rates. One possibility is to define the delta of a portfolio as the change in value for a one-basis-point parallel shift in the zero curve. This is sometimes termed a DV01. It is the same as the

Table 4.8 Deltas for portfolio in Table 4.7. Value of Portfolio is $1 million. The dollar impact of a one-basis-point shift in points on the zero curve is shown.

Maturity (years)	1	2	3	4	5	7	10	*Total*
Delta	200	160	60	20	−50	−180	−190	20

duration of the portfolio multiplied by the value of the portfolio multiplied by 0.0001.

In practice, analysts like to calculate several deltas to reflect their exposures to all the different ways in which the yield curve can move. There are a number of different ways this can be done. One approach corresponds to the partial duration approach that we outlined in the previous section. It involves computing the impact of a one-basis-point change similar to the one illustrated in Figure 4.4 for each point on the zero-coupon yield curve. This delta is the partial duration calculated in Table 4.7 multiplied by the value of the portfolio multiplied by 0.0001. The sum of the deltas for all the points on the yield curve equals the DV01. Suppose that the portfolio in Table 4.7 is worth $1 million. The deltas are shown in Table 4.8.

A variation on this approach is to divide the yield curve into a number of segments or "buckets" and calculate for each bucket the impact of changing all the zero rates corresponding to the bucket by one basis point while keeping all other zero rates unchanged. This approach is often used in asset–liability management (see Section 1.5) and is referred to as GAP management. Figure 4.6 shows the type of change that would

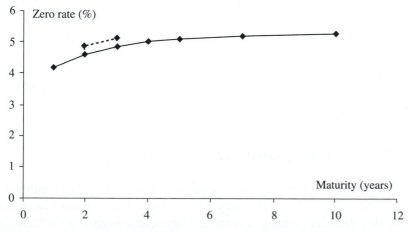

Figure 4.6 Change considered to yield curve when bucketing approach is used.

be considered for the segment of the zero curve between 2.0 and 3.0 years in Figure 4.3. Again, the sum of the deltas for all the segments equals the DV01.

Calculating Deltas to Facilitate Hedging

One of the problems with the delta measures that we have considered so far is that they are not designed to make hedging easy. Consider the deltas in Table 4.8. If we plan to hedge our portfolio with zero-coupon bonds, we can calculate the position in a one-year zero-coupon bond to zero out the $200 per basis point exposure to the one-year rate, the position in a two-year zero-coupon bond to zero out the exposure to the two-year rate, and so on. But, if other instruments are used, a much more complicated analysis is necessary.

In practice, traders tend to use positions in the instruments that have been used to construct the zero curve to hedge their exposure. For example, a government bond trader is likely to take positions in the actively traded government bonds that were used to construct the Treasury zero curve when hedging. A trader of instruments dependent on the LIBOR/swap yield curve is likely to take positions in LIBOR deposits, Eurodollar futures, and swaps when hedging.

To facilitate hedging, traders therefore often calculate the impact of small changes in the quotes for each of the instruments used to construct the zero curve. Consider a trader responsible for interest rate caps and swap options. Suppose that the trader's exposure to a one-basis-point change in a Eurodollar futures quote is $500. Each Eurodollar futures contract changes in value by $25 for a one-basis-point change in the Eurodollar futures quote. It follows that the trader's exposure can be hedged with 20 contracts. Suppose that the exposure to a one-basis-point change in the five-year swap rate is $4,000 and that a five-year swap with a notional principal of $1 million changes in value by $400 for a one-basis-point change in the five-year swap rate. The exposure can be hedged by trading swaps with a notional principal of $10 million.

4.10 PRINCIPAL COMPONENTS ANALYSIS

The approaches we have just outlined can lead to analysts calculating 10 to 15 different deltas for every zero curve. This seems like overkill because the variables being considered are quite highly correlated with each other. For example, when the yield on a five-year bond moves up by

Table 4.9 Factor loadings for US Treasury data.

	PC1	PC2	PC3	PC4	PC5	PC6	PC7	PC8	PC9	PC10
3m	0.21	−0.57	0.50	0.47	−0.39	−0.02	0.01	0.00	0.01	0.00
6m	0.26	−0.49	0.23	−0.37	0.70	0.01	−0.04	−0.02	−0.01	0.00
12m	0.32	−0.32	−0.37	−0.58	−0.52	−0.23	−0.04	−0.05	0.00	0.01
2y	0.35	−0.10	−0.38	0.17	0.04	0.59	0.56	0.12	−0.12	−0.05
3y	0.36	0.02	−0.30	0.27	0.07	0.24	−0.79	0.00	−0.09	−0.00
4y	0.36	0.14	−0.12	0.25	0.16	−0.63	0.15	0.55	−0.14	−0.08
5y	0.36	0.17	−0.04	0.14	0.08	−0.10	0.09	−0.26	0.71	0.48
7y	0.34	0.27	0.15	0.01	0.00	−0.12	0.13	−0.54	0.00	−0.68
10y	0.31	0.30	0.28	−0.10	−0.06	0.01	0.03	−0.23	−0.63	0.52
30y	0.25	0.33	0.46	−0.34	−0.18	0.33	−0.09	0.52	0.26	−0.13

a few basis points, most of the time the yield on a ten-year bond does the same. Arguably a trader should not be worried when a portfolio has a large positive exposure to the five-year rate and a similar large negative exposure to the ten-year rate.

One approach to handling the risk arising from groups of highly correlated market variables is principal components analysis. This takes historical data on movements in the market variables and attempts to define a set of components or factors that explain the movements.

The approach is best illustrated with an example. The market variables we will consider are ten US Treasury rates with maturities between three months and 30 years. Tables 4.9 and 4.10 show results produced by Frye for these market variables using 1,543 daily observations between 1989 and 1995.[8] The first column in Table 4.9 shows the maturities of the rates that were considered. The remaining ten columns in the table show the ten factors (or principal components) describing the rate moves. The first factor, shown in the column labeled PC1, corresponds to a roughly parallel shift in the yield curve. When we have one unit of that factor,

Table 4.10 Standard deviation of factor scores (basis points).

PC1	PC2	PC3	PC4	PC5	PC6	PC7	PC8	PC9	PC10
17.49	6.05	3.10	2.17	1.97	1.69	1.27	1.24	0.80	0.79

---

[8] See J. Frye, "Principals of Risk: Finding VAR through Factor-Based Interest Rate Scenarios." In *VAR: Understanding and Applying Value at Risk*, Risk Publications, London, 1997, pp. 275–288.

the three-month rate increases by 0.21 basis points, the six-month rate increases by 0.26 basis points, and so on. The second factor is shown in the column labeled PC2. It corresponds to a "twist" or change of slope of the yield curve. Rates between three months and two years move in one direction; rates between three years and 30 years move in the other direction. The third factor corresponds to a "bowing" of the yield curve. Rates at the short end and long end of the yield curve move in one direction; rates in the middle move in the other direction. The interest rate move for a particular factor is known as *factor loading*. In our example, the first factor's loading for the three-month rate is 0.21.[9]

As there are ten rates and ten factors, the interest rate changes observed on any given day can always be expressed as a linear sum of the factors by solving a set of ten simultaneous equations. The quantity of a particular factor in the interest rate changes on a particular day is known as the *factor score* for that day.

The importance of a factor is measured by the standard deviation of its factor score. The standard deviations of the factor scores in our example are shown in Table 4.10 and the factors are listed in order of their importance. The numbers in Table 4.10 are measured in basis points. A quantity of the first factor equal to one standard deviation, therefore, corresponds to the three-month rate moving by $0.21 \times 17.49 = 3.67$ basis points, the six-month rate moving by $0.26 \times 17.49 = 4.55$ basis points, and so on.

The technical details of how the factors are determined are not covered here. It is sufficient for us to note that the factors are chosen so that the factor scores are uncorrelated. For instance, in our example, the first factor score (amount of parallel shift) is uncorrelated with the second factor score (amount of twist) across the 1,543 days. The variances of the factor scores (i.e., the squares of the standard deviations) have the property that they add up to the total variance of the data. From Table 4.10, the total variance of the original data (i.e., sum of the variance of the observations on the three-month rate, the variance of the observations on the six-month rate, and so on) is

$$17.49^2 + 6.05^2 + 3.10^2 + \cdots + 0.79^2 = 367.9$$

From this, it can be seen that the first factor accounts for $17.49^2/367.9 = 83.1\%$ of the variance in the original data; the first two factors account for $(17.49^2 + 6.05^2)/367.9 = 93.1\%$ of the variance in the

---

[9] The factor loadings have the property that the sum of their squares for each factor is 1.0.

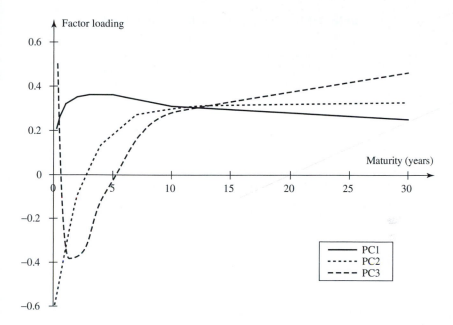

Figure 4.7 The three most important factors driving yield curve movements.

data; the third factor accounts for a further 2.6% of the variance. This shows that most of the risk in interest rate moves is accounted for by the first two or three factors. It suggests that we can relate the risks in a portfolio of interest-rate-dependent instruments to movements in these factors instead of considering all ten interest rates. The three most important factors from Table 4.9 are plotted in Figure 4.7.[10]

Using Principal Components Analysis to Calculate Deltas

To illustrate how a principal components analysis can provide an alternative way of calculating deltas, suppose we have a portfolio with the exposures to interest rate moves shown in Table 4.11. A one-basis-point change in the one-year rate causes the portfolio value to increase by $10 million; a one-basis-point change in the two-year rate causes it to increase by $4 million; and so on. We use the first two factors to model rate moves. (As mentioned earlier, this captures over 90% of the uncertainty in rate moves.) Using the data in Table 4.9, our delta exposure to the first factor (measured in millions of dollars per factor-score basis

---

[10] Results similar to those described here, with respect to the nature of the factors and the amount of the total risk they account for, are obtained when a principal components analysis is used to explain the movements in almost any yield curve in any country.

Table 4.11   Change in portfolio value for a
one-basis-point rate move ($ millions).

1-year rate	2-year rate	3-year rate	4-year rate	5-year rate
+10	+4	−8	−7	+2

point) is

$$10 \times 0.32 + 4 \times 0.35 - 8 \times 0.36 - 7 \times 0.36 + 2 \times 0.36 = -0.08$$

and our delta exposure to the second factor is

$$10 \times (-0.32) + 4 \times (-0.10) - 8 \times 0.02 - 7 \times 0.14 + 2 \times 0.17 = -4.40$$

The approach being used here is similar to the approach described in Section 4.8 where partial durations are used to estimate the impact of nonparallel shifts. The advantage of using a principal components analysis is that it tells you which are the most appropriate shifts to consider. It also provides information on the relative importance of different shifts. In the example we have considered, our exposure to the second shift is about 50 times greater than our exposure to the first shift. However, the first shift is about three times as important in terms of the extent to which it occurs. (We base this last statement on the standard deviation of factor scores reported in Table 4.10.)

4.11 GAMMA AND VEGA

When several delta measures are calculated, there are many possible gamma measures. Suppose that ten instruments are used to compute the zero curve and that we measure deltas with respect to changes in the quotes for each of these. Gamma is a second partial derivative of the form $\partial^2 P / \partial x_i \, \partial x_j$, where P is the portfolio value. We have ten choices for x_i and ten choices for x_j and a total of 55 different gamma measures. This may be "information overload". One approach is to ignore cross-gammas and focus on the ten partial derivatives where $i = j$. Another is to calculate a single gamma measure as the second partial derivative of the value of the portfolio with respect to a parallel shift in the zero curve. A further possibility is to calculate gammas with respect to the first two factors in a principal components analysis.

The vega of a portfolio of interest rate derivatives measures its exposure to volatility changes. Different volatilities are used to price different interest rate derivatives. One approach is to make the same small change to all volatilities and calculate the effect on the value of the portfolio. Another is to carry out a principal components analysis to calculate factors that reflect the patterns of volatility changes across different instruments that tend to occur in practice. Vega measures can be calculated for the first two or three factors.

SUMMARY

The compounding frequency used for an interest rate defines the units in which it is measured. The difference between an annually compounded rate and a quarterly compounded rate is analogous to the difference between a distance measured in miles and a distance measured in kilometers. Analysts frequently use continuous compounding when analyzing derivatives.

Many different types of interest rates are quoted in financial markets and calculated by analysts. The n-year zero rate or n-year spot rate is the rate applicable to an investment lasting for n years when all of the return is realized at the end. Forward rates are the rates applicable to future periods of time implied by today's zero rates.

A zero-coupon yield curve shows the zero rate as a function of maturity. Two important zero-coupon yield curves for risk managers are the Treasury zero curve and the LIBOR/swap zero curve. The method most commonly used to calculate zero curves is known as the bootstrap method. It involves starting with short-term instruments and moving to progressively longer-term instruments making sure that the zero rates calculated at each stage are consistent with the prices of the instruments.

An important concept in interest rate markets is duration. Duration measures the sensitivity of the value of a portfolio to a small parallel shift in the zero-coupon yield curve. An approximate relationship is

$$\Delta P = -PD\,\Delta y$$

where P is the value of the portfolio, D is the duration of the portfolio, Δy is the size of a small parallel shift in the zero curve, and ΔP is the resultant effect on the value of the portfolio. A more precise relationship is

$$\Delta P = -PD\,\Delta y + \tfrac{1}{2}CP(\Delta y)^2$$

where C is the convexity of the portfolio. This relationship is accurate for relatively large parallel shifts in the yield curve but does not quantify the exposure to nonparallel shifts.

To quantify exposure to all the different ways the yield curve can change through time, several duration or delta measures are necessary. There are a number of ways these can be defined. A principal components analysis can be a useful alternative to calculating multiple deltas. It shows that the yield curve shifts that occur in practice are to a large extent a linear sum of two or three standard shifts. If a portfolio manager is hedged against these standard shifts, he or she is therefore also well hedged against the shifts that occur in practice.

FURTHER READING

Allen, S. L., and A. D. Kleinstein. *Valuing Fixed-Income Investments and Derivative Securities*. New York Institute of Finance, 1991.

Duffie, D. "Debt Management and Interest Rate Risk," in W. Beaver and G. Parker (eds.) *Risk Management: Challenges and Solutions*. New York: McGraw-Hill, 1994.

Fabozzi, F. J. *Fixed-Income Mathematics: Analytical and Statistical Techniques*. New York: McGraw-Hill, 1996.

Fabozzi, F. J. *Duration, Convexity, and Other Bond Risk Measures*, Frank J. Fabozzi Associates, 1999.

Grinblatt, M., and F. A. Longstaff. "Financial Innovation and the Role of Derivatives Securities: An Empirical Analysis of the Treasury Strips Program," *Journal of Finance*, 55, 3 (2000): 1415–1436.

Jorion, P. *Big Bets Gone Bad: Derivatives and Bankruptcy in Orange County*. New York: Academic Press, 1995.

Stigum, M., and F. L. Robinson. *Money Markets and Bond Calculations*. Chicago: Irwin, 1996.

QUESTIONS AND PROBLEMS (Answers at End of Book)

4.1. A bank quotes you an interest rate of 14% per annum with quarterly compounding. What is the equivalent rate with (a) continuous compounding and (b) annual compounding?

4.2. An investor receives $1,100 in one year in return for an investment of $1,000 now. Calculate the percentage return per annum with (a) annual compounding, (b) semiannual compounding, (c) monthly compounding, and (d) continuous compounding.

4.3. A deposit account pays 12% per annum with continuous compounding, but interest is actually paid quarterly. How much interest will be paid each quarter on a $10,000 deposit?

4.4. What rate of interest with continuous compounding is equivalent to 15% per annum with monthly compounding?

4.5. Suppose that zero interest rates with continuous compounding are as follows:

Maturity (years)	Rate (% per annum)
1	2.0
2	3.0
3	3.7
4	4.2
5	4.5

Calculate forward interest rates for the second, third, fourth, and fifth years.

4.6. Suppose that zero interest rates with continuous compounding are as follows:

Maturity (months)	Rate (% per annum)
3	8.0
6	8.2
9	8.4
12	8.5
15	8.6
18	8.7

Calculate forward interest rates for the second, third, fourth, fifth, and sixth quarters.

4.7. The term structure of interest rates is upward sloping. Put the following in order of magnitude: (a) the five-year zero rate, (b) the yield on a five-year coupon-bearing bond, and (c) the forward rate corresponding to the period between 5 and 5.25 years in the future. What is the answer to this question when the term structure of interest rates is downward sloping?

4.8. The six-month and one-year zero rates are both 10% per annum. For a bond that has a life of 18 months and pays a coupon of 8% per annum (with semiannual payments and one having just been made), the yield is 10.4% per annum. What is the bond's price? What is the 18-month zero rate? All rates are quoted with semiannual compounding.

4.9. Suppose that 6-month, 12-month, 18-month, 24-month, and 30-month zero rates are 4%, 4.2%, 4.4%, 4.6%, and 4.8% per annum, respectively, with continuous compounding. Estimate the cash price of a bond with a face value of 100 that will mature in 30 months and pays a coupon of 4% per annum semiannually.

4.10. A three-year bond provides a coupon of 8% semiannually and has a cash price of 104. What is the bond's yield?

4.11. Why are US Treasury rates significantly lower than other rates that are close to risk free?

4.12. What does duration tell you about the sensitivity of a bond portfolio to interest rates. What are the limitations of the duration measure?

4.13. A five-year bond with a yield of 11% (continuously compounded) pays an 8% coupon at the end of each year. (a) What is the bond's price? (b) What is the bond's duration? (c) Use the duration to calculate the effect on the bond's price of a 0.2% decrease in its yield. (d) Recalculate the bond's price on the basis of a 10.8% per annum yield and verify that the result is in agreement with your answer to (c).

4.14. Repeat Problem 4.13 on the assumption that the yield is compounded annually. Use modified durations.

4.15. A six-year bond with a continuously compounded yield of 4% provides a 5% coupon at the end of each year. Use duration and convexity to estimate the effect of a 1% increase in the yield on the price of the bond. How accurate is the estimate?

4.16. Explain three ways in which a vector of deltas can be calculated to manage nonparallel yield curve shifts.

4.17. Estimate the delta of the portfolio in Table 4.8 with respect to the first two factors in Table 4.9.

ASSIGNMENT QUESTIONS

4.18. An interest rate is quoted as 5% per annum with semiannual compounding. What is the equivalent rate with (a) annual compounding, (b) monthly compounding, and (c) continuous compounding.

4.19. Portfolio A consists of a 1-year zero-coupon bond with a face value of $2,000 and a 10-year zero-coupon bond with a face value of $6,000. Portfolio B consists of a 5.95-year zero-coupon bond with a face value of $5,000. The current yield on all bonds is 10% per annum (continuously compounded). (a) Show that both portfolios have the same duration. (b) Show that the percentage changes in the values of the two portfolios for a 0.1% per annum increase in yields are the same. (c) What are the percentage changes in the values of the two portfolios for a 5% per annum increase in yields?

4.20. What are the convexities of the portfolios in Problem 4.19? To what extent does (a) duration and (b) convexity explain the difference between the percentage changes calculated in part (c) of Problem 4.19?

4.21. When the partial durations are as in Table 4.7 estimate the effect of a shift in the yield curve where the 10-year rate stays the same, the 1-year rate moves up by $9e$ and the movements in intermediate rates are calculated by interpolation between $9e$ and 0. How could your answer be calculated from the results for a rotation presented in Section 4.8?

4.22. Suppose that the change in a portfolio value for a 1-basis-point shift in the 3-month, 6-month, 1-year, 2-year, 3-year, 4-year, and 5-year rates are (in $million) +5, −3, −1, +2, +5, +7, and +8, respectively. Estimate the delta of the portfolio with respect to the first three factors in Table 4.9. Quantify the relative importance of the three factors for this portfolio.

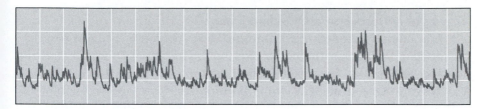

Volatility

5

Hedging schemes such as those described in the last two chapters eliminate much of the risks from trading activities. This is because traders are required to ensure that Greek letters such as delta, gamma, and vega are within certain limits. But trading portfolios are not totally free of risk. At any given time, a financial institution still has a residual exposure to changes in hundreds or even thousands of market variables such as interest rates, exchange rates, equity prices, and commodity prices. The volatility of a market variable measures uncertainty about the future value of the variable. It is important for risk managers to monitor the volatilities of market variables in order to assess potential losses. This chapter describes the procedures they use to carry out the monitoring.

We begin by defining volatility and then explain how volatility can be implied from option prices or estimated from historical data. The common assumption that percentage returns from market variables are normally distributed is examined and we present the power law as an alternative. After that we move on to consider models with imposing names such as exponentially weighted moving average (EWMA), autoregressive conditional heteroscedasticity (ARCH), and generalized autoregressive conditional heteroscedasticity (GARCH). The distinctive feature of these models is that they recognize that volatility is not constant: during some periods it may be relatively low, whereas during others it may be relatively high. The models attempt to keep track of the variations in the volatility through time.

5.1 DEFINITION OF VOLATILITY

The volatility σ of a variable is defined as the standard deviation of the return provided by the variable per unit of time when the return is expressed using continuous compounding. When volatility is used for option pricing, the unit of time is usually one year, so that volatility is the standard deviation of the continuously compounded return per year. However, when volatility is used for risk management, the unit of time is usually one day, so that volatility is the standard deviation of the continuously compounded return per day.

In general, $\sigma\sqrt{T}$ is equal to the standard deviation of $\ln(S_T/S_0)$, where S_T is the value of the market variable at time T and S_0 is its value today. The expression $\ln(S_T/S_0)$ equals the total return (not the return per unit time) earned in time T expressed with continuous compounding. If σ is per day, T is measured in days; if σ is per year, T is measured in years.

When T is small, the continuously compounded return of a market variable is close to the percentage change. It follows that, for small T, $\sigma\sqrt{T}$ is approximately equal to the standard deviation of the percentage change in the market variable in time T. Suppose, for example, that a stock price is \$50 and its volatility is 30% per year. The standard deviation of the percentage change in the stock price in one week is approximately

$$30 \times \sqrt{1/52} = 4.16\%$$

A one-standard-deviation move in the stock price in one week is therefore 50×0.0416, or \$2.08.

When the time horizons considered are short, our uncertainty about a future stock price, as measured by its standard deviation, increases (at least approximately) with the square root of how far ahead we are looking. For example, the standard deviation of the stock price in four weeks is approximately twice the standard deviation in one week. This corresponds to the adage "uncertainty increases with the square root of time".

Variance Rate

Risk managers often focus on the variance rate rather than the volatility. The *variance rate* is defined as the square of the volatility. The variance rate per year is the variance of the continuously compounded return in one year; the variance rate per day is the variance of the continuously compounded return in one day. Whereas the standard deviation of the return in time T increases with the square root of time, the variance of

---

Business Snapshot 5.1 What Causes Volatility?

It is natural to assume that the volatility of a stock price is caused by new information reaching the market. This information causes people to revise their opinions on the value of the stock. The price of the stock changes and volatility results. However, this view of what causes volatility is not supported by research. With several years of daily stock price data, researchers can calculate:

1. The variance of stock price returns between the close of trading on one day and the close of trading on the next day when there are no intervening nontrading days

2. The variance of the stock price returns between the close of trading on Friday and the close of trading on Monday

The second variance is the variance of returns over a three-day period. The first is a variance over a one-day period. We might reasonably expect the second variance to be three times as great as the first variance. Fama (1965), French (1980), and French and Roll (1986) show that this is not the case. These three research studies estimate the second variance to be 22%, 19%, and 10.7% higher than the first variance, respectively.

At this stage you might be tempted to argue that these results are explained by more news reaching the market when the market is open for trading. But research by Roll (1984) does not support this explanation. Roll looked at the prices of orange juice futures. By far the most important news for orange juice futures prices is news about the weather and news about the weather is equally likely to arrive at any time. When Roll did a similar analysis to that just described for stocks, he found that the second (Friday-to-Monday) variance is only 1.54 times the first variance.

The only reasonable conclusion from all this is that volatility is to a large extent caused by trading itself. (Traders usually have no difficulty accepting this conclusion!)

---

this return increases linearly with time. If we wanted to be pedantic, we could say that it is correct to talk about the variance rate per day but that volatility is "per square root of day".

Trading Days vs. Calendar Days

When volatilities are calculated and used, an issue that crops up is whether time should be measured in calendar days or trading days. As shown in Business Snapshot 5.1, research shows that volatility is much higher when the exchange is open for trading than when it is closed. As a result, when estimating volatility from historical data, analysts tend to ignore days when the exchange is closed. The usual assumption is that there are 252 days per year.

Define σ_{yr} as the volatility per year of a certain asset, while σ_{day} is the equivalent volatility per day of the asset. The standard deviation of the continuously compounded return on the asset in one year is either σ_{yr} or $\sigma_{day}\sqrt{252}$. It follows that

$$\sigma_{yr} = \sigma_{day}\sqrt{252}$$

or

$$\sigma_{day} = \frac{\sigma_{yr}}{\sqrt{252}}$$

with the result that the daily volatility is about 6% of annual volatility.

5.2 IMPLIED VOLATILITIES

As shown in Appendix C at the end of this book, the one parameter in option pricing formulas that cannot be directly observed is the volatility of the asset price. This allows traders to imply a volatility from option prices.

To illustrate how implied volatilities are calculated, suppose that the market price of a three-month European call option on a non-dividend-paying stock is $1.875 when the stock price is $21, the strike price is $20 and the risk-free rate is 10%. The implied volatility is the value of volatility that, when substituted into the Black–Scholes option pricing formula, gives an option price of $1.875. Unfortunately, it is not possible to invert the Black–Scholes formula so that volatility is expressed as a function of the option price and other variables. However, an iterative search procedure can be used to find the implied volatility σ. For example, we can start by trying $\sigma = 0.20$. This gives a value for the option price equal to $1.76, which is less than the market price of $1.875. Since the option price is an increasing function of σ, a higher value of σ is required. We can next try $\sigma = 0.3$. This gives a value for the option price equal to $2.10, which is too high and means that σ must lie between 0.20 and 0.30. Next, we try a value of 0.25 for σ. This also proves to be too high, showing that the implied volatility lies between 0.20 and 0.25. Proceeding in this way, we can halve the range of values for σ at each iteration and calculate its correct value to any required accuracy.[1] In this example, the

---

[1] This method is presented for illustration. Other more powerful search procedures are used to calculate implied volatilities in practice.

implied volatility is 0.235, or 23.5% per annum. A similar procedure can be used in conjunction with binomial trees to find implied volatilities for American options.

Implied volatilities are used extensively by traders, as we will explain in Chapter 15. However, risk management is largely based on historical volatilities. The rest of this chapter will be concerned with developing procedures for using historical data to monitor volatility.

5.3 ESTIMATING VOLATILITY FROM HISTORICAL DATA

When the volatility of a variable is estimated using historical data, it is usually observed at fixed intervals of time (e.g., every day, week, or month). Define:

$n + 1$: Number of observations

S_i: Value of variable at end of ith interval, where $i = 0, 1, \ldots, n$

τ: Length of time interval

and let

$$u_i = \ln\left(\frac{S_i}{S_{i-1}}\right)$$

for $i = 1, 2, \ldots, n$.

The usual estimate s of the standard deviation of the u_i is given by

$$s = \sqrt{\frac{1}{n-1} \sum_{i=1}^{n} (u_i - \bar{u})^2}$$

or

$$s = \sqrt{\frac{1}{n-1} \sum_{i=1}^{n} u_i^2 - \frac{1}{n(n-1)} \left(\sum_{i=1}^{n} u_i\right)^2}$$

where $\bar{u}$ is the mean of the u_i.

As explained in Section 5.1, the standard deviation of the u_i is $\sigma\sqrt{\tau}$, where σ is the volatility of the variable. The variable s is, therefore, an estimate of $\sigma\sqrt{\tau}$. It follows that σ itself can be estimated as $\hat{\sigma}$, where

$$\hat{\sigma} = \frac{s}{\sqrt{\tau}}$$

The standard error of this estimate can be shown to be approximately

$\hat{\sigma}/\sqrt{2n}$. If τ is measured in years, the volatility calculated is a volatility per year; if τ is measured in days, the volatility that is calculated is a daily volatility.

Example 5.1

Table 5.1 shows a possible sequence of stock prices during 21 consecutive trading days. In this case,

$$\sum u_i = 0.09531 \quad \text{and} \quad \sum u_i^2 = 0.00326$$

and the estimate of the standard deviation of the daily return is

$$\sqrt{\frac{0.00326}{19} - \frac{0.09531^2}{380}} = 0.01216$$

or 1.216%. To calculate a daily volatility, we set $\tau = 1$ and obtain a volatility of 1.216%. To calculate a volatility per year, we set $\tau = 1/252$ and the data

Table 5.1   Computation of volatility.

Day	Closing stock price ($)	Price relative S_i/S_{i-1}	Daily return $u_i = \ln(S_i/S_{i-1})$
0	20.00		
1	20.10	1.00500	0.00499
2	19.90	0.99005	−0.01000
3	20.00	1.00503	0.00501
4	20.50	1.02500	0.02469
5	20.25	0.98780	−0.01227
6	20.90	1.03210	0.03159
7	20.90	1.00000	0.00000
8	20.90	1.00000	0.00000
9	20.75	0.99282	−0.00720
10	20.75	1.00000	0.00000
11	21.00	1.01205	0.01198
12	21.10	1.00476	0.00475
13	20.90	0.99052	−0.00952
14	20.90	1.00000	0.00000
15	21.25	1.01675	0.01661
16	21.40	1.00706	0.00703
17	21.40	1.00000	0.00000
18	21.25	0.99299	−0.00703
19	21.75	1.02353	0.02326
20	22.00	1.01149	0.01143

give an estimate for the volatility per annum of $0.01216\sqrt{252} = 0.193$, or 19.3%. The standard error of the daily volatility estimate is

$$\frac{0.01216}{\sqrt{2 \times 20}} = 0.0019$$

or 0.19% per day. The standard error of the volatility per year is

$$\frac{0.193}{\sqrt{2 \times 20}} = 0.031$$

or 3.1% per annum.

5.4 ARE DAILY PERCENTAGE CHANGES IN FINANCIAL VARIABLES NORMAL?

The Black–Scholes model and its extensions (see Appendix C) make the assumption that asset prices change continuously and have constant volatility. This means that the return in a short period of time Δt always has a normal distribution with a standard deviation of $\sigma\sqrt{\Delta t}$. Suppose that the volatility of an exchange rate is estimated as 12% per year. This corresponds to $12/\sqrt{252}$, or 0.756%, per day. Assuming normally distributed returns, we see from the tables at the end of this book that the probability of the value of the foreign currency changing by more than one standard deviation (i.e., by more than 0.756%) in one day is 31.73%; the probability that the exchange rate will change by more than two standard deviations (i.e., by more than 1.512%) is 4.55%; the probability that it will change by more than three standard deviations (i.e., by more than 2.268%) is 0.27%; and so on.[2]

In practice, exchange rates, as well as most other market variables, tend to have heavier tails than the normal distribution. Table 5.2 illustrates this by examining the daily movements in 12 different exchange rates over a ten-year period.[3] The first step in the production of this table is to calculate the standard deviation of daily percentage changes in each exchange rate. The next stage is to note how often the actual percentage changes exceeded one standard deviation, two standard deviations, and so on. These numbers are then compared with the corresponding numbers for the normal distribution.

---

[2] We are making a small approximation here that the one-day continuously compounded return is the same as the one-week return with daily compounding.

[3] This table is taken from J. C. Hull and A. White, "Value at Risk When Daily Changes in Market Variables Are Not Normally Distributed." *Journal of Derivatives*, 5, No. 3 (Spring 1998): 9–19.

Business Snapshot 5.2 Making Money from Foreign Currency Options

Suppose that most market participants think that exchange rates are log-normally distributed. They will be comfortable using the same volatility to value all options on a particular exchange rate. You have just done the analysis in Table 5.2 and know that the lognormal assumption is not a good one for exchange rates. What should you do?

The answer is that you should buy deep-out-of-the-money call and put options on a variety of different currencies—and wait. These options will be relatively inexpensive and more of them will close in the money than the lognormal model predicts. The present value of your payoffs will on average be much greater than the cost of the options.

In the mid-1980s a few traders knew about the heavy tails of foreign exchange probability distributions. Everyone else thought that the lognormal assumption of Black–Scholes was reasonable. The few traders who were well informed followed the strategy we have described—and made lots of money. By the late 1980s everyone realized that out-of-the money options should have a higher implied volatility than at-the-money options and the trading opportunities disappeared.

Daily percentage changes exceed three standard deviations on 1.34% of the days. The normal model for returns predicts that this should happen on only 0.27% of days. Daily percentage changes exceed four, five, and six standard deviations on 0.29%, 0.08%, and 0.03% of days, respectively. The normal model predicts that we should hardly ever observe this happening. The table, therefore, provides evidence to support the existence of heavy tails. Business Snapshot 5.2 shows how you could have made money if you had done the analysis in Table 5.2 in 1985!

Table 5.2 Percentage of days when absolute size of daily exchange rate moves is greater than $1, 2, \ldots, 6$ standard deviations. (SD = standard deviation of daily percentage change.)

	Real world (%)	*Normal model* (%)
>1 SD	25.04	31.73
>2 SD	5.27	4.55
>3 SD	1.34	0.27
>4 SD	0.29	0.01
>5 SD	0.08	0.00
>6 SD	0.03	0.00

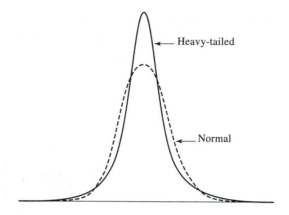

Figure 5.1 Comparison of normal distribution with a heavy-tailed distribution. The two distributions have the same mean and standard deviation.

Figure 5.1 compares a typical heavy-tailed distribution (such as the one for foreign exchange) with a normal distribution that has the same mean and standard deviation.[4] The heavy-tailed distribution is more peaked than the normal distribution. In Figure 5.1, we can distinguish three parts of the distribution: the middle, the tails, the intermediate parts (between the middle and the tails). When we move from the normal distribution to the heavy-tailed distribution, probability mass shifts from the intermediate parts of the distribution to both the tails and the middle. If we are considering the percentage change in a market variable, the heavy-tailed distribution has the property that small and large changes in the variable are more likely than they would be if a normal distribution were assumed. Intermediate changes are less likely.

An Alternative to Normal Distributions: The Power Law

The power law asserts that, for many variables that are encountered in practice, it is approximately true that the value v of the variable has the property that, when x is large,

$$\text{Prob}(v > x) = Kx^{-\alpha} \tag{5.1}$$

where K and α are constants. This equation has been found to be

---

[4] *Kurtosis* measures the size of a distribution's tails. A *leptokurtic* distribution has heavier tails than the normal distribution. A *platykurtic* distribution has less heavy tails than the normal distribution. A distribution with tails of the same size as the normal distribution is termed *mesokurtic*.

approximately true for variables as diverse as the income of individuals, the size of cities, and the number of visits to a website. Suppose that $\alpha = 3$ and we observe that the probability that $v > 10$ is 0.05. In this case $K = 50$ and we can estimate that the probability that $v > 20$ is 0.00625; the probability that $v > 30$ is 0.0019; and so on.

Equation (5.1) implies that

$$\ln[\text{Prob}(v > x)] = \ln K - \alpha \ln x$$

We can therefore do a quick test of whether it holds by plotting $\ln[\text{Prob}(v > x)]$ against $\ln x$. We do this for our exchange rate data in Figure 5.2. The logarithm of the probability of the exchange rate increasing by more than x standard deviations is approximately linearly dependent on $\ln x$ for $x > 3$ showing that the power law holds. The parameter α is about 5.5. When producing Figure 5.2, we assume that the distribution of exchange rate changes in Table 5.2 is symmetrical, so that the probability of a change greater than one standard deviation is $0.5 \times 25.04 = 12.52\%$, greater than two standard deviations is $0.5 \times 5.27 = 2.635\%$, and so on.

We will examine the power law more formally and explain better

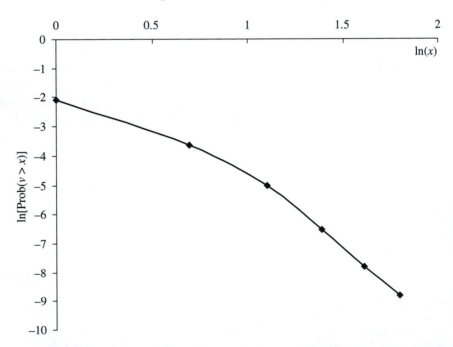

Figure 5.2 Log–log plot for exchange rate increases: x is number of standard deviations; v is the exchange rate increase.

procedures for estimating the parameters when we consider extreme value theory in Chapter 9. We will also explain how it can be used in the assessment of operational risk in Chapter 14.

5.5 MONITORING DAILY VOLATILITY

Risk managers cannot assume that asset prices are well behaved with a constant volatility. It is important for them to monitor volatility daily.

Define σ_n as the volatility of a market variable on day n, as estimated at the end of day $n-1$. The variance rate is σ_n^2. Suppose that the value of the market variable at the end of day i is S_i. As in Section 5.3, we define the variable u_i as the continuously compounded return during day i (between the end of day $i-1$ and the end of day i), so that

$$u_i = \ln \frac{S_i}{S_{i-1}}$$

One approach to estimating σ_n is to set it equal to the historical volatility as calculated in Section 5.3. When m days of observations on the u_i are used, this approach gives

$$\sigma_n^2 = \frac{1}{m-1} \sum_{i=1}^{m} (u_{n-i} - \bar{u})^2 \tag{5.2}$$

where $\bar{u}$ is the mean of the u_i:

$$\bar{u} = \frac{1}{m} \sum_{i=1}^{m} u_{n-i}$$

For risk management purposes, the formula in equation (5.2) is usually changed in a number of ways:

1. u_i is defined as the percentage change in the market variable between the end of day $i-1$ and the end of day i so that

$$u_i = \frac{S_i - S_{i-1}}{S_{i-1}} \tag{5.3}$$

This makes very little difference to the values of u_i that are computed.
2. $\bar{u}$ is assumed to be zero. The justification for this is that the expected change in a variable in one day is very small when compared with the standard deviation of changes.
3. $m-1$ is replaced by m. This moves us from an unbiased estimate of volatility to a maximum-likelihood estimate (see Section 5.9).

These three changes allow the formula for the variance rate to be simplified to

$$\sigma_n^2 = \frac{1}{m} \sum_{i=1}^{m} u_{n-i}^2 \tag{5.4}$$

where u_i is given by equation (5.3).

Weighting Schemes

Equation (5.4) gives equal weight to all $u_{n-1}^2, u_{n-2}^2, \ldots, u_{n-m}^2$. Our objective is to estimate the current level of volatility, σ_n. It therefore makes sense to give more weight to recent data. A model that does this is

$$\sigma_n^2 = \sum_{i=1}^{m} \alpha_i u_{n-i}^2 \tag{5.5}$$

The variable α_i is the amount of weight given to the observation i days ago. The α's are positive. If we choose them so that $\alpha_i < \alpha_j$ when $i > j$, less weight is given to older observations. The weights must sum to unity, so that

$$\sum_{i=1}^{m} \alpha_i = 1$$

An extension of the idea in equation (5.5) is to assume that there is a long-run average variance rate and that this should be given some weight. This leads to the model that takes the form

$$\sigma_n^2 = \gamma V_L + \sum_{i=1}^{m} \alpha_i u_{n-i}^2 \tag{5.6}$$

where V_L is the long-run variance rate and γ is the weight assigned to V_L. Since the weights must sum to unity, we have

$$\gamma + \sum_{i=1}^{m} \alpha_i = 1$$

This is known as an ARCH(m) model. It was first suggested by Engle.[5] The estimate of the variance is based on a long-run average variance and m observations. The older an observation, the less weight it is given.

---

[5] See R. Engle, "Autoregressive Conditional Heteroscedasticity with Estimates of the Variance of UK Inflation," *Econometrica*, 50 (1982), 987–1008. Robert Engle won the Nobel prize for economics in 2003 for his work on ARCH models.

Defining $\omega = \gamma V_L$, we can write the model in equation (5.6) as

$$\sigma_n^2 = \omega + \sum_{i=1}^{m} \alpha_i u_{n-i}^2 \tag{5.7}$$

In the next two sections we discuss two important approaches to monitoring volatility using the ideas in equations (5.5) and (5.6).

5.6 THE EXPONENTIALLY WEIGHTED MOVING AVERAGE MODEL

The exponentially weighted moving average (EWMA) model is a particular case of the model in equation (5.5) where the weights α_i decrease exponentially as we move back through time. Specifically, $\alpha_{i+1} = \lambda \alpha_i$, where λ is a constant between 0 and 1.

It turns out that this weighting scheme leads to a particularly simple formula for updating volatility estimates. The formula is

$$\sigma_n^2 = \lambda \sigma_{n-1}^2 + (1 - \lambda) u_{n-1}^2 \tag{5.8}$$

The estimate σ_n of the volatility for day n (made at the end of day $n - 1$) is calculated from σ_{n-1} (the estimate of the volatility for day $n - 1$ that was made at the end of day $n - 2$) and u_{n-1} (the most recent daily percentage change).

To understand why equation (5.8) corresponds to weights that decrease exponentially, we substitute for σ_{n-1}^2 to get

$$\sigma_n^2 = \lambda [\lambda \sigma_{n-2}^2 + (1 - \lambda) u_{n-2}^2] + (1 - \lambda) u_{n-1}^2$$

or

$$\sigma_n^2 = (1 - \lambda)(u_{n-1}^2 + \lambda u_{n-2}^2) + \lambda^2 \sigma_{n-2}^2$$

Substituting in a similar way for σ_{n-2}^2 gives

$$\sigma_n^2 = (1 - \lambda)(u_{n-1}^2 + \lambda u_{n-2}^2 + \lambda^2 u_{n-3}^2) + \lambda^3 \sigma_{n-3}^2$$

Continuing in this way, we see that

$$\sigma_n^2 = (1 - \lambda) \sum_{i=1}^{m} \lambda^{i-1} u_{n-i}^2 + \lambda^m \sigma_{n-m}^2$$

For a large m, the term $\lambda^m \sigma_{n-m}^2$ is sufficiently small to be ignored, so that equation (5.8) is the same as equation (5.5) with $\alpha_i = (1 - \lambda)\lambda^{i-1}$. The weights for the u's decline at rate λ as we move back through time. Each weight is λ times the previous weight.

Example 5.2

Suppose that λ is 0.90, the volatility estimated for a market variable for day $n - 1$ is 1% per day, and during day $n - 1$ the market variable increased by 2%. This means that $\sigma_{n-1}^2 = 0.01^2 = 0.0001$ and $u_{n-1}^2 = 0.02^2 = 0.0004$. Equation (5.8) gives

$$\sigma_n^2 = 0.9 \times 0.0001 + 0.1 \times 0.0004 = 0.00013$$

The estimate σ_n of the volatility for day n is therefore $\sqrt{0.00013}$, or 1.14%, per day. Note that the expected value of u_{n-1}^2 is σ_{n-1}^2, or 0.0001. In this example, the realized value of u_{n-1}^2 is greater than the expected value, and as a result our volatility estimate increases. If the realized value of u_{n-1}^2 had been less than its expected value, our estimate of the volatility would have decreased.

The EWMA approach has the attractive feature that relatively little data need to be stored. At any given time, we need to remember only the current estimate of the variance rate and the most recent observation on the value of the market variable. When we get a new observation on the value of the market variable, we calculate a new daily percentage change and use equation (5.8) to update our estimate of the variance rate. The old estimate of the variance rate and the old value of the market variable can then be discarded.

The EWMA approach is designed to track changes in the volatility. Suppose there is a big move in the market variable on day $n - 1$, so that u_{n-1}^2 is large. From equation (5.8), this causes our estimate of the current volatility to move upward. The value of λ governs how responsive the estimate of the daily volatility is to the most recent daily percentage change. A low value of λ leads to a great deal of weight being given to the u_{n-1}^2 when σ_n is calculated. In this case, the estimates produced for the volatility on successive days are themselves highly volatile. A high value of λ (i.e., a value close to 1.0) produces estimates of the daily volatility that respond relatively slowly to new information given by the daily percentage change.

The RiskMetrics database, which was originally created by J. P. Morgan and made publicly available in 1994, uses the EWMA model with $\lambda = 0.94$ for updating daily volatility estimates. The company found that, across a range of different market variables, this value of λ gives forecasts of the variance rate that come closest to the realized variance rate.[6] The realized

---

[6] See J.P. Morgan, *RiskMetrics Monitor*, Fourth Quarter, 1995. We will explain an alternative (maximum-likelihood) approach to estimating parameters later in the chapter.

variance rate on a particular day was calculated as an equally weighted average of the u_i^2 on the subsequent 25 days (see Problem 5.20).

5.7 THE GARCH(1, 1) MODEL

We now move on to discuss what is known as the GARCH(1, 1) model, proposed by Bollerslev in 1986.[7] The difference between the GARCH(1, 1) model and the EWMA model is analogous to the difference between equation (5.5) and equation (5.6). In GARCH(1, 1), σ_n^2 is calculated from a long-run average variance rate, V_L, as well as from σ_{n-1} and u_{n-1}. The equation for GARCH(1, 1) is

$$\sigma_n^2 = \gamma V_L + \alpha u_{n-1}^2 + \beta \sigma_{n-1}^2 \qquad (5.9)$$

where γ is the weight assigned to V_L, α is the weight assigned to u_{n-1}^2, and β is the weight assigned to σ_{n-1}^2. Since the weights must sum to one, we have

$$\gamma + \alpha + \beta = 1$$

The EWMA model is a particular case of GARCH(1, 1) where $\gamma = 0$, $\alpha = 1 - \lambda$, and $\beta = \lambda$.

The "(1, 1)" in GARCH(1, 1) indicates that σ_n^2 is based on the most recent observation of u^2 and the most recent estimate of the variance rate. The more general GARCH(p,q) model calculates σ_n^2 from the most recent p observations on u^2 and the most recent q estimates of the variance rate.[8] GARCH(1, 1) is by far the most popular of the GARCH models.

Setting $\omega = \gamma V_L$, we can also write the GARCH(1, 1) model as

$$\sigma_n^2 = \omega + \alpha u_{n-1}^2 + \beta \sigma_{n-1}^2 \qquad (5.10)$$

This is the form of the model that is usually used for the purposes of

---

[7] See T. Bollerslev. "Generalized Autoregressive Conditional Heteroscedasticity," *Journal of Econometrics*, 31 (1986), 307–327.

[8] Other GARCH models have been proposed that incorporate asymmetric news. These models are designed so that σ_n depends on the sign of u_{n-1}. Arguably, these models are more appropriate than GARCH(1, 1) for equities. This is because the volatility of an equity's price tends to be inversely related to the price, so that a negative u_{n-1} should have a bigger effect on σ_n than the same positive u_{n-1}. For a discussion of models for handling asymmetric news, see D. Nelson, "Conditional Heteroscedasticity and Asset Returns; A New Approach," *Econometrica*, 59 (1990), 347–370 and R. F. Engle and V. Ng, "Measuring and Testing the Impact of News on Volatility," *Journal of Finance*, 48 (1993), 1749–1778.

estimating the parameters. Once ω, α, and β have been estimated, we can calculate γ as $1 - \alpha - \beta$. The long-term variance V_L can then be calculated as ω/γ. For a stable GARCH(1, 1) process, we require $\alpha + \beta < 1$. Otherwise the weight applied to the long-term variance is negative.

Example 5.3

Suppose that a GARCH(1, 1) model is estimated from daily data as

$$\sigma_n^2 = 0.000002 + 0.13u_{n-1}^2 + 0.86\sigma_{n-1}^2$$

This corresponds to $\alpha = 0.13$, $\beta = 0.86$, and $\omega = 0.000002$. Since $\gamma = 1 - \alpha - \beta$, it follows that $\gamma = 0.01$, and, since $\omega = \gamma V_L$, we have $V_L = 0.0002$. In other words, the long-run average variance per day implied by the model is 0.0002. This corresponds to a volatility of $\sqrt{0.0002} = 0.014$, or 1.4%, per day.

Suppose that the estimate of the volatility on day $n - 1$ is 1.6% per day, so that $\sigma_{n-1}^2 = 0.016^2 = 0.000256$, and that on day $n - 1$ the market variable decreased by 1%, so that $u_{n-1}^2 = 0.01^2 = 0.0001$. Then

$$\sigma_n^2 = 0.000002 + 0.13 \times 0.0001 + 0.86 \times 0.000256 = 0.00023516$$

The new estimate of the volatility is therefore $\sqrt{0.00023516} = 0.0153$, or 1.53%, per day.

The Weights

Substituting for σ_{n-1}^2 in equation (5.10), we obtain

$$\sigma_n^2 = \omega + \alpha u_{n-1}^2 + \beta(\omega + \alpha u_{n-2}^2 + \beta\sigma_{n-2}^2)$$

or

$$\sigma_n^2 = \omega + \beta\omega + \alpha u_{n-1}^2 + \alpha\beta u_{n-2}^2 + \beta^2\sigma_{n-2}^2$$

Substituting for σ_{n-2}^2, we get

$$\sigma_n^2 = \omega + \beta\omega + \beta^2\omega + \alpha u_{n-1}^2 + \alpha\beta u_{n-2}^2 + \alpha\beta^2 u_{n-3}^2 + \beta^3\sigma_{n-3}^2$$

Continuing in this way, we see that the weight applied to u_{n-i}^2 is $\alpha\beta^{i-1}$. The weights decline exponentially at rate β. The parameter β can be interpreted as a "decay rate". It is similar to λ in the EWMA model. It defines the relative importance of the u's in determining the current variance rate. For example, if $\beta = 0.9$, then u_{n-2}^2 is only 90% as important as u_{n-1}^2; u_{n-3}^2 is 81% as important as u_{n-1}; and so on. The GARCH(1, 1) model is the same as the EWMA model except that, in addition to assigning weights that decline exponentially to past u^2, it also assigns some weight to the long-run average volatility.

5.8 CHOOSING BETWEEN THE MODELS

In practice, variance rates do tend to be pulled back to a long-run average level. This is known as *mean reversion*. The GARCH(1, 1) model incorporates mean reversion whereas the EWMA model does not. GARCH(1, 1) is therefore theoretically more appealing than the EWMA model.

In the next section, we shall discuss how best-fit parameters ω, α, and β in GARCH(1, 1) can be estimated. When the parameter ω is zero, the GARCH(1, 1) reduces to EWMA. In circumstances where the best-fit value of ω turns out to be negative, the GARCH(1, 1) model is not stable and it makes sense to switch to the EWMA model.

5.9 MAXIMUM-LIKELIHOOD METHODS

It is now appropriate to discuss how the parameters in the models we have been considering are estimated from historical data. The approach used is known as the *maximum-likelihood method*. It involves choosing values for the parameters that maximize the chance (or likelihood) of the data occurring.

To illustrate the method, we start with a very simple example. Suppose that we sample ten stocks at random on a certain day and find that the price of one of them declined on that day and the prices of the other nine either remained the same or increased. What is our best estimate of the probability of a price decline? The natural answer is 0.1. Let us see if this is the result given by the maximum-likelihood method.

Suppose that the probability of a price decline is p. The probability that one particular stock declines in price and the other nine do not is $p(1 - p)^9$. (There is a probability p that it will decline and $1 - p$ that each of the other nine will not.) Using the maximum-likelihood approach, the best estimate of p is the one that maximizes $p(1 - p)^9$. Differentiating this expression with respect to p and setting the result equal to zero, we find that $p = 0.1$ maximizes the expression. This shows that the maximum-likelihood estimate of p is 0.1, as expected.

Estimating a Constant Variance

As our next example of maximum-likelihood methods, we consider the problem of estimating the variance of a variable X from m observations on X when the underlying distribution is normal with mean zero. We assume that the observations are $u_1, u_2, \ldots, u_m$ and that the mean of the underlying distribution is zero. Denote the variance by v. The likelihood of u_i being observed is the probability density function for X when $X = u_i$. This is

$$\frac{1}{\sqrt{2\pi v}} \exp\left(\frac{-u_i^2}{2v}\right)$$

The likelihood of m observations occurring in the order in which they are observed is

$$\prod_{i=1}^{m}\left[\frac{1}{\sqrt{2\pi v}} \exp\left(\frac{-u_i^2}{2v}\right)\right] \tag{5.11}$$

Using the maximum-likelihood method, the best estimate of v is the value that maximizes this expression.

Maximizing an expression is equivalent to maximizing the logarithm of the expression. Taking logarithms of the expression in equation (5.11) and ignoring constant multiplicative factors, it can be seen that we wish to maximize

$$\sum_{i=1}^{m}\left[-\ln(v) - \frac{u_i^2}{v}\right] \tag{5.12}$$

or

$$-m\ln(v) - \sum_{i=1}^{m}\frac{u_i^2}{v}$$

Differentiating this expression with respect to v and setting the resultant equation to zero, we see that the maximum-likelihood estimator of v is[9]

$$\frac{1}{m}\sum_{i=1}^{m}u_i^2$$

Estimating GARCH(1, 1) Parameters

We now consider how the maximum-likelihood method can be used to estimate the parameters when GARCH(1, 1) or some other volatility updating scheme is used. Define $v_i = \sigma_i^2$ as the estimated variance for day i. We assume that the probability distribution of u_i conditional on the variance is normal. A similar analysis to the one just given shows the best

---

[9] The unbiased estimator has m replaced by $m - 1$.

parameters are the ones that maximize

$$\prod_{i=1}^{m}\left[\frac{1}{\sqrt{2\pi v_i}}\exp\left(\frac{-u_i^2}{2v_i}\right)\right]$$

Taking logarithms, we see that this is equivalent to maximizing

$$\sum_{i=1}^{m}\left[-\ln(v_i)-\frac{u_i^2}{v_i}\right] \tag{5.13}$$

This is the same as the expression in equation (5.12), except that v is replaced by v_i. We search iteratively to find the parameters in the model that maximize the expression in equation (5.13).

The spreadsheet in Table 5.3 indicates how the calculations could be organized for the GARCH(1, 1) model. The table analyzes data on the Japanese yen exchange rate between January 6, 1988, and August 15, 1997. The numbers in the table are based on trial estimates of the three GARCH(1, 1) parameters: ω, α, and β. The first column in the table records the date. The second counts the days. The third shows the exchange rate S_i at the end of day i. The fourth shows the proportional change in the exchange rate between the end of day $i-1$ and the end of

Table 5.3   Estimation of parameters in GARCH(1, 1) model.

Date	Day i	S_i	u_i	$v_i = \sigma_i^2$	$-\ln(v_i) - u_i^2/v_i$
06-Jan-88	1	0.007728			
07-Jan-88	2	0.007779	0.006599		
08-Jan-88	3	0.007746	−0.004242	0.00004355	9.6283
11-Jan-88	4	0.007816	0.009037	0.00004198	8.1329
12-Jan-88	5	0.007837	0.002687	0.00004455	9.8568
13-Jan-88	6	0.007924	0.011101	0.00004220	7.1529
⋮	⋮	⋮	⋮	⋮	⋮
13-Aug-97	2421	0.008643	0.003374	0.00007626	9.3321
14-Aug-97	2422	0.008493	−0.017309	0.00007092	5.3294
15-Aug-97	2423	0.008495	0.000144	0.00008417	9.3824
					22,063.5763

Trial estimates of GARCH parameters:

ω	α	β
0.00000176	0.0626	0.8976

day i. This is $u_i = (S_i - S_{i-1})/S_{i-1}$. The fifth column shows the estimate of the variance rate, $v_i = \sigma_i^2$, for day i made at the end of day $i - 1$. On day three, we start things off by setting the variance equal to u_2^2. On subsequent days equation (5.10) is used. The sixth column tabulates the likelihood measure, $-\ln(v_i) - u_i^2/v_i$. The values in the fifth and sixth columns are based on the current trial estimates of ω, α, and β. We are interested in choosing ω, α, and β to maximize the sum of the numbers in the sixth column. This involves an iterative search procedure.[10]

In our example, the optimal values of the parameters turn out to be

$$\omega = 0.00000176, \quad \alpha = 0.0626, \quad \beta = 0.8976$$

and the maximum value of the function in equation (5.13) is 22,063.5763. The numbers shown in Table 5.3 were calculated on the final iteration of the search for the optimal ω, α, and β.

The long-term variance rate, V_L, in our example is

$$\frac{\omega}{1 - \alpha - \beta} = \frac{0.00000176}{0.0398} = 0.00004422$$

The long-term volatility is $\sqrt{0.00004422}$, or 0.665%, per day.

Figure 5.3 shows the way in which the GARCH(1, 1) volatility for the Japanese yen changed over the ten-year period covered by the data. Most of the time, the volatility was between 0.4% and 0.8% per day, but volatilities over 1% were experienced during some periods.

An alternative and more robust approach to estimating parameters in GARCH(1, 1) is known as *variance targeting*.[11] This involves setting the long-run average variance rate, V_L, equal to the sample variance calculated from the data (or to some other value that is believed to be reasonable.) The value of ω then equals $V_L(1 - \alpha - \beta)$ and only two parameters have to be estimated. For the data in Table 5.3 the sample variance is 0.00004341, which gives a daily volatility of 0.659%. Setting V_L equal to the sample variance, we find that the values of α and β that maximize the objective function in equation (5.13) are 0.0607 and 0.8990, respectively. The value of the objective function is 22,063.5274, only

---

[10] As discussed later, a general purpose algorithm such as Solver in Microsoft's Excel can be used. Alternatively, a special purpose algorithm, such as Levenberg–Marquardt, can be used. See, for example, W. H. Press, B. P. Flannery, S. A. Teukolsky, and W. T. Vetterling. *Numerical Recipes in C: The Art of Scientific Computing*, Cambridge University Press, 1988.

[11] See R. Engle and J. Mezrich, "GARCH for Groups," *Risk*, August 1996, 36–40.

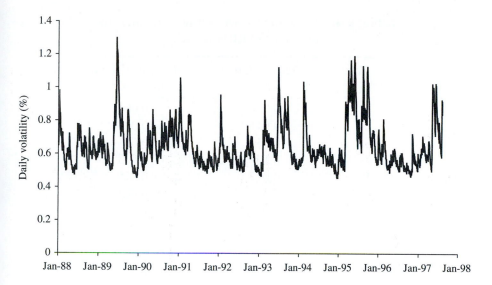

Figure 5.3 Daily volatility of the yen/USD exchange rate, 1988–97.

marginally below the value of 22,063.5763 obtained using the earlier procedure.

When the EWMA model is used, the estimation procedure is relatively simple. We set $\omega = 0$, $\alpha = 1 - \lambda$, and $\beta = \lambda$, and only one parameter has to be estimated. In the data in Table 5.3, the value of λ that maximizes the objective function in equation (5.13) is 0.9686 and the value of the objective function is 21,995.8377.

Both GARCH(1, 1) and the EWMA method can be implemented by using the Solver routine in Excel to search for the values of the parameters that maximize the likelihood function. The routine works well provided that we structure our spreadsheet so that the parameters we are searching for have roughly equal values. For example, in GARCH(1, 1) we could let cells A1, A2, and A3 contain $\omega \times 10^5$, α, and 0.1β. We could then set B1 = A1/100,000, B2 = A2, and B3 = 10 * A3. We could use B1, B2, and B3 to calculate the likelihood function and then ask Solver to calculate the values of A1, A2, and A3 that maximize the likelihood function.

How Good Is the Model?

The assumption underlying a GARCH model is that volatility changes with the passage of time. During some periods volatility is relatively high; during others it is relatively low. To put this another way, when u_i^2 is high,

Table 5.4 Autocorrelations before and after the
use of a GARCH model.

Time lag	Autocorrelation for u_i^2	Autocorrelation for u_i^2/σ_i^2
1	0.072	0.004
2	0.041	−0.005
3	0.057	0.008
4	0.107	0.003
5	0.075	0.016
6	0.066	0.008
7	0.019	−0.033
8	0.085	0.012
9	0.054	0.010
10	0.030	−0.023
11	0.038	−0.004
12	0.038	−0.021
13	0.057	−0.001
14	0.040	0.002
15	0.007	−0.028

there is a tendency for $u_{i+1}^2, u_{i+2}^2, \ldots$ to be high; when u_i^2 is low, there is a tendency for $u_{i+1}^2, u_{i+2}^2, \ldots$ to be low. We can test how true this is by examining the autocorrelation structure of the u_i^2.

Let us assume that the u_i^2 do exhibit autocorrelation. If a GARCH model is working well, it should remove the autocorrelation. We can test whether it has done this by considering the autocorrelation structure for the variables u_i^2/σ_i^2. If these show very little autocorrelation, our model for σ_i has succeeded in explaining autocorrelations in the u_i^2.

Table 5.4 shows results for the yen/USD exchange rate data referred to earlier. The first column shows the lags considered when the autocorrelation is calculated. The second column shows autocorrelations for u_i^2; the third column shows autocorrelations for u_i^2/σ_i^2.[12] The table shows that the autocorrelations are positive for u_i^2 for all lags between 1 and 15. In the case of u_i^2/σ_i^2, some of the autocorrelations are positive and some are negative. They tend to be smaller in magnitude than the autocorrelations for u_i^2.

The GARCH model appears to have done a good job in explaining the

---

[12] For a series x_i, the autocorrelation with a lag of k is the coefficient of correlation between x_i and x_{i+k}.

data. For a more scientific test, we can use what is known as the Ljung–Box statistic.[13] If a certain series has m observations the Ljung–Box statistic is

$$m \sum_{k=1}^{K} w_k \eta_k^2$$

where η_k is the autocorrelation for a lag of k, K is the number of lags considered, and

$$w_k = \frac{m+2}{m-k}$$

For $K = 15$, zero autocorrelation can be rejected with 95% confidence when the Ljung–Box statistic is greater than 25.

From Table 5.4, the Ljung–Box statistic for the u_i^2 series is about 123. This is strong evidence of autocorrelation. For the u_i^2/σ_i^2 series the Ljung–Box statistic is 8.2, suggesting that the autocorrelation has been largely removed by the GARCH model.

5.10 USING GARCH(1, 1) TO FORECAST FUTURE VOLATILITY

The variance rate estimated at the end of day $n - 1$ for day n, when GARCH(1, 1) is used, is

$$\sigma_n^2 = (1 - \alpha - \beta)V_L + \alpha u_{n-1}^2 + \beta \sigma_{n-1}^2$$

so that

$$\sigma_n^2 - V_L = \alpha(u_{n-1}^2 - V_L) + \beta(\sigma_{n-1}^2 - V_L)$$

On day $n + t$ in the future, we have

$$\sigma_{n+t}^2 - V_L = \alpha(u_{n+t-1}^2 - V_L) + \beta(\sigma_{n+t-1}^2 - V_L)$$

The expected value of u_{n+t-1}^2 is σ_{n+t-1}^2. Hence,

$$E[\sigma_{n+t}^2 - V_L] = (\alpha + \beta)E[\sigma_{n+t-1}^2 - V_L]$$

where E denotes expected value. Using this equation repeatedly yields

$$E[\sigma_{n+t}^2 - V_L] = (\alpha + \beta)^t (\sigma_n^2 - V_L)$$

---

[13] See G. M. Ljung and G. E. P. Box, "On a Measure of Lack of Fit in Time Series Models," *Biometrica*, 65 (1978), 297–303.

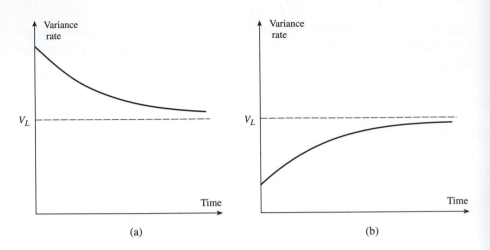

Figure 5.4 Expected path for the variance rate when (a) current variance rate is above long-term variance rate and (b) current variance rate is below long-term variance rate.

or

$$E[\sigma_{n+t}^2] = V_L + (\alpha + \beta)^t(\sigma_n^2 - V_L) \tag{5.14}$$

This equation forecasts the volatility on day $n + t$ using the information available at the end of day $n - 1$. In the EWMA model, $\alpha + \beta = 1$ and equation (5.14) shows that the expected future variance rate equals the current variance rate. When $\alpha + \beta < 1$, the final term in the equation becomes progressively smaller as t increases. Figure 5.4 shows the expected path followed by the variance rate for situations where the current variance rate is different from V_L. As mentioned earlier, the variance rate exhibits mean reversion with a reversion level of V_L and a reversion rate of $1 - \alpha - \beta$. Our forecast of the future variance rate tends toward V_L as we look further and further ahead. This analysis emphasizes the point that we must have $\alpha + \beta < 1$ for a stable GARCH(1, 1) process. When $\alpha + \beta > 1$, the weight given to the long-term average variance is negative and the process is "mean fleeing" rather than "mean reverting".

In the yen/USD exchange rate example considered earlier, $\alpha + \beta = 0.9602$ and $V_L = 0.00004422$. Suppose that our estimate of the current variance rate per day is 0.00006. (This corresponds to a volatility of 0.77% per day.) In ten days the expected variance rate is

$$0.00004422 + 0.9602^{10}(0.00006 - 0.00004422) = 0.00005473$$

The expected volatility per day is 0.74%, still well above the long-term volatility of 0.665% per day. However, the expected variance rate in 100 days is

$$0.00004422 + 0.9602^{100}(0.00006 - 0.00004422) = 0.00004449$$

and the expected volatility per day is 0.667%, very close the long-term volatility.

Volatility Term Structures

Suppose it is day n. Define

$$V(t) = E(\sigma_{n+t}^2) \quad \text{and} \quad a = \ln \frac{1}{\alpha + \beta}$$

so that equation (5.14) becomes

$$V(t) = V_L + e^{-at}[V(0) - V_L]$$

Here $V(t)$ is an estimate of the instantaneous variance rate in t days. The average variance rate per day between today and time T is

$$\frac{1}{T} \int_0^T V(t)\, dt = V_L + \frac{1 - e^{-aT}}{aT}[V(0) - V_L]$$

The longer the life of the option, the closer this is to V_L. Define $\sigma(T)$ as the volatility per annum that should be used to price a T-day option under GARCH(1, 1). Assuming 252 days per year, $\sigma(T)^2$ is 252 times the average variance rate per day, so that

$$\sigma(T)^2 = 252 \left\{ V_L + \frac{1 - e^{-aT}}{aT}[V(0) - V_L] \right\} \tag{5.15}$$

As we discuss in Chapter 15, the market prices of different options on the same asset are often used to calculate a *volatility term structure*. This is the relationship between the implied volatilities of the options and their maturities. Equation (5.15) can be used to estimate a volatility term structure based on the GARCH(1, 1) model. The estimated volatility term structure is not usually the same as the actual volatility term structure. However, as we will show, it is often used to predict the way that the actual volatility term structure will respond to volatility changes.

When the current volatility is above the long-term volatility, the

GARCH(1, 1) model estimates a downward-sloping volatility term structure. When the current volatility is below the long-term volatility, it estimates an upward-sloping volatility term structure. In the case of the yen/USD exchange rate $a = \ln(1/0.9602) = 0.0406$ and $V_L = 0.00004422$. Suppose that the current variance rate per day, $V(0)$ is estimated as 0.00006 per day. It follows from equation (5.15) that

$$\sigma(T)^2 = 252\left[0.00004422 + \frac{1 - e^{-0.0406T}}{0.0406T}(0.00006 - 0.000044220)\right]$$

where T is measured in days. Table 5.5 shows the volatility per year for different values of T.

Impact of Volatility Changes

Equation (5.15) can be written as

$$\sigma(T)^2 = 252\left\{V_L + \frac{1 - e^{-aT}}{aT}\left(\frac{\sigma(0)^2}{252} - V_L\right)\right\}$$

When $\sigma(0)$ changes by $\Delta\sigma(0)$, $\sigma(T)$ changes by

$$\frac{1 - e^{-aT}}{aT}\frac{\sigma(0)}{\sigma(T)}\Delta\sigma(0) \qquad\qquad (5.16)$$

Table 5.6 shows the effect of a volatility change on options of varying maturities for our yen/USD exchange rate example. We assume as before that $V(0) = 0.00006$, so that $\sigma(0) = 12.30\%$. The table considers a 100-basis-point change in the instantaneous volatility from 12.30% per year to 13.30% per year. This means that $\Delta\sigma(0) = 0.01$, or 1%.

Many financial institutions use analyses such as this when determining the exposure of their books to volatility changes. Rather than consider an across-the-board increase of 1% in implied volatilities when calculating vega, they relate the size of the volatility increase that is considered to the maturity of the option. Based on Table 5.6, a 0.84% volatility increase

Table 5.5   Yen/USD volatility term structure predicted from GARCH(1, 1).

Option life (days):	10	30	50	100	500
Option volatility (% per annum):	12.00	11.59	11.33	11.00	10.65

Table 5.6   Impact of 1% change in the instantaneous volatility predicted from GARCH(1, 1).

Option life (days):	10	30	50	100	500
Increase in volatility (%):	0.84	0.61	0.46	0.27	0.06

would be considered for a 10-day option, a 0.61% increase for a 30-day option, a 0.46% increase for a 50-day option, and so on.

SUMMARY

In option pricing we define the volatility of a variable as the standard deviation of its continuously compounded return per year. Volatilities are either estimated from historical data or implied from option prices. In risk management the daily volatility of a market variable is defined as the standard deviation of the percentage daily change in the market variable. The daily variance rate is the square of the daily volatility. Volatility tends to be much higher on trading days than on nontrading days. As a result nontrading days are ignored in volatility calculations. It is tempting to assume that daily changes in market variables are normally distributed. In fact, this is far from true. Most market variables have distributions for percentage daily changes with much heavier tails than the normal distribution. The power law has been found to be a good description of the tails of many distributions that are encountered in practice, and is often used for the tails of the distributions of percentage changes in many market variables.

Most popular option pricing models, such as Black–Scholes, assume that the volatility of the underlying asset is constant. This assumption is far from perfect. In practice, the volatility of an asset, like its price, is a stochastic variable. However, unlike the asset price, it is not directly observable. This chapter has discussed schemes for attempting to keep track of the current level of volatility.

We define u_i as the percentage change in a market variable between the end of day $i - 1$ and the end of day i. The variance rate of the market variable (i.e., the square of its volatility) is calculated as a weighted average of the u_i^2. The key feature of the schemes that have been discussed here is that they do not give equal weight to the observations on the u_i^2. The more recent an observation, the greater the weight assigned to it. In the EWMA model and the GARCH(1, 1) model, the weights assigned to observations decrease exponentially as the observations become older. The GARCH(1, 1) model differs from the EWMA model in that some weight is also assigned to the long-run average variance rate. Both the EWMA and GARCH(1, 1) models have structures that enable forecasts of the future level of variance rate to be produced relatively easily.

Maximum-likelihood methods are usually used to estimate parameters in GARCH(1, 1) and similar models from historical data. These methods involve using an iterative procedure to determine the parameter values that maximize the chance or likelihood that the historical data will occur. Once its parameters have been determined, a model can be judged by how well it removes autocorrelation from the u_i^2.

FURTHER READING

On the Causes of Volatility

Fama, E. F., "The Behavior of Stock Market Prices," *Journal of Business*, 38 (January 1965): 34–105.

French, K. R., "Stock Returns and the Weekend Effect," *Journal of Financial Economics*, 8 (March 1980): 55–69.

French, K. R, and R. Roll, "Stock Return Variances: The Arrival of Information and the Reaction of Traders," *Journal of Financial Economics*, 17 (September 1986): 5–26.

Roll, R., "Orange Juice and Weather," *American Economic Review*, 74, No. 5 (December 1984): 861–880.

On GARCH

Bollerslev, T., "Generalized Autoregressive Conditional Heteroscedasticity," *Journal of Econometrics*, 31 (1986): 307–327.

Cumby, R., S. Figlewski, and J. Hasbrook, "Forecasting Volatilities and Correlations with EGARCH Models," *Journal of Derivatives*, 1, No. 2 (Winter 1993): 51–63.

Engle, R. F., "Autoregressive Conditional Heteroscedasticity with Estimates of the Variance of UK Inflation," *Econometrica*, 50 (1982): 987–1008.

Engle, R. F. and J. Mezrich, "Grappling with GARCH," *Risk*, September 1995: 112–117.

Engle, R. F., and V. Ng, "Measuring and Testing the Impact of News on Volatility," *Journal of Finance*, 48 (1993): 1749–1778.

Nelson, D., "Conditional Heteroscedasticity and Asset Returns; A New Approach," *Econometrica*, 59 (1990): 347–370.

Noh, J., R. F. Engle, and A. Kane, "Forecasting Volatility and Option Prices of the S&P 500 Index," *Journal of Derivatives*, 2 (1994): 17–30.

QUESTIONS AND PROBLEMS (Answers at End of Book)

5.1. The volatility of a stock price is 30% per annum. What is the standard deviation of the percentage price change in one week?

5.2. The volatility of an asset is 25% per annum. What is the standard deviation of the percentage price change in one trading day. Assuming a normal distribution, estimate 95% confidence limits for the percentage price change in one day.

5.3. Why do traders assume 252 rather than 365 days in a year when using volatilities?

5.4. What is *implied volatility*? How can it be calculated? In practice, different options on the same asset have different implied volatilities. What conclusions do you draw from this?

5.5. Suppose that observations on an exchange rate at the end of the last 11 days have been 0.7000, 0.7010, 0.7070, 0.6999, 0.6970, 0.7003, 0.6951, 0.6953, 0.6934, 0.6923, 0.6922. Estimate the daily volatility using both the approach in Section 5.3 and the simplified approach in equation (5.4).

5.6. The number of visitors to a website follows the power law given in equation (5.1) with $\alpha = 2$. Suppose that 1% of sites get 500 or more visitors per day. What percentage of sites get (a) 1000 and (b) 2000 or more visitors per day.

5.7. Explain the exponentially weighted moving average (EWMA) model for estimating volatility from historical data.

5.8. What is the difference between the exponentially weighted moving average model and the GARCH(1, 1) model for updating volatilities?

5.9. The most recent estimate of the daily volatility of an asset is 1.5% and the price of the asset at the close of trading yesterday was $30.00. The parameter λ in the EWMA model is 0.94. Suppose that the price of the asset at the close of trading today is $30.50. How will this cause the volatility to be updated by the EWMA model?

5.10. A company uses an EWMA model for forecasting volatility. It decides to change the parameter λ from 0.95 to 0.85. Explain the likely impact on the forecasts.

5.11. Assume that S&P 500 at close of trading yesterday was 1,040 and the daily volatility of the index was estimated as 1% per day at that time. The parameters in a GARCH(1, 1) model are $\omega = 0.000002$, $\alpha = 0.06$, and

$\beta = 0.92$. If the level of the index at close of trading today is 1,060, what is the new volatility estimate?

5.12. The most recent estimate of the daily volatility of the USD/GBP exchange rate is 0.6% and the exchange rate at 4 p.m. yesterday was 1.5000. The parameter λ in the EWMA model is 0.9. Suppose that the exchange rate at 4 p.m. today proves to be 1.4950. How would the estimate of the daily volatility be updated?

5.13. A company uses the GARCH(1, 1) model for updating volatility. The three parameters are ω, α, and β. Describe the impact of making a small increase in each of the parameters while keeping the others fixed.

5.14. The parameters of a GARCH(1, 1) model are estimated as $\omega = 0.000004$, $\alpha = 0.05$, and $\beta = 0.92$. What is the long-run average volatility and what is the equation describing the way that the variance rate reverts to its long-run average? If the current volatility is 20% per year, what is the expected volatility in 20 days?

5.15. Suppose that the daily volatility of the FTSE 100 stock index (measured in GBP) is 1.8% and the daily volatility of the USD/GBP exchange rate is 0.9%. Suppose further that the correlation between the FTSE 100 and the USD/GBP exchange rate is 0.4. What is the volatility of the FTSE 100 when it is translated to US dollars? Assume that the USD/GBP exchange rate is expressed as the number of US dollars per pound sterling. (*Hint*: When $Z = XY$, the percentage daily change in Z is approximately equal to the percentage daily change in X plus the percentage daily change in Y.)

5.16. Suppose that GARCH(1, 1) parameters have been estimated as $\omega = 0.000003$, $\alpha = 0.04$, and $\beta = 0.94$. The current daily volatility is estimated to be 1%. Estimate the daily volatility in 30 days.

5.17. Suppose that GARCH(1, 1) parameters have been estimated as $\omega = 0.000002$, $\alpha = 0.04$, and $\beta = 0.94$. The current daily volatility is estimated to be 1.3%. Estimate the volatility per annum that should be used to price a 20-day option.

ASSIGNMENT QUESTIONS

5.18. Suppose that observations on a stock price (in US dollars) at the end of each of 15 consecutive weeks are as follows:

30.2, 32.0, 31.1, 30.1, 30.2, 30.3, 30.6, 33.0, 32.9, 33.0, 33.5, 33.5, 33.7, 33.5, 33.2

Estimate the stock price volatility. What is the standard error of your estimate?

5.19. Suppose that the price of gold at close of trading yesterday was $300 and its volatility was estimated as 1.3% per day. The price at the close of trading today is $298. Update the volatility estimate using (a) the EWMA model with $\lambda = 0.94$ and (b) the GARCH(1, 1) model with $\omega = 0.000002$, $\alpha = 0.04$, and $\beta = 0.94$.

5.20. An Excel spreadsheet containing over 900 days of daily data on a number of different exchange rates and stock indices can be downloaded from the author's website: http://www.rotman.utoronto.ca/~hull. Choose one exchange rate and one stock index. Estimate the value of λ in the EWMA model that minimizes the value of

$$\sum_i (v_i - \beta_i)^2$$

where v_i is the variance forecast made at the end of day $i - 1$ and β_i is the variance calculated from data between day i and day $i + 25$. Use the Solver tool in Excel. To start the EWMA calculations, set the variance forecast at the end of the first day equal to the square of the return on that day.

5.21. Suppose that the parameters in a GARCH(1, 1) model are $\alpha = 0.03$, $\beta = 0.95$, and $\omega = 0.000002$. (a) What is the long-run average volatility? (b) If the current volatility is 1.5% per day, what is your estimate of the volatility in 20, 40, and 60 days? (c) What volatility should be used to price 20-, 40-, and 60-day options? (d) Suppose that there is an event that increases the current volatility by 0.5% to 2% per day. Estimate the effect on the volatility in 20, 40, and 60 days. (e) Estimate by how much the event increases the volatilities used to price 20-, 40-, and 60-day options.

5.22. An Excel spreadsheet containing over 900 days of daily data on a number of different exchange rates and stock indices can be downloaded from the author's website: http://www.rotman.utoronto.ca/~hull. Use the data and maximum-likelihood methods to estimate for the TSE and S&P indices the best-fit parameters in an EWMA model and a GARCH(1, 1) model for the variance rate.

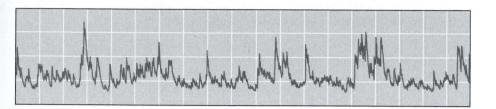

6

C H A P T E R

Correlations
and Copulas

Suppose a company has an exposure to two different market variables. In the case of each variable it gains $10 million if there is a one-standard-deviation increase and loses $10 million if there is a one-standard-deviation decrease. If changes in the two variables have a high positive correlation, the company's total exposure is very high; if they have a correlation of zero, the exposure is less, but still quite large; if they have a high negative correlation, the exposure is quite low because a loss on one of the variables is likely to be offset by a gain on the other. This example shows that it is important for a risk manager to estimate correlations between the changes in market variables as well as their volatilities when assessing risk exposures.

This chapter explains how correlations can be monitored in a similar way to volatilities. It also covers what are known as copulas. These are tools that provide a way of defining a correlation structure between two or more variables, regardless of the shapes of their probability distributions. Copulas will prove to be important in a number of future chapters. For example, a knowledge of copulas enables some of the formulas underlying the Basel II capital requirements to be understood (Chapter 7). Copulas are also useful in modeling default correlation for the purposes of valuing credit derivatives (Chapter 13) and in the calculation of economic capital (Chapter 16). The final section of this chapter explains how copulas can be used to model defaults on portfolios of loans.

6.1 DEFINITION OF CORRELATION

The coefficient of correlation, ρ, between two variables V_1 and V_2 is defined as

$$\rho = \frac{E(V_1 V_2) - E(V_1)E(V_2)}{SD(V_1)SD(V_2)} \qquad (6.1)$$

where $E(\cdot)$ denotes expected value and $SD(\cdot)$ denotes standard deviation. If there is no correlation between the variables, then $E(V_1 V_2) = E(V_1)E(V_2)$ and $\rho = 0$. If $V_1 = V_2$, then the numerator and the denominator in the expression for ρ are both equal to the variance of V_1. As we would expect, $\rho = 1$ in this case.

The *covariance* between V_1 and V_2 is defined as

$$\text{cov}(V_1, V_2) = E(V_1 V_2) - E(V_1)E(V_2) \qquad (6.2)$$

so that the correlation can be written

$$\rho = \frac{\text{cov}(V_1, V_2)}{SD(V_1)SD(V_2)}$$

Although it is easier to develop intuition about the meaning of a correlation than a covariance, it is covariances that will prove to be the fundamental variables of our analysis. An analogy here is that variance rates were the fundamental variables for the EWMA and GARCH methods in Chapter 5, even though volatilities are easier to understand.

Correlation vs. Dependence

Two variables are defined as statistically independent if knowledge about one of them does not affect the probability distribution for the other. Formally, V_1 and V_2 and independent if

$$f(V_2 \mid V_1 = x) = f(V_2)$$

for all x, where $f(\cdot)$ denotes the probability density function.

If the coefficient of correlation between two variables is zero, does this mean that there is no dependence between the variables? The answer is no. We can illustrate this with a simple example. Suppose that there are three equally likely values for V_1: -1, 0, and $+1$. If $V_1 = -1$ or $V_1 = +1$, then $V_2 = 1$. If $V_1 = 0$, then $V_2 = 0$. In this case there is clearly a dependence between V_1 and V_2. If we observe the value of V_1, we know the value of V_2. Also, a knowledge of the value of V_2 will cause us to

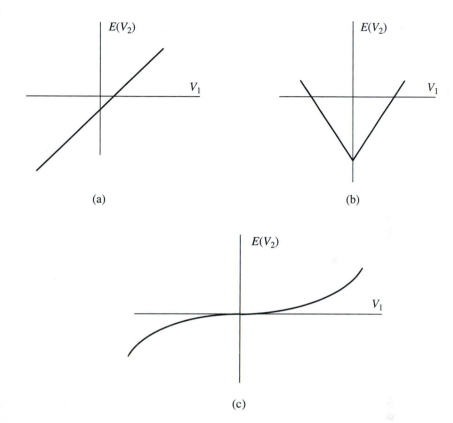

Figure 6.1 Examples of ways in which V_2 can depend on V_1.

change our probability distribution for V_1. However, the coefficient of correlation between V_1 and V_2 is zero.

This example emphasizes the point that the coefficient of correlation measures one particular type of dependence between two variables. This is linear dependence. There are many other ways in which two variables can be related. We can characterize the nature of the dependence between V_1 and V_2 by plotting $E(V_2)$ against V_1. Three examples are shown in Figure 6.1. Figure 6.1a shows linear dependence where the expected value of V_2 depends linearly on V_1. Figure 6.1b shows a V-shaped relationship between the expected value of V_2 and V_1. (This is similar to the example we have just considered; a symmetrical V-shaped relationship, however strong, leads to zero coefficient of correlation.) Figure 6.1c shows a type of dependence that is often seen when V_1 and V_2 are percentage changes in financial variables. For the values of V_1 normally encountered, there is very little relation between V_1 and V_2. However, extreme values of V_1 tend to lead to extreme values of V_2. To quote one commentator: "During a crisis the correlations all go to one."

6.2 MONITORING CORRELATION

Chapter 5 explained how EWMA and GARCH methods can be developed to monitor the variance rate of a variable. Similar approaches can be used to monitor the covariance rate between two variables. The variance rate per day of a variable is the variance of daily returns. Similarly the *covariance rate* per day between two variables is defined as the covariance between the daily returns of the variables.

Suppose that X_i and Y_i are the values of two variables X and Y at the end of day i. The returns on the variables on day i are

$$x_i = \frac{X_i - X_{i-1}}{X_{i-1}} \quad \text{and} \quad y_i = \frac{Y_i - Y_{i-1}}{Y_{i-1}}$$

The covariance rate between X and Y on day n is, from equation (6.2),

$$\text{cov}_n = E(x_n y_n) - E(x_n)E(y_n)$$

In Section 5.5 we explained that risk managers assume that expected daily returns are zero when the variance rate per day is calculated. They do the same when calculating the covariance rate per day. This means that the covariance rate per day between X and Y on day n is simply

$$\text{cov}_n = E(x_n y_n)$$

Using equal weighting for the last m observations on x_i and y_i

$$\text{cov}_n = \frac{1}{m} \sum_{i=1}^{m} x_{n-i} y_{n-i} \tag{6.3}$$

A similar weighting scheme for variances gives an estimate for the variance rate on day n for variable X as

$$\text{var}_{x,n} = \frac{1}{m} \sum_{i=1}^{m} x_{n-i}^2$$

and for variable Y as

$$\text{var}_{y,n} = \frac{1}{m} \sum_{i=1}^{m} y_{n-i}^2$$

The correlation estimate on day n is

$$\frac{\text{cov}_n}{\sqrt{\text{var}_{x,n}\text{var}_{y,n}}}$$

Using EWMA

Most risk managers would agree that observations from far back in the past should not have as much weight as recent observations. In Chapter 5 we discussed the use of the EWMA model for variances. We saw that it leads to weights that decline exponentially as we move back through time. A similar weighting scheme can be used for covariances. The formula for updating a covariance estimate in the EWMA model is, similarly to equation (5.8),

$$\text{cov}_n = \lambda\text{cov}_{n-1} + (1 - \lambda)x_{n-1}y_{n-1}$$

A similar analysis to that presented for the EWMA volatility model shows that the weight given to $x_{n-i}y_{n-i}$ declines as i increases (i.e., as we move back through time). The lower the value of λ, the greater the weight that is given to recent observations.

Example 6.1

Suppose that $\lambda = 0.95$ and that the estimate of the correlation between two variables X and Y on day $n - 1$ is 0.6. Suppose further that the estimate of the volatilities for X and Y on day $n - 1$ are 1% and 2%, respectively. From the relationship between correlation and covariance, the estimate of the covariance rate between X and Y on day $n - 1$ is

$$0.6 \times 0.01 \times 0.02 = 0.00012$$

Suppose that the percentage changes in X and Y on day $n - 1$ are 0.5% and 2.5%, respectively. The variance rates and covariance rate for day n would be updated as follows:

$$\sigma_{x,n}^2 = 0.95 \times 0.01^2 + 0.05 \times 0.005^2 = 0.00009625$$

$$\sigma_{y,n}^2 = 0.95 \times 0.02^2 + 0.05 \times 0.025^2 = 0.00041125$$

$$\text{cov}_n = 0.95 \times 0.00012 + 0.05 \times 0.005 \times 0.025 = 0.00012025$$

The new volatility of X is $\sqrt{0.00009625} = 0.981\%$ and the new volatility of Y is $\sqrt{0.00041125} = 2.028\%$. The new correlation between X and Y is

$$\frac{0.00012025}{0.00981 \times 0.02028} = 0.6044$$

Using GARCH

GARCH models can also be used for updating covariance rate estimates and forecasting the future level of covariance rates. For example, the GARCH(1, 1) model for updating a covariance rate between X and Y is

$$\text{cov}_n = \omega + \alpha x_{n-1} y_{n-1} + \beta \text{cov}_{n-1}$$

This formula, like its counterpart in equation (5.10) for updating variances, gives some weight to a long-run average covariance, some to the most recent covariance estimate, and some to the most recent observation on covariance (which is $x_{n-1} y_{n-1}$). The long-term average covariance rate is $\omega/(1 - \alpha - \beta)$. Formulas similar to those in equations (5.14) and (5.15) can be developed for forecasting future covariance rates and calculating the average covariance rate during the life of an option.

Consistency Condition for Covariances

Once variance and covariance rates have been calculated for a set of market variables, a variance–covariance matrix can be constructed. When $i \neq j$, the (i, j)th element of this matrix shows the covariance rate between the variables i and j; when $i = j$, it shows the variance rate of variable i.

Not all variance–covariance matrices are internally consistent. The condition for an $N \times N$ variance–covariance matrix Ω to be internally consistent is

$$w^{\mathsf{T}} \Omega w \geqslant 0 \tag{6.4}$$

for all $N \times 1$ vectors w, where w^{T} is the transpose of w. A matrix that satisfies this property is known as *positive-semidefinite*.

To understand why the condition in equation (6.4) must hold, suppose that w^{T} is $[w_1, w_2, \ldots, w_n]$. The expression $w^{\mathsf{T}} \Omega w$ is the variance rate of $w_1 z_1 + w_2 z_2 + \cdots + w_n z_n$, where z_i is the value of variable i. As such, it cannot be negative.

To ensure that a positive-semidefinite matrix is produced, variances and covariances should be calculated consistently. For example, if variance rates are calculated by giving equal weight to the last m data items, the same should be done for covariance rates. If variance rates are updated using an EWMA model with $\lambda = 0.94$, the same should be done for covariance rates. Multivariate GARCH models, where variance rates and covariance rates for a set of variables are updated in a consistent way, can also be developed.[1]

An example of a variance–covariance matrix that is not internally consistent is

$$\begin{bmatrix} 1 & 0 & 0.9 \\ 0 & 1 & 0.9 \\ 0.9 & 0.9 & 1 \end{bmatrix}$$

The variance of each variable is 1.0 and so the covariances are also coefficients of correlation in this case. The first variable is highly correlated with the third variable, and the second variable is also highly correlated with the third variable. However, there is no correlation at all between the first and second variables. This seems strange. When we set w equal to $(1, 1, -1)$, we find that the condition in equation (6.4) is not satisfied, proving that the matrix is not positive-semidefinite.[2]

Variance–covariance matrices that are calculated in a consistent way from observations on the underlying variables are always positive-semidefinite. For example, if we have 500 days of data on three different variables and use it to calculate a variance–covariance matrix using EWMA with $\lambda = 0.94$, it will be positive-semidefinite. If we make a small change to the matrix (e.g., for the purposes of doing a sensitivity analysis), it is likely that the matrix will remain positive-semidefinite. However, if we do the same thing for observations on 1000 variables, we have to be much more careful. The 1000×1000 matrix that we calculate from the 500 days of data is positive-semidefinite, but if we make an arbitrary small change to the matrix it is quite likely that it will no longer be positive-semidefinite.

6.3 MULTIVARIATE NORMAL DISTRIBUTIONS

Multivariate normal distributions are well understood and relatively easy to deal with. As we will explain in the next section, they can be useful

---

[1] See R. Engle and J. Mezrich, "GARCH for Groups," *Risk*, August 1996, 36–40, for a discussion of alternative approaches.

[2] It can be shown that the condition for a 3×3 matrix of correlations to be internally consistent is

$$\rho_{12}^2 + \rho_{13}^2 + \rho_{23}^2 - 2\rho_{12}\rho_{13}\rho_{23} \leqslant 1$$

where ρ_{ij} is the coefficient of correlation between variables i and j.

tools for specifying the correlation structure between variables—even when the distributions of the variables are not normal.

We start by considering a bivariate normal distribution, where there are only two variables, V_1 and V_2. Suppose that we know V_1 has some value v_1. Conditional on this, the value of V_2 is normal with mean

$$\mu_2 + \rho \frac{v_1 - \mu_1}{\sigma_1}$$

and standard deviation

$$\sigma_2 \sqrt{1 - \rho^2}$$

Here μ_1 and μ_2 are the unconditional means of V_1 and V_2; σ_1 and σ_2 are their unconditional standard deviations; and ρ is the coefficient of correlation between V_1 and V_2. Note that the expected value of V_2 conditional on V_1 is linearly dependent on the value of V_1. This corresponds to Figure 6.1a. Also the standard deviation of V_2 conditional on the value of V_1 is the same for all values of V_1.

Generating Random Samples from Normal Distributions

Most programming languages have routines for sampling a random number between 0 and 1 and many have routines for sampling from a normal distribution.[3] If no routine for sampling from a standardized normal distribution is readily available, an approximate random sample can be calculated as

$$\epsilon = \sum_{i=1}^{12} R_i - 6 \tag{6.5}$$

where the R_i $(1 \leqslant i \leqslant 12)$ are independent random numbers between 0 and 1, and ϵ is the required sample. This approximation is satisfactory for most purposes.

When two correlated samples ϵ_1 and ϵ_2 from bivariate distributions are required, an appropriate procedure is as follows. Independent samples z_1 and z_2 from a univariate standardized normal distribution are obtained as just described. The required samples ϵ_1 and ϵ_2 are then calculated as follows:

$$\epsilon_1 = z_1 \quad \text{and} \quad \epsilon_2 = \rho z_1 + z_2 \sqrt{1 - \rho^2}$$

where ρ is the coefficient of correlation.

---

[3] In Excel the instruction =NORMSINV(RAND()) gives a random sample from a normal distribution.

Consider next the situation where we require n correlated samples from normal distributions and the coefficient of correlation between sample i and sample j is $\rho_{i,j}$. We first sample n independent variables z_i ($1 \leqslant i \leqslant n$) from univariate standardized normal distributions. The required samples are ϵ_i ($1 \leqslant i \leqslant n$), where

$$\epsilon_i = \sum_{k=1}^{i} \alpha_{ik} z_k$$

and the α_{ik} are parameters chosen to give the correct variances and correlations for the ϵ's.

For $1 \leqslant j < i$, we have

$$\sum_{k=1}^{i} \alpha_{ik}^2 = 1$$

and, for all $j < i$,

$$\sum_{k=1}^{j} \alpha_{ik} \alpha_{jk} = \rho_{ij}$$

The first sample, ϵ_1, is set equal to z_1. These equations for the α's can be solved so that ϵ_2 is calculated from z_1 and z_2, ϵ_3 is calculated from z_1, z_2 and z_3, and so on. The procedure is known as the *Cholesky decomposition*.

If we find ourselves trying to take the square root of a negative number when using the Cholesky decomposition, the variance–covariance matrix assumed for the variables is not internally consistent. As explained in Section 6.2, this is equivalent to saying that the matrix is not positive-semidefinite.

Factor Models

Sometimes the correlations between normally distributed variables are defined using a factor model. Suppose that $U_1, U_2, \ldots, U_N$ have standard normal distributions (i.e., normal distributions with mean 0 and standard deviation 1). In a one-factor model each U_i has a component dependent on a common factor F and a component that is uncorrelated with the other variables. Formally,

$$U_i = a_i F + \sqrt{1 - a_i^2}\, Z_i \qquad (6.6)$$

where F and the Z_i have a standard normal distributions and a_i is a constant between -1 and $+1$. The Z_i are uncorrelated with each other and uncorrelated with F. In this model all the correlation between U_i and U_j arises from their dependence on the common factor F. The coefficient of correlation between U_i and U_j is $a_i a_j$.

The advantage of a one-factor model is that it imposes some structure on the correlations. Without assuming a factor model the number of correlations that have to be estimated for the N variables is $N(N-1)/2$. With the one-factor model we need only estimate N parameters: $a_1, a_2, \ldots, a_N$. An example of a one-factor model from the world of investments is the capital asset pricing model, where the return on a stock has a component dependent on the return from the market and an idiosyncratic (nonsystematic) component that is independent of the return on other stocks (see Section 1.1).

The one-factor model can be extended to a two-, three-, or M-factor model. In the M-factor model,

$$U_i = a_{i1}F_1 + a_{i2}F_2 + \cdots + a_{iM}F_M + \sqrt{1 - a_{i1}^2 - a_{i2}^2 - \cdots - a_{iM}^2}\, Z_i \quad \textbf{(6.7)}$$

The factors $F_1, F_2, \ldots, F_M$ have uncorrelated standard normal distributions and the Z_i are uncorrelated both with each other and with the F's. In this case the correlation between U_i and U_j is

$$\sum_{m=1}^{M} a_{im} a_{jm}$$

6.4 COPULAS

Consider two correlated variables V_1 and V_2. The *marginal distribution* of V_1 (sometimes also referred to as the unconditional distribution) is its distribution assuming we know nothing about V_2; similarly, the marginal distribution of V_2 is its distribution assuming we know nothing about V_1. Suppose we have estimated the marginal distributions of V_1 and V_2. How can we make an assumption about the correlation structure between the two variables to define their joint distribution?

If the marginal distributions of V_1 and V_2 are normal, an assumption that is convenient and easy to work with is that the joint distribution of the variables is bivariate normal.[4] Similar assumptions are possible for some other marginal distributions. But often there is no natural way of defining a correlation structure between two marginal distributions. This is where copulas come in.

---

[4] Although this is a convenient assumption it is not the only one that can be made. There are many other ways in which two normally distributed variables can be dependent on each other. See, for example, Problem 6.11.

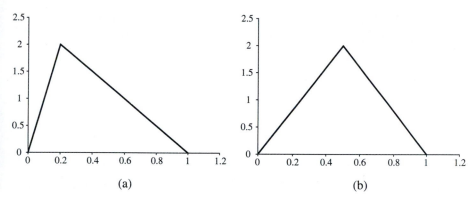

Figure 6.2   Triangular distributions for (a) V_1 and (b) V_2.

As an example of the application of copulas, suppose that the marginal distributions of V_1 and V_2 are the triangular probability density functions shown in Figure 6.2. Both variables have values between 0 and 1. The density function for V_1 peaks at 0.2, and the density function for V_2 peaks at 0.5. For both density functions, the maximum height is 2.0. To use what is known as a *Gaussian copula*, we map V_1 and V_2 into new variables U_1 and U_2 that have standard normal distributions. (A standard normal distribution is a normal distribution with mean 0 and standard deviation 1.) The mapping is effected on a percentile-to-percentile basis. The 1-percentile point of the V_1 distribution is mapped to the 1-percentile point of the U_1 distribution; the 10-percentile point of the V_1 distribution is mapped to the 10-percentile point of the U_1 distribution; and so on. The variable V_2 is mapped into U_2 in a similar way. Table 6.1 shows how values of V_1 are

Table 6.1   Mapping of V_1, which has the triangular distribution in Figure 6.2a, to U_1, which has a standard normal distribution.

V_1 value	Percentile of distribution	U_1 value
0.1	5.00	−1.64
0.2	20.00	−0.84
0.3	38.75	−0.29
0.4	55.00	0.13
0.5	68.75	0.49
0.6	80.00	0.84
0.7	88.75	1.21
0.8	95.00	1.64
0.9	98.75	2.24

Table 6.2 Mapping of V_2, which has the triangular distribution in Figure 6.2b, to U_2, which has a standard normal distribution.

V_2 value	Percentile of distribution	U_2 value
0.1	2.00	−2.05
0.2	8.00	−1.41
0.3	18.00	−0.92
0.4	32.00	−0.47
0.5	50.00	0.00
0.6	68.00	0.47
0.7	82.00	0.92
0.8	92.00	1.41
0.9	98.00	2.05

mapped into values of U_1 and Table 6.2 how values of V_2 are mapped into values of U_2. Consider the $V_1 = 0.1$ calculation in Table 6.1. The cumulative probability that V_1 is less than 0.1 is (by calculating areas of triangles) $0.5 \times 0.1 \times 1 = 0.05$, or 5%. The value 0.1 for V_1 therefore gets mapped to the 5-percentile point of the standard normal distribution. This is −1.64.[5]

The variables U_1 and U_2 have normal distributions. We assume that they are jointly bivariate normal. This in turn implies a joint distribution and a correlation structure between V_1 and V_2. The essence of copulas is therefore that, instead of defining a correlation structure between V_1 and V_2 directly, we do so indirectly. We map V_1 and V_2 into other variables which have "well-behaved" distributions and for which it is easy to define a correlation structure.

The way in which a copula defines a joint distribution is illustrated in Figure 6.3. Let us assume that the correlation between U_1 and U_2 is 0.5. The joint cumulative probability distribution between V_1 and V_2 is shown in Table 6.3. To illustrate the calculations, consider the first one where we are calculating the probability that $V_1 < 0.1$ and $V_2 < 0.1$. From Tables 6.1 and 6.2, this is the same as the probability that $U_1 < -1.64$ and $U_2 < -2.05$. From the cumulative bivariate normal distribution, this is 0.006 when $\rho = 0.5$.[6] (The probability would be only $0.02 \times 0.05 = 0.001$ if $\rho = 0$.)

---

[5] It can be calculated using Excel: NORMSINV(0.05) = −1.64.

[6] An Excel function for calculating the cumulative bivariate normal distribution can be found on the author's website: www.rotman.utoronto.ca/~hull.

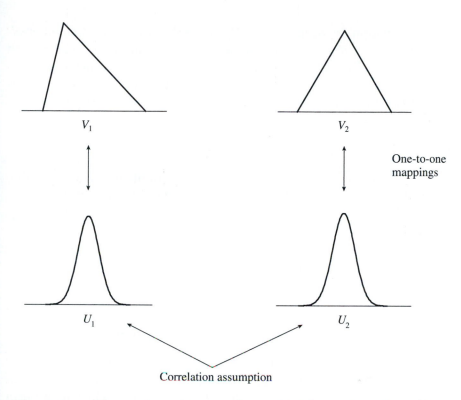

Figure 6.3   The way in which a copula model defines a joint distribution.

Table 6.3   Cumulative joint probability distribution for V_1 and V_2 in a Gaussian copula model. Correlation parameter $= 0.5$. Table shows the joint probability that V_1 and V_2 are less than the specified values.

V_1	V_2								
	0.1	0.2	0.3	0.4	0.5	0.6	0.7	0.8	0.9
0.1	0.006	0.017	0.028	0.037	0.044	0.048	0.049	0.050	0.050
0.2	0.013	0.043	0.081	0.120	0.156	0.181	0.193	0.198	0.200
0.3	0.017	0.061	0.124	0.197	0.273	0.331	0.364	0.381	0.387
0.4	0.019	0.071	0.149	0.248	0.358	0.449	0.505	0.535	0.548
0.5	0.019	0.076	0.164	0.281	0.417	0.537	0.616	0.663	0.683
0.6	0.020	0.078	0.173	0.301	0.456	0.600	0.701	0.763	0.793
0.7	0.020	0.079	0.177	0.312	0.481	0.642	0.760	0.837	0.877
0.8	0.020	0.080	0.179	0.318	0.494	0.667	0.798	0.887	0.936
0.9	0.020	0.080	0.180	0.320	0.499	0.678	0.816	0.913	0.970

The correlation between U_1 and U_2 is referred to as the *copula correlation*. This is not, in general, the same as the correlation between V_1 and V_2. Since U_1 and U_2 are bivariate normal, the conditional mean of U_2 is linearly dependent on U_1 and the conditional standard deviation of U_2 is constant (as discussed in Section 6.3). However, a similar result does not in general apply to V_1 and V_2.

Expressing the Approach Algebraically

For a more formal description of the Gaussian copula approach, suppose that F_1 and F_2 are the cumulative marginal probability distributions of V_1 and V_2. We map $V_1 = v_1$ to $U_1 = u_1$ and $V_2 = v_2$ to $U_2 = u_2$, where

$$F_1(v_1) = N(u_1) \quad \text{and} \quad F_2(v_2) = N(u_2)$$

and N is the cumulative normal distribution function. This means that

$$u_1 = N^{-1}[F_1(v_1)], \qquad u_2 = N^{-1}[F_2(v_2)]$$

and

$$v_1 = F_1^{-1}[N(u_1)], \qquad v_2 = F_2^{-1}[N(u_2)]$$

The variables U_1 and U_2 are then assumed to be bivariate normal. The key property of a copula model is that it preserves the marginal distributions of V_1 and V_2 (however unusual these may be) while defining a correlation structure between them.

Other Copulas

The Gaussian copula is just one copula that can be used to define a correlation structure between V_1 and V_2. There are many other copulas leading to many other correlation structures. One that is sometimes used is the *Student t-copula*. This works in the same way as the Gaussian copula except that the variables U_1 and U_2 are assumed to have a bivariate Student t-distribution. To sample from a bivariate Student t-distribution with f degrees of freedom and correlation ρ, we proceed as follows:

1. Sample from the inverse chi-square distribution to get a value χ. (In Excel, the CHIINV function can be used. The first argument is RAND() and the second is f.)

2. Sample from a bivariate normal distribution with correlation ρ as described in Section 6.3.

3. Multiply the normally distributed samples by $\sqrt{f/\chi}$.

Figure 6.4 shows plots of 5000 random samples from a bivariate normal, while Figure 6.5 does the same for the bivariate Student t. The correlation parameter is 0.5 and the number of degrees of freedom for the Student t is 4. Define a "tail value" of a distribution as a value in the left or right 1% tail of the distribution. There is a tail value for the normal distribution when the variable is greater than 2.33 or less than -2.33. Similarly there is a tail value in the t-distribution when the value of the variable is greater than 3.75 or less than -3.75. Vertical and horizontal lines in the figures indicate when tail values occur. The figures illustrate that it is more common for both variables to have tail values in the bivariate t-distribution than in the bivariate normal distribution. To put this another way, the *tail correlation* is higher in a bivariate t-distribution that in a bivariate normal distribution. We made the point earlier that correlations between market variables tend to increase in extreme market conditions so that Figure 6.1c is sometimes a better description of the correlation structure between two variables than Figure 6.1a. This has led some researchers to argue that the Student t-copula provides a better description of the joint behavior of market variables than the Gaussian copula.

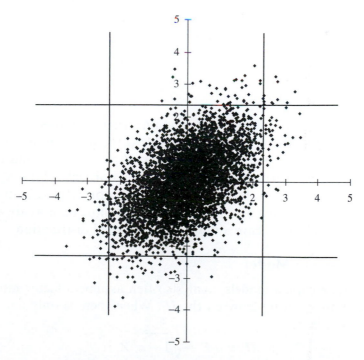

Figure 6.4   5000 random samples from a bivariate normal distribution.

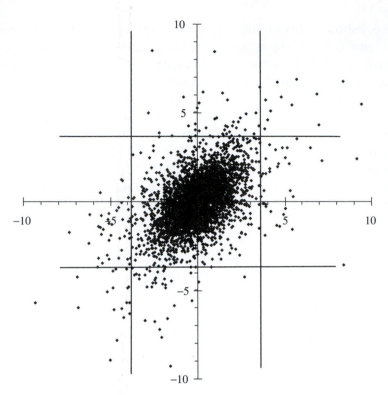

Figure 6.5 5000 random samples from a bivariate Student t-distribution.

Multivariate Copulas

Copulas can be used to define a correlation structure between more than two variables. The simplest example of this is the multivariate Gaussian copula. Suppose that there are N variables, V_1, V_2, ..., V_N, and that we know the marginal distribution of each variable. For each i ($1 \leqslant i \leqslant N$), we transform V_i into U_i, where U_i has a standard normal distribution (the transformation is effected on a percentile-to-percentile basis as above). We then assume that the U_i have a multivariate normal distribution.

A Factor Copula Model

In multivariate copula models, analysts often assume a factor model for the correlation structure between the U_i. When there is only one factor, equation (6.6) gives

$$U_i = a_i F + \sqrt{1 - a_i^2}\, Z_i \tag{6.8}$$

where F and the Z_i have standard normal distributions. The Z_i are uncorrelated with each other and uncorrelated with F. Other factor copula models are obtained by choosing F and the Z_i to have other zero-mean unit-variance distributions. For example, if Z_i is normal and F has a Student t-distribution, we obtain a multivariate Student t-distribution for U_i. These distributional choices affect the nature of the dependence between the variables.

6.5 APPLICATION TO LOAN PORTFOLIOS

We now present an application of the one-factor Gaussian copula that will prove useful in understanding the Basel II capital requirements in Chapter 7. Consider a portfolio of N companies. Define T_i $(1 \leqslant i \leqslant N)$ as the time when company i defaults. (We assume that all companies will default eventually—but that the default time may be a long time, perhaps even hundreds of years, in the future.) Denote the cumulative probability distribution of T_i by Q_i.

In order to define a correlation structure between the T_i using the one-factor Gaussian copula model, we map, for each i, T_i to a variable U_i that has a standard normal distribution on a percentile-to-percentile basis. We assume the factor model in equation (6.8) for the correlation structure between the U_i:

$$U_i = a_i F + \sqrt{1 - a_i^2}\, Z_i \qquad (6.9)$$

where the variables F and Z_i have independent standard normal distributions. The mappings between the U_i and T_i imply

$$\text{Prob}(U_i < U) = \text{Prob}(T_i < T)$$

when

$$U = N^{-1}[Q_i(T)] \qquad (6.10)$$

From equation (6.9), the probability that $U_i < U$ conditional on the factor value F is

$$\text{Prob}(U_i < U \mid F) = N\left[\frac{U - a_i F}{\sqrt{1 - a_i^2}}\right]$$

This is also $\text{Prob}(T_i < T \mid F)$ when equation (6.10) is satisfied. Hence,

$$\text{Prob}(T_i < T \mid F) = N\left(\frac{N^{-1}[Q_i(T)] - a_i F}{\sqrt{1 - a_i^2}}\right) \tag{6.11}$$

To simplify matters, we suppose that the distribution Q_i of time to default is the same for all i and equal to Q. We also assume that the copula correlation between any two names is the same and equals ρ. Since the copula correlation between companies i and j is $a_i a_j$, this means that the $a_i = \sqrt{\rho}$ for all i. Equation (6.11) becomes

$$\text{Prob}(T_i < T \mid F) = N\left(\frac{N^{-1}[Q(T)] - \sqrt{\rho}\,F}{\sqrt{1 - \rho}}\right)$$

For a large portfolio of loans, this equation provides a good estimate of the proportion of loans in the portfolio that default by time T. We will refer to this as the *default rate*.

As F decreases, the default rate increases. How bad can the default rate become? Because F has a standard normal distribution, the probability that F will be less than $N^{-1}(Y)$ is Y. There is therefore a probability of Y that the default rate will be greater than

$$N\left(\frac{N^{-1}[Q(T)] - \sqrt{\rho}\,N^{-1}(Y)}{\sqrt{1 - \rho}}\right)$$

Define $V(T, X)$ as the default rate that will not be exceeded with probability X, so that we are $X\%$ certain that the default rate will not exceed $V(T, X)$. The value of $V(T, X)$ is determined by substituting $Y = 1 - X$ into the above expression:

$$V(T, X) = N\left(\frac{N^{-1}[Q(T)] + \sqrt{\rho}\,N^{-1}(X)}{\sqrt{1 - \rho}}\right) \tag{6.12}$$

This result was first developed by Vasicek in 1987.[7]

Example 6.2

Suppose that a bank has lent a total of $100 million to its retail clients. The one-year probability of default on every loan is 2% and the amount recovered in the event of a default averages 60%. The copula correlation parameter is

---

[7] See O. Vasicek "Probability of Loss on a Loan Portfolio," Working Paper KMV, 1987. Vasicek's results were published in *Risk* in December 2002 under the title "Loan Portfolio Value".

estimated as 0.1. In this case,

$$V(1, 0.999) = N\left(\frac{N^{-1}(0.02) + \sqrt{0.1}\, N^{-1}(0.999)}{\sqrt{1 - 0.1}}\right) = 0.128$$

showing that we are 99.9% certain that the default rate will not be worse than 12.8%. Losses when this worst-case loss rate occur are $100 \times 0.128 \times (1 - 0.6)$, or $5.13 million.

SUMMARY

The measure usually considered by a risk manager to describe the relationship between two variables is the covariance rate. The daily covariance rate is the correlation between the daily returns on the variables multiplied by the product of their daily volatilities. The methods for monitoring a covariance rate are similar to those described in Chapter 5 for monitoring a variance rate. Either EWMA or GARCH models can be used. In practice, risk managers need to keep track of a variance–covariance matrix for all the variables to which they are exposed.

The marginal distribution of a variable is the unconditional distribution of the variable. Very often an analyst is in a situation where he or she has estimated the marginal distributions of a set of variables and wants to make an assumption about their correlation structure. If the marginal distributions of the variables happen to be normal, it is natural to assume that the variables have a multivariate normal distribution. In other situations copulas are used. The marginal distributions are transformed on a percentile-to-percentile basis to normal distributions (or to some other distribution for which there is a multivariate counterpart). The correlation structure between the variables of interest is then defined indirectly from an assumed correlation structure between the transformed variables.

When many variables are involved, analysts often use a factor model. This is a way of reducing the number of correlation estimates that have to be made. The correlation between any two variables is assumed to derive solely from their correlations with the factors. The default correlation between different companies can be modeled using a factor-based Gaussian copula model of their times to default.

FURTHER READING

Cherubini, U., E. Luciano, and W. Vecchiato, *Copula Methods in Finance*, Wiley, 2004.

Demarta, S., and A. J. McNeil, "The t Copula and Related Copulas," Working Paper, Department of Mathematics, ETH Zentrum, Zurich, Switzerland.

Engle, R. F., and J. Mezrich, "GARCH for Groups," *Risk*, August 1996, 36–40.

Vasicek, O. "Probability of Loss on a Loan Portfolio," Working Paper, KMV, 1987. [Published in *Risk* in December 2002 under the title "Loan Portfolio Value".]

QUESTIONS AND PROBLEMS (Answers at End of Book)

6.1. If you know the correlation between two variables, what extra information do you need to calculate the covariance?

6.2. What is the difference between correlation and dependence? Suppose that $y = x^2$ and x is normally distributed with mean 0 and standard deviation 1. What is the correlation between x and y?

6.3. What is a factor model? Why are factor models useful when defining a correlation structure between large numbers of variables?

6.4. What is meant by a positive-semidefinite matrix? What are the implications of a correlation matrix not being positive-semidefinite?

6.5. Suppose that the current daily volatilities of asset A and asset B are 1.6% and 2.5%, respectively. The prices of the assets at close of trading yesterday were \$20 and \$40 and the estimate of the coefficient of correlation between the returns on the two assets made at that time was 0.25. The parameter λ used in the EWMA model is 0.95. (a) Calculate the current estimate of the covariance between the assets. (b) On the assumption that the prices of the assets at close of trading today are \$20.50 and \$40.50, update the correlation estimate.

6.6. Suppose that the current daily volatilities of asset X and asset Y are 1.0% and 1.2%, respectively. The prices of the assets at close of trading yesterday were \$30 and \$50 and the estimate of the coefficient of correlation between the returns on the two assets made at this time was 0.50. Correlations and volatilities are updated using a GARCH(1,1) model. The estimates of the model's parameters are $\alpha = 0.04$ and $\beta = 0.94$. For the correlation, $\omega = 0.000001$, and, for the volatilities, $\omega = 0.000003$. If the prices of the two assets at close of trading today are \$31 and \$51, how is the correlation estimate updated?

6.7. Suppose that in Problem 5.15 the correlation between the S&P 500 Index (measured in dollars) and the FTSE 100 Index (measured in sterling) is 0.7, the correlation between the S&P 500 Index (measured in dollars) and the USD/GBP exchange rate is 0.3, and the daily volatility of the S&P 500 Index is 1.6%. What is the correlation between the S&P 500 Index (measured in dollars) and the FTSE 100 Index when it is translated to dollars? (*Hint*: For three variables X, Y, and Z, the covariance between $X + Y$ and Z equals the covariance between X and Z plus the covariance between Y and Z.)

6.8. Suppose that two variables V_1 and V_2 have uniform distributions where all values between 0 and 1 are equally likely. Use a Gaussian copula to define the correlation structure between V_1 and V_2 with a copula correlation of 0.3. Produce a table similar to Table 6.3 considering values of 0.25, 0.5, and 0.75 for V_1 and V_2. (A spreadsheet for calculating the cumulative bivariate normal distribution can be found on the author's website: www.rotman.utoronto.ca/~hull.)

6.9. Assume that you have independent random samples z_1, z_2, and z_3 from a standard normal distribution and want to convert them to samples e_1, e_2, and e_3 from a trivariate normal distribution using the Cholesky decomposition. Derive three formulas expressing e_1, e_2, and e_3 in terms of z_1, z_2, and z_3 and the three correlations that are needed to define the trivariate normal distribution.

6.10. Explain what is meant by tail dependence. How can you vary tail dependence by the choice of copula?

6.11. Suppose that the marginal distributions of V_1 and V_2 are standard normal distributions but that a Student t-copula with four degrees of freedom and a correlation parameter of 0.5 is used to define the correlation between the variables. How would you construct a chart showing samples from the joint distribution?

6.12. In Table 6.3 what is the probability density function of V_2 conditional on $V_1 < 0.1$. Compare it with the unconditional distribution of V_2.

6.13. What is the median of the distribution of V_2 when V_1 equals 0.2 in the example in Tables 6.1 and 6.2.

6.14. Suppose that a bank has made a large number of loans of a certain type. The total amount lent is $500 million. The one-year probability of default on each loan is 1.5% and the loss when a default occurs is 70% of the amount owed. The bank uses a Gaussian copula for time to default. The copula correlation parameter is 0.2. Estimate the loss on the portfolio that is not expected to be exceeded with a probability of 99.5%.

ASSIGNMENT QUESTIONS

6.15. Suppose that the price of gold at close of trading yesterday was $300 and its volatility was estimated as 1.3% per day. The price of gold at the close of trading today is $298. Suppose further that the price of silver at the close of trading yesterday was $8, its volatility was estimated as 1.5% per day, and its correlation with gold was estimated as 0.8. The price of silver at the close of trading today is unchanged at $8. Update the volatility of gold and silver and the correlation between gold and silver using (a) the EWMA model with $\lambda = 0.94$, and (b) the GARCH(1, 1) model with $\omega = 0.000002$, $\alpha = 0.04$, and $\beta = 0.94$. In practice, is the ω parameter likely to be the same for gold and silver?

6.16. The probability density function for an exponential distribution is $\lambda e^{-\lambda x}$, where x is the value of the variable and λ is a parameter. The cumulative probability distribution is $1 - e^{-\lambda x}$. Suppose that two variables V_1 and V_2 have exponential distributions with λ's of 1.0 and 2.0, respectively. Use a Gaussian copula to define the correlation structure between V_1 and V_2 with a copula correlation of −0.2. Produce a table similar to Table 6.3 using values of 0.25, 0.5, 0.75, 1, 1.25, 1.5 for V_1 and V_2. (A spreadsheet for calculating the cumulative bivariate normal distribution can be found on the author's website: www.rotman.utoronto.ca/~hull.

6.17. Create an Excel spreadsheet to produce a chart similar to Figure 6.5 showing samples from a bivariate Student t-distribution with four degrees of freedom where the correlation is 0.5. Next suppose that the marginal distributions of V_1 and V_2 are Student t with four degrees of freedom but that a Gaussian copula with a copula correlation parameter of 0.5 is used to define the correlation between the two variables. Construct a chart showing samples from the joint distribution. Compare the two charts you have produced.

6.18. Suppose that a bank has made a large number loans of a certain type. The one-year probability of default on each loan is 1.2%. The bank uses a Gaussian copula for time to default. It is interested in estimating a "99.97% worst case" for the percentage of loans that default on the portfolio. Show how this varies with the copula correlation.

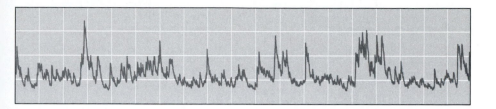

CHAPTER 7

Bank Regulation and Basel II

An important objective of governments is to provide a stable economic environment for private individuals and businesses. One way they do this is by providing a reliable banking system where bank failures are rare and depositors are protected. Shortly after the disastrous crash of 1929, the United States took a number of steps to increase confidence in the banking system and protect depositors. It created the Federal Deposit Insurance Corporation (FDIC) to provide safeguards to depositors in the event of a failure by a bank. It also passed the famous Glass–Steagall Act that prevented deposit-taking commercial banks from engaging in investment banking activities.

Deposit insurance continues to exist in the United States and many other countries today. However, many of the provisions of the Glass–Steagall Act in the United States have now been repealed. There has been a trend worldwide toward the development of progressively more complicated rules on the capital that banks are required to keep. This is because, as shown in Section 1.3, the ability of a bank to absorb unexpected losses is critically dependent on the amount of equity and other forms of capital held. In this chapter we review the evolution of the regulation of bank capital from the 1980s and explain the new Basel II capital requirements, which are scheduled to be implemented starting in 2007.

It is widely accepted that the capital a financial institution requires should cover the difference between expected losses over some time horizon and "worst-case losses" over the same time horizon. The worst-case loss is

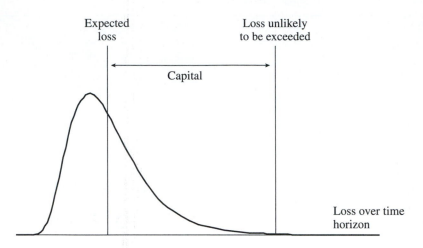

Figure 7.1 The loss probability density function and the capital required by a financial institution.

the loss that is not expected to be exceeded with some high degree of confidence. The high degree of confidence might be 99% or 99.9%. The idea here is that expected losses are usually covered by the way a financial institution prices its products. For example, the interest charged by a bank is designed to recover expected loan losses. Capital is a cushion to protect the bank from an extremely unfavorable outcome. This is illustrated in Figure 7.1.

Banks compete in some financial markets with securities firms and insurance companies. These types of financial institutions are often subject to different regulations from banks. In the United States securities firms are regulated by the Securities and Exchange Commission (SEC), and insurance companies are regulated at the state level with national guidelines being set by the National Association of Insurance Commissioners (NAIC). However, the regulators of all financial institutions face similar problems. Bank regulators want to protect depositors and ensure a stable financial system; insurance regulators want to protect policyholders from defaults by insurance companies and ensure that the public has confidence in the insurance industry; securities regulators want to protect the clients of brokers from defaults and ensure that markets operate smoothly. In some instances the three types of regulators find themselves specifying capital for the same financial instruments. If they do not do this in the same way, there is liable to be what is known as *regulatory arbitrage*, with risks being shifted to those financial institutions that are required to carry least capital for the financial instruments.

There have been some signs of convergence in the regulation of financial institutions. Insurance regulators and securities regulators are adopting similar approaches to bank regulators in prescribing minimum levels for capital. In the European Union the Capital Requirements Directive (CRD) legislation will require the regulatory capital for securities firms to be calculated in a similar way to that for banks. Another initiative by the European Union, Solvency II, is likely to lead to the capital for insurance companies in Europe being calculated in a broadly similar way to that for banks.

Bank regulators are in many ways taking the lead in developing a methodology for setting capital requirements for financial institutions. The regulation of banks is based on international standards, whereas the regulation of other types of financial institutions varies more from country to country. For this reason the regulation of banks will be the main focus of this chapter.

7.1 REASONS FOR REGULATING BANK CAPITAL

It is tempting to argue as follows: "Bank regulation is unnecessary. Even if there were no regulations, banks would manage their risks prudently and would strive to keep a level of capital that is commensurate with the risks they are taking." Unfortunately, history does not altogether support this view. There is little doubt that regulation has played an important role in increasing bank capital, making banks more aware of the risks they are taking.

If markets operated totally without government intervention, banks that took risks by keeping low levels of equity capital would find it difficult to attract deposits and might experience a "run on deposits", where large numbers of depositors try to withdraw funds at the same time. As mentioned earlier, most governments do provide some form of deposit insurance because they want depositors to have confidence that their money is safe. However, the existence of deposit insurance has the effect of encouraging banks to reduce equity capital (thereby increasing expected return on equity) because they no longer have to worry about depositors losing confidence.[1] From the government's perspective there is therefore a risk that the existence of deposit insurance leads to more bank

---

[1] This is an example of what insurance companies term *moral hazard*. The existence of an insurance contract changes the behavior of the insured party. We will discuss moral hazard further in Chapter 14.

Business Snapshot 7.1   Systemic Risk

Systemic risk is the risk that a default by one financial institution will create a "ripple effect" that leads to defaults by other financial institutions and threatens the stability of the financial system. The financial system has survived defaults such as Drexel in 1990 and Barings in 1995 very well, but regulators continue to be concerned. There are huge numbers of over-the-counter transactions between banks. If Bank A fails, Bank B may take a huge loss on the transactions it has with Bank A. This in turn could lead to Bank B failing. Bank C that has many outstanding transactions with both Bank A and Bank B might then take a large loss and experience severe financial difficulties, and so on.

---

failures and an increase in the cost of deposit insurance programs. As a result governments have found it necessary to combine deposit insurance with regulations on the capital banks must hold. In addition, governments are concerned about what is termed *systemic risk*. This is discussed in Business Snapshot 7.1.

7.2 PRE-1988

Prior to 1988 bank regulators in different countries tended to regulate bank capital by setting minimum levels for the ratio of capital to total assets. However, definitions of capital and the ratios considered acceptable varied from country to country. Some countries enforced their regulations more diligently than others. Banks were competing globally and a bank operating in a country where capital regulations were slack was considered to have a competitive edge over one operating in a country with tighter more strictly enforced capital regulations. In addition the huge exposures of the major international banks to less developed countries such as Mexico, Brazil, and Argentina and the accounting games sometimes used to manage those exposures were starting to raise questions about the adequacy of capital levels.

Another problem was that the types of transactions entered into by banks were becoming more complicated. The over-the-counter derivatives market for products such as interest rate swaps, currency swaps, and foreign exchange options was growing fast. These contracts increase the credit risks being taken by a bank. Consider, for example, an interest rate swap. If the counterparty in an interest rate swap transaction defaults when the swap has a positive value to the bank and a negative value to the counterparty, the bank loses money. Many of these newer transactions were "off balance sheet". This means that they had no effect on the level of assets reported by a bank. As a result, they had no effect on the amount of capital the bank was required to keep. It became apparent to regulators that total assets was no longer a good indicator of the total risks being taken. A more sophisticated approach than that of setting minimum levels for the ratio of capital to total balance sheet assets was needed.

These problems led supervisory authorities for Belgium, Canada, France, Germany, Italy, Japan, Luxembourg, the Netherlands, Sweden, Switzerland, the United Kingdom, and the United States to form the Basel Committee on Banking Supervision. They met regularly in Basel, Switzerland, under the patronage of the Bank for International Settlements. The first major result of these meetings was a document entitled "International Convergence of Capital Measurement and Capital Standards". This was referred to as "The 1988 BIS Accord" or just "The Accord". More recently it has come to be known as Basel I.

7.3 THE 1988 BIS ACCORD

The 1988 BIS Accord was the first attempt to set international risk-based standards for capital adequacy. It has been subject to much criticism as being too simple and somewhat arbitrary. In fact, the Accord was a huge achievement. It was signed by all 12 members of the Basel Committee and paved the way for significant increases in the resources banks devote to measuring, understanding, and managing risks.

The BIS Accord defined two minimum standards for meeting acceptable capital adequacy requirements. The first standard was similar to that existing prior to 1988 and required banks to have an assets-to-capital multiple of at most 20. The second standard introduced what became known as the Cooke ratio. For most banks there was no problem in satisfying the capital multiple rule. The Cooke ratio was the key regulatory requirement.

The Cooke Ratio

In calculating the Cooke ratio both on-balance-sheet and off-balance-sheet items are considered. They are used to calculate what is known as the bank's total *risk-weighted assets* (also sometimes referred to as the *risk-weighted amount*). It is a measure of the bank's total credit exposure.

Table 7.1   Risk weights for on-balance-sheet items.

Risk weight (%)	Asset category
0	Cash, gold bullion, claims on OECD governments such as Treasury bonds or insured residential mortgages
20	Claims on OECD banks and OECD public sector entities such as securities issued by US government agencies or claims on municipalities
50	Uninsured residential mortgage loans
100	All other claims, such as corporate bonds and less-developed country debt, claims on non-OECD banks, real estate, premises, plant, and equipment

Consider first on-balance-sheet items. Each on-balance-sheet item is assigned a risk weight reflecting its risk. A sample of the risk weights specified in the Accord are shown in Table 7.1. Cash and securities issued by OECD governments are considered to have virtually zero risk and have a risk weight of zero. Loans to corporations have a risk weight of 100%. Loans to OECD banks and government agencies have a risk weight of 20%. Uninsured residential mortgages have a risk weight of 50%. The total risk-weighted assets for N on-balance-sheet items equals

$$\sum_{i=1}^{N} w_i L_i$$

where L_i is the principal amount of the ith item and w_i is its risk weight.

Example 7.1

The assets of a bank consist of $100 million of corporate loans, $10 million of OECD government bonds, and $50 million of residential mortgages. The total of risk-weighted assets is

$$1.0 \times 100 + 0.0 \times 10 + 0.5 \times 50 = 125$$

or $125 million.

Off-balance-sheet items are expressed as a *credit equivalent amount*. Loosely speaking, the credit equivalent amount is the loan principal that is considered to have the same credit risk. For nonderivative instruments the credit equivalent amount is calculated by applying a conversion factor to the principal amount of the instrument. Instruments that from a credit perspective are considered to be similar to loans, such as bankers' acceptances, have a conversion factor of 100%. Others, such as note issuance facilities (where a bank agrees that a company can issue short-term paper on pre-agreed terms in the future), have lower conversion factors.

For an over-the-counter derivative, such as an interest rate swap or a forward contract, the credit equivalent amount is calculated as

$$\max(V, 0) + aL \tag{7.1}$$

where V is the current value of the derivative, a is an *add-on factor*, and L is the principal amount. The first term in equation (7.1) is the current exposure. The add-on factor is an allowance for the possibility of the exposure increasing in the future. The add-on factors are shown in Table 7.2.

Example 7.2
A bank has entered into a $100 million interest rate swap with a remaining life of 4 years. The current value of the swap is $2.0 million. In this case the add-on amount is 0.5% of the principal, so that the credit equivalent amount is $2.0 million plus $0.5 million, or $2.5 million.

The credit equivalent amount for an off-balance-sheet item is multiplied by the risk weight for the counterparty in order to calculate the risk-weighted assets. The risk weights for off-balance-sheet items are similar to those in Table 7.1 except that the risk weight for a corporation is 0.5 rather than 1.0 when off-balance-sheet items are considered.

Example 7.3
Consider again the bank in Example 7.2. If the interest rate swap is with a corporation, the risk-weighted assets are 2.5 × 0.5, or $1.25 million. If it is with an OECD bank, the risk-weighted assets are 2.5 × 0.2, or $0.5 million.

Table 7.2 Add-on factors (as a percentage of principal) for derivatives.

Remaining maturity (years)	Interest rate	Exchange rate and gold	Equity	Precious metals except gold	Other commodities
< 1	0.0	1.0	6.0	7.0	10.0
1 to 5	0.5	5.0	8.0	7.0	12.0
> 5	1.5	7.5	10.0	8.0	15.0

Putting all this together, the total risk-weighted assets for a bank with N on-balance-sheet items and M off-balance-sheet items is

$$\sum_{i=1}^{N} w_i L_i + \sum_{j=1}^{M} w_j^* C_j \qquad (7.2)$$

Here, L_i is the principal of the ith on-balance-sheet item and w_i is its risk weight for the counterparty; C_j is the credit equivalent amount for the jth off-balance-sheet item and w_j^* is the risk weight for the counterparty.

Capital Requirement

The Accord required banks to keep capital equal to at least 8% of the risk-weighted assets. The capital had two components:

1. *Tier 1 Capital.* This consists of items such as equity, noncumulative perpetual preferred stock[2] less goodwill.

2. *Tier 2 Capital.* This is sometimes referred to as Supplementary Capital. It includes instruments such as cumulative perpetual preferred stock,[3] certain types of 99-year debenture issues, and subordinated debt with an original life of more than five years.

At least 50% of the required capital (i.e., 4% of the risk-weighted assets) must be in Tier 1. The Basel Committee updated its definition of instruments that are eligible for Tier 1 capital in a 1998 press release.

7.4 THE G-30 POLICY RECOMMENDATIONS

In 1993 a working group consisting of end users, dealers, academics, accountants, and lawyers involved in derivatives published a report that contained 20 risk management recommendations for dealers and end users of derivatives and four recommendations for legislators, regulators, and supervisors. The report was based on a detailed survey of 80 dealers and 72 end users worldwide. The survey involved both questionnaires and in-depth interviews. The report is not a regulatory document, but it has been very influential in the development of risk management practices.

---

[2] Noncumulative perpetual preferred stock is preferred stock lasting forever where there is a predetermined dividend rate. Unpaid dividends do not cumulate (i.e., the dividends for one year are not carried forward to the next year).

[3] In cumulative preferred stock unpaid dividends cumulate. Any backlog of dividends must be paid before dividends are paid on the common stock.

A brief summary of the important recommendations is as follows:

1. A company's policies on risk management should be clearly defined and approved by senior management, ideally at the board of directors level. Managers at all levels should enforce the policies.

2. Derivatives positions should be marked to market at least once a day.

3. Derivatives dealers should measure market risk using a consistent measure such as value at risk. (This will be discussed further in Chapter 8.) Limits to the market risks that are taken should be set.

4. Derivatives dealers should carry out stress tests to determine potential losses under extreme market conditions.

5. The risk management function should be set up so that it is independent from the trading operation.

6. Credit exposures arising from derivatives trading should be assessed based on the current replacement value of existing positions and potential future replacement costs.

7. Credit exposures to a counterparty should be aggregated in a way that reflects enforceable netting agreements. (We talk about netting in the next section.)

8. The individuals responsible for setting credit limits should be independent of those involved in trading.

9. Dealers and end users should assess carefully both the costs and benefits of credit risk mitigation techniques such as collateralization and downgrade triggers. In particular, they should assess their own capacity and that of their counterparties to meet the cash flow requirement of downgrade triggers. (Credit mitigation techniques are discussed in Chapter 12.)

10. Only individuals with the appropriate skills and experience should be allowed to have responsibility for trading derivatives, supervising the trading, carrying out back-office functions in relation to the trading, etc.

11. There should be adequate systems in place for data capture, processing, settlement, and management reporting.

12. Dealers and end users should account for the derivatives transactions used to manage risks so as to achieve a consistency of income recognition treatment between those instruments and the risks being managed.

7.5 NETTING

The word *netting* refers to a clause in over-the-counter contracts which states that if a counterparty defaults on one contract it has with a financial institution then it must default on all outstanding contracts with that financial institution.

Netting can have the effect of substantially reducing credit risk. Consider a bank that has three swap contracts outstanding with a particular counterparty. The contracts are worth +$24 million, −$17 million, and +$8 million to the bank. Suppose that the counterparty experiences financial difficulties and defaults on its outstanding obligations. To the counterparty, the three contracts have values of −$24 million, +$17 million, and −$8 million, respectively. Without netting, the counterparty would default on the first contract, keep the second contract, and default on the third contract. The loss to the bank would be $32 (= 24 + 8) million. With netting, the counterparty is required to default on the second contract as well. The loss to bank is then $15 (= 24 − 17 + 8) million.[4]

Suppose that a financial institution has a portfolio of N derivative contracts outstanding with a particular counterparty and that the current value of the ith contract is V_i. Without netting, the financial institution's exposure in the event of a default today is

$$\sum_{i=1}^{N} \max(V_i, 0)$$

With netting, it is

$$\max\left(\sum_{i=1}^{N} V_i, 0\right)$$

Without netting, the exposure is the payoff from a portfolio of options; with netting, the exposure is the payoff from an option on a portfolio.

The 1988 Accord does not take netting into account in setting capital requirements. From equation (7.1) the credit equivalent amount for a portfolio of derivatives with a counterparty under the Accord is

$$\sum_{i=1}^{N} [\max(V_i, 0) + a_i L_i]$$

---

[4] Note that if the second contract had been worth −$40 million to the bank then the counterparty is better off if it chooses not to default on its contracts with the bank.

where a_i is the add-on factor for the ith transaction and L_i is the principal for the ith transaction.

By 1995 netting had been successfully tested in the courts in many jurisdictions. As a result, the 1988 Accord was modified to allow banks to reduce their credit equivalent totals when enforceable bilateral netting agreements were in place. The first step was to calculate the net replacement ratio, NRR. This is the ratio of the current exposure with netting to the current exposure without netting:

$$\text{NRR} = \frac{\max(\sum_{i=1}^{N} V_i, 0)}{\sum_{i=1}^{N} \max(V_i, 0)}$$

The credit equivalent amount was modified to

$$\max\left(\sum_{i=1}^{N} V_i, 0\right) + (0.4 + 0.6 \times \text{NRR}) \sum_{i=1}^{N} a_i L_i$$

Example 7.4

Consider the example in Table 7.3 which shows a portfolio of three derivatives contracts that a bank has with a particular counterparty. The third column shows the current marked-to-market values of the transactions and the fourth column shows the add-on amount calculated from Table 7.2. The current exposure with netting is $-60 + 70 + 55 = 65$. The current exposure without netting is $0 + 70 + 55 = 125$. The net replacement ratio is given by

$$\text{NRR} = \frac{65}{125} = 0.52$$

The total of the add-on amounts, $\sum a_i L_i$, is $5 + 75 + 30 = 110$. The credit equivalent amount, when netting agreements are in place is $65 + (0.4 + 0.6 \times 0.52) \times 110 = 143.32$. Without netting agreements, the credit equivalent amount is $125 + 110 = 235$. Suppose that the counterparty is an OECD bank so that the risk weight is 0.2. This means that the risk-weighted assets with netting is $0.2 \times 143.32 = 28.66$. Without netting, it is $0.2 \times 235 = 47$.

Table 7.3 Portfolio of derivatives with a particular counterparty.

Transaction	Principal, L_i	Current value, V_i	Table 7.2 add-on amount, $a_i L_i$
3-year interest rate swap	1000	−60	5
6-year foreign exchange forward	1000	70	75
9-month option on a stock	500	55	30

7.6 THE 1996 AMENDMENT

In 1995 the Basel Committee issued a consultative proposal to amend the 1988 Accord. This became known as the "1996 Amendment". It was implemented in 1998 and was then sometimes referred to as "BIS 98".

The 1996 Amendment requires financial institutions to hold capital to cover their exposure to market risks as well as credit risks. The Amendment distinguishes between a bank's trading book and its banking book. The banking book consists primarily of loans and is not usually marked to market for managerial and accounting purposes. The trading book consists of the myriad of different instruments that are traded by the bank (stocks, bonds, swaps, forward contract, exotic derivatives, etc.). The trading book is normally marked to market daily.

Under the 1996 Amendment, the credit risk capital charge in the 1988 Accord continued to apply to all on-balance-sheet and off-balance-sheet items in the trading and banking book, except positions in the trading book that consisted of (a) debt and equity traded securities and (b) positions in commodities and foreign exchange. In addition there was a market risk capital charge for all items in the trading book whether they were on balance sheet or off balance sheet.[5]

The 1996 Amendment outlined a standardized approach for measuring the capital charge for market risk. The standardized approach assigned capital separately to each of debt securities, equity securities, foreign exchange risk, commodities risk, and options. No account was taken of correlations between different types of instruments. The more sophisticated banks with well-established risk management functions were allowed to use an "internal model-based approach" for setting market risk capital. This involved calculating a value-at-risk measure and converting it into a capital requirement using a formula specified in the 1996 amendment. (We discuss value at risk and the alternative approaches companies use to calculate it in Chapters 8, 9, and 10). Most large banks preferred to use the internal model-based approach because it better reflected the benefits of diversification and led to lower capital requirements.

The value-at-risk measure used by regulators for market risk is the loss on the trading book that can be expected to occur over a 10-day period 1% of the time. Suppose that the value at risk is $1 million. This means

---

[5] Certain nontrading book positions that are used to hedge positions in the trading book can be included in the calculation of the market risk capital charge.

that the bank is 99% confident that there will not be a loss greater than $1 million over the next 10 days.

The market risk capital requirement for banks when they use the internal model-based approach is calculated at any given time as

$$k * \text{VaR} + \text{SRC} \tag{7.3}$$

where k is a multiplicative factor, and SRC is a specific risk charge. The value at risk, VaR, is the greater of the previous day's value at risk and the average value at risk over the last 60 days. The minimum value for k is 3. Higher values may be chosen by regulators for a particular bank if tests reveal inadequacies in the bank's value-at-risk model.

The specific risk charge, SRC, is a capital charge for the idiosyncratic risks related to individual companies. One security that gives rise to idiosyncratic risk is a corporate bond. There are two components to the risk of this security: interest rate risk and credit risk. The interest rate risk is captured by the bank's market value-at-risk measure; the credit risk is specific risk.[6] The 1996 Amendment proposed standard methods for assessing a specific risk capital charge, but allowed banks to use internal models for arriving at a capital charge for specific risk similarly to the way they calculate a capital charge for market risks. We discuss specific risk and its calculation further in Chapter 12.

The total capital a bank was required to keep after the implementation of the 1996 Amendment was (for banks adopting the internal model-based approach) the sum of (a) credit risk capital equal to 8% of the risk-weighted assets (RWA), as given by equation (7.2) and (b) market risk capital as given by equation (7.3). For convenience, an RWA for market risk capital is defined as 12.5 multiplied by the amount given in equation (7.3). This means that the total capital required for credit and market risk is given by

$$\text{Total capital} = 0.08 \times (\text{Credit risk RWA} + \text{Market risk RWA}) \tag{7.4}$$

A bank has more flexibility in the type of capital it uses for market risk. It can use Tier 1 or Tier 2 capital. It can also use what is termed Tier 3 capital. This consists of short-term subordinated debt with an original maturity of at least two years that is unsecured and fully paid up.

For most banks the majority of the capital is for credit risk rather than

---

[6] As mentioned earlier, the 1988 credit capital charge did not apply to debt securities in the trading book under the 1996 Amendment.

market risk. In a typical situation 70% of required capital might be for credit risk and 30% for market risk.

7.7 BASEL II

The 1988 Basel Accord led to significant increases in the capital held by banks over the following ten years. It deserves a great deal of credit for improving the stability of the global banking system. However, it does have significant weaknesses. Under the 1988 Basel Accord, all loans by a bank to a corporation have a risk weight of 100% and require the same amount of capital. A loan to a corporation with a AAA credit rating is treated in the same way as one to a corporation with a B credit rating.[7] Furthermore, in Basel I, there was no model of default correlation.

In June 1999 the Basel Committee proposed new rules that have become known as Basel II. These were revised in January 2001 and April 2003. A number of quantitative impact studies (QISs) were carried out to test the application of the new rules and the amount of capital that will be required. A final set of rules agreed to by all members of the Basel Committee was published in June 2004. This was updated in November 2005. Implementation of the rules is expected to begin in 2007 after a further QIS.[8]

The Basel II capital requirements apply to "internationally active" banks. In the United States there are many small regional banks and the US regulatory authorities have decided that Basel II will not apply to them. (These banks will be regulated under what is termed Basel IA, which is similar to Basel I.) It is likely that some of the larger regional banks will voluntarily implement Basel II—perhaps to signal to their shareholders that they manage risks in a sophisticated way. In Europe all banks, large or small, will be regulated under Basel II. In addition, the European Union requires the Basel II rules to be applied to securities companies as well as banks. Basel II is based on three "pillars":

1. Minimum capital requirements
2. Supervisory review
3. Market discipline

---

[7] Credit ratings are discussed in Chapter 11.

[8] One point to note about the QIS studies is that they do not take account of changes banks may choose to make to their portfolios to minimize their capital requirements once Basel II is implemented.

In Pillar 1, the minimum capital requirement for credit risk in the banking book is calculated in a new way that reflects the credit ratings of counterparties. The capital requirement for market risk remains unchanged from the 1996 Amendment and there is a new capital charge for operational risk. The general requirement in Basel I that banks hold a total capital equal to 8% of risk-weighted assets remains unchanged. A risk-weighted asset for operational risk is defined as 12.5 times the calculated operational risk capital and equation (7.4) becomes

Total capital = 0.08 ×

(Credit risk RWA + Market risk RWA + Operational risk RWA) (7.5)

Pillar 2, which is concerned with the supervisory review process, allows regulators in different countries some discretion in how rules are applied (so that they can take account of local conditions) but seeks to achieve overall consistency in the application of the rules. It places more emphasis on early intervention when problems arise. Supervisors are required to do far more than just ensure that the minimum capital required under Basel II is held. Part of their role is to encourage banks to develop and use better risk management techniques and to evaluate these techniques. They should evaluate risks that are not covered by Pillar 1 and enter into an active dialogue with banks when deficiencies are identified.

The third pillar, market discipline, will require banks to disclose more information about the way they allocate capital and the risks they take. The idea here is that banks will be subjected to added pressure to make sound risk management decisions if shareholders and potential shareholders have more information about those decisions.

7.8 CREDIT RISK CAPITAL UNDER BASEL II

For credit risk, banks will have three choices under Basel II:

1. The standardized approach
2. The foundation internal ratings based (IRB) approach
3. The advanced IRB approach

The overall structure of the calculations is similar to that under Basel I. For an on-balance-sheet item a risk weight is applied to the principal to calculate risk-weighted assets reflecting the creditworthiness of the counterparty. For off-balance-sheet items the risk weight is applied to a credit equivalent amount. This is calculated using either credit conversion factors or add-on amounts. The adjustments for netting are similar to those in Basel I (see Section 7.5).

The Standardized Approach

The standardized approach is to be used by banks that are not sufficiently sophisticated (in the eyes of the regulators) to use the internal ratings approaches. (In the United States, Basel II will apply only to the largest banks and US regulators have decided that these banks must use the IRB approach.) Some of the rules for determining risk weights are summarized in Table 7.4. Comparing Table 7.4 with Table 7.1, we see that the OECD status of a bank or a country is no longer important under Basel II. The risk weight for a country (sovereign) exposure ranges from 0% to 150% and the risk weight for an exposure to another bank or a corporation ranges from 20% to 150%. In Table 7.1 OECD banks were implicitly assumed to be lesser credit risks than corporations. An OECD bank attracted a risk weight of 20%, while a corporation attracted a risk weight of 100%. Table 7.4 treats banks and corporation much more equitably. An interesting observation from Table 7.4 for a country, corporation, or bank that wants to borrow money is that it may be better to have no credit rating at all than a very poor credit rating! Supervisors are allowed to apply lower risk weights (20% rather than 50%, 50% rather than 100%, and 100% rather than 150%) when exposures are to a bank's country of incorporation or that country's central bank.

Table 7.4 Risk weights (as a percentage of principal) for exposures to country, banks, and corporations under Basel II's standardized approach as a function of their ratings.

	AAA to AA−	A+ to A−	BBB+ to BBB−	BB+ to BB−	B+ to B−	Below B−	Unrated
Country*	0	20	50	100	100	150	100
Banks**	20	50	50	100	100	150	50
Corporations	20	50	100	100	150	150	100

*   Includes exposures to central banks of the country.
** National supervisors have options as outlined in the text.

For claims on banks, the rules are somewhat complicated. Instead of using the risk weights in Table 7.4, national supervisors can choose to base capital requirements on the rating of the country in which the bank is incorporated. The risk weight assigned to the bank will be 20% if the country of incorporation has a rating between AAA and AA−, 50% if it is between A+ and A−, 100% if it is between BBB+ and B−, 150% if it is below B−, and 100% if it is unrated. Another complication is that, if national supervisors elect to use the rules in Table 7.4, then they can choose to treat claims with a maturity less than three months more favorably, so that the risk weights are 20% if the rating is between AAA+ and BBB−, 50% if it is between BB+ and B−, 150% if it is below B−, and 20% if it is unrated.

The standard rule for retail lending is that a risk weight of 75% be applied. (This compares with 100% in the 1988 Accord.) When claims are secured by a residential mortgage, the risk weight is 35%. (This compares with 50% in the 1988 Accord.) Owing to poor historical loss experience, the risk weight for claims secured by commercial real estate is 100%.

Example 7.5

Suppose that the assets of a bank consist of $100 million of loans to corporations rated A, $10 million of government bonds rated AAA, and $50 million of residential mortgages. Under the Basel II standardized approach, the total risk-weighted assets is

$$0.5 \times 100 + 0.0 \times 10 + 0.35 \times 50 = 67.5$$

or $67.5 million. This compares with $125 million under Basel I (see Example 7.1).

Adjustments for Collateral

There are two ways banks can adjust risk weights for collateral. The first is termed the *simple approach* and is similar to an approach used in Basel I. The second is termed the *comprehensive approach*. Banks have a choice as to which approach is used in the banking book, but they must use the comprehensive approach to calculate capital for counterparty credit risk in the trading book.

Under the simple approach, the risk weight of the counterparty is replaced by the risk weight of the collateral for the part of the exposure covered by the collateral. (The exposure is calculated after netting.) For any exposure not covered by the collateral, the risk weight of the counterparty is used. The minimum level for the risk weight applied to the collateral is 20%.[9] A requirement is that the collateral must be revalued at least every six months and must be pledged for at least the life of the exposure.

Under the comprehensive approach, banks adjust the size of their exposure upward to allow for possible increases and adjust the value of the collateral downward to allow for possible decreases in the value of the collateral.[10] (The adjustments depend on the volatility of the exposure and the loan.) A new exposure equal to the excess of the adjusted exposure over the adjusted value of the collateral is calculated and the counterparty's risk weight is applied to this exposure. The adjustments applied to the exposure and the collateral can be calculated using rules specified in Basel II or, with regulatory approval, using a bank's internal models. Where netting arrangements apply, exposures and collateral are separately netted and the adjustments made are weighted averages.

Example 7.6

Suppose that an $80 million exposure to a particular counterparty is secured by collateral worth $70 million. The collateral consists of bonds issued by an A-rated company. The counterparty has a rating of B+. The risk weight for the counterparty is 150% and the risk weight for the collateral is 50%. The risk-weighted assets applicable to the exposure using the simple approach is therefore

$$0.5 \times 70 + 1.50 \times 10 = 50$$

or $50 million.

Consider next the comprehensive approach. Assume that the adjustment to exposure to allow for possible future increases in the exposure is +10% and the adjustment to the collateral to allow for possible future decreases in its value is −15%. The new exposure is

$$1.1 \times 80 - 0.85 \times 70 = 28.5$$

or $28.5 million and a risk weight of 150% is applied to this exposure to give risk-adjusted assets equal to $42.75 million.

The IRB Approach

The model underlying the internal ratings based (IRB) approach is the one-factor Gaussian copula model of time to default that we discussed in Section 6.5.

---

[9] An exception is when the collateral consists of cash or government securities with the currency of the collateral being the same as the currency of the exposure.

[10] An adjustment to the exposure is not likely to be necessary on a loan, but is likely to be necessary on an over-the-counter derivative. The adjustment is in addition to the add on factor.

Table 7.5 Dependence of WCDR on PD and ρ.

	PD = 0.1%	PD = 0.5%	PD = 1%	PD = 1.5%	PD = 2.0%
$\rho = 0.0$	0.1%	0.5%	1.0%	1.5%	2.0%
$\rho = 0.2$	2.8%	9.1%	14.6%	18.9%	22.6%
$\rho = 0.4$	7.1%	21.1%	31.6%	39.0%	44.9%
$\rho = 0.6$	13.5%	38.7%	54.2%	63.8%	70.5%
$\rho = 0.8$	23.3%	66.3%	83.6%	90.8%	94.4%

Consider a large portfolio of N loans. Define:

WCDR: The worst-case default rate during the next year that we are 99.9% certain will not be exceeded

PD: The probability of default for each loan in one year

EAD: The exposure at default on each loan (in dollars)

LGD: The loss given default. This is the proportion of the exposure that is lost in the event of a default

Suppose that the copula correlation between each pair of obligors is ρ.[11] Equation (6.12) shows that

$$\text{WCDR} = N\left[\frac{N^{-1}(\text{PD}) + \sqrt{\rho}\,N^{-1}(0.999)}{\sqrt{1-\rho}}\right] \qquad (7.6)$$

It follows that there is a 99.9% chance that the loss on the portfolio will be less than N times

$$\text{EAD} \times \text{LGD} \times \text{WCDR}$$

It can be shown that, as a good approximation, this result can be extended to the case where the loans have different sizes and different default probabilities. In a general portfolio of loans, there is a 99.9% chance that the total loss will be less than the sum of $\text{EAD} \times \text{LGD} \times \text{WCDR}$ for the individual loans.[12] This result is the theoretical underpinning of the IRB approach.

Table 7.5 shows how WCDR depends on PD and ρ. When the correlation ρ is zero, $\text{WCDR} = \text{PD}$ because in that case there is no default correlation and the default rate in all years is the same. As ρ increases, WCDR increases.

---

[11] Note that the Basel Committee publications use R, not ρ, to denote the copula correlation.

[12] The WCDR for an individual loan is calculated by substituting the PD and ρ parameter for the loan into equation (7.6).

Corporate, Sovereign, and Bank Exposures

In the case of corporate, sovereign, and bank exposures, Basel II assumes a relationship between the correlation parameter ρ and the probability of default PD in equation (7.6) based on empirical research.[13] The formula is

$$\rho = 0.12\frac{1 - \exp(-50 \times PD)}{1 - \exp(-50)} + 0.24\left[1 - \frac{1 - \exp(-50 \times PD)}{1 - \exp(-50)}\right]$$

Because $\exp(-50)$ is a very small number, this formula is to all intents and purposes

$$\rho = 0.12(1 + e^{-50 \times PD}) \qquad (7.7)$$

As PD increases, ρ decreases. The reason for this inverse relationship is as follows. As a company becomes less creditworthy, its PD increases and its probability of default becomes more idiosyncratic and less affected by overall market conditions.

Combining equation (7.7) with equation (7.6), we obtain the relationship between WCDR and PD in Table 7.6. We find that WCDR is, as we would expect, an increasing function of PD. However, it does not increase as fast as it would if ρ were assumed to be independent of PD.

The formula for the capital required is

$$\text{EAD} \times \text{LGD} \times (\text{WCDR} - \text{PD}) \times \text{MA} \qquad (7.8)$$

The first three terms in this expression can be understood from our earlier discussion. We use $WCDR - PD$ instead of WCDR because we are interested in providing capital for the excess of the 99.9% worst-case loss over the expected loss. The variable MA is the maturity adjustment and is defined as

$$\text{MA} = \frac{1 + (M - 2.5) \times b}{1 - 1.5 \times b} \qquad (7.9)$$

Table 7.6 Relationship between WCDR and PD for corporate, sovereign, and bank exposures.

PD:	0.1%	0.5%	1.0%	1.5%	2.0%
WCDR:	3.4%	9.8%	14.0%	16.9%	19.0%

[13] See J. Lopez, "The Empirical Relationship Between Average asset Correlation, Firm Probability of Default and Asset Size," *Journal of Financial Intermediation*, 13, 2 (2004), 265–283.

where

$$b = [0.11852 - 0.05478 \times \ln(PD)]^2$$

and M is the maturity of the exposure.

The maturity adjustment is designed to allow for the fact that, if an instrument lasts longer than one year, there is a one-year credit exposure arising from a possible decline in the creditworthiness of the counterparty as well as from a possible default by the counterparty. (Note that when $M = 1$ the MA is 1.0 and has no effect.) As mentioned earlier, the risk-weighted assets (RWA) are calculated as 12.5 times the capital required

$$RWA = 12.5 \times EAD \times LGD \times (WCDR - PD) \times MA$$

so that the capital is 8% of RWA.

Under the foundation IRB approach, banks supply PD, while LGD, EAD, and M are supervisory values set by the Basel Committee. PD is largely determined by a bank's own estimate of the creditworthiness of the counterparty. It is subject to a floor of 0.03% for bank and corporate exposures. LGD is set at 45% for senior claims and 75% for subordinated claims. When there is eligible collateral, in order to correspond to the comprehensive approach that we described earlier, LGD is reduced by the ratio of the adjusted value of the collateral to the adjusted value of the exposure, both calculated using the comprehensive approach. The EAD is calculated in a manner similar to the credit equivalent amount in Basel I and includes the impact of netting. M is set at 2.5 in most circumstances.

Under the advanced IRB approach, banks supply their own estimates of the PD, LGD, EAD, and M for corporate, sovereign, and bank exposures. The PD can be reduced by credit mitigants such as credit triggers. (As in the case of the foundation IRB approach, it is subject to a floor of 0.03% for bank and corporate exposures.) The two main factors influencing the LGD are the seniority of the debt and the collateral. In calculating EAD, banks can with regulatory approval use their own estimates of credit conversion factors.

The capital given by equation (7.8) is intended to be sufficient to cover unexpected losses over a one-year period that we are 99% sure will not be exceeded. Losses from the one-year "average" probability of default, PD, should be covered by a bank in the way it prices its products. The WCDR is the probability of default that occurs once every thousand years. The Basel Committee reserves the right to apply a scaling factor (less than or greater than 1.0) to the result of the calculations in equation (7.8) if it finds that the aggregate capital requirements are too high or low. At the time of writing, this factor is estimated at 1.06.

Example 7.7

Suppose that the assets of a bank consist of $100 million of loans to A-rated corporations. The PD for the corporations is estimated as 0.1% and LGD is 60%. The average maturity is 2.5 years for the corporate loans. This means that

$$b = [0.11852 - 0.05478 \times \ln(0.001)]^2 = 0.247$$

so that

$$\text{MA} = \frac{1}{1 - 1.5 \times 0.247} = 1.59$$

From Table 7.6, the WCDR is 3.4%. Under the Basel II IRB approach, the risk-weighted assets for the corporate loans are

$$12.5 \times 100 \times 0.6 \times (0.034 - 0.001) \times 1.59 = 39.3$$

or $39.3 million. This compares with $100 million under Basel I and $50 million under the standardized approach of Basel II. (See Examples 7.1 and 7.5, where a $100 million corporate loan is part of the portfolio.)

Retail Exposures

The model underlying the calculation of capital for retail exposures is similar to that underlying the calculation of corporate, sovereign, and banking exposures. However, the foundation IRB and advanced IRB approaches are merged and all banks using the IRB approach provide their own estimates of PD, EAD, and LGD. There is no maturity adjustment. The capital requirement is therefore

$$\text{EAD} \times \text{LGD} \times (\text{WCDR} - \text{PD})$$

and the risk-weighted assets are

$$12.5 \times \text{EAD} \times \text{LGD} \times (\text{WCDR} - \text{PD})$$

WCDR is calculated as in equation (7.6). For residential mortgages, ρ is set equal to 0.15 in this equation. For qualifying revolving exposures, ρ is set equal to 0.04. For all other retail exposures, a relationship between ρ and PD is specified for the calculation of WCDR. This is

$$\rho = 0.03 \frac{1 - \exp(-35 \times \text{PD})}{1 - \exp(-35)} + 0.16 \left[1 - \frac{1 - \exp(-35 \times \text{PD})}{1 - \exp(-35)} \right]$$

Because $\exp(-35)$ is a very small number, this formula is to all intents

Table 7.7 Relationship between WCDR and PD for retail exposures.

PD:	0.1%	0.5%	1.0%	1.5%	2.0%
WCDR:	2.1%	6.3%	9.1%	11.0%	12.3%

and purposes

$$\rho = 0.03 + 0.13e^{-35 \times PD} \tag{7.10}$$

Comparing equation (7.10) with equation (7.7), we see that correlations are assumed to be much lower for retail exposures. Table 7.7 is the table corresponding to Table 7.6 for retail exposures.

Example 7.8

Suppose that the assets of a bank consist of $50 million of residential mortgages where the PD is 0.005 and the LGD is 20%. In this case, $\rho = 0.15$ and

$$WCDR = N\left[\frac{N^{-1}(0.005) + \sqrt{0.15}\, N^{-1}(0.999)}{\sqrt{1 - 0.15}}\right] = 0.067$$

The risk-weighted assets are

$$12.5 \times 50 \times 0.2 \times (0.067 - 0.005) = 7.8$$

or $7.8 million. This compares with $25 million under Basel I and $17.5 million under the standardized approach of Basel II. (See Examples 7.1 and 7.5, where $50 million of residential mortgages is part of the portfolio.)

Guarantees and Credit Derivatives

The approach traditionally taken by the Basel Committee for handling guarantees is the credit substitution approach. Suppose that an AA-rated company guarantees a loan to a BBB-rated company. For the purposes of calculating capital, the credit rating of the guarantor is substituted for the credit rating of the borrower, so that capital is calculated as though the loan had been made to the AA-rated company. This overstates the credit risk because, for the lender to lose money, both the guarantor and the borrower have to default (with the guarantor defaulting before the borrower). The Basel Committee has addressed this issue. In July 2005 it published a document concerned with the treatment of double defaults under Basel II.[14] As an alternative to using the credit substitution

---

[14] See "The Application of Basel II to Trading Activities and the Treatment of Double Defaults," July 2005, available on www.bis.org.

approach, the capital requirement can be calculated as the capital that would be required without the guarantee but multiplied by $0.15 + 160 \times PD_g$, where PD_g is the one-year probability of default by the guarantor. Credit default swaps, which we talk about in Chapter 13, provide a type of insurance against default and are handled similarly to guarantees for regulatory purposes.

7.9 OPERATIONAL RISK UNDER BASEL II

In addition to improving the way banks calculate credit risk capital, Basel II will require banks to keep capital for operational risk. It seems that regulators are introducing a capital charge for operational risk for three reasons. The first is that in an increasingly complex environment banks face many risks arising from the possibilities of human and computer error.[15] The second is that regulators want banks to pay more attention to their internal systems to avoid catastrophes like that at Barings Bank. The third is that the effect of the Basel II credit risk calculation will be to reduce the capital requirements for most banks and regulators want another capital charge to bring the total capital back to roughly where it was before. The regulators are currently offering three approaches:

1. The basic indicator approach
2. The standardized approach
3. The advanced measurement approach

Which of these is used depends on the sophistication of the bank. The simplest approach is the basic indicator approach. This sets the operational risk capital equal to the bank's average annual gross income over the last three years multiplied by 0.15.[16] The standardized approach is similar to the basic indicator approach except that a different factor is applied to the gross income from different business lines. In the advanced measurement approach the bank uses its own internal models to calculate the operational risk loss that it is 99.9% certain will not be exceeded in one year. One advantage of the advanced measurement approach is that it

---

[15] All errors are ultimately human errors. In the case of a "computer error", someone at a some stage made a mistake programming the computer.

[16] Gross income is defined as net interest income plus noninterest income. Net interest income is the excess of income earned on loans over interest paid on deposits and other instruments that are used to fund the loans. Years where gross income is negative are not included in the calculations.

Business Snapshot 7.2 Basel III?

Basel II does not allow a bank to use its own credit risk diversification calculations when setting capital requirements for credit risk within the banking book. Equation (7.6) with prescribed values of ρ must be used. In theory a bank with $1 billion of lending to BBB-rated companies in a single industry is liable to be asked to keep the same capital as a bank that has $1 billion of lending to a much more diverse group of BBB-rated corporations. As banks develop better credit value-at-risk models, we may see a Basel III standard where the capital requirement in the banking book is based on a bank's own model of the aggregate credit risks it is taking.

The total required capital under Basel II is the sum of the capital for credit risk, market risk, and operational risk. This implicitly assumes that the risks are perfectly correlated. For example, it assumes that the 99.9% worst-case loss for credit risk occurs at the same time as the 99.9% worst-case loss for operational risk. Possibly, the calculations in Basel III (if it ever comes to pass) will allow banks to assume less than perfect correlation between losses from different types of risk when determining regulatory capital requirements.

---

allows banks to recognize the risk-mitigating impact of insurance, subject to certain conditions. We discuss the calculation of operational risk further in Chapter 14.

There is no question that the calculations in Pillar 1 of Basel II are a huge step forward over those in Basel I. In order to comply with Basel II, banks are finding that they have to become much more sophisticated in the way they handle credit risk and operational risk. Whether there will be further major changes to the way capital requirements are calculated for banks remains to be seen. Business Snapshot 7.2 speculates on what may be the major changes in Basel III.

7.10 SUPERVISORY REVIEW

Pillar 2 of Basel II is concerned with the supervisory review process. Four key principles of supervisory review are specified:

1. Banks should have a process for assessing their overall capital adequacy in relation to their risk profile and a strategy for maintaining their capital levels.
2. Supervisors should review and evaluate banks' internal capital adequacy assessments and strategies, as well as their ability to

monitor and ensure compliance with regulatory capital ratios. Supervisors should take appropriate supervisory action if they are not satisfied with the result of this process.

3. Supervisors should expect banks to operate above the minimum regulatory capital and should have the ability to require banks to hold capital in excess of this minimum.

4. Supervisors should seek to intervene at an early stage to prevent capital from falling below the minimum levels required to support the risk characteristics of a particular bank and should require rapid remedial action if capital is not maintained or restored.

The Basel Committee suggests that regulators pay particular attention to interest rate risk in the banking book, credit risk, and operational risk. Key issues in credit risk are stress tests used, default definitions used, credit risk concentration, and the risks associated with the use of collateral, guarantees, and credit derivatives.

The Basel Committee also stresses that there should be transparency and accountability in the procedures used by bank supervisors. This is particularly important when a supervisor exercises discretion in the procedures used or sets capital requirements above the minimum specified in Basel II.

7.11 MARKET DISCIPLINE

Pillar 3 of Basel II is concerned with market discipline. The Basel Committee wants to encourage banks to increase disclosure to the market of their risk assessment procedures and capital adequacy. The extent to which regulators can force banks to increase disclosure varies from jurisdiction to jurisdiction. However, banks are unlikely to ignore directives on this from their supervisors, given the potential of supervisors to make their life difficult. Also, in some instances, banks will have to increase their disclosure in order to be allowed to use particular methodologies for calculating capital.

Regulatory disclosures are likely to be different in form from accounting disclosures and need not be made in annual reports. It is largely left to the bank to choose disclosures that are material and relevant. Among the items that banks should disclose are:

1. The entities in the banking group to which Basel II is applied and adjustments made for entities to which it is not applied

2. The terms and conditions of the main features of all capital instruments

3. A list of the instruments constituting Tier 1 capital and the amount of capital provided by each item

4. The total amount of Tier 2 and Tier 3 capital

5. Capital requirements for credit, market, and operational risk

6. Other general information on the risks to which a bank is exposed and the assessment methods used by the bank for different categories of risk

7. The structure of the risk management function and how it operates

SUMMARY

This chapter has provided an overview of capital requirements for banks throughout the world. The way in which regulators calculate the minimum capital a bank is required to hold has changed dramatically since the 1980s. Prior to 1988, regulators determined capital requirements by specifying minimum ratios for capital to assets or maximum ratios for assets to capital. In the late 1980s, both bank supervisors and the banks themselves agreed that changes were necessary. Off-balance-sheet derivatives trading was increasing fast. In addition, banks were competing globally and it was considered important to create a level playing field by making regulations uniform throughout the world.

The 1988 Basel Accord assigned capital for credit risk both on and off the balance sheet. This involved calculating a risk-weighted asset for each item. The risk-weighted asset for an on-balance-sheet loan was calculated by multiplying the principal by a risk weight for the counterparty. In the case of derivatives such as swaps, banks were first required to calculate a credit equivalent amount. The risk-weighted asset was obtained by multiplying the credit equivalent amount by a risk weight for the counterparty. Banks were required to keep capital equal to 8% of the total risk-weighted assets. In 1995 the capital requirements for credit risk were modified to incorporate netting.

In 1996, the Accord was modified to include a capital charge for market risk. Sophisticated banks could base the capital charge on a value-at-risk calculation. In 1999, the Basel Committee proposed significant changes, which are expected to be implemented in 2007. The capital for market risk is unchanged. Credit risk capital will be calculated in a more sophisticated way that will reflect either (a) credit ratings from agencies such as Moody's or S&P or (b) a bank's own internal estimates of default probabilities. In addition, there will be a capital requirement for operational risk.

FURTHER READING

Bank for International Settlements, "Basel II: International Convergence of Capital Measurement and Capital Standards: A Revised Framework," November 2005, www.bis.org.

Crouhy, M., D. Galai, and R. Mark, *Risk Management*. New York: McGraw-Hill, 2001.

Gordy, M. B., "A Risk-factor Model Foundation for Ratings-Based Bank Capital Ratios," *Journal of Financial Intermediation*, 12 (2003): 199–232.

Lopez, J. A., "The Empirical Relationship Between Average Asset Correlation, Firm Probability of Default, and Asset Size," *Journal of Financial Intermediation*, 13, No. 2 (2004): 265–283.

Vasicek, O., "Probability of Loss on a Loan Portfolio," Working Paper, KMV, 1987. [Published in *Risk* in December 2002 under the title "Loan Portfolio Value".]

QUESTIONS AND PROBLEMS (Answers at End of Book)

7.1. "When a steel company goes bankrupt, other companies in the same industry benefit because they have one less competitor. But when a bank goes bankrupt, other banks do not necessarily benefit." Explain this statement.

7.2. "The existence of deposit insurance makes it particularly important for there to be regulations on the amount of capital banks hold." Explain this statement.

7.3. As explained in Section 2.3 an interest rate swap involves the exchange of a fixed rate of interest for a floating rate of interest with both being applied to the same principal. The principals are not exchanged. What is the nature of the credit risk for a bank when it enters into a five-year interest rate swap with a notional principal of $100 million? Assume the swap is worth zero initially.

7.4. In a currency swap, interest on a principal in one currency is exchanged for interest on a principal in another currency. The principals in the two currencies are exchanged at the end of the life of the swap. Why is the credit risk on a currency swap greater than that on an interest rate swap?

7.5. An interest rate swap currently has a negative value to a financial institution. Is the financial institution exposed to credit risk on the transaction? Explain your answer.

7.6. Estimate the capital required under Basel I for a bank that has the following transactions with a corporation (assume no netting): (a) a 9-year interest rate swap with a notional principal of $250 million and a current market value of −$2 million; (b) a 4-year interest rate swap with a notional principal of $100 million and a current value of $3.5 million; and (c) a 6-month derivative on a commodity with a principal of $50 million that is currently worth $1 million.

7.7. What is the capital required in Problem 7.6 under Basel I assuming that the 1995 netting amendment applies?

7.8. All the contracts a bank has with a corporate client are loans to the client. What is the value to the bank of netting provisions in the loan agreement?

7.9. Explain why the final stage in the Basel II calculations for credit risk, market risk, and operational risk is to multiply by 12.5.

7.10. What is the difference between the trading book and the banking book for a bank? A bank currently has a loan of $10 million dollars to a corporate client. At the end of the life of the loan the client would like to sell debt securities to the bank instead of borrowing. How does this change affect the nature of the bank's regulatory capital calculations?

7.11. Under Basel I, banks do not like lending to highly creditworthy companies and prefer to help them issue debt securities. Why is this? Do you expect the banks' attitude to this type of lending to change under Basel II?

7.12. What is regulatory arbitrage?

7.13. Equation (7.8) gives the formula for the capital required under Basel II. It involves four terms being multiplied together. Explain each of these terms.

7.14. Explain the difference between the simple and the comprehensive approach for adjusting for collateral.

7.15. Explain the difference between the standardized approach, the IRB approach, and the advanced IRB approach for calculating credit risk capital under Basel II.

7.16. Explain the difference between the basic indicator approach, the standardized approach, and the advanced measurement approach for calculating operational risk capital under Basel II.

7.17. Suppose that the assets of a bank consist of $200 of retail loans (not mortgages). The PD is 1% and the LGD is 70%. What is the risk-weighted assets under the Basel II IRB approach? How much Tier 1 and Tier 2 capital is required.

ASSIGNMENT QUESTIONS

7.18. Why is there an add-on amount in Basel I for derivatives transactions? "Basel I could be improved if the add-on amount for a derivatives transaction depended on the value of the transaction." How would you argue this viewpoint?

7.19. Estimate the capital required under Basel I for a bank that has the following transactions with another bank (assume no netting): (a) a 2-year forward contract on a foreign currency, currently worth $2 million, to buy foreign currency worth $50 million; (b) a long position in a 6-month option on the S&P 500 with a principal of $20 million and a current value of $4 million; and (c) a 2-year swap involving oil with a principal of $30 million and a current swap value of –$5 million. What difference does it make if the netting amendment applies?

7.20. A bank has the following transaction with an AA-rated corporation: (a) a 2-year interest rate swap with a principal of $100 million worth $3 million; (b) a 9-month foreign exchange forward contract with a principal of $150 million worth –$5 million; and (c) a 6-month long option on gold with a principal of $50 worth $7 million. What is the capital requirement under Basel I if there is no netting? What difference does it make if the netting amendment applies? What is the capital required under Basel II when the standardized approach is used?

7.21. Suppose that the assets of a bank consist of $500 million of loans to BBB-rated corporations. The PD for the corporations is estimated as 0.3%. The average maturity is 3 years and the LGD is 60%. What is the risk-weighted assets for credit risk under the Basel II advanced IRB approach? How much Tier 1 and Tier 2 capital is required. How does this compare with the capital required under the Basel II standardized approach and under Basel I?

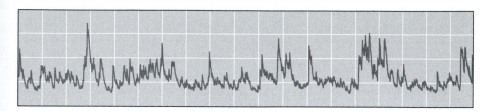

CHAPTER 8

The VaR Measure

In Chapter 3 we examined measures such as delta, gamma, and vega for describing different aspects of the risk in a portfolio of derivatives. A financial institution usually calculates each of these measures each day for every market variable to which it is exposed. Often there are hundreds, or even thousands, of these market variables. A delta–gamma–vega analysis therefore leads to a huge number of different risk measures being produced each day. These risk measures provide valuable information for a trader who is responsible for managing the part of the financial institution's portfolio that is dependent on a particular market variable. However, they do not provide a way of measuring the total risk to which the financial institution is exposed.

Value at risk (VaR) is an attempt to provide a single number that summarizes the total risk in a portfolio of financial assets. It was pioneered by J.P. Morgan (see Business Snapshot 8.1), and it has become widely used by corporate treasurers and fund managers as well as by financial institutions. As we saw in Chapter 7, the VaR measure is used by the Basel Committee in setting capital requirements for banks throughout the world.

In this chapter we explain the VaR measure and discuss its strengths and weaknesses. We also cover back testing and stress testing. In the next two chapters we will explain the two main approaches for estimating VaR for market risk. In Chapter 12 we will consider how VaR can be estimated for credit risk.

Business Snapshot 8.1   Historical Perspectives on VaR

J.P. Morgan is credited with helping to make VaR a widely accepted measure. The Chairman, Dennis Weatherstone, was dissatisfied with the long risk reports he received every day. These contained a huge amount of detail on the Greek letters for different exposures, but very little that was really useful to top management. He asked for something simpler that focused on the bank's total exposure over the next 24 hours measured across the bank's entire trading portfolio. At first his subordinates said this was impossible, but eventually they adapted the Markowitz portfolio theory (see Section 1.1) to develop a VaR report. This became known as the 4:15 report because it was placed on the chairman's desk at 4:15 p.m. every day after the close of trading.

Producing the report entailed a huge amount of work involving the collection of data daily on the positions held by the bank around the world, the handling of different time zones, the estimation of correlations and volatilities, and the development of computer systems. The work was completed in about 1990. The main benefit of the new system was that senior management had a better understanding of the risks being taken by the bank and were better able to allocate capital within the bank. Other banks had been working on similar approaches for aggregating risks and by 1993 VaR was established as an important risk measure.

Banks usually keep the details about the models they develop internally a secret. However, in 1994 J.P. Morgan made a simplified version of their own system, which they called RiskMetrics, available on the internet. RiskMetrics included variances and covariances for a very large number of different market variables. This attracted a lot of attention and led to debates about the pros and cons of different VaR models. Software firms started offering their own VaR models, some of which used the RiskMetrics database. After that, VaR was rapidly adopted as a standard by financial institutions and some nonfinancial institutions. The BIS Amendment, which was based on VaR (see Section 7.6), was announced in 1996 and implemented in 1998. Later the RiskMetrics group within J.P. Morgan was spun off as a separate company. This company developed CreditMetrics for handling credit risks in 1997 and Corporate-Metrics for handling the risks faced by nonfinancial corporations in 1999.

8.1 DEFINITION OF VaR

When using the value-at-risk measure, we are interested in making a statement of the following form:

We are X percent certain that we will not lose more than V dollars in the next N days.

The variable V is the VaR of the portfolio. It is a function of two parameters: the time horizon (N days) and the confidence level ($X\%$). It is the loss level over N days that we are $X\%$ certain will not be exceeded. VaR is the loss corresponding to the $(100 - X)$th percentile of the distribution of the change in the value of the portfolio over the next N days. (Gains are positive changes; losses are negative changes.) For example, when $N = 5$ and $X = 97$, VaR is the third percentile of the distribution of changes in the value of the portfolio over the next five days. In Figure 8.1, VaR is illustrated for the situation where the change in the value of the portfolio is approximately normally distributed.

Figure 8.1 shows the distribution of the portfolio's daily gain, with losses being counted as negative gains. As mentioned, VaR is the $(100 - X)$th percentile of this distribution. Instead, we can calculate the distribution of the portfolio's daily loss, with a gain being counted as a negative loss. VaR is the Xth percentile of this distribution.

As discussed in Section 7.6, the 1996 BIS Amendment calculates capital for the trading book using the VaR measure with $N = 10$ and $X = 99$. This means that it focuses on the revaluation loss over a 10-day period that is expected to be exceeded only 1% of the time. The capital it requires the bank to hold is k times this VaR measure (with an adjustment for what are termed specific risks.) The multiplier k is chosen on a bank-by-bank basis by the regulators and must be at least 3.0. For a bank with excellent well-tested VaR estimation procedures, it is likely that k will be set equal to the minimum value of 3.0. For other banks it may be higher. As we will discuss in Section 8.6, when tests show a bank's VaR model would not have performed well during the last 250 days, k may be as high as 4.0.

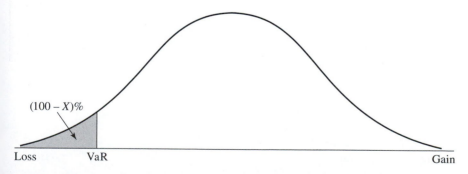

Figure 8.1   Calculation of VaR from the probability distribution of the change in the portfolio value; confidence level is $X\%$.

8.2 VaR vs. EXPECTED SHORTFALL

VaR is an attractive measure because it is easy to understand. In essence, it asks the simple question: "How bad can things get?" This is the question all senior managers want answered. They are very comfortable with the idea of compressing all the Greek letters for all the market variables underlying a portfolio into a single number. VaR is also relatively easy to back test, as we shall see later in this chapter.

However, when VaR is used in an attempt to limit the risks taken by a trader, it can lead to undesirable results. Suppose that a bank tells a trader that the one-day 99% VaR of the trader's portfolio must be kept at less than $10 million. The trader can construct a portfolio where there is a 99% chance that the daily loss is less than $10 million and a 1% chance that it is $500 million. The trader is satisfying the risk limits imposed by the bank but is clearly taking unacceptable risks.

This behavior by a trader is not as unlikely as it sounds. Many traders like taking high risks in the hope of realizing high returns. If they can find ways of taking high risks without violating risk limits, they will do so. To quote one trader the author has talked to: "I have never met a risk control system that I cannot trade around." The problem we are talking about is summarized by Figures 8.1 and 8.2. The figures show the probability distribution for the gain or loss on a portfolio during N days. Both portfolios have the same VaR, but the portfolio in Figure 8.2 is much riskier than that in Figure 8.1 because expected losses are much larger.

Expected Shortfall

A measure that produces better incentives for traders than VaR is *expected shortfall*. This is also sometimes referred to as *conditional VaR* or *tail loss*.

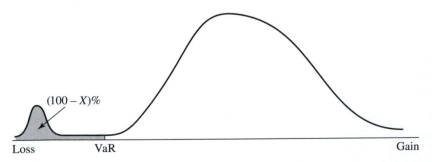

Figure 8.2   Alternative situation to Figure 8.1; VaR is the same, but the potential loss is larger.

Whereas VaR asks how bad can things get, expected shortfall asks: "If things do get bad, what is the expected loss?" Expected shortfall, like VaR, is a function of two parameters: N (the time horizon in days) and X (the percent confidence level). It is the expected loss during an N-day period conditional on the loss being greater than the Xth percentile of the loss distribution.[1] For example, with $X = 99$ and $N = 10$, the expected shortfall is the average amount we lose over a ten-day period assuming that the loss is greater than the 99th percentile of the loss distribution.

As we show in the next section, expected shortfall has better properties than VaR in that it encourages diversification. One disadvantage is that it does not have the simplicity of VaR and, as a result, is slightly more difficult to understand. Another is that it is more difficult to back test. VaR has become the most popular measure of risk among both regulators and risk managers in spite of its weaknesses. Therefore, in most of our discussions in this chapter and the next two, we will focus on how VaR can be measured and used. Many of the points we make apply equally to expected shortfall and other risk measures.

8.3 PROPERTIES OF RISK MEASURES

A *risk measure* used for specifying capital requirements can be thought of as the amount of cash (or capital) that must be added to a position to make its risk acceptable to regulators. Artzner *et al.* have proposed a number of properties that such a risk measure should have.[2] These are:

1. *Monotonicity*: If a portfolio has lower returns than another portfolio for every state of the world, its risk measure should be greater.

2. *Translation invariance*: If we add an amount of cash K to a portfolio, its risk measure should go down by K.

3. *Homogeneity*: Changing the size of a portfolio by a factor λ while keeping the relative amounts of different items in the portfolio the same should result in the risk measure being multiplied by λ.

4. *Subadditivity*: The risk measure for two portfolios after they have been merged should be no greater than the sum of their risk measures before they were merged.

---

[1] As mentioned earlier, gains are calculated as negative losses, and so all outcomes are considered when a loss distribution is constructed.

[2] See P. Artzner, F. Delbaen, J.-M. Eber, and D. Heath, "Coherent Measures of Risk," *Mathematical Finance*, 9 (1999): 203–228.

The first three conditions are straightforward, given that the risk measure is the amount of cash needed to be added to the portfolio to make its risk acceptable. The fourth condition states that diversification helps reduce risks. When we aggregate two risks, the total of the risk measures corresponding to the risks should either decrease or stay the same. VaR satisfies the first three conditions. However, it does not always satisfy the fourth one, as is illustrated by the following example.

Example 8.1

Consider two $10 million one-year loans each of which has a 1.25% chance of defaulting. If a default occurs on one of the loans, the recovery of the loan principal is uncertain, with all recoveries between 0% and 100% being equally likely. If the loan does not default, a profit of $0.2 million is made. To simplify matters, we suppose that if one loan defaults then it is certain that the other loan will not default.[3]

For a single loan, the one-year 99% VaR is $2 million. This is because there is a 1.25% chance of a loss occurring, and conditional on a loss there is an 80% chance that the loss is greater than $2 million. The unconditional probability that the loss is greater than $2 million is therefore 80% of 1.25%, or 1%.

Consider next the portfolio of two loans. Each loan defaults 1.25% of the time and they never default together. There is therefore a 2.5% probability that a default will occur. The VaR in this case turns out to be $5.8 million. This is because there is a 2.5% chance of one of the loans defaulting, and conditional on this event there is an 40% chance that the loss on the loan that defaults is greater than $6 million. The unconditional probability that the loss on the defaulting loan is greater than $6 million is therefore 40% of 2.5%, or 1%. A profit of $0.2 million is made on the other loan showing that the one-year 99%VaR is $5.8 million.

The total VaR of the loans considered separately is $2 + 2 = 4$ million. The total VaR after they have been combined in the portfolio is $1.8 million greater at $5.8 million. This is in spite of the fact that there are very attractive diversification benefits from combining the loans in a single portfolio.

Coherent Risk Measures

Risk measures satisfying all four conditions are referred to as *coherent*. Example 8.1 illustrates that VaR is not coherent. It can be shown that the expected shortfall measure we discussed earlier is coherent. The following

---

[3] This is to simplify the calculations. If the loans default independently of each other, so that two defaults can occur, the numbers are slightly different and the VaR of the portfolio is still greater than the sum of the VaRs of the individual loans.

example illustrates this by calculating expected shortfalls for the situation in Example 8.1.

Example 8.2

Consider again the situation in Example 8.1. We showed that the VaR for a single loan is $2 million. The expected shortfall from a single loan when the time horizon is one year and the confidence level is 99% is therefore the expected loss on the loan conditional on a loss greater than $2 million. Given that losses are uniformly distributed between zero and $10 million, this is halfway between $2 million and $10 million, or $6 million.

The VaR for a portfolio consisting of the two loans was calculated in Example 8.1 as $5.8 million. The expected shortfall from the portfolio is therefore the expected loss on the portfolio conditional on the loss being greater than $5.8 million. When a loan defaults, the other (by assumption) does not and outcomes are uniformly distributed between a gain of $0.2 million and a loss of $9.8 million. The expected loss given that we are in the part of the distribution between $5.8 million and $9.8 million is $7.8 million. This is therefore the expected shortfall of the portfolio.

Because $6 + 6 > 7.8$, the expected shortfall does satisfy the subadditivity condition.

A risk measure can be characterized by the weights it assigns to quantiles of the loss distribution.[4] VaR gives a 100% weighting to the Xth quantile and zero to other quantiles. Expected shortfall gives equal weight to all quantiles greater than the Xth quantile and zero weight to all quantiles below the Xth quantile. We can define what is known as a *spectral risk measure* by making other assumptions about the weights assigned to quantiles. A general result is that a spectral risk measure is coherent (i.e., it satisfies the subadditivity condition) if the weight assigned to the qth quantile of the loss distribution is a nondecreasing function of q. Expected shortfall satisfies this condition. However, VaR does not, because the weights assigned to quantiles greater than X are less than the weight assigned to the Xth quantile. Some researchers have proposed measures where the weights assigned to the qth quantile of the loss distribution increase relatively fast with q. One idea is to make the weight assigned to the qth quantile proportional to $e^{-(1-q)/\gamma}$, where γ is a constant. This is referred to as the *exponential spectral risk measure*. Figure 8.3 shows the weights assigned to loss quantiles for expected shortfall and for the exponential spectral risk measure when γ has two different values.

---

[4] Quantiles are also referred to as percentiles or fractiles.

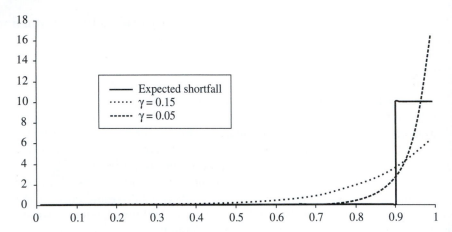

Figure 8.3 Weights as a function of quantiles for (a) expected shortfall when $X = 90\%$, (b) exponential spectral risk measure with $\gamma = 0.15$, and (c) exponential spectral risk measure with $\gamma = 0.05$.

8.4 CHOICE OF PARAMETERS FOR VaR

We now return to a consideration of VaR. The user must choose two parameters: the time horizon and the confidence level. As mentioned in Chapter 7, the Basel Committee has chosen a time horizon of ten days and a confidence level of 99% for market risks in the trading book. It has also chosen a time horizon of one year and a confidence level of 99.9% for credit risks under the internal-ratings-based approach and for operational risk under the advanced measurement approach. Other parameter values are chosen in different situations. For example, Microsoft in its financial statements says that it calculates VaR with a 97.5% confidence level and a 20-day time horizon.

A common, though questionable, assumption is that the change in the portfolio value over the time horizon is normally distributed. The mean change in the portfolio value is usually assumed to be zero. These assumptions are convenient because they lead to a simple formula for VaR:

$$\text{VaR} = \sigma N^{-1}(X) \tag{8.1}$$

where X is the confidence level, σ is the standard deviation of the portfolio change over the time horizon, and $N^{-1}(\cdot)$ is the inverse cumulative normal distribution (which can be calculated using NORMSINV in Excel). This equation shows that, regardless of the time horizon, VaR for a particular confidence level is proportional to σ.

Example 8.3

Suppose that the change in the value of a portfolio over a ten-day time horizon is normal with a mean of zero and a standard deviation of $20 million. The ten-day 99% VaR is

$$20N^{-1}(0.99) = 46.5$$

or $46.5 million.

The Time Horizon

An appropriate choice for the time horizon depends on the application. The trading desks of banks calculate the profit and loss daily. Their positions are usually fairly liquid and actively managed. For internal use, it therefore makes sense to calculate a VaR over a time horizon of one trading day. If VaR is unacceptable, the portfolio can be adjusted fairly quickly. Also, a VaR with a longer time horizon might not be meaningful because of changes in the composition of the portfolio.

For an investment portfolio held by a pension fund, a time horizon of one month is often chosen. This is because the portfolio is traded less actively and some of the instruments in the portfolio are less liquid. Also the performance of pension fund portfolios is often monitored monthly.

Whatever the application, when market risks are being considered analysts almost invariably start by calculating VaR for a time horizon of one day. The usual assumption is

$$N\text{-day VaR} = 1\text{-day VaR} \times \sqrt{N} \tag{8.2}$$

This formula is exactly true when the changes in the value of the portfolio on successive days have independent identical normal distributions with mean zero. In other cases it is an approximation. The formula follows from equation (8.1) and the following results:

1. The standard deviation of the sum on N independent identically distributions is $\sqrt{N}$ times the standard deviation of each distribution

2. The sum of independent normal distributions is normal

Regulatory Capital

As mentioned earlier, the regulatory capital for market risk in the trading book is based on the ten-day 99% VaR. Regulators explicitly state that the ten-day 99% VaR can be calculated using equation (8.2) as $\sqrt{10}$ times the one-day 99% VaR. This means that when the capital requirement for a bank is specified as three times the ten-day 99% VaR it is to all intents and purposes $3 \times \sqrt{10} = 9.49$ times the one-day 99% VaR. In the next two chapters we will focus entirely on the calculation of one-day VaR for market risks.

Impact of Autocorrelation

In practice, the changes in the value of a portfolio from one day to the next are not always totally independent. Define ΔP_i as the change in the value of a portfolio on day i. A simple assumption is first-order autocorrelation where the correlation between ΔP_i and ΔP_{i-1} is ρ for all i. Suppose that the variance of ΔP_i is σ^2 for all i. Using the usual formula for the variance of the sum of two variables, the variance of $\Delta P_{i-1} + \Delta P_i$ is

$$\sigma^2 + \sigma^2 + 2\rho\sigma^2 = (2 + \rho)\sigma^2$$

The correlation between ΔP_{i-j} and ΔP_i is ρ^j. This leads to the following formula for the variance of $\sum_{i=1}^{N} \Delta P_i$ (see Problem 8.12):

$$\sigma^2[N + 2(N - 1)\rho + 2(N - 2)\rho^2 + 2(N - 3)\rho^3 + \cdots + 2\rho^{N-1}] \qquad \textbf{(8.3)}$$

Table 8.1 shows the impact of autocorrelation on the N-day VaR that is calculated from the one-day VaR. It assumes that the distribution of daily changes in the portfolio are identical normals with mean zero. Note that the ratio of the N-day VaR to the one-day VaR does not depend on the daily standard deviation σ or on the confidence level. This follows from the result in equation (8.1) and the property of equation (8.3) that the N-day standard deviation is proportional to the one-day standard deviation. Comparing the $\rho = 0$ row in Table 8.1 with the other rows shows that the existence of autocorrelation results in the VaR estimates calculated from equation (8.1) being a little low.

Table 8.1 Ratio of N-day VaR to one-day VaR for different values of N when there is first-order correlation; distribution of change in portfolio value each day is assumed to have the same normal distribution with mean zero; ρ is the autocorrelation parameter.

	$N = 1$	$N = 2$	$N = 5$	$N = 10$	$N = 50$	$N = 250$
$\rho = 0$	1.00	1.41	2.24	3.16	7.07	15.81
$\rho = 0.05$	1.00	1.45	2.33	3.31	7.43	16.62
$\rho = 0.1$	1.00	1.48	2.42	3.46	7.80	17.47
$\rho = 0.2$	1.00	1.55	2.62	3.79	8.62	19.35

Example 8.4

Suppose that the standard deviation of daily changes in the portfolio value is $3 million and the first-order autocorrelation of daily changes is 0.1. From equation (8.3), the variance of the change in the portfolio value over five days is

$$3^2[5 + 2 \times 4 \times 0.1 + 2 \times 3 \times 0.1^2 + 2 \times 2 \times 0.1^3 + 2 \times 1 \times 0.1^4] = 52.7778$$

The standard deviation of the change in the value of the portfolio over five days is $\sqrt{52.7778}$, or 7.265. The five-day 95% VaR is therefore $7.265 \times N^{-1}(0.95) = 11.95$, or $11.95 million. Note that the ratio of the five-day standard deviation of portfolio changes to the one-day standard deviation is $7.265/3 = 2.42$. Since VaRs are proportional to standard deviations under the assumptions we are making, this is the number in Table 8.1 for $\rho = 0.1$ and $N = 5$.

Confidence Level

The confidence level chosen for VaR is likely to depend on a number of factors. Suppose a bank wants to maintain an AA credit rating and calculates that companies with this credit rating have a 0.03% chance of defaulting over a one-year period. It might choose to use a 99.97% confidence level in conjunction with a one-year time horizon for internal risk management purposes. (It might also communicate the analysis to rating agencies as evidence that it deserves its AA rating.)

The confidence level that is actually used for the first VaR calculation is often much less than the one that is eventually reported. This is because it is very difficult to estimate a VaR directly when the confidence level is very high. If daily portfolio changes are assumed to be normally distributed with zero mean, we can use equation (8.1) to convert a VaR calculated with one confidence level to a VaR with another confidence level. Suppose that σ is the standard deviation of the change in the portfolio value over a certain time horizon and that the expected change in the portfolio value is zero. Denote VaR for a confidence level of X by VaR(X). From equation (8.1), we have

$$\text{VaR}(X) = \sigma N^{-1}(X)$$

for all confidence levels X. It follows that

$$\text{VaR}(X^*) = \text{VaR}(X) \frac{N^{-1}(X^*)}{N^{-1}(X)} \tag{8.4}$$

Unfortunately this formula is critically dependent on the shape of the tails of the loss distribution being normal. When they are not normal, the formula may be quite a bad approximation. Extreme value theory, which is covered in Chapter 9, provides an alternative way of extrapolating tails of loss distributions.

Equation (8.4) assumes that the two VaR measures have the same time horizon. If we want to change the time horizon, we can use equation (8.4) in conjunction with equation (8.2) or (8.3).

Example 8.5

Suppose that the one-day VaR with a confidence level of 95% is $1.5 million. Using the assumption that the distribution of portfolio value changes is normal with mean zero, the one-day 99% VaR is

$$1.5 \times \frac{2.326}{1.645} = 2.12$$

or $2.12 million. If we assume daily changes are independent, the ten-day 99% VaR is $\sqrt{10}$ times this or $6.71 million and the 250-day VaR is $\sqrt{250}$ times this, or $33.54 million.

8.5 MARGINAL VaR, INCREMENTAL VaR, AND COMPONENT VaR

Analysts often calculate additional measures in order to understand VaR. Consider a portfolio with a number of components where the investment in the ith component is x_i. The *marginal VaR* is the sensitivity of VaR to the amount invested in the ith component. It is

$$\frac{\partial(\text{VaR})}{\partial x_i}$$

For an investment portfolio, marginal VaR is closely related to the capital asset pricing model's beta (see Section 1.1). If an asset's beta is high, its marginal VaR will tend to be high; if its beta is low, the marginal VaR tends to be low. In some circumstances marginal VaR is negative, indicating that increasing the weighting of a particular asset reduces the risk of the portfolio.

Incremental VaR is the incremental effect on VaR of a new trade or the incremental effect of closing out an existing trade. It asks the question: "What is the difference between VaR with and without the trade." It is of particular interest to traders who are wondering what the effect of a new trade will be on their regulatory capital. If a component is small in relation to the size of a portfolio, it may be reasonable to assume that the marginal VaR remains constant as x_i is reduced all the way to zero. This leads to the following approximate formula for the incremental VaR of the ith component:

$$\frac{\partial(\text{VaR})}{\partial x_i} x_i \tag{8.5}$$

The *component VaR* for the ith component of the portfolio is the part of the VaR of the portfolio that can be attributed to this component. Component VaRs should have the following properties:

1. The ith component VaR for a large portfolio should be approximately equal to the incremental VaR for that component.
2. The sum of all the component VaRs should equal the portfolio VaR.

Owing to nonlinearities in the calculation of VaR, we cannot satisfy the first condition exactly if we also want to satisfy the second condition. A result known as Euler's theorem can be used to calculate component VaRs. This is[5]

$$\text{VaR} = \sum_{i=1}^{N} \frac{\partial(\text{VaR})}{\partial x_i} x_i$$

where N is the number of components. We can therefore set

$$C_i = \frac{\partial(\text{VaR})}{\partial x_i} x_i \tag{8.6}$$

where C_i is the component VaR for the ith component. From the Euler's theorem result, these satisfy the second condition specified above:

$$\text{VaR} = C_1 + C_2 + \cdots + C_N$$

Also, as indicated by equation (8.5), they satisfy the first condition. Interestingly, the definition of C_i in equation (8.6) is equivalent to the alternative definition that C_i is the expected loss on the ith position, conditional on the loss on the portfolio equaling the VaR level.

Marginal, incremental, and component expected shortfall can be defined analogously to marginal, incremental, and component VaR. Euler's

---

[5] The condition that we need for Euler's theorem is that when each of the x_i is multiplied by λ the portfolio VaR is multiplied by λ. This condition is known as linear homogeneity and is clearly satisfied.

theorem applies, so component expected shortfall can be defined by
equation (8.6) with VaR replaced by expected shortfall.

8.6 BACK TESTING

Whatever the method used for calculating VaR, an important reality
check is *back testing*. It involves testing how well the VaR estimates
would have performed in the past. Suppose that we have developed a
procedure for calculating a one-day 99% VaR. Back testing involves
looking at how often the loss in a day exceeded the one-day 99% VaR
calculated using the procedure for that day. Days when the actual change
exceeds VaR are referred to as *exceptions*. If exceptions happen on about
1% of the days, we can feel reasonably comfortable with the methodology for calculating VaR. If they happen on, say, 7% of days, the
methodology is suspect and it is likely that VaR is underestimated. From
a regulatory perspective, the capital calculated using the VaR estimation
procedure is then too low. On the other hand, if exceptions happen on,
say 0.3% of days it is likely that the procedure is overestimating VaR and
the capital calculated is too high.

One issue in back testing VaR is whether we take account of changes
made in the portfolio during the time period considered. There are two
possibilities. The first is to compare VaR with the hypothetical change in
the portfolio value calculated on the assumption that the composition of
the portfolio remains unchanged during the time period. The other is to
compare VaR to the actual change in the value of the portfolio during the
time period. VaR itself is invariably calculated on the assumption that the
portfolio will remain unchanged during the time period, and so the first
comparison based on hypothetical changes is more logical. However, it is
actual changes in the portfolio value that we are ultimately interested in.
In practice, risk managers usually compare VaR to both hypothetical
portfolio changes and actual portfolio changes. (In fact, regulators insist
on seeing the results of back testing using actual as well as hypothetical
changes.) The actual changes are adjusted for items unrelated to the
market risk—such as fee income and profits from trades carried out at
prices different from the mid-market price.

Suppose that the time horizon is one day and the confidence limit is
$X\%$. If the VaR model used is accurate, the probability of the VaR
being exceeded on any given day is $p = 1 - X$. Suppose that we look at
a total of n days and we observe that the VaR limit is exceeded on m of

the days where $m/n > p$. Should we reject the model for producing values of VaR that are too low? Expressed formally, we can consider two alternative hypotheses:

1. The probability of an exception on any given day is p.
2. The probability of an exception on any given day is greater than p.

From the properties of the binomial distribution, the probability of the VaR limit being exceeded on m or more days is

$$\sum_{k=m}^{n} \frac{n!}{k!\,(n-k)!}\, p^k (1-p)^{n-k}$$

This can be calculated using the **BINOMDIST** function in Excel. An often-used confidence level in statistical tests is 5%. If the probability of the VaR limit being exceeded on m or more days is less than 5%, we reject the first hypothesis that the probability of an exception is p. If this probability of the VaR limit being exceeded on m or more days is greater than 5%, then the hypothesis is not rejected.

Example 8.6

Suppose that we back test a VaR model using 600 days of data. The VaR confidence level is 99% and we observe nine exceptions. The expected number of exceptions is six. Should we reject the model? The probability of nine or more exceptions can be calculated in Excel as

$$1 - \text{BINOMDIST}(8, 600, 0.01, \text{TRUE})$$

It is 0.152. At a 5% confidence level, we should not therefore reject the model. However, if the number of exceptions had been 12, we would have calculated the probability of 12 or more exceptions as 0.019 and rejected the model. The model is rejected when the number of exceptions is 11 or more. (The probability of 10 or more exceptions is greater than 5%, but the probability of 11 or more is less than 5%.)

When the number of exceptions, m, is lower than the expected number of exceptions, we can similarly test whether the true probability of an exception is 1%. (In this case, our alternative hypothesis is that the true probability of an exception is less than 1%.) The probability of m or less exceptions is

$$\sum_{k=0}^{m} \frac{n!}{k!\,(n-k)!}\, p^k (1-p)^{n-k}$$

and this is compared with the 5% threshold.

Example 8.7

Suppose again that we back test a VaR model using 600 days of data when the VaR confidence level is 99% and we observe one exception, well below the expected number of six. Should we reject the model? The probability of one or zero exceptions can be calculated in Excel as

$$\text{BINOMDIST}(1, 600, 0.01, \text{TRUE})$$

It is 0.017. At a 5% confidence level, we should therefore reject the model. However, if the number of exceptions had been two or more, we would not have rejected the model.

The tests we have considered so far have been one-tailed tests. In Example 8.6 we assumed that the true probability of an exception was either 1% or greater than 1%. In Example 8.7 we assumed that it was 1% or less than 1%. Kupiec has proposed a relatively powerful two-tailed test.[6] If the probability of an exception under the VaR model is p and m exceptions are observed in n trials, then

$$-2\ln[(1-p)^{n-m}p^m] + 2\ln[(1-m/n)^{n-m}(m/n)^m] \qquad \textbf{(8.7)}$$

should have a chi-square distribution with one degree of freedom. Values of the statistic are high for either very low or very high numbers of exceptions. There is a probability of 5% that the value of a chi-square variable with one degree of freedom will be greater than 3.84. It follows that we should reject the model whenever the expression in equation (8.7) is greater than 3.84.

Example 8.8

Suppose that as in the previous two examples we back test a VaR model using 600 days of data when the VaR confidence level is 99%. The value of the statistic in equation (8.7) is greater that 3.84 when the number of exceptions, m, is one or less and when the number of exceptions is 12 or more. We therefore accept the VaR model when $2 \leqslant m \leqslant 11$, and reject it otherwise.

Generally speaking the difficulty of back testing a VaR model increases as the VaR confidence level increases. This is an argument in favor of not using very high confidence levels for VaR.

Basel Committee Rules

The 1986 BIS Amendment (see Section 7.6) requires VaR models to be back tested. Banks should use both actual and hypothetical changes in

---

[6] See P. Kupiec, "Techniques for Verifying the Accuracy of Risk Management Models," *Journal of Derivatives*, 3 (1995), 73–84.

the daily profit and loss to test a one-day VaR model that has a confidence level of 99%. If the number of exceptions during the previous 250 days is less than 5, the regulatory multiplier for VaR is set at its minimum value of 3. If the number of exceptions are 5, 6, 7, 8, and 9, values of the multiplier equal to 3.4, 3.5, 3.65, 3.75, and 3.85, respectively, are specified. The bank supervisor has some discretion as to whether the higher multipliers are used. The penalty will normally apply when the reason for the exceptions is identified as a deficiency in the VaR model being used. If changes in positions during the day result in exceptions, the higher multiplier should be considered. When the only reason that is identified is bad luck, no guidance is provided for the supervisor. In circumstances where the number of exceptions is 10 or more the Basel Amendment requires the multiplier to be set at 4. The statistical tests we have presented can be used to determine the confidence limits the Basel Committee is implicitly using for its decision to accept or reject a model (see Problem 8.13).

Bunching

A separate issue from the number of exceptions is *bunching*. If daily portfolio changes are independent, exceptions should be spread evenly through the period used for back testing. In practice, they are often bunched together, suggesting that losses on successive days are not independent. One approach for testing for bunching is to use the test for autocorrelation in Section 5.9. Another approach is to use the following test statistic suggested by Christofferson[7]

$$-2\ln[(1-\pi)^{u_{00}+u_{10}}\pi^{u_{01}+u_{11}}] + 2\ln[(1-\pi_{01})^{u_{00}}\pi_{01}^{u_{01}}(1-\pi_{11})^{u_{10}}\pi_{11}^{u_{11}}]$$

where u_{ij} is the number of observations in which we go from a day where we are in state i to a day where we are in state j. This statistic is chi-square with one degree of freedom if there is no bunching. State 0 is a day where there is no exception while state 1 is a day where there is an exception. Also,

$$\pi = \frac{u_{01} + u_{11}}{u_{00} + u_{10} + u_{10} + u_{11}}$$

$$\pi_{01} = \frac{u_{01}}{u_{00} + u_{01}}, \qquad \pi_{11} = \frac{u_{11}}{u_{10} + u_{11}}$$

---

[7] See P. F. Christofferson, "Evaluating Interval Forecasts," *International Economic Review*, 39 (1998), 841–862.

8.7 STRESS TESTING

In addition to requiring that a model for market risk be back tested, the Basel Committee requires market risk VaR calculations be accompanied by a "rigorous and comprehensive" stress-testing program. Stress testing involves estimating how the portfolio would have performed under extreme market moves. These extreme market moves typically have a very low (virtually zero) probability under most VaR models—but they do happen!

Stress testing is a way of taking into account extreme events that are virtually impossible according to the probability distributions assumed for market variables, but do occur from time to time. A five-standard-deviation daily move in a market variable is one such extreme event. Under the assumption of a normal distribution, it happens about once every 7,000 years, but, in practice, it is not uncommon to see a five-standard-deviation daily move once or twice every ten years.

Some stress tests focus on particular market variables. Examples of stress tests that have been recommended include:

1. Shifting a yield curve by 100 basis points
2. Changing implied volatilities for an asset by 20% of current values
3. Changing an equity index by 10%
4. Changing an exchange rate for a major currency by 6% or changing the exchange rate for a minor currency by 20%

Stress tests more often involve making changes to several market variables. A common practice is to use historical scenarios. For example, to test the impact of an extreme movement in US equity prices, a company might set the percentage changes in all market variables equal to those on October 19, 1987 (when the S&P 500 moved by 22.3 standard deviations). If this is considered too extreme, the company might choose January 8, 1988 (when the S&P 500 moved by 6.8 standard deviations). To test the effect of extreme movements in UK interest rates, the company might set the percentage changes in all market variables equal to those on April 10, 1992 (when ten-year bond yields moved by 8.7 standard deviations).

The scenarios used in stress testing are also sometimes generated by senior management. One technique sometimes used is to ask senior management to meet periodically and "brainstorm" to develop extreme scenarios that might occur given the current economic environment and global uncertainties. Whatever the procedure used to generate the stress tests, there should be a "buy in" to the idea of stress testing by senior management and it should be senior management that reviews the results of stress tests.

If movements in only a few variables are specified in a stress test, one approach is to set changes in all other variables to zero. Another approach is to regress the nonstressed variables on the variables that are being stressed to obtain forecasts for them, conditional on the changes being made to the stressed variables. These forecasts can be incorporated into the stress test. This is known as *conditional stress testing* and is discussed by Kupiec.[8]

SUMMARY

A value-at-risk (VaR) calculation is aimed at making a statement of the form: "We are X percent certain that we will not lose more than V dollars in the next N days." The variable V is the VaR, $X\%$ is the confidence level, and N days is the time horizon. It has become a very popular risk measure. An alternative measure that has rather better theoretical properties is expected shortfall. This is the expected loss conditional on the loss being greater than the VaR level.

When changes in a portfolio value are normally distributed, a VaR estimate with one confidence level can be used to calculate a VaR level with another confidence level. Also, if one-day changes have independent normal distributions, an N-day VaR equals the one-day VaR multiplied by $\sqrt{N}$. When the independence assumption is relaxed other somewhat more complicated formulas can be used to go from the one-day VaR to the N-day VaR.

The marginal VaR with respect to the ith position is the partial derivative of VaR with respect to the size of the position. The incremental VaR with respect to a particular position is the incremental effect of that position on VaR. There is a formula that can be used for dividing VaR into components that correspond to the positions taken. The component VaRs sum to VaR and each component is, for a large portfolio of relatively small positions, approximately equal to the corresponding incremental VaR.

Back testing is an important part of a VaR system. It examines how well the VaR model would have performed in the past. There are two ways in which back testing may indicate weaknesses in a VaR model. One

---

[8] P. Kupiec, "Stress Testing in a Value at Risk Framework," *Journal of Derivatives*, 6 (1999), 7–24.

is in the percentage of exceptions, that is, the percentage of times the actual loss exceeds VaR. The other is in the extent to which exceptions are bunched. There are statistical tests to determine whether a VaR model should be rejected because of the percentage of exceptions or the amount of bunching. Regulators have rules for increasing the VaR multiplier when market risk capital is calculated if they consider the results from back testing over 250 days to be unsatisfactory.

Stress testing is an important complement to VaR calculations. It considers scenarios that either have occurred in the past or are considered possibilities for the future. Typically, the scenarios have a very low probability of occurring under the models used for calculating VaR.

FURTHER READING

Artzner P., F. Delbaen, J.-M. Eber, and D. Heath, "Coherent Measures of Risk," *Mathematical Finance*, 9 (1999): 203–228.

Basak, S., and A. Shapiro, "Value-at-Risk-Based Risk Management: Optimal Policies and Asset Prices," *Review of Financial Studies*, 14, No. 2 (2001): 371–405.

Beder, T., "VaR: Seductive But Dangerous," *Financial Analysts Journal*, 51, No. 5 (1995): 12–24.

Boudoukh, J., M. Richardson, and R. Whitelaw, "The Best of Both Worlds," *Risk*, May 1998: 64–67.

Dowd, K., *Measuring Market Risk*. 2nd edn. New York: Wiley, 2005.

Duffie, D., and J. Pan, "An Overview of Value at Risk," *Journal of Derivatives*, 4, No. 3 (Spring 1997): 7–49.

Hopper, G., "Value at Risk: A New Methodology for Measuring Portfolio Risk," *Business Review*, Federal Reserve Bank of Philadelphia, July/August 1996: 19–29.

Hua P., and P. Wilmott, "Crash Courses," *Risk*, June 1997: 64–67.

Jackson, P., D. J. Maude, and W. Perraudin, "Bank Capital and Value at Risk," *Journal of Derivatives*, 4, No. 3 (Spring 1997): 73–90.

Jorion, P., *Value at Risk*. 2nd edn. New York: McGraw-Hill, 2001.

Longin, F. M., "Beyond the VaR," *Journal of Derivatives*, 8, No. 4 (Summer 2001): 36–48.

Marshall, C., and M. Siegel, "Value at Risk: Implementing a Risk Measurement Standard," *Journal of Derivatives*, 4, No. 3 (Spring 1997): 91–111.

QUESTIONS AND PROBLEMS (Answers at End of Book)

8.1. What is the difference between expected shortfall and VaR? What is the theoretical advantage of expected shortfall over VaR?

8.2. What is a spectral risk measure? What conditions must be satisfied by a spectral risk measure for the subadditivity condition in Section 8.3 to be satisfied?

8.3. A fund manager announces that the fund's 1-month 95% VaR is 6% of the size of the portfolio being managed. You have an investment of $100,000 in the fund. How do you interpret the portfolio manager's announcement?

8.4. A fund manager announces that the fund's one-month 95% expected shortfall is 6% of the size of the portfolio being managed. You have an investment of $100,000 in the fund. How do you interpret the portfolio manager's announcement?

8.5. Suppose that each of two investments has a 0.9% chance of a loss of $10 million, a 99.1% of a loss of $1 million, and zero probability of a gain. The investments are independent of each other. (a) What is the VaR for one of the investments when the confidence level is 99%? (b) What is the expected shortfall for one of the investments when the confidence level is 99%? (c) What is the VaR for a portfolio consisting of the two investments when the confidence level is 99%? (d) What is the expected shortfall for a portfolio consisting of the two investments when the confidence level is 99%? (e) Show that in this example VaR does not satisfy the subadditivity condition whereas expected shortfall does.

8.6. Suppose that the change in the value of a portfolio over a 1-day time period is normal with a mean of zero and a standard deviation of $2 million, What is (a) the 1-day 97.5% VaR, (b) the 5-day 97.5% VaR, and (c) the 5-day 99% VaR?

8.7. What difference does it make to your answers to (b) and (c) of Problem 8.6 if there is first-order daily autocorrelation with correlation parameter equal to 0.16?

8.8. Explain carefully the differences between marginal VaR, incremental VaR, and component VaR for a portfolio consisting of a number of assets.

8.9. Suppose that we back test a VaR model using 1,000 days of data. The VaR confidence level is 99% and we observe 17 exceptions. Should we reject the model at the 5% confidence level? Use a one-tailed test.

8.10. Explain what is meant by *bunching*.

8.11. Describe two ways extreme scenarios can be developed for stress testing.

8.12. Prove equation (8.3).

8.13. The back-testing rules of the Basel Committee can lead to questions about a VaR model when there are 5 or more exceptions in 250 trials. What is the chance of this if the VaR methodology is perfectly accurate?

ASSIGNMENT QUESTIONS

8.14. Suppose that each of two investments has a 4% chance of a loss of $10 million, a 2% chance of a loss of $1 million, and a 94% chance of a profit of $1 million. They are independent of each other. (a) What is the VaR for one of the investments when the confidence level is 95%? (b) What is the expected shortfall when the confidence level is 95%? (c) What is the VaR for a portfolio consisting of the two investments when the confidence level is 95%? (d) What is the expected shortfall for a portfolio consisting of the two investments when the confidence level is 95%? (e) Show that, in this example, VaR does not satisfy the subadditivity condition whereas expected shortfall does.

8.15. Suppose that daily changes for a portfolio have first-order correlation with correlation parameter 0.12. The 10-day VaR, calculated by multiplying the 1-day VaR by $\sqrt{10}$, is $2 million. What is a better estimate of the VaR that takes account of autocorrelation?

8.16. The probability that the loss from a portfolio will be greater than $10 million in 1 month is estimated to be 5%. (a) What is the 1-month 99% VaR assuming the change in value of the portfolio is normally distributed. (b) What is the 1-month 99% VaR assuming that the power law described in Section 5.4 applies with $\alpha = 3$.

8.17. Suppose that we back test a VaR model using 1,000 days of data. The VaR confidence level is 99% and we observe 15 exceptions. Should we reject the model at the 5% confidence level. Use Kupiec's two-tailed test.

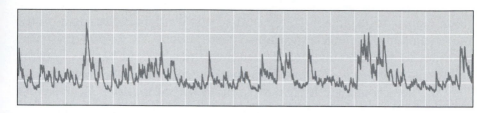

Market Risk VaR: Historical Simulation Approach

In this chapter and the next we cover the two main approaches for calculating VaR for market risk. The approach we consider in this chapter is known as *historical simulation*. This involves using historical day-to-day changes in the values of market variables in a direct way to estimate the probability distribution of the change in the value of the current portfolio between today and tomorrow.

After describing the mechanics of the historical simulation approach, we explain how to calculate the standard error of the VaR estimate and how to modify the procedure to take into account the latest information about volatility. We also describe how extreme value theory can be used in conjuction with a historical simulation to improve VaR estimates and to deal with situations where the VaR confidence level is very high.

9.1 THE METHODOLOGY

Historical simulation involves using past data as a guide to what will happen in the future. Suppose that we want to calculate VaR for a portfolio using a one-day time horizon, a 99% confidence level, and 500 days of data. (The time horizon and confidence level are those typically used for a market risk VaR calculation; 500 is a popular choice for the number of days of data used.) The first step is to identify the market variables affecting the portfolio. These will typically be exchange rates, equity prices, interest rates, and so on. We then collect data on the movements in these market variables over the most recent 500 days. This provides us with 500 alternative scenarios for what can happen between today and tomorrow. Denote the first day for which we have data as Day 0, the second day as Day 1, and so on. Scenario 1 is where the percentage changes in the values of all variables are the same as they were between Day 0 and Day 1; Scenario 2 is where they are the same as between Day 1 and Day 2; and so on. For each scenario we calculate the dollar change in the value of the portfolio between today and tomorrow. This defines a probability distribution for daily changes in the value of our portfolio. The first percentile of the distribution can be estimated as the fifth worst outcome.[1] The estimate of VaR is the loss when we are at this first percentile point. We are 99% certain that we would not have taken a loss greater than our VaR estimate if the changes in market variables are a random sample from the last 500 days.

The historical simulation methodology is illustrated in Tables 9.1 and 9.2. Table 9.1 shows observations on market variables over the last 500 days. The observations are taken at some particular point in time during the day (usually the close of trading). There are assumed to be a total of 1,000 market variables.

Table 9.2 shows the values of the market variables tomorrow if their percentage changes between today and tomorrow are the same as they

Table 9.1 Data for VaR historical simulation calculation.

Day	Market variable 1	Market variable 2	. . .	Market variable 1,000
0	20.33	0.1132	. . .	65.37
1	20.78	0.1159	. . .	64.91
2	21.44	0.1162	. . .	65.02
3	20.97	0.1184	. . .	64.90
⋮	⋮	⋮	⋮	⋮
498	25.72	0.1312	. . .	62.22
499	25.75	0.1323	. . .	61.99
500	25.85	0.1343	. . .	62.10

---

[1] There are alternatives here. A case could be made for using the fifth worst outcome or the sixth worst outcome, or an average of the two, as the first percentile of the distribution when there are 500 outcomes. In Excel's PERCENTILE function, when there are n observations and k is an integer, the $k/(n-1)$ percentile is the observation ranked $k + 1$. Other percentiles are calculated using linear interpolation.

Table 9.2 Scenarios generated for tomorrow (Day 501) using data in Table 9.1. Value of portfolio on Day 500 is $23.50 million

Scenario number	Market variable 1	Market variable 2	...	Market variable 1,000	Portfolio value ($ millions)	Change in value ($ millions)
1	26.42	0.1375	...	61.66	23.71	0.21
2	26.67	0.1346	...	62.21	23.12	−0.38
3	25.28	0.1368	...	61.99	22.94	−0.56
⋮	⋮	⋮	⋮	⋮	⋮	⋮
499	25.88	0.1354	...	61.87	23.63	0.13
500	25.95	0.1363	...	62.21	22.87	−0.63

were between Day $i-1$ and Day i for $1 \leqslant i \leqslant 500$. The first row in Table 9.2 shows the values of market variables tomorrow assuming their percentage changes between today and tomorrow are the same as they were between Day 0 and Day 1; the second row shows the values of market variables tomorrow assuming their percentage changes are the same as those between Day 1 and Day 2; and so on. The 500 rows in Table 9.2 are the 500 scenarios considered.

Define v_i as the value of a market variable on Day i and suppose that today is Day n. The ith scenario assumes that the value of the market variable tomorrow will be

$$v_n \frac{v_i}{v_{i-1}} \tag{9.1}$$

In our example, $n = 500$. For the first variable, the value today, v_{500}, is 25.85. In addition, $v_0 = 20.33$ and $v_1 = 20.78$. It follows that the value of the first market variable in the first scenario is

$$25.85 \times \frac{20.78}{20.33} = 26.42$$

The penultimate column of Table 9.2 shows the value of the portfolio tomorrow for each of the 500 scenarios. We suppose the value of the portfolio today is $23.50 million. This leads to the numbers in the final column for the change in the value between today and tomorrow for all the different scenarios. For Scenario 1 the change in value is +$210,000; for Scenario 2 it is −$380,000; and so on.

We are interested in the one-percentile point of the distribution of changes in the portfolio value. As indicated earlier, because there are a total of 500 scenarios in Table 9.2, we can estimate this as the fifth worst number in the final column of the table. Alternatively, we can use extreme value theory, which will be described later in the chapter. As mentioned in Section 8.4, the ten-day VaR for a 99% confidence level is usually calculated as $\sqrt{10}$ times the one-day VaR.

Each day the VaR estimate in our example would be updated using the most recent 500 days of data. Consider, for example, what happens on Day 501. We find out new values for all the market variables and are able to calculate a new value for our portfolio.[2] We then go through the procedure we have outlined to calculate a new VaR. We use data on the market variables from Day 1 to Day 501. (This gives us the required 500 observations on percentage changes in market variables; the Day 0 values of the market variables are no longer used.) Similarly, on Day 502, we use data from Day 2 to Day 502 to determine VaR, and so on.

9.2 ACCURACY

The historical simulation approach estimates the distribution of portfolio changes based on a finite number of observations of what happened in the past. As a result, the estimates of quantiles of the distribution are not perfectly accurate.

Kendall and Stuart describe how to calculate a confidence interval for the quantile of a probability distribution when it is estimated from sample data.[3] Suppose that the q-quantile of the distribution is estimated as x. The standard error of the estimate is

$$\frac{1}{f(x)}\sqrt{\frac{q(1-q)}{n}}$$

where n is the number of observations and $f(x)$ is the probability density function of the loss evaluated at x. The latter can be estimated by fitting the empirical data to a standard distribution.

Example 9.1

Suppose we are interested in estimating the 0.01 quantile ($= 1$ percentile) of a loss distribution from 500 observations so that $n = 500$ and $q = 0.01$. We can estimate $f(x)$ by approximating the actual empirical distribution with a

---

[2] Note that the portfolio's composition may have changed between Day 500 and Day 501.

[3] See M.G. Kendall and A. Stuart, *The Advanced Theory of Statistics*, Vol. 1: *Distribution Theory*, 4th edn. London: Griffin, 1972.

standard distribution. Suppose that the approximate empirical distribution is normal with mean zero and standard deviation $10 million. Using Excel, the 0.01 quantile is NORMINV$(0.01, 0, 10)$, or 23.26. The value of $f(x)$ is NORMDIST$(23.26, 0, 10, \text{FALSE})$, or 0.0027. The standard error of the estimate that is made is

$$\frac{1}{0.0027} \times \sqrt{\frac{0.01 \times 0.99}{500}} = 1.67$$

If the estimate of the 0.01 quantile using historical simulation is $25 million, a 95% confidence interval is from $25 - 1.96 \times 1.67$ to $25 + 1.96 \times 1.67$, that is, from $21.7 million to $28.3 million.

As Example 9.1 illustrates, the standard error of a VaR estimated using historical simulation tends to be quite high. It increases as the VaR confidence level is increased. For example, if in Example 9.1 the VaR confidence level had been 95% instead of 99%, the standard error would be $0.95 million instead of $1.67 million. The standard error declines as the sample size is increased—but only as the square root of the sample size. If we quadrupled the sample size in Example 9.1 from 500 to 2,000 (i.e., from approximately two to approximately eight years of data), the standard error halves from $1.67 million to about $0.83 million.

Additionally, we should bear in mind that historical simulation assumes that the joint distribution of daily changes in market variables is stationary through time. This is unlikely to be exactly true and creates additional uncertainty about the value of VaR.

9.3 EXTENSIONS

In this section we cover a number of extensions of the basic historical simulation methodology that we discussed in Section 9.1.

Weighting of Observations

The basic historical simulation approach assumes that each day in the past is given equal weight. More formally, if we have observations for n day-to-day changes, each of them is given a weighting of $1/n$. Boudoukh *et al.* suggest that more recent observations should be given more weight because they are more reflective of current volatilities and current macroeconomic variables.[4] The natural weighting scheme to use is one where

---

[4] See J. Boudoukh, M. Richardson, and R. Whitelaw, "The Best of Both Worlds: A Hybrid Approach to Calculating Value at Risk," *Risk*, 11 (May 1998), 64–67.

weights decline exponentially. We used this in Section 5.6 when developing the exponentially weighted moving average model for monitoring variance. Suppose that we are now at the end of day n. The weight assigned to the change in the portfolio value between day $n - i$ and day $n - i + 1$ is λ times that assigned to the change between day $n - i + 1$ and day $n - i + 2$. In order for the weights to add up to 1, the weight given to the change between day $n - i$ and $n - i + 1$ is

$$\frac{\lambda^{i-1}(1 - \lambda)}{1 - \lambda^n}$$

where n is the number of days. As $\lambda \to 1$, this weighting scheme approaches the basic historical simulation approach, where all observations are given a weight of $1/n$ (see Problem 9.2).

VaR is calculated by ranking the observations from the worst outcome to the best. Starting at the worst outcome, weights are summed until the required quantile of the distribution is reached. For example, if we are calculating VaR with a 99% confidence level, we continue summing weights until the sum just exceeds 0.01. We have then reached the 99% VaR level. The best value of λ can be obtained by experimenting to see which value back tests best. One disadvantage of the exponential weighting approach relative to the basic historical simulation approach is that the effective sample size is reduced. However, we can compensate for this by using a larger value of n. Indeed it is not really necessary to discard old days as we move forward in time because they are given very little weight.

Incorporating Volatility Updating

Hull and White suggest a way of incorporating volatility updating into the historical simulation approach.[5] A volatility updating scheme, such as EWMA or GARCH(1, 1) (both of which were described in Chapter 5) is used in parallel with the historical simulation approach for all market variables. Suppose that the daily volatility for a particular market variable estimated at the end of day $i - 1$ is σ_i. This is an estimate of the daily volatility between the end of day $i - 1$ and the end of day i. Suppose it is now day n. The current estimate of the volatility of the market variable is σ_{n+1}. This applies to the time period between today and tomorrow, which is the time period over which we are calculating VaR.

Suppose that σ_{n+1} is twice σ_i. This means that we estimate the daily

[5] See J. Hull and A. White, "Incorporating Volatility Updating into the Historical Simulation Method for Value-at-Risk," *Journal of Risk*, 1, No. 1 (Fall 1998), 5–19.

volatility of this particular market variable to be twice as great today as on day $i - 1$. This means that we expect to see changes between today and tomorrow that are twice as big as changes between day $i - 1$ and day i. When carrying out the historical simulation and creating a sample of what could happen between today and tomorrow based on what happened between day $i - 1$ and day i, it therefore makes sense to multiply the latter by 2. In general, when this approach is used, the expression in equation (9.1) for the value of a market variable under the ith scenario becomes

$$v_n \frac{v_{i-1} + (v_i - v_{i-1})\sigma_{n+1}/\sigma_i}{v_{i-1}} \tag{9.2}$$

Each market variable is handled in the same way. This approach takes account of volatility changes in a natural and intuitive way and produces VaR estimates that incorporate more current information. The VaR estimates can be greater than any of the historical losses that would have occurred for our current portfolio on the days we consider. Hull and White produce evidence using exchange rates and stock indices to show that this approach is superior to traditional historical simulation and to the exponential weighting scheme described earlier. More complicated models can be developed where observations are adjusted for the latest information on correlations as well as for the latest information on volatilities.

Bootstrap Method

The bootstrap method is another variation on the basic historical simulation approach. It involves creating a set of changes in the portfolio value based on historical movements in market variables in the usual way. We then sample with replacement from these changes to create many new similar data sets. We calculate the VaR for each of the new data sets. Our 95% confidence interval for VaR is the range between the 2.5 and the 97.5 percentile point of the distribution of the VaRs calculated from the data sets.

Suppose, for example, that we have 500 days of data. We could sample with replacement 500,000 times from the data to obtain 1,000 different sets of 500 days of data. We calculate the VaR for each set. We then rank the VaRs. Suppose that the 25th largest VaR is $5.3 million and the 475th largest VaR is $8.9 million. The 95% confidence limit for VaR is $5.3 million to $8.9 million. Usually the 95% confidence range calculated for VaR using the bootstrap method is less than that calculated using the procedure in Section 9.2.

9.4 EXTREME VALUE THEORY

In Section 5.4 we introduced the power law and explained that it can be used to estimate the tails of a wide range of distributions. We now provide the theoretical underpinnings for the power law and present more sophisticated estimation procedures than those used in Section 5.4. The term used to describe the science of estimating the tails of a distribution is *extreme value theory*. In this section we show how extreme value theory can be used to improve VaR estimates and to deal with situations where the VaR confidence level is very high. It provides a way of smoothing and extrapolating the tails of an empirical distribution.

The Key Result

A key result in extreme value theory was proved by Gnedenko in 1943.[6] This concerns the properties of the tails of a wide range of different probability distributions.

Suppose that $F(x)$ is the cumulative distribution function for a variable x and that u is a value of x in the right-hand tail of the distribution. The probability that x lies between u and $u + y$ ($y > 0$) is $F(u + y) - F(u)$. The probability that x is greater than u is $1 - F(u)$. Define $F_u(y)$ as the probability that x lies between u and $u + y$ conditional on $x > u$. This is

$$F_u(y) = \frac{F(u + y) - F(u)}{1 - F(u)}$$

The variable $F_u(y)$ defines the right tail of the probability distribution. It is the cumulative probability distribution for the amount by which x exceeds u given that it does exceed u.

Gnedenko's result states that, for a wide class of distributions $F(x)$, the distribution of $F_u(y)$ converges to a generalized Pareto distribution as the threshold u is increased. The generalized Pareto distribution is

$$G_{\xi,\beta}(y) = 1 - \left(1 + \xi \frac{y}{\beta}\right)^{-1/\xi} \tag{9.3}$$

The distribution has two parameters that have to be estimated from the data. These are ξ and β. The parameter ξ is the shape parameter and

[6] See D. V. Gnedenko, "Sur la distribution limité du terme d'une série aléatoire," *Ann. Math.*, 44 (1943), 423–453.

determines the heaviness of the tail of the distribution. The parameter β is a scale parameter.

When the underlying variable x has a normal distribution, $\xi = 0$.[7] As the tails of the distribution become heavier, the value of ξ increases. For most financial data, ξ is positive and in the range 0.1 to 0.4.[8]

Estimating ξ and β

The parameters ξ and β can be estimated using maximum-likelihood methods (see Section 5.9 for a discussion of these methods). The probability density function $g_{\xi,\beta}(y)$ of the cumulative distribution in equation (9.3) is calculated by differentiating with respect to y. It is

$$g_{\xi,\beta}(y) = \frac{1}{\beta}\left(1 + \frac{\xi y}{\beta}\right)^{-1/\xi-1}$$

We first choose a value for u. This could be a value close to the 95 percentile point of the empirical distribution. We then rank the observations on x from the highest to the lowest and focus our attention on those observations for which $x > u$. Suppose there are n_u such observations and they are x_i ($1 \leqslant i \leqslant n_u$). The likelihood function (assuming that $\xi \neq 0$) is

$$\prod_{i=1}^{n_u} \frac{1}{\beta}\left(1 + \frac{\xi(x_i - u)}{\beta}\right)^{-1/\xi-1}$$

Maximizing this function is the same as maximizing its logarithm:

$$\sum_{i=1}^{n_u} \ln\left[\frac{1}{\beta}\left(1 + \frac{\xi(x_i - u)}{\beta}\right)^{-1/\xi-1}\right] \tag{9.4}$$

Standard numerical procedures can be used to find the values of ξ and β that maximize this expression.

---

[7] When $\xi = 0$, the generalized Pareto distribution becomes

$$G_{\xi,\beta}(y) = 1 - \exp\left(-\frac{y}{\beta}\right)$$

[8] One of the properties of the distribution in equation (9.3) is that the kth moment $E(x^k)$ of x is infinite for $k \geqslant 1/\xi$. For a normal distribution, all moments are finite. When $\xi = 0.25$, only the first three moments are finite; when $\xi = 0.5$, only the first moment is finite; and so on.

Estimating the Tail of the Distribution

The probability that $x > u + y$ conditional that $x > u$ is $1 - G_{\xi,\beta}(y)$. The probability that $x > u$ is $1 - F(u)$. The unconditional probability that $x > u + y$ is therefore

$$[1 - F(u)][1 - G_{\xi,\beta}(y)]$$

If n is the total number of observations, an estimate of $1 - F(u)$ calculated from the empirical data is n_u/n. The unconditional probability that $x > u + y$ is therefore

$$\frac{n_u}{n}[1 - G_{\xi,\beta}(y)] = \frac{n_u}{n}\left(1 + \xi\frac{y}{\beta}\right)^{-1/\xi}$$

This means that our estimator of the tail of the cumulative probability distribution of x when x is large is

$$F(x) = 1 - \frac{n_u}{n}\left(1 + \xi\frac{x - u}{\beta}\right)^{-1/\xi} \tag{9.5}$$

Equivalence to the Power Law

If we set $u = \beta/\xi$, equation (9.5) reduces to

$$F(x) = 1 - \frac{n_u}{n}\left(\frac{\xi x}{\beta}\right)^{-1/\xi}$$

so that the probability of the variable being greater than x is

$$K x^{-\alpha}$$

where

$$K = \frac{n_u}{n}\left(\frac{\xi}{\beta}\right)^{-1/\xi}$$

and $\alpha = 1/\xi$. This shows that equation (9.5) is consistent with the power law introduced in Section 5.4.

The Left Tail

The analysis so far has assumed that we are interested in the right tail of the probability distribution. If we are interested in the left tail, we can use the methodology just presented on the variable $-x$.

Calculation of VaR

To calculate VaR with a confidence level of q it is necessary to solve the equation

$$F(\text{VaR}) = q$$

From equation (9.5), we have

$$q = 1 - \frac{n_u}{n}\left(1 + \xi\frac{\text{VaR} - u}{\beta}\right)^{-1/\xi}$$

so that

$$\text{VaR} = u + \frac{\beta}{\xi}\left[\left(\frac{n}{n_u}(1 - q)\right)^{-\xi} - 1\right] \tag{9.6}$$

9.5 APPLICATION

We now illustrate the results in the previous section using data for daily returns on the S&P 500 between July 11, 1988, and July 10, 1998. During this period the total number of observations, n, on the daily return were 2,256 and the observations ranged from -6.87% to $+5.12\%$. We consider the left tail of the distribution of returns. This means that in the equations given above the variable x is the negative of the daily return on the S&P 500. We choose a value for u equal to 0.02. There were a total of 28 returns less than -2%. This means than $n_u = 28$. The returns and the x-values are shown in the first two columns of Table 9.3. The third column shows the value of

$$\ln\left[\frac{1}{\beta}\left(1 + \frac{\xi(x_i - u)}{\beta}\right)^{-1/\xi - 1}\right]$$

for particular values of x_i and β. (The test values of ξ and β in Table 9.3 are $\xi = 0.2$ and $\beta = 0.01$.) The sum of the numbers in the third column is the log-likelihood function in equation (9.4). Once we have set up the spreadsheet, we search for the best-fit values of ξ and β that maximize the log-likelihood function.[9] It turns out that these are

$$\xi = 0.3232, \quad \beta = 0.0055$$

and maximum log-likelihood is 108.48.

---

[9] The Solver routine in Excel works well provided that the spreadsheet is set up so that the values being searched for are similar in magnitude. In this example, we could set up the spreadsheet to search for ξ and 100β.

Table 9.3 Estimation of extreme value theory parameters.

Daily return	x_i	$\ln\left[\dfrac{1}{\beta}\left(1+\dfrac{\xi(x_i - u)}{\beta}\right)^{-1/\xi - 1}\right]$
−0.068667	0.068667	0.5268
−0.061172	0.061172	1.0008
−0.036586	0.036586	2.8864
−0.034445	0.034445	3.0825
−0.031596	0.031596	3.3537
−0.030827	0.030827	3.4291
−0.029979	0.029979	3.5133
−0.029654	0.029654	3.5460
−0.029084	0.029084	3.6035
−0.027283	0.027283	3.7893
−0.025859	0.025859	3.9403
−0.025364	0.025364	3.9937
−0.024675	0.024675	4.0689
−0.024000	0.024000	4.1434
−0.023485	0.023485	4.2009
−0.023397	0.023397	4.2108
−0.023234	0.023234	4.2291
−0.022675	0.022675	4.2925
−0.022542	0.022542	4.3076
−0.022343	0.022343	4.3304
−0.022249	0.022249	4.3412
−0.022020	0.022020	4.3676
−0.021813	0.021813	4.3915
−0.021025	0.021025	4.4835
−0.020843	0.020843	4.5049
−0.020625	0.020625	4.5306
−0.020546	0.020546	4.5400
−0.020243	0.020243	4.5761
		106.1842

Trial estimates of EVT parameters

ξ	β
0.2	0.01

Suppose that we wish to estimate the probability that x will be less than 0.04. From equation (9.5), this is

$$1 - \frac{28}{2256}\left(1 + 0.3232\frac{0.04 - 0.02}{0.0055}\right)^{-1/0.3232} = 0.9989$$

This means that we estimate the probability that the daily return will be less than -4% to be $1 - 0.9989 = 0.0011$. (This is more accurate than an estimate obtained by counting observations.) The probability that x will be less than 0.06 is similarly 0.9997. This means that we estimate the probability that the daily return will be less than -6% to be $1 - 0.9997 = 0.0003$.

From equation (9.6) the value of the one-day 99% VaR for a portfolio where \$1 million is invested in the S&P 500 is \$1 million times

$$0.02 + \frac{0.0055}{0.3232}\left[\left(\frac{2256}{28}(1 - 0.99)\right)^{-0.3232} - 1\right] = 0.0212$$

or \$21,200. More generally, our estimate of the one-day 99% VaR for a portfolio invested in the S&P 500 is 2.12% of the portfolio value.

Choice of u

A natural question is how the results depend on the choice of u. In our example the values of ξ and β do depend on u, but the estimates of $F(x)$ remain roughly the same. For example, if we choose $u = 0.015$, the best-fit values of ξ and β are 0.264 and 0.0046, respectively. The estimate for $F(x)$ when $x = 0.04$ and $x = 0.06$ are 0.9989 and 0.9997 (much the same as before). The estimate of VaR also does not change too much provided that the confidence level is not too high. The one-day 99% VaR for an investment in the S&P 500 when $u = 0.015$ is 2.13% (compared with 2.12% when $u = 0.02$) of the value of the portfolio.

SUMMARY

Historical simulation is a very popular approach for estimating VaR. It involves creating a database consisting of the daily movements in all market variables over a period of time. The first simulation trial assumes that the percentage change in each market variable is the same as that on the first day covered by the database; the second simulation trial assumes that the percentage changes are the same as those on the second day; and so on. The change in the portfolio value, ΔP, is calculated for each simulation trial, and VaR is calculated as the appropriate percentile of the probability distribution of ΔP. The procedure assumes that the future will in some sense be like the past. The standard error for a VaR that is estimated using historical simulation tends to be quite high. The higher the VaR confidence level required, the higher the standard error.

There are a number of extensions of the basic historical simulation approach. The weights given to observations can be allowed to decrease exponentially as we look further and further into the past. Volatility updating schemes can be used to take account of differences between the volatilities of market variables today and their volatilities at different times during the period covered by the historical data.

Extreme value theory is a way of smoothing the tails of the probability distribution of portfolio daily changes calculated using historical simulation. It leads to estimates of VaR that reflect the whole shape of the tail of the distribution, not just the positions of a few losses in the tails. Extreme value theory can also be used to estimate VaR when the VaR confidence level is very high. For example, even if we have only 500 days of data, it could be used to come up an estimate of VaR for a VaR confidence level of 99.9%.

FURTHER READING

Boudoukh, J., M. Richardson, and R. Whitelaw, "The Best of Both Worlds," *Risk*, 11 (May 1998): 64–67.

Embrechts, P., C. Kluppelberg, and T. Mikosch, *Modeling Extremal Events for Insurance and Finance*. New York: Springer, 1997.

Hendricks, D., "Evaluation of Value-at-Risk Models Using Historical Data," *Economic Policy Review*, Federal Reserve Bank of New York, Vol. 2 (April 1996): 39–69.

Hull, J. C., and A. White, "Incorporating Volatility Updating into the Historical Simulation Method for Value at Risk," *Journal of Risk*, 1, No. 1 (Fall 1998): 5–19.

McNeil, A. J., "Extreme Value Theory for Risk Managers," in *Internal Modeling and CAD II*, Risk Books, 1999. See also: www.math.ethz.ch/~mcneil.

Neftci, S. N., "Value at Risk Calculations, Extreme Events and Tail Estimation," *Journal of Derivatives*, 7, No. 3 (Spring 2000): 23–38.

QUESTIONS AND PROBLEMS (Answers at End of Book)

9.1. What assumptions are being made when VaR is calculated using the historical simulation approach and 500 days of data.

9.2. Show that when λ approaches 1, the weighting scheme in Section 9.3 approaches the basic historical simulation approach.

9.3. Calculate the 1-day 99% VaR on February 10, 2006, for a £100 million portfolio invested in the FTSE 100 Index. Use the previous 1,000 days of data (available on the author's website) and historical simulation.

9.4. Repeat Problem 9.3 using the exponential weighting scheme in Section 9.3 with $\lambda = 0.99$.

9.5. Repeat Problem 9.3 using the volatility updating scheme discussed in Section 9.3. Use EWMA with $\lambda = 0.94$ to update volatilities. Assume that the volatility is initially equal to the standard deviation of daily returns calculated from the whole sample.

9.6. How does extreme value theory modify your answer to Problem 9.3. Try values of u equal to 0.005, 0.01, and 0.015.

9.7. Suppose we estimate the 1-day 95% VaR from 1,000 observations as $5 million. By fitting a standard distribution to the observations, the probability density function of the loss distribution at the 95% point is estimated to be 0.01 when losses are measured in millions. What is the standard error of the VaR estimate?

ASSIGNMENT QUESTIONS

9.8. Values for the NASDAQ composite index during the 1,500 days preceding March 10, 2006, can be downloaded from the author's website. Calculate the 1-day 99% VaR on March 10, 2006, for a $10 million portfolio invested in the index using (a) the basic historical simulation approach, (b) the exponential weighting scheme in Section 9.3 with $\lambda = 0.995$, (c) the volatility updating scheme in Section 9.3 with $\lambda = 0.94$ (assume that the volatility is initially equal to the standard deviation of daily returns calculated from the whole sample), (d) extreme value theory with $u = 0.03$, (e) a model where daily returns are assumed to be normally distributed (use both an approach where observations are given equal weights and the EWMA approach with $\lambda = 0.94$ to estimate the standard deviation of daily returns). Discuss the reasons for the differences between the results you get.

9.9. Suppose that a 1-day 97.5% VaR is estimated as $13 million from 2,000 observations. The observation on the 1-day changes are approximately normal with mean 0 and standard deviation \$6 million. Estimate a 99% confidence interval for the VaR estimate.

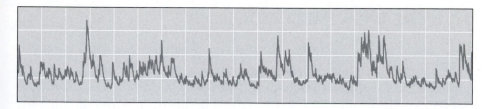

10

Market Risk VaR: Model-Building Approach

The main alternative to the historical simulation approach for estimating VaR for market risk is what is known as the *model-building* approach or the *variance–covariance* approach. In this approach, we assume a model for the joint distribution of changes in market variables and use historical data to estimate the model parameters.

The model-building approach is based on ideas pioneered by Harry Markowitz. We used these ideas for assessing the risk–return trade-offs in portfolios of stocks in Section 1.1. They can also be used to calculate VaR. Estimates of the current levels of the variances and covariances of market variables are made using the approaches described in Chapters 5 and 6. If the probability distributions of the daily percentage changes in market variables are assumed to be normal and the dollar change in the value of the portfolio is assumed to be linearly dependent on percentage changes in market variables, VaR can be obtained very quickly.

In this chapter we explain the model-building approach and show how it can be used for portfolios consisting of stocks, bonds, forward contracts, and interest rate swaps. We discuss attempts to extend it to situations where the portfolio is not linearly dependent on the market variables and to situations where the distributions of daily percentage changes in market variables are not normal. Finally, we evaluate the strengths and weaknesses of both the model-building approach and the historical simulation approach.

10.1 THE BASIC METHODOLOGY

In option pricing, volatility is normally measured as "volatility per year". When using the model-building approach to calculate VaR, we usually measure the volatility of an asset as "volatility per day". As explained in Section 5.1, the relationship between the volatility per day and the volatility per year is

$$\sigma_{day} = \sigma_{yr}/\sqrt{252}$$

where σ_{yr} is the volatility per year and σ_{day} is the corresponding volatility per day. This equation shows that the daily volatility is about 6% of annual volatility.

As also pointed out in Chapter 5, σ_{day} is approximately equal to the standard deviation of the percentage change in the asset price in one day. For the purposes of calculating VaR, we assume exact equality. We define the daily volatility of an asset price (or any other variable) as equal to the standard deviation of the percentage change in one day.

Single-Asset Case

We now consider how VaR is calculated using the model-building approach in a very simple situation where the portfolio consists of a position in a single stock. The portfolio we consider is one consisting of $10 million in shares of Microsoft. We suppose that the time horizon is ten days and the VaR confidence level is 99%, so that we are interested in the loss level over ten days that we are 99% confident will not be exceeded. Initially, we consider a one-day time horizon.

We assume that the volatility of Microsoft is 2% per day (corresponding to about 32% per year). Because the size of the position is $10 million, the standard deviation of daily changes in the value of the position is 2% of $10 million, or $200,000.

It is customary in the model-building approach to assume that the expected change in a market variable over the time period considered is zero. This is not exactly true, but it is a reasonable assumption. The expected change in the price of a market variable over a short time period is generally small when compared to the standard deviation of the change. Suppose, for example, that Microsoft has an expected return of 20% per annum. Over a one-day period, the expected return is 0.20/252, or about 0.08%, whereas the standard deviation of the return is 2%. Over a ten-day period, the expected return is 0.08×10, or about 0.8%, whereas the standard deviation of the return is $2\sqrt{10}$, or about 6.3%.

So far, we have established that the change in the value of the portfolio of Microsoft shares over a one-day period has a standard deviation of $200,000 and (at least approximately) a mean of zero. We assume that the change is normally distributed.[1] Since $N(-2.33) = 0.01$, this means that there is a 1% probability that a normally distributed variable will decrease in value by more than 2.33 standard deviations. Equivalently, it means that we are 99% certain that a normally distributed variable will not decrease in value by more than 2.33 standard deviations. The one-day 99% VaR for our portfolio consisting of a $10 million position in Microsoft is therefore

$$2.33 \times 200,000 = \$466,000$$

Assuming that the changes in Microsoft's stock price on successive days are independent, the N-day VaR is calculated as $\sqrt{N}$ times the one-day VaR. The ten-day 99% VaR for Microsoft is therefore

$$466,000 \times \sqrt{10} = \$1,473,621$$

Consider next a portfolio consisting of a $5 million position in AT&T, and suppose the daily volatility of AT&T is 1% (approximately 16% per year). A similar calculation to that for Microsoft shows that the standard deviation of the change in the value of the portfolio in one day is

$$5,000,000 \times 0.01 = 50,000$$

Assuming that the change is normally distributed, the one-day 99% VaR is

$$50,000 \times 2.33 = \$116,500$$

and the ten-day 99% VaR is

$$116,500 \times \sqrt{10} = \$368,405$$

Two-Asset Case

Now consider a portfolio consisting of both $10 million of Microsoft shares and $5 million of AT&T shares. We suppose that the returns on the two shares have a bivariate normal distribution with a correlation of 0.3. A standard result in statistics tells us that, if two variables X and Y have standard deviations equal to σ_X and σ_Y with the coefficient of

---

[1] We could assume that the price of Microsoft is lognormal tomorrow. Since one day is such a short period of time, this is almost indistinguishable from the assumption we do make—that the change in the stock price between today and tomorrow is normal.

correlation between them being equal to ρ, the standard deviation of $X + Y$ is given by

$$\sigma_{X+Y} = \sqrt{\sigma_X^2 + \sigma_Y^2 + 2\rho\sigma_X\sigma_Y}$$

To apply this result, we set X equal to the change in the value of the position in Microsoft over a one-day period and Y equal to the change in the value of the position in AT&T over a one-day period, so that

$$\sigma_X = 200,000 \quad \text{and} \quad \sigma_Y = 50,000$$

The standard deviation of the change in the value of the portfolio consisting of both stocks over a one-day period is therefore

$$\sqrt{200,000^2 + 50,000^2 + 2 \times 0.3 \times 200,000 \times 50,000} = 220,227$$

The mean change is assumed to be zero. The change is normally distributed. So the one-day 99% VaR is therefore

$$220,227 \times 2.33 = \$513,129$$

The ten-day 99% VaR is $\sqrt{10}$ times this or \$1,622,657.

The Benefits of Diversification

In the example we have just considered:

1. The ten-day 99% VaR for the portfolio of Microsoft shares is \$1,473,621.
2. The ten-day 99% VaR for the portfolio of AT&T shares is \$368,405.
3. The ten-day 99% VaR for the portfolio of both Microsoft and AT&T shares is \$1,622,657.

The amount
$$(1,473,621 + 368,405) - 1,622,657 = \$219,369$$

represents the benefits of diversification. If Microsoft and AT&T were perfectly correlated, the VaR for the portfolio of both Microsoft and AT&T would equal the VaR for the Microsoft portfolio plus the VaR for the AT&T portfolio. Less than perfect correlation leads to some of the risk being "diversified away".[2]

---

[2] VaR reflects the benefits of diversification when the distribution of the portfolio-value changes is normal. As we saw in Section 8.3, VaR does not always reflect the benefits of diversification. The VaR of two portfolios can be greater than the sum of their separate VaRs.

10.2 THE LINEAR MODEL

The examples we have just considered are simple illustrations of the use of the linear model for calculating VaR. Suppose that we have a portfolio worth P consisting of n assets with an amount α_i being invested in asset i ($1 \leqslant i \leqslant n$). Define Δx_i as the return on asset i in one day. The dollar change in the value of our investment in asset i in one day is $\alpha_i \Delta x_i$ and

$$\Delta P = \sum_{i=1}^{n} \alpha_i \Delta x_i \qquad (10.1)$$

where ΔP is the dollar change in the value of the whole portfolio in one day.

In the example considered in the previous section, $10 million was invested in the first asset (Microsoft) and $5 million was invested in the second asset (AT&T) so that (in millions of dollars) $\alpha_1 = 10$, $\alpha_2 = 5$, and

$$\Delta P = 10\Delta x_1 + 5\Delta x_2$$

If we assume that the Δx_i in equation (10.1) are multivariate normal, ΔP is normally distributed. To calculate VaR, we therefore need to calculate only the mean and standard deviation of ΔP. We assume, as discussed in the previous section, that the expected value of each Δx_i is zero. This implies that the mean of ΔP is zero.

To calculate the standard deviation of ΔP, we define σ_i as the daily volatility of the ith asset and ρ_{ij} as the coefficient of correlation between returns on asset i and asset j.[3] This means that σ_i is the standard deviation of Δx_i, and ρ_{ij} is the coefficient of correlation between Δx_i and Δx_j. The variance of ΔP, which we will denote by σ_P^2, is given by

$$\sigma_P^2 = \sum_{i=1}^{n} \sum_{j=1}^{n} \rho_{ij} \alpha_i \alpha_j \sigma_i \sigma_j$$

This equation can also be written as

$$\sigma_P^2 = \sum_{i=1}^{n} \alpha_i^2 \sigma_i^2 + 2 \sum_{i=1}^{n} \sum_{j<i} \rho_{ij} \alpha_i \alpha_j \sigma_i \sigma_j \qquad (10.2)$$

---

[3] The ρ_{ij} are sometimes calculated using a factor model (see Section 6.3).

The standard deviation of the change over N days is $\sigma_P\sqrt{N}$, and the 99% VaR for an N-day time horizon is $2.33\sigma_P\sqrt{N}$.

In the example considered in the previous section, $\sigma_1 = 0.02$, $\sigma_2 = 0.01$, and $\rho_{12} = 0.3$. As already noted, $\alpha_1 = 10$ and $\alpha_2 = 5$, so that

$$\sigma_P^2 = 10^2 \times 0.02^2 + 5^2 \times 0.01^2 + 2 \times 10 \times 5 \times 0.3 \times 0.02 \times 0.01 = 0.0485$$

and $\sigma_P = 0.220$. This is the standard deviation of the change in the portfolio value per day (in millions of dollars). The ten-day 99% VaR is $2.33 \times 0.220 \times \sqrt{10} = \$1.623$ million. This agrees with the calculation in the previous section.

10.3 HANDLING INTEREST RATES

It is not possible to define a separate market variable for every single bond price or interest rate to which a company is exposed. Some simplifications are necessary when the model-building approach is used. One possibility is to assume that only parallel shifts in the yield curve occur. It is then necessary to define only one market variable: the size of the parallel shift. The changes in the value of bond portfolio can then be calculated using the approximate duration relationship in equation (4.15):

$$\Delta P = -DP\Delta y$$

where P is the value of the portfolio, ΔP is the change in P in one day, D is the modified duration of the portfolio, and Δy is the parallel shift in one day. This approach gives a linear relationship between ΔP and Δy, but it does not usually give enough accuracy because the relationship is not exact and does not take account of nonparallel shifts in the yield curve.

The procedure usually followed is to choose as market variables the prices of zero-coupon bonds with standard maturities: 1 month, 3 months, 6 months, 1 year, 2 years, 5 years, 7 years, 10 years, and 30 years. For the purposes of calculating VaR, the cash flows from instruments in the portfolio are mapped into cash flows occurring on the standard maturity dates.

Consider a $1 million position in a Treasury bond lasting 0.8 years that pays a coupon of 10% semiannually. A coupon is paid in 0.3 years and 0.8 years and the principal is paid in 0.8 years. This bond is therefore in the first instance regarded as a $50,000 position in 0.3-year zero-coupon bond plus a $1,050,000 position in a 0.8-year zero-coupon bond. The position in the 0.3-year bond is then replaced by an equivalent position in 3-month and 6-month zero-coupon bonds and the position in the 0.8-year bond is replaced by an equivalent position in 6-month and 1-year zero-coupon bonds. The result is that the position in the 0.8-year coupon-bearing bond is for VaR purposes regarded as a position in zero-coupon bonds having maturities of 3 months, 6 months, and 1 year. This procedure is known as *cash-flow mapping*.

Illustration of Cash-Flow Mapping

We now illustrate how cash-flow mapping works by continuing with the example we have just introduced. It should be emphasized that the procedure we use is just one of several that have been proposed.

Consider first the $1,050,000 that will be received in 0.8 years. We suppose that zero rates, daily bond price volatilities, and correlations between bond returns are as shown in Table 10.1. The first stage is to interpolate between the 6-month rate of 6.0% and the 1-year rate of 7.0% to obtain a 0.8-year rate of 6.6% (annual compounding is assumed for all rates). The present value of the $1,050,000 cash flow to be received in 0.8 years is

$$\frac{1,050,000}{1.066^{0.8}} = 997,662$$

We also interpolate between the 0.1% volatility for the 6-month bond and the 0.2% volatility for the 1-year bond to get a 0.16% volatility for the 0.8-year bond.

Table 10.1 Data to illustrate cash-flow mapping procedure.

Maturity	*3-month bond*	*6-month bond*	*1-year bond*
Zero rate (% with ann. comp.):	5.50	6.00	7.00
Bond price volatility (% per day):	0.06	0.10	0.20
Correlation between daily returns	*3-month bond*	*6-month bond*	*1-year bond*
3-month bond	1.0	0.9	0.6
6-month bond	0.9	1.0	0.7
1-year bond	0.6	0.7	1.0

Suppose we allocate α of the present value to the 6-month bond and $1 - \alpha$ of the present value to the 1-year bond. Using equation (10.2) and matching variances, we obtain

$$0.0016^2 = 0.001^2\alpha^2 + 0.002^2(1 - \alpha)^2 + 2 \times 0.7 \times 0.001 \times 0.002\alpha(1 - \alpha)$$

This is a quadratic equation that can be solved in the usual way to give $\alpha = 0.320337$. This means that 32.0337% of the value should be allocated to a 6-month zero-coupon bond and 67.9663% of the value should be allocated to a 1-year zero-coupon bond. The 0.8-year bond worth $997,662 is therefore replaced by a 6-month bond worth

$$997,662 \times 0.320337 = \$319,589$$

and a 1-year bond worth

$$997,662 \times 0.679663 = \$678,074$$

This cash-flow-mapping scheme has the advantage that it preserves both the value and the variance of the cash flow. Also, it can be shown that the weights assigned to the two adjacent zero-coupon bonds are always positive.

For the $50,000 cash flow received at time 0.3 years, we can carry out similar calculations (see Problem 10.7). It turns out that the present value of the cash flow is $49,189. This can be mapped to a position worth $37,397 in a 3-month bond and a position worth $11,793 in a 6-month bond.

The results of the calculations are summarized in Table 10.2. The 0.8-year coupon-bearing bond is mapped to a position worth $37,397 in a 3-month bond, a position worth $331,382 in a 6-month bond, and a position worth $678,074 in a 1-year bond. Using the volatilities and correlations in Table 10.1, equation (10.2) gives the variance of the

Table 10.2   The cash-flow-mapping result.

	$50,000 received in 0.3 years	$1,050,000 received in 0.8 years	Total
Position in 3-month bond ($):	37,397		37,397
Position in 6-month bond ($):	11,793	319,589	331,382
Position in 1-year bond ($):		678,074	678,074

change in the price of the 0.8-year bond with $n = 3$, $\alpha_1 = 37,397$, $\alpha_2 = 331,382$, $\alpha_3 = 678,074$; $\sigma_1 = 0.0006$, $\sigma_2 = 0.001$ and $\sigma_3 = 0.002$; and $\rho_{12} = 0.9$, $\rho_{13} = 0.6$, $\rho_{23} = 0.7$. This variance is 2,628,518. The standard deviation of the change in the price of the bond is therefore $\sqrt{2,628,518} = 1,621.3$. Because we are assuming that the bond is the only instrument in the portfolio, the ten-day 99% VaR is

$$1621.3 \times \sqrt{10} \times 2.33 = 11,946$$

or about $11,950.

Principal Components Analysis

As we explained in Section 4.10, a principal components analysis (PCA) can be used to reduce the number of deltas that are calculated for movements in a zero-coupon yield curve. A PCA can also be used (in conjunction with cash-flow mapping) to handle interest rates when VaR is calculated using the model-building approach. For any given portfolio, we can convert a set of delta exposures, such as those given in Table 4.11, into a delta exposure to the first PCA factor, a delta exposure to the second PCA factor, and so on. This is done in Section 4.10. In the example in Table 4.11 the exposure to the first factor is calculated as -0.08 and the exposure to the second factor is calculated as -4.40. (The first two factors capture over 90% of the variation in interest rates.) Suppose that f_1 and f_2 are the factor scores. The change in the portfolio value is approximately

$$\Delta P = -0.08 f_1 - 4.40 f_2$$

The factor scores in a PCA are uncorrelated. From Table 4.10 their standard deviations of the first two factors are 17.49 and 6.05. The standard deviation of ΔP is therefore

$$\sqrt{0.08^2 \times 17.49^2 + 4.40^2 \times 6.05^2} = 26.66$$

The one-day 99% VaR is therefore $26.66 \times 2.33 = 62.12$. Note that the portfolio we are considering has very little exposure to the first factor and significant exposure to the second factor. Using only one factor would significantly understate VaR (see Problem 10.9). The duration-based method for handling interest rates would also significantly understate VaR as it considers only parallel shifts in the yield curve.

Chapter 10

10.4 APPLICATIONS OF THE LINEAR MODEL

The simplest application of the linear model is to a portfolio with no derivatives consisting of positions in stocks, bonds, foreign exchange, and commodities. In this case the change in the value of the portfolio is linearly dependent on the percentage changes in the prices of the assets comprising the portfolio. Note that, for the purposes of VaR calculations, all asset prices are measured in the domestic currency. The market variables considered by a large bank in the United States are therefore likely to include the value of the Nikkei 225 Index measured in dollars, the price of a ten-year sterling zero-coupon bond measured in dollars, and so on.

Examples of derivatives that can be handled by the linear model are forward contracts on foreign exchange and interest rate swaps. Suppose a forward foreign exchange contract matures at time T. It can be regarded as the exchange of a foreign zero-coupon bond maturing at time T for a domestic zero-coupon bond maturing at time T. Therefore, for the purposes of calculating VaR, the forward contract is treated as a long position in the foreign bond combined with a short position in the domestic bond. (As just mentioned, the foreign bond is valued in the domstic currency.) Each bond can be handled using a cash-flow-mapping procedure so that it is a linear combination of bonds with standard maturities.

Consider next an interest rate swap. This can be regarded as the exchange of a floating-rate bond for a fixed-rate bond. The fixed-rate bond is a regular coupon-bearing bond (see Appendix B). The floating-rate bond is worth par just after the next payment date. It can be regarded as a zero-coupon bond with a maturity date equal to the next payment date. The interest rate swap therefore reduces to a portfolio of long and short positions in bonds and can be handled using a cash-flow-mapping procedure.

10.5 THE LINEAR MODEL AND OPTIONS

We now consider how the linear model can be used when there are options. Consider first a portfolio consisting of options on a single stock whose current price is S. Suppose that the delta of the position (calculated in the way described in Chapter 3) is δ.[4] Because δ is the rate of change of

---

[4] In Chapter 3 we denote the delta and gamma of a portfolio by Δ and Γ. In this section and the next, we use the lower case Greek letters δ and γ to avoid overworking Δ.

the value of the portfolio with S, it is approximately true that

$$\delta = \frac{\Delta P}{\Delta S}$$

or

$$\Delta P = \delta \Delta S \tag{10.3}$$

where ΔS is the dollar change in the stock price in one day and ΔP is, as usual, the dollar change in the portfolio in one day. We define Δx as the return on the stock in one day, so that

$$\Delta x = \frac{\Delta S}{S}$$

It follows that an approximate relationship between ΔP and Δx is

$$\Delta P = S \delta \Delta x$$

When we have a position in several underlying market variables that includes options, we can derive an approximate linear relationship between ΔP and the Δx_i similarly. This relationship is

$$\Delta P = \sum_{i=1}^{n} S_i \delta_i \, \Delta x_i \tag{10.4}$$

where S_i is the value of the ith market variable and δ_i is the delta of the portfolio with respect to the ith market variable. This is equation (10.1):

$$\Delta P = \sum_{i=1}^{n} \alpha_i \, \Delta x_i \tag{10.5}$$

with $\alpha_i = S_i \delta_i$. Equation (10.5) can therefore be used to calculate the standard deviation of ΔP.

Example 10.1

A portfolio consists of options on Microsoft and AT&T. The options on Microsoft have a delta of 1,000, and the options on AT&T have a delta of 20,000. The Microsoft share price is $120, and the AT&T share price is $30. From equation (10.4), it is approximately true that

$$\Delta P = 120 \times 1{,}000 \times \Delta x_1 + 30 \times 20{,}000 \times \Delta x_2$$

or

$$\Delta P = 120{,}000 \Delta x_1 + 600{,}000 \Delta x_2$$

where Δx_1 and Δx_2 are the returns from Microsoft and AT&T in one day and ΔP is the resultant change in the value of the portfolio. (The portfolio is assumed to be equivalent to an investment of \$120,000 in Microsoft and \$600,000 in AT&T.) Assuming that the daily volatility of Microsoft is 2% and the daily volatility of AT&T is 1% and the correlation between the daily changes is 0.3, the standard deviation of ΔP (in thousands of dollars) is

$$\sqrt{(120 \times 0.02)^2 + (600 \times 0.01)^2 + 2 \times 120 \times 0.02 \times 600 \times 0.01 \times 0.3} = 7.099$$

Because $N(-1.65) = 0.05$, the five-day 95% VaR is

$$1.65 \times \sqrt{5} \times 7,099 = \$26,193$$

Weakness of the Model

When a portfolio includes options, the linear model is an approximation. It does not take account of the gamma of the portfolio. As discussed in Chapter 3, delta is defined as the rate of change of the portfolio value with respect to an underlying market variable and gamma is defined as the rate of change of the delta with respect to the market variable. Gamma measures the curvature of the relationship between the portfolio value and an underlying market variable.

Figure 10.1 shows the impact of a nonzero gamma on the probability distribution of the value of the portfolio. When gamma is positive, the probability distribution tends to be positively skewed; when gamma is negative, it tends to be negatively skewed. Figures 10.2 and 10.3 illustrate the reason for this result. Figure 10.2 shows the relationship between the value of a long call option and the price of the underlying asset. A long call is an example of an option position with positive gamma. The figure shows that, when the probability distribution for the price of the under-lying asset at the end of one day is normal, the probability distribution

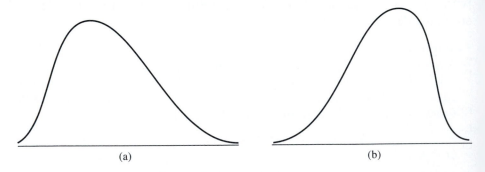

(a)   (b)

Figure 10.1   Probability distribution for value of portfolio: (a) positive gamma; (b) negative gamma.

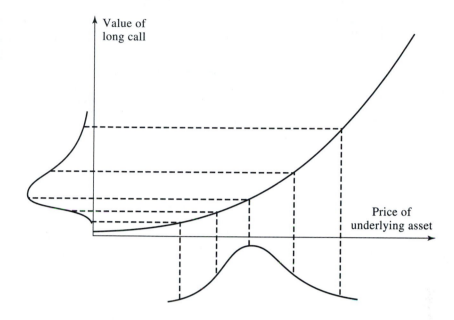

Figure 10.2 Translation of normal probability distribution for an asset into probability distribution for value of a long call on that asset.

for the option price is positively skewed. Figure 10.3 shows the relationship between the value of a short call position and the price of the underlying asset. A short call position has a negative gamma. In this case, we see that a normal distribution for the price of the underlying asset at the end of one day gets mapped into a negatively skewed distribution for the value of the option position.[5]

The VaR for a portfolio is critically dependent on the left tail of the probability distribution of the portfolio value. For example, when the confidence level used is 99%, the VaR is the value in the left tail below which only 1% of the distribution resides. As indicated in Figures 10.1a and 10.2, a positive gamma portfolio tends to have a less heavy left tail than the normal distribution. If we assume the distribution is normal, we will tend to calculate a VaR that is too high. Similarly, as indicated in Figures 10.1b and 10.3, a negative gamma portfolio tends to have a heavier left tail than the normal distribution. If we assume the distribution is normal, we will tend to calculate a VaR that is too low.

---

[5] The normal distribution is a good approximation to the lognormal distribution for short time periods.

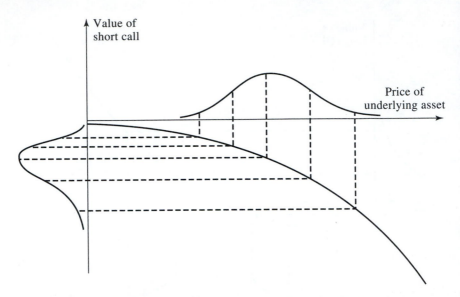

Figure 10.3   Translation of normal probability distribution for an asset into probability distribution for value of a short call on that asset.

10.6 THE QUADRATIC MODEL

For a more accurate estimate of VaR than that given by the linear model, we can use both delta and gamma measures to relate ΔP to the Δx_i. Consider a portfolio dependent on a single asset whose price is S. Suppose δ and γ are the delta and gamma of the portfolio. As indicated in Chapter 3, a Taylor Series expansion gives

$$\Delta P = \delta \Delta S + \tfrac{1}{2}\gamma(\Delta S)^2$$

as an improvement over the approximation in equation (10.3).[6] Setting

$$\Delta x = \frac{\Delta S}{S}$$

reduces this to

$$\Delta P = S\delta \Delta x + \tfrac{1}{2}S^2\gamma(\Delta x)^2 \qquad (\textbf{10.6})$$

---

[6] A fuller Taylor series expansion suggests the approximation

$$\Delta P = \Theta \Delta t + \delta \Delta S + \tfrac{1}{2}\gamma(\Delta S)^2$$

when terms of higher order than Δt are ignored. In practice, the $\Theta \Delta t$ term is so small that it is usually ignored.

In this case, we have

$$E(\Delta P) = 0.5 S^2 \gamma \sigma^2$$
$$E(\Delta P^2) = S^2 \delta^2 \sigma^2 + 0.75 S^4 \gamma^2 \sigma^4$$
$$E(\Delta P^3) = 4.5 S^4 \delta^2 \gamma \sigma^4 + 1.875 S^6 \gamma^3 \sigma^6$$

where σ is the daily volatility of the variable.

For a portfolio with n underlying market variables, with each instrument in the portfolio being dependent on only one of the market variables, equation (10.6) becomes

$$\Delta P = \sum_{i=1}^{n} S_i \delta_i \, \Delta x_i + \sum_{i=1}^{n} \tfrac{1}{2} S_i^2 \gamma_i (\Delta x_i)^2$$

where S_i is the value of the ith market variable, and δ_i and γ_i are the delta and gamma of the portfolio with respect to the ith market variable. When some of the individual instruments in the portfolio are dependent on more than one market variable, this equation takes the more general form

$$\Delta P = \sum_{i=1}^{n} S_i \delta_i \, \Delta x_i + \sum_{i=1}^{n} \sum_{j=1}^{n} \tfrac{1}{2} S_i S_j \gamma_{ij} \, \Delta x_i \, \Delta x_j \qquad \textbf{(10.7)}$$

where γ_{ij} is a "cross gamma", defined as

$$\gamma_{ij} = \frac{\partial^2 P}{\partial S_i \, \partial S_j}$$

Equation (10.7) is not as easy to work with as equation (10.5), but it can be used to calculate moments for ΔP.

Cornish–Fisher Expansion

A result in statistics known as the Cornish–Fisher expansion can be used to estimate quantiles of a probability distribution from its moments. We illustrate this by showing how the first three moments can be used to produce a VaR estimate that takes account of the skewness of the probability distribution. Define μ_P and σ_P as the mean and standard deviation of ΔP, so that

$$\mu_P = E(\Delta P) \quad \text{and} \quad \sigma_P^2 = E[(\Delta P)^2] - [E(\Delta P)]^2$$

The skewness ξ_P of the probability distribution of ΔP is defined as

$$\xi_P = \frac{1}{\sigma_P^3} E[(\Delta P - \mu_P)^3] = \frac{E[(\Delta P)^3] - 3E[(\Delta P)^2]\mu_P + 2\mu_P^3}{\sigma_P^3}$$

Using the first three moments of ΔP, the Cornish–Fisher expansion estimates the q-quantile of the distribution of ΔP as

$$\mu_P + w_q \sigma_P$$

where

$$w_q = z_q + \frac{1}{6}(z_q^2 - 1)\xi_P$$

and z_q is q-quantile of the standard normal distribution.

Example 10.2

Suppose that for a certain portfolio we calculate $\mu_P = -0.2$, $\sigma_P = 2.2$, and $\xi_P = -0.4$, and we are interested in the 0.01 quantile ($q = 0.01$). In this case, $z_q = -2.33$. If we assume that the probability distribution of ΔP is normal, then the 0.01 quantile is

$$-0.2 - 2.33 \times 2.2 = -5.326$$

In other words, we are 99% certain that

$$\Delta P > -5.326$$

When we use the Cornish–Fisher expansion to adjust for skewness and set $q = 0.01$, we obtain

$$w_q = -2.33 - \frac{1}{6}(2.33^2 - 1) \times 0.4 = -2.625$$

so that the 0.01 quantile of the distribution is

$$-0.2 - 2.625 \times 2.2 = -5.976$$

Taking account of skewness, therefore, changes the VaR from 5.326 to 5.976.

10.7 MONTE CARLO SIMULATION

As an alternative to the approaches described so far, we can implement the model-building approach using Monte Carlo simulation to generate the probability distribution for ΔP. Suppose we wish to calculate a one-day VaR for a portfolio. The procedure is as follows:

1. Value the portfolio today in the usual way using the current values of market variables.

2. Sample once from the multivariate normal probability distribution of the Δx_i.[7]

3. Use the sampled values of the Δx_i to determine the value of each market variable at the end of one day.

4. Revalue the portfolio at the end of the day in the usual way.

5. Subtract the value calculated in Step 1 from the value in Step 4 to determine a sample ΔP.

6. Repeat Steps 2 to 5 many times to build up a probability distribution for ΔP.

The VaR is calculated as the appropriate percentile of the probability distribution of ΔP. Suppose, for example, that we calculate 5,000 different sample values of ΔP in the way just described. The one-day 99% VaR is the 50th worst outcome; the one-day 95% VaR is the 250th worst outcome; and so on.[8] The N-day VaR is usually assumed to be the one-day VaR multiplied by $\sqrt{N}$.[9]

The drawback of Monte Carlo simulation is that it tends to be computationally slow because a company's complete portfolio (which might consist of hundreds of thousands of different instruments) has to be revalued many times.[10] One way of speeding things up is to assume that equation (10.7) describes the relationship between ΔP and the Δx_i. We can then jump straight from Step 2 to Step 5 in the Monte Carlo simulation and avoid the need for a complete revaluation of the portfolio. This is sometimes referred to as the *partial simulation approach*.

10.8 USING DISTRIBUTIONS THAT ARE NOT NORMAL

When Monte Carlo simulation is used, there are ways of extending the model-building approach so that market variables are no longer assumed to be normal. One possibility is to assume that the variables have a multivariate t-distribution. As indicated in Figures 6.4 and 6.5, this has

---

[7] One way of doing so is given in Chapter 6.

[8] As in the case of historical simulation, extreme value theory can be used to "smooth the tails", so that better estimates of extreme percentiles are obtained.

[9] This is only approximately true when the portfolio includes options, but it is the assumption that is made in practice for most VaR calculation methods.

[10] An approach for limiting the number of portfolio revaluations is proposed in F. Jamshidian and Y. Zhu, "Scenario Simulation Model: Theory and Methodology," *Finance and Stochastics*, 1 (1997), 43–67.

the effect of giving a higher value to the probability that extreme values for several variables occur simultaneously.

We can assume any set of distributions for the Δx_i in conjunction with a copula model.[11] Suppose, for example, that we use a Gaussian copula model. As explained in Chapter 6, this means that, when the changes Δx_i in market variables are transformed on a percentile-to-percentile basis to normally distributed variables u_i, the u_i are multivariate normal. We can follow the five steps given earlier except that Step 2 is changed and a step is inserted between Steps 2 and 3 as follows:

2. Sample once from the multivariate probability distribution for the u_i.

2a. Transform each u_i to Δx_i on a percentile-to-percentile basis.

If a bank has already implemented the Monte Carlo simulation approach for calculating VaR assuming percentage changes in market variables are normal, it should be relatively easy to modify calculations to implement the approach we describe here. Just before the portfolio is valued it is necessary to insert a line or two of code into the computer program to do the transformation in Step 2a. The marginal distributions of the Δx_i can be calculated by fitting a more general distribution than the normal distribution to empirical data.

10.9 MODEL BUILDING vs. HISTORICAL SIMULATION

In the last chapter and this one, we have discussed two methods for estimating VaR: the historical simulation approach and the model-building approach. The advantages of the model-building approach are that results can be produced very quickly and it can easily be used in conjunction with volatility and correlation updating schemes such as those described in Chapters 5 and 6. As mentioned in Section 9.3, volatility updating can be incorporated into the historical simulation approach—but in a rather more artificial way. The main disadvantage of the model-building approach is that (at least in the simplest version of the approach) it assumes that the market variables have a multivariate normal distribution. In practice, daily changes in market variables often have distributions that are quite different from normal (see, for example, Table 5.2). A user of the model-building approach is hoping that some

---

[11] See J. Hull and A. White, "Value at Risk When Daily Changes Are Not Normally Distributed," *Journal of Derivatives*, 5, No. 3 (Spring 1998), 9–19.

form of the central limit theorem of statistics applies to the portfolio, so that the probability distribution of daily gains/losses on the portfolio is normally distributed—even though the gains/losses on the component parts of the portfolio are not normally distributed.

The historical simulation approach has the advantage that historical data determines the joint probability distribution of the market variables. It is also easier to handle interest rates in a historical simulation because on each trial a complete zero-coupon yield curve for both today and tomorrow can be calculated. The somewhat messy cash-flow-mapping procedure described in Section 10.3 is avoided. The main disadvantage of historical simulation is that it is computationally much slower than the model-building approach. It is sometimes necessary to use an approximation such as equation (10.7) when using the historical simulation approach. This is because a full revaluation for each of the 500 different scenarios is not possible.[12]

The model-building approach is often used for investment portfolios. (It is after all closely related to the popular Markowitz mean–variance method of portfolio analysis.) It is less commonly used for calculating the VaR for the trading operations of a financial institution. This is because, as explained in Chapter 3, financial institutions like to maintain their deltas with respect to market variables close to zero. Neither the linear model nor the quadratic model work well when deltas are low and portfolios are nonlinear.

SUMMARY

Whereas historical simulation lets the data determine the joint probability distribution of daily percentage changes in market variables, the model-building approach assumes a particular form for this distribution. The most common assumption is that percentage changes in the variables have a multivariate normal distribution. For situations where the change in the value of the portfolio is linearly dependent on percentage changes in the market variables, VaR can be calculated exactly in a straightforward way. In other situations approximations are necessary. One approach is to use a quadratic approximation for the change in the value of the portfolio as a

---

[12] This is particularly likely to be the case if Monte Carlo simulation is the numerical procedure used by the financial institution to value a deal. Monte Carlo simulations within historical simulations lead to extremely time-consuming computations.

function of percentage changes in the market variables. Another (much slower) approach is to use Monte Carlo simulation.

The model-building approach is frequently used for investment portfolios. It is less popular for the trading portfolios of financial institutions because it does not work well when deltas are low.

FURTHER READING

Frye, J., "Principals of Risk: Finding VAR through Factor-Based Interest Rate Scenarios," in *VAR: Understanding and Applying Value at Risk*, pp. 275–288. London: Risk Publications, 1997.

Hull, J. C., and A. White, "Value at Risk When Daily Changes in Market Variables Are Not Normally Distributed," *Journal of Derivatives*, 5 (Spring 1998): 9–19.

Jamshidian, F., and Y. Zhu, "Scenario Simulation Model: Theory and Methodology," *Finance and Stochastics*, 1 (1997): 43–67.

Rich, D., "Second Generation VaR and Risk-Adjusted Return on Capital," *Journal of Derivatives*, 10, No. 4 (Summer 2003): 51–61.

QUESTIONS AND PROBLEMS (Answers at End of Book)

10.1. Consider a position consisting of a $100,000 investment in asset A and a $100,000 investment in asset B. Assume that the daily volatilities of both assets are 1% and that the coefficient of correlation between their returns is 0.3. What is the 5-day 99% VaR for the portfolio?

10.2. Describe three ways of handling interest-rate-dependent instruments when the model building approach is used to calculate VaR.

10.3. Explain how an interest rate swap is mapped into a portfolio of zero-coupon bonds with standard maturities for the purposes of a VaR calculation.

10.4. A financial institution owns a portfolio of options on the USD/GBP exchange rate. The delta of the portfolio is 56.0. The current exchange rate is 1.5000. Derive an approximate linear relationship between the change in the portfolio value and the percentage change in the exchange rate. If the daily volatility of the exchange rate is 0.7%, estimate the ten-day 99% VaR.

10.5. Suppose you know that the gamma of the portfolio in Problem 10.4 is 16.2. How does this change your estimate of the relationship between the change in the portfolio value and the percentage change in the exchange rate?

10.6. Suppose that the 5-year rate is 6%, the seven year rate is 7% (both expressed with annual compounding), the daily volatility of a 5-year zero-coupon bond is 0.5%, and the daily volatility of a 7-year zero-coupon bond is 0.58%. The correlation between daily returns on the two bonds is 0.6. Map a cash flow of $1,000 received at time 6.5 years into a position in a 5-year bond and a position in a 7-year bond. What cash flows in 5 and 7 years are equivalent to the 6.5-year cash flow?

10.7. Verify that the 0.3-year zero-coupon bond in the cash-flow-mapping example in Table 10.2 is mapped into a $37,397 position in a 3-month bond and a $11,793 position in a 6-month bond.

10.8. Suppose that the daily change in the value of a portfolio is, to a good approximation, linearly dependent on two factors, calculated from a principal components analysis. The delta of a portfolio with respect to the first factor is 6 and the delta with respect to the second factor is –4. The standard deviations of the factor are 20 and 8, respectively. What is the 5-day 90% VaR?

10.9. The text calculates a VaR estimate for the example in Table 4.11 assuming two factors. How does the estimate change if you assume (a) one factor and (b) three factors.

10.10. A bank has a portfolio of options on an asset. The delta of the options is –30 and the gamma is –5. Explain how these numbers can be interpreted. The asset price is 20 and its volatility is 1% per day. Using the quadratic model calculate the first three moments of the change in the portfolio value. Calculate a 1-day 99% VaR using (a) the first two moments and (b) the first three moments.

10.11. Suppose that in Problem 10.10 the vega of the portfolio is –2 per 1% change in the annual volatility. Derive a model relating the change in the portfolio value in 1 day to delta, gamma, and vega. Explain, without doing detailed calculations, how you would use the model to estimate a VaR.

10.12. Explain why the linear model can provide only approximate estimates of VaR for a portfolio containing options.

10.13. Some time ago a company entered into a forward contract to buy £1 million for $1.5 million. The contract now has 6 months to maturity. The daily volatility of a 6-month zero-coupon sterling bond (when its price is translated to dollars) is 0.06% and the daily volatility of a 6-month zero-coupon dollar bond is 0.05%. The correlation between returns from the two bonds is 0.8. The current exchange rate is 1.53. Calculate the standard deviation of the change in the dollar value of the forward contract in 1 day. What is the 10-day 99% VaR? Assume that the 6-month interest rate in both sterling and dollars is 5% per annum with continuous compounding.

ASSIGNMENT QUESTIONS

10.14. Consider a position consisting of a $300,000 investment in gold and a $500,000 investment in silver. Suppose that the daily volatilities of these two assets are 1.8% and 1.2% respectively, and that the coefficient of correlation between their returns is 0.6. What is the 10-day 97.5% VaR for the portfolio? By how much does diversification reduce the VaR?

10.15. Consider a portfolio of options on a single asset. Suppose that the delta of the portfolio is 12, the value of the asset is $10, and the daily volatility of the asset is 2%. Estimate the 1-day 95% VaR for the portfolio from the delta.

10.16. Suppose you know that the gamma of the portfolio in Problem 10.15 is −2.6. Derive a quadratic relationship between the change in the portfolio value and the percentage change in the underlying asset price in 1 day. (a) Calculate the first three moments of the change in the portfolio value. (b) Using the first two moments and assuming that the change in the portfolio is normally distributed, calculate the 1-day 95% VaR for the portfolio. (c) Use the third moment and the Cornish–Fisher expansion to revise your answer to (b).

10.17. A company has a long position in a 2-year bond and a 3-year bond as well as a short position in a 5-year bond. Each bond has a principal of $100 and pays a 5% coupon annually. Calculate the company's exposure to the 1-year, 2-year, 3-year, 4-year, and 5-year rates. Use the data in Tables 4.8 and 4.9 to calculate a 20-day 95% VaR on the assumption that rate changes are explained by (a) one factor, (b) two factors, and (c) three factors. Assume that the zero-coupon yield curve is flat at 5%.

10.18. A company has a position in bonds worth $6 million. The modified duration of the portfolio is 5.2 years. Assume that only parallel shifts in the yield curve can take place and that the standard deviation of the daily yield change (when yield is measured in percent) is 0.09. Use the duration model to estimate the 20-day 90% VaR for the portfolio. Explain carefully the weaknesses of this approach to calculating VaR. Explain two alternatives that give more accuracy.

10.19. A bank has written a call option on one stock and a put option on another stock. For the first option the stock price is 50, the strike price is 51, the volatility is 28% per annum, and the time to maturity is 9 months. For the second option the stock price is 20, the strike price is 19, the volatility is 25% per annum, and the time to maturity is 1 year. Neither stock pays a dividend, the risk-free rate is 6% per annum, and the correlation between stock price returns is 0.4. Calculate a 10-day 99% VaR (a) using only deltas, (b) using the partial simulation approach, and (c) using the full simulation approach.

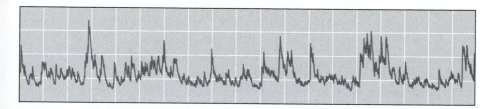

Credit Risk: Estimating Default Probabilities

This is the first of three chapters concerned with credit risk. Credit risk arises from the possibility that borrowers, bond issuers, and counter-parties in derivatives transactions may default. As explained in Chapter 7, regulators have for a long time required banks to keep capital for credit risk. In Basel II, banks can, with approval from bank supervisors, use their own estimates of default probabilities to determine the amount of capital they are required to keep. This has led banks to devote a lot of resources to developing better ways of estimating default probabilities.

In this chapter we discuss a number of different approaches to estimating default probabilities and explain the key difference between risk-neutral and real-world estimates. The material we cover will be used in both Chapters 12 and 13. In Chapter 12 we examine the nature of the credit risk in over-the-counter derivatives transactions and discuss the calculation of credit value at risk. In Chapter 13 we cover credit derivatives.

11.1 CREDIT RATINGS

Rating agencies such as Moody's and S&P are in the business of provid-ing ratings describing the creditworthiness of corporate bonds. Using the Moody's system, the best rating is Aaa. Bonds with this rating are considered to have almost no chance of defaulting. The next best rating is Aa. Following that comes A, Baa, Ba, B, and Caa. Only bonds with ratings of Baa or above are considered to be *investment grade*. The S&P ratings corresponding to Moody's Aaa, Aa, A, Baa, Ba, B, and Caa are AAA, AA, A, BBB, BB, B, and CCC, respectively. To create finer rating measures, Moody's divides the Aa rating category into Aa1, Aa2, and Aa3; it divides A into A1, A2 and A3; and so on. Similarly S&P divides its AA rating category into AA+, AA, and AA−; it divides its A rating category into A+, A, and A−; and so on. (Only the Aaa category for Moody's and the AAA category for S&P are not subdivided.)

A credit rating is designed to provide information about default probabilities. As such one might expect frequent changes in a company's credit rating as positive and negative information reaches the market.[1] In fact, ratings change relatively infrequently. When rating agencies assign ratings, one of their objectives is ratings stability. For example, they want to avoid ratings reversals where a company is downgraded and then upgraded a few weeks later. Ratings therefore change only when there is reason to believe that a long-term change in the company's credit-worthiness has taken place. The reason for this is that bond traders are major users of ratings. Often they are subject to rules governing what the credit ratings of the bonds they hold must be. If these ratings changed frequently they might have to do a large amount of trading (and incur high transactions costs) just to satisfy the rules.

A related point is that rating agencies try to "rate through the cycle". Suppose that the economy exhibits a downturn and this has the effect of increasing the probability of a company defaulting in the next six months, but makes very little difference to the company's cumulative probability of defaulting over the next three to five years. A rating agency would not change the company's credit rating.

Internal Credit Ratings

Most banks have procedures for rating the creditworthiness of their corporate and retail clients. This is a necessity. The ratings published by rating agencies are only available for relatively large corporate clients. Many small and medium-sized businesses do not issue publicly traded bonds and therefore are not rated by rating agencies. As explained in Chapter 7, the internal ratings based (IRB) approach in Basel II allows banks to use their internal ratings in determining the probability of

---

[1] In theory, a credit rating is an attribute of a bond issue, not a company. However, in most cases all bonds issued by a company have the same rating. A rating is therefore often referred to as an attribute of a company.

default, PD. Under the advanced IRB approach, they are also allowed to use their own internal procedures for estimating the loss given default, LGD, the exposure at default, EAD, and the maturity, M.

Internal ratings based approaches for PD typically involve profitability ratios, such as return on assets, and balance-sheet ratios, such as the current ratio and the debt-to-equity ratio. Banks recognize that it is cash rather than profits that is necessary to repay a loan. They typically take the financial information provided by a company and convert it to the type of cash-flow statement that allows them to estimate how easy it will be for a company to service its debt.

Altman's Z-Score

Edward Altman has pioneered the use of accounting ratios to predict default. In 1968 he developed what has become known as the Z-score.[2] Using a statistical technique known as discriminant analysis, he attempted to predict defaults from five accounting ratios:

X_1: Working capital/Total Assets

X_2: Retained earnings/Total assets

X_3: Earnings before interest and taxes/Total assets

X_4: Market value of equity/Book value of total liabilities

X_5: Sales/Total assets

The Z-score was calculated as

$$Z = 1.2X_1 + 1.4X_2 + 3.3X_3 + 0.6X_4 + 0.999X_5 \qquad (11.1)$$

If the Z-score is greater than 3.0, the company is unlikely to default. If it is between 2.7 and 3.0, we should be "on alert". If it is between 1.8 and 2.7, there is a good chance of default. If it is less than 1.8, the probability of a financial embarrassment is very high. The Z-score was calculated from a sample of 66 publicly traded manufacturing companies. Of these, 33 failed within one year and 33 did not fail. The model proved very accurate when tested on a sample of firms different from that used to obtain equation (11.1). Both Type I errors (companies that were predicted not to go bankrupt but did do so) and Type II errors (companies that were predicted to go bankrupt, but did not do so) were small.[3] Variations on the model

---

[2] See E. I. Altman, "Financial Ratios, Discriminant Analysis, and the Prediction of Corporate Bankruptcy," *Journal of Finance*, 23, No. 4 (September 1968), 589–609.

[3] Clearly Type I errors are much more costly to the lending department of a commercial bank than Type II errors.

have been developed for manufacturing companies that are not publicly traded and nonmanufacturing companies.

Example 11.1

Consider a company for which working capital is 170,000, total assets are 670,000, earnings before interest and taxes is 60,000, sales are 2,200,000, the market value of equity is 380,000, total liabilities is 240,000, and retained earnings is 300,000. In this case $X_1 = 0.254$, $X_2 = 0.448$, $X_3 = 0.0896$, $X_4 = 1.583$, and $X_5 = 3.284$. The Z-score is

$$1.2 \times 0.254 + 1.4 \times 0.448 + 3.3 \times 0.0896 + 0.6 \times 1.583 + 0.999 \times 3.284 = 5.46$$

The Z-score indicates that the company is not in danger of defaulting in the near future.

11.2 HISTORICAL DEFAULT PROBABILITIES

Table 11.1 is typical of the data that is produced by rating agencies. It shows the default experience through time of companies that started with a certain credit rating. For example, Table 11.1 shows that a bond issue with an initial credit rating of Baa has a 0.20% chance of defaulting by the end of the first year, a 0.57% chance of defaulting by the end of the second year, and so on. The probability of a bond defaulting during a particular year can be calculated from the table. For example, the probability that a bond initially rated Baa will default during the second year of its life is $0.57 - 0.20 = 0.37\%$.

Table 11.1 shows that, for investment-grade bonds, the probability of default in a year tends to be an increasing function of time. (For example,

Table 11.1   Average cumulative default rates (%), 1970–2003 (*Source*: Moody's).

Rating	Term (years)								
	1	2	3	4	5	7	10	15	20
Aaa	0.00	0.00	0.00	0.04	0.12	0.29	0.62	1.21	1.55
Aa	0.02	0.03	0.06	0.15	0.24	0.43	0.68	1.51	2.70
A	0.02	0.09	0.23	0.38	0.54	0.91	1.59	2.94	5.24
Baa	0.20	0.57	1.03	1.62	2.16	3.24	5.10	9.12	12.59
Ba	1.26	3.48	6.00	8.59	11.17	15.44	21.01	30.88	38.56
B	6.21	13.76	20.65	26.66	31.99	40.79	50.02	59.21	60.73
Caa	23.65	37.20	48.02	55.56	60.83	69.36	77.91	80.23	80.23

the probability of an A-rated bond defaulting during years 1, 2, 3, 4, and 5 are 0.02%, 0.07%, 0.14%, 0.15%, and 0.16%, respectively.) This is because the bond issuer is initially considered to be creditworthy, and the more time that elapses, the greater the possibility that its financial health will decline. For bonds with a poor credit rating, the probability of default is often a decreasing function of time. (For example, the probabilities that a Caa-rated bond will default during years 1, 2, 3, 4, and 5 are 23.65%, 13.55%, 10.82%, 7.54%, and 5.27%, respectively.) The reason here is that, for a bond with a poor credit rating, the next year or two may be critical. If the issuer survives this period, its financial health is likely to have improved.

Default Intensities

From Table 11.1 we can calculate the probability of a Caa bond defaulting during the third year as $48.02 - 37.20 = 10.82\%$. We will refer to this as the *unconditional default probability*. It is the probability of default during the third year as seen at time zero. The probability that the Caa-rated bond will survive until the end of year 2 is $100 - 37.20 = 62.80\%$. The probability that it will default during the third year, conditional on no earlier default, is therefore 0.1082/0.6280, or 17.23%.

The 17.23% we have just calculated is for a one-year time period. By considering the probability of default between times t and $t + \Delta t$ conditional on no earlier default, we obtain what is known as the *default intensity* or *hazard rate* at time t. The default intensity $\lambda(t)$ at time t is defined so that $\lambda(t)\,\Delta t$ is the probability of default between time t and $t + \Delta t$ conditional on no default between time 0 and time t. If $V(t)$ is the cumulative probability of the company surviving to time t (i.e., no default by time t), then

$$V(t + \Delta t) - V(t) = -\lambda(t)V(t)\,\Delta t$$

Taking limits, we obtain

$$\frac{dV(t)}{dt} = -\lambda(t)V(t)$$

from which we get

$$V(t) = e^{-\int_0^t \lambda(\tau)\,d\tau}$$

or

$$V(t) = e^{-\bar{\lambda}t}$$

where $\bar{\lambda}$ is the average default intensity between time zero and time t.

Define $Q(t)$ as the probability of default by time t. It follows that

$$Q(t) = 1 - V(t) = 1 - e^{-\int_0^t \lambda(\tau)\,d\tau}$$

or

$$Q(t) = 1 - e^{-\bar{\lambda}t} \tag{11.2}$$

11.3 RECOVERY RATES

When a company goes bankrupt, those that are owed money by the company file claims against the assets of the company.[4] Sometimes there is a reorganization in which these creditors agree to a partial payment of their claims. In other cases the assets are sold by the liquidator and the proceeds are used to meet the claims as far as possible. Some claims typically have priorities over other claims and are met more fully.

The *recovery rate* for a bond is normally defined as the bond's market value immediately after a default as a percent of its face value. It equals one minus the loss given default, LGD. Table 11.2 provides historical data on average recovery rates for different categories of bonds in the United States. It shows that senior secured debtholders had an average recovery rate of 57.4 cents per dollar of face value, while junior subordinated debtholders had an average recovery rate of only 28.9 cents per dollar of face value.

Recovery rates are significantly negatively correlated with default rates. Moody's looked at average recovery rates and average default rates each

Table 11.2 Recovery rates on corporate bonds as a percent of face value, 1982–2004. *Source*: Moody's.

Class	Average recovery rate (%)
Senior secured	57.4
Senior unsecured	44.9
Senior subordinated	39.1
Subordinated	32.0
Junior subordinated	28.9

[4] In the United States, the claim made by a bondholder is the bond's face value plus accrued interest.

year between 1983 and 2004. It found that the following relationship provides a good fit to the data:[5]

Average recovery rate $= 0.52 - 6.9 \times$ Average default rate

This relationship means that a bad year for the default rate is usually doubly bad because it is accompanied by a low recovery rate. For example, when the average default rate in a year is only 0.1%, we expect the recovery rate to be relatively high at 51.3%. When it is relatively high at 3%, we expect the recovery rate to be 31.3%.

11.4 ESTIMATING DEFAULT PROBABILITIES FROM BOND PRICES

The probability of default for a company can be estimated from the prices of bonds it has issued. The usual assumption is that the only reason a corporate bond sells for less than a similar risk-free bond is the possibility of default.[6]

Consider first an approximate calculation. Suppose that a bond yields 200 basis points more than a similar risk-free bond and that the expected recovery rate in the event of a default is 40%. The holder of a corporate bond must be expecting to lose 200 basis points (or 2% per year) from defaults. Given the recovery rate of 40%, this leads to an estimate of the probability of a default per year conditional on no earlier default of $0.02/(1 - 0.4)$, or 3.33%. In general,

$$h = \frac{s}{1 - R} \tag{11.3}$$

where h is the default intensity per year, s is the spread of the corporate bond yield over the risk-free rate, and R is the expected recovery rate.

---

[5] See D. T. Hamilton, P. Varma, S. Ou, and R. Cantor, "Default and Recovery Rates of Corporate Bond Issuers, 1920–2004," Moody's Investor's Services, January 2005. The R^2 of the regression is 0.65. The correlation is also identified and discussed in E. I. Altman, B. Brady, A. Resti, and A. Sironi, "The Link between Default and Recovery Rates: Implications for Credit Risk Models and Procyclicality," Working Paper, New York University, 2003.

[6] We discuss this point later. The assumption is not perfect. In practice, the price of a corporate bond is also affected by its liquidity. The lower the liquidity, the lower the price.

A More Exact Calculation

For a more exact calculation, suppose that the corporate bond we have been considering lasts for five years, provides a coupon of 6% per annum (paid semiannually), and yields 7% per annum (with continuous compounding). The yield on a similar default-free bond is 5% (with continuous compounding). The yields imply that the price of the corporate bond is 95.34 and the price of the default-free bond is 104.09. The expected loss from default over the five-year life of the bond is therefore 104.09 − 95.34, or $8.75. Suppose that the probability of default per year (assumed in this simple example to be the same each year) is Q. Table 11.3 calculates the expected loss from default in terms of Q on the assumption that defaults can happen at times 0.5, 1.5, 2.5, 3.5, and 4.5 years (immediately before coupon payment dates). Risk-free rates for all maturities are assumed to be 5% (with continuous compounding).

To illustrate the calculations, consider the 3.5-year row in Table 11.3. The expected value of the default-free bond at time 3.5 years (calculated using forward interest rates) is

$$3 + 3e^{-0.05 \times 0.5} + 3e^{-0.05 \times 1.0} + 103e^{-0.05 \times 1.5} = 104.34$$

Given the definition of recovery rates in the previous section, the amount recovered if there is a default is 40, so that the loss is 104.34 − 40, or $64.34. The present value of this loss is 54.01 and the expected loss is therefore $54.01Q$.

The total expected loss is $288.48Q$. Setting this equal to 8.75, we obtain a value for Q equal to 3.03%. The calculations we have given assume that

Table 11.3   Calculation of loss from default on a bond in terms of the default probabilities per year, Q. Notional principal = $100.

Time (years)	Default probability	Recovery amount ($)	Default-free value ($)	Loss ($)	Discount factor	PV of expected loss ($)
0.5	Q	40	106.73	66.73	0.9753	$65.08Q$
1.5	Q	40	105.97	65.97	0.9277	$61.20Q$
2.5	Q	40	105.17	65.17	0.8825	$57.52Q$
3.5	Q	40	104.34	64.34	0.8395	$54.01Q$
4.5	Q	40	103.46	63.46	0.7985	$50.67Q$
Total						$288.48Q$

the default probability is the same each year and that defaults take place once a year. We can extend the calculations to assume that defaults can take place more frequently. Furthermore, instead of assuming a constant unconditional probability of default, we can assume a constant default intensity or a particular pattern for the variation of default probabilities with time.

With several bonds we can estimate several parameters describing the term structure of default probabilities. Suppose, for example, we have bonds maturing in 3, 5, 7, and 10 years. We could use the first bond to estimate a default probability per year for the first three years, the second to estimate a default probability per year for years 4 and 5, the third to estimate a default probability for years 6 and 7, and the fourth to estimate a default probability for years 8, 9, and 10 (see Problems 11.11 and 11.17). The approach is analogous to the bootstrap procedure we discussed in Chapter 4 for calculating a zero-coupon yield curve.

The Risk-Free Rate

A key issue when bond prices are used to estimate default probabilities is the meaning of the terms "risk-free rate" and "risk-free bond". In equation (11.3) the spread s is the excess of the corporate bond yield over the yield on a similar risk-free bond. In Table 11.3 the default-free value of the bond must be calculated using risk-free rates. The benchmark risk-free rate that is usually used in quoting corporate bond yields is the yield on similar Treasury bonds (e.g., a bond trader might quote the yield on a particular corporate bond as being a spread of 250 basis points over Treasuries).

As discussed in Section 4.4, traders usually use LIBOR/swap rates as proxies for risk-free rates when valuing derivatives. Traders also use LIBOR/swap rates as risk-free rates when calculating default probabilities. For example, when they determine default probabilities from bond prices, the spread s in equation (11.3) is the spread of the bond yield over the LIBOR/swap rate. Also, the risk-free discount rates used in the calculations such as those in Table 11.3 are LIBOR/swap zero rates.

Credit default swaps (which will be discussed in Chapter 13) can be used to imply the risk-free rate assumed by traders. The rate used appears to be approximately equal to the LIBOR/swap rate minus 10 basis points on average.[7] This estimate is plausible. As explained in Section 4.4, the

---

[7] See J. Hull, M. Predescu, and A. White, "The Relationship between Credit Default Swap Spreads, Bond Yields, and Credit Rating Announcements," *Journal of Banking and Finance*, 28 (November 2004), 2789–2811.

credit risk in a swap rate is the credit risk from making a series of six-month loans to AA-rated counterparties and 10 basis points is a reasonable default risk premium for an AA-rated six-month instrument.

Asset Swaps

In practice, traders often use asset swap spreads as a way of extracting default probabilities from bond prices. This is because asset swap spreads provide a direct estimate of the spread of bond yields over the LIBOR/swap curve.

To explain how asset swaps work, consider the situation where an asset swap spread for a particular bond is quoted as 150 basis points. There are three possible situations:

1. The bond sells for its par value of 100. The swap then involves one side (Company A) paying the coupon on the bond and the other side (Company B) paying LIBOR plus 150 basis points.[8]
2. The bond sells below its par value, say, for 95. The swap is then structured so that, in addition to the coupons, Company A pays $5 per $100 of notional principal at the outset.
3. The underlying bond sells above par, say, for 108. The swap is then structured so that Company B makes a payment of $8 per $100 of principal at the outset. After that, Company A pays the bond's coupons and Company B pays LIBOR plus 150 basis points.

The effect of all this is that the present value of the asset swap spread is the amount by which the price of the corporate bond is exceeded by the price of a similar risk-free bond, where the risk-free rate is assumed to be given by the LIBOR/swap curve (see Problem 11.12). Consider again the example in Table 11.3 where the LIBOR/swap zero curve is flat at 5%. Suppose that instead of knowing the bond's price we know that the asset swap spread is 150 basis points. This means that the amount by which the value of the risk-free bond exceeds the value of the corporate bond is the present value of 150 basis points per year for five years. Assuming semiannual payments, this is $6.55 per $100 of principal.

The total loss in Table 11.3 would be set equal to $6.55 in this case. This means that the default probability per year, Q, would be 6.55/288.48, or 2.27%.

---

[8] Note that it is the promised coupons that are exchanged. The exchanges take place regardless of whether the bond defaults.

11.5 COMPARISON OF DEFAULT PROBABILITY ESTIMATES

The default probabilities estimated from historical data are much less than those derived from bond prices. Table 11.4 illustrates this.[9] It shows, for companies that start with a particular rating, the seven-year average annual default intensity calculated from (a) historical data and (b) bond prices.

The calculation of default intensities using historical data is based on equation (11.2) and Table 11.1. From equation (11.2), we have

$$\bar{\lambda}(t) = -\frac{1}{t}\ln[1 - Q(t)]$$

where $\bar{\lambda}(t)$ is the average default intensity (or hazard rate) by time t and $Q(t)$ is the cumulative probability of default by time t. The values of $Q(7)$ are taken directly from Table 11.1. Consider, for example, an A-rated company. The value of $Q(7)$ is 0.0091. The average seven-year default intensity is therefore

$$\bar{\lambda}(7) = -\tfrac{1}{7}\ln(0.9909) = 0.0013$$

or 0.13%.

The calculations using bond prices are based on equation (11.3) and bond yields published by Merrill Lynch. The results shown are averages between December 1996 and July 2004. The recovery rate is assumed to be 40% and, for the reasons discussed in the previous section, the risk-free interest rate is assumed to be the seven-year swap rate minus 10 basis points. For example, for A-rated bonds the average Merrill Lynch yield was

Table 11.4 Seven-year average default intensities (% per annum).

Rating	Historical default intensity	Default intensity from bonds	Ratio	Difference
Aaa	0.04	0.67	16.8	0.63
Aa	0.06	0.78	13.0	0.72
A	0.13	1.28	9.8	1.15
Baa	0.47	2.38	5.1	1.91
Ba	2.40	5.07	2.1	2.67
B	7.49	9.02	1.2	1.53
Caa	16.90	21.30	1.3	4.40

[9] Tables 11.4 and 11.5 are taken from J. Hull, M. Predescu, and A. White, "Bond Prices, Default Probabilities, and Risk Premiums," *Journal of Credit Risk*, 1, No. 2 (2004), 53–60.

Table 11.5   Expected excess return on bonds (basis points).

Rating	Bond yield spread over Treasuries	Spread of risk-free rate over Treasuries	Spread for historical defaults	Expected excess return
Aaa	83	43	2	38
Aa	90	43	4	43
A	120	43	8	69
Baa	186	43	28	115
Ba	347	43	144	160
B	585	43	449	93
Caa	1321	43	1014	264

6.274%. The average swap rate was 5.605%, so that the average risk free rate was 5.505%. This gives the average seven-year default probability as

$$\frac{0.06274 - 0.05505}{1 - 0.4} = 0.0128$$

or 1.28%.

Table 11.4 shows that the ratio of the default probability backed out of bond prices to the default probability calculated from historical data is high for investment-grade companies and tends to decline as the credit quality declines. By contrast, the difference between the two default probabilities tends to increase as credit quality declines.

Table 11.5 gives another way of looking at these results. It shows the excess return over the risk-free rate (still assumed to be the seven-year swap rate minus 10 basis points) earned by investors in bonds with different credit ratings. Consider again an A-rated bond. The average spread over Treasuries is 120 basis points. Of this, 43 basis points represent the average spread between seven-year Treasuries and our proxy for the risk-free rate. A spread of 8 basis points is necessary to cover expected defaults. (This equals the real-world probability of default from Table 11.4 times 1 minus the assumed recovery rate of 0.4.) This leaves an expected excess return (after expected defaults have been taken into account) of 69 basis points.

Tables 11.4 and 11.5 show that a large percentage difference between default probability estimates translates into a relatively small expected excess return on the bond. For Aaa-rated bonds the ratio of the two default probabilities is 16.8, but the expected excess return is only 38 basis points. The expected return tends to increase as credit quality declines.[10]

---

[10]   The results for B-rated bonds in Tables 11.4 and 11.5 run counter to the overall pattern.

Business Snapshot 11.1   Risk-Neutral Valuation

The single most important idea in the valuation of derivatives is risk-neutral valuation. It shows that we can value a derivative by

1. Assuming that all investors are risk neutral
2. Calculating expected cash flows
3. Discounting the cash flows at the risk-free rate

As a simple example of the application of risk-neutral valuation, suppose that the price of a non-dividend-paying stock is $30 and consider a derivative that pays off $100 in one year if the stock price is greater than $40 at that time. (This is known as a binary cash-or-nothing call option.) Suppose that the risk-free rate (continuously compounded) is 5%, the expected return on the stock (also continuously compounded) is 10%, and the stock price volatility is 30% per annum. In a risk-neutral world the expected growth of the stock price is 5%. It can be shown (with the usual Black–Scholes lognormal assumptions) that when the stock price has this growth rate the probability that the stock price will be greater than $40 in one year is 0.1730. The expected payoff from the derivatives is therefore $100 \times 0.1730 = \$17.30$. The value of the derivative is calculated by discounting this at 5%. It is $16.46.

The real-world (physical) probability of the stock price being greater than $40 in one year is calculated by assuming a growth rate of 10%. It is 0.2190. The expected payoff in the real world is therefore $21.90. The problem with using this expected cash flow is that we do not know the correct discount rate. The stock price has risk associated with it that is priced by the market (otherwise the expected return on the stock would not be 5% more than the risk-free rate). The derivative has the effect of "leveraging this risk", so that a very high discount rate is required for its expected payoff. Since we know the correct value of the derivative is $16.46, we can deduce that the correct discount rate to apply to the real-world expected payoff of $21.90 must be 28.6%.

Interestingly, the excess return on bonds varies through time. It increased steadily between 1997 and 2002 and then declined sharply in 2003 and 2004. For example, for the A-rated category the excess return ranged from 35 basis points in 1997 to 119 basis points in 2002.

Real-World vs. Risk-Neutral Probabilities

The risk-neutral valuation argument is explained in Business Snapshot 11.1. It shows that we can value cash flows on the assumption that all investors are risk neutral (i.e., on the assumption that they do not require a premium for bearing risks). When we do this, we get the right answer in the real world as well as in the risk-neutral world.

The default probabilities implied from bond yields are risk-neutral default probabilities (i.e., they are the probabilities of default in a world where all investors are risk neutral). To understand why this is so, consider the calculations of default probabilities in Table 11.3. These assume that expected default losses can be discounted at the risk-free rate. The risk-neutral valuation principle shows that this is a valid procedure provided the expected losses are calculated in a risk-neutral world. This means that the default probability Q in Table 11.3 must be a risk-neutral probability.

By contrast, the default probabilities implied from historical data are real-world default probabilities (sometimes also called *physical probabilities*). The expected excess return in Table 11.5 arises directly from the difference between real-world and risk-neutral default probabilities. If there was no expected excess return, the real-world and risk-neutral default probabilities would be the same, and vice versa.

Reasons for the Difference

Why do we see such big differences between real-world and risk-neutral default probabilities? As we have just argued, this is the same as asking why corporate bond traders earn more than the risk-free rate on average. There are a number of potential reasons:

1. Corporate bonds are relatively illiquid and bond traders demand an extra return to compensate for this. This may account for perhaps 25 basis points of the excess return. This is a significant part of the excess return for high-quality bonds, but a relatively small part for bonds rated Baa and below.

2. The subjective default probabilities of bond traders may be much higher than the those given in Table 11.1. Bond traders may be allowing for depression scenarios much worse than anything seen during the 1970 to 2003 period. To test this, we can look at a table produced by Moody's that is similar to Table 11.1, but applies to the 1920 to 2003 period instead of 1970 to 2003 period. When the analysis is based on this table, historical default intensities for investment-grade bonds in Table 11.4 rise somewhat. The Aaa default intensity increases from 4 to 6 basis points; the Aa increases from 6 to 22 basis points; the A increases from 13 to 29 basis points; the Baa increases from 47 to 73 basis points. However, non-investment-grade historical default intensities decline somewhat.

3. Bonds do not default independently of each other. This is the most important reason for the results in Tables 11.4 and 11.5. There are

periods of time when default rates are very low and periods of time when they are very high. (Evidence for this can be obtained by looking at the defaults rates in different years. Moody's statistics show that between 1970 and 2003 the default rate per year ranged from a low of 0.09% in 1979 to a high of 3.81% in 2001.) This gives rise to systematic risk (i.e., risk that cannot be diversified away) and bond traders should require an expected excess return for bearing the risk. The variation in default rates from year to year may be because of overall economic conditions or because a default by one company has a ripple effect resulting in defaults by other companies. (The latter is referred to by researchers as *credit contagion*.)

4. Bond returns are highly skewed with limited upside. As a result it is much more difficult to diversify risks in a bond portfolio than in an equity portfolio.[11] A very large number of different bonds must be held. In practice, many bond portfolios are far from fully diversified. As a result bond traders may require an extra return for bearing unsystematic risk as well as for bearing the systematic risk mentioned in 3 above.

Which Estimates Should Be Used?

At this stage it is natural to ask whether we should use real-world or risk-neutral default probabilities in the analysis of credit risk. The answer depends on the purpose of the analysis. When valuing credit derivatives or estimating the impact of default risk on the pricing of instruments, we should use risk-neutral default probabilities. This is because the analysis calculates the present value of expected future cash flows and almost invariably (implicitly or explicitly) involves using risk-neutral valuation. When carrying out scenario analyses to calculate potential future losses from defaults, we should use real-world default probabilities. The PD used to calculate regulatory capital is a real-world default probability.

11.6 USING EQUITY PRICES TO ESTIMATE DEFAULT PROBABILITIES

When we use a table such as Table 11.1 to estimate a company's real-world probability of default, we are relying on the company's credit

---

[11] See J. D. Amato and E. M. Remolona, "The Credit Spread Puzzle," *BIS Quarterly Review*, 5 (December 2003), 51–63.

rating. Unfortunately, credit ratings are revised relatively infrequently. This has led some analysts to argue that equity prices can provide more up-to-date information for estimating default probabilities.

In 1974, Merton proposed a model where a company's equity is an option on the assets of the company.[12] Suppose, for simplicity, that a firm has one zero-coupon bond outstanding and that the bond matures at time T. Define:

V_0: Value of company's assets today

V_T: Value of company's assets at time T

E_0: Value of company's equity today

E_T: Value of company's equity at time T

D: Amount of debt interest and principal due to be repaid at time T

σ_V: Volatility of assets (assumed constant)

σ_E: Instantaneous volatility of equity

If $V_T < D$, it is (at least in theory) rational for the company to default on the debt at time T. The value of the equity is then zero. If $V_T > D$, the company should make the debt repayment at time T and the value of the equity at this time is $V_T - D$. Merton's model, therefore, gives the value of the firm's equity at time T as

$$E_T = \max(V_T - D, 0)$$

This shows that the equity of a company is a call option on the value of the assets of the company with a strike price equal to the repayment required on the debt. The Black–Scholes formula (see Appendix C at the end of this book) gives the value of the equity today as

$$E_0 = V_0 N(d_1) - De^{-rT} N(d_2) \tag{11.4}$$

where

$$d_1 = \frac{\ln V_0/D + (r + \sigma_V^2/2)T}{\sigma_V\sqrt{T}} \quad \text{and} \quad d_2 = d_1 - \sigma_V\sqrt{T}$$

and N is the cumulative normal distribution function. The value of the debt today is $V_0 - E_0$.

The risk-neutral probability that the company will default on the debt is $N(-d_2)$. To calculate this, we require V_0 and σ_V. Neither of these are

---

[12] See R. Merton "On the Pricing of Corporate Debt: The Risk Structure of Interest Rates," *Journal of Finance*, 29 (1974), 449–470 .

directly observable. However, if the company is publicly traded, we can observe E_0. This means that equation (11.4) provides one condition that must be satisfied by V_0 and σ_V. We can also estimate σ_E. From a result in stochastic calculus known as Itô's lemma, we have

$$\sigma_E E_0 = \frac{\partial E}{\partial V} \sigma_V V_0$$

or

$$\sigma_E E_0 = N(d_1)\sigma_V V_0 \qquad (11.5)$$

This provides another equation that must be satisfied by V_0 and σ_V. Equations (11.4) and (11.5) provide a pair of simultaneous equations that can be solved for V_0 and σ_V.[13]

Example 11.2

The value of a company's equity is \$3 million and the volatility of the equity is 80%. The debt that will have to be paid in one year is \$10 million. The risk-free rate is 5% per annum. In this case, $E_0 = 3$, $\sigma_E = 0.80$, $r = 0.05$, $T = 1$, and $D = 10$. Solving equations (11.4) and (11.5) yields $V_0 = 12.40$ and $\sigma_V = 0.2123$. The parameter d_2 is 1.1408, so that the probability of default is $N(-d_2) = 0.127$, or 12.7%. The market value of the debt is $V_0 - E_0$, or 9.40. The present value of the promised payment on the debt is $10e^{-0.05 \times 1} = 9.51$. The expected loss on the debt is therefore $(9.51 - 9.40)/9.51$, or about 1.2% of its no-default value. Comparing this with the probability of default gives the expected recovery in the event of a default as $(12.7 - 1.2)/12.7$, or about 91%.

Distance to Default

Moody's KMV has coined the term *distance to default* to describe the output from Merton's model. This is the number of standard deviations by which the asset price must change for default to be triggered T years in the future. It is given by

$$\frac{\ln V_0 - \ln D + (r - \sigma_V^2/2)T}{\sigma_V \sqrt{T}}$$

As the distance to default decreases, the company becomes more likely to default. In Example 11.2 the one-year distance to default is 1.14 standard deviations.

---

[13] To solve two nonlinear equations of the form $F(x, y) = 0$ and $G(x, y) = 0$, we can use the Solver routine in Excel to find the values of x and y that minimize $[F(x, y)]^2 + [G(x, y)]^2$.

Extensions of the Basic Model

The basic Merton model we have just presented has been extended in a number of ways. For example, one version of the model assumes that a default occurs whenever the value of the assets falls below a barrier level. Another allows payments on debt instruments to be required at more than one time. Many analysts have found the implied volatility of equity issued by a company to be a good predictor of the probability of default. (The higher the implied volatility, the higher the probability of default.) Hull *et al.* show that this is consistent with Merton's model.[14] They provide a way of implementing Merton's model using two equity implied volatilities and show that the resulting model provides results comparable to those provided by the usual implementation of the model.

Performance of the Model

How well do the default probabilities produced by Merton's model and its extensions correspond to actual default experience? The answer is that Merton's model and its extensions produce a good ranking of default probabilities (risk neutral or real world). This means that a monotonic transformation can be estimated to convert the probability of default output from Merton's model into a good estimate of either the real-world or risk-neutral default probability.[15] It may seem strange to use a default probability, $N(-d_2)$, that is in theory a risk-neutral default probability to estimate a real-world default probability. Given the nature of the calibration process we have just described, the underlying assumption is that the ranking of risk-neutral default probabilities of different companies is the same as that of their real-world default probabilities.

SUMMARY

The probability that a company will default during a particular period of time in the future can be estimated from historical data, bond prices, or equity prices. The default probabilities calculated from bond prices are risk-neutral probabilities, whereas those calculated from historical data

---

[14] See J. Hull, I. Nelken, and A. White, "Merton's Model, Credit Risk, and Volatility Skews," *Journal of Credit Risk*, 1, No. 1 (2004), 1–27.

[15] Moody's KMV provides a service that transforms a default probability produced by Merton's model into a real-world default probability (which it refers to as an EDF, short for expected default frequency). CreditGrades uses Merton's model to estimate credit spreads, which are closely linked to risk-neutral default probabilities.

are real-world probabilities. The default probabilities calculated from equity prices using Merton's model are in theory risk-neutral default probabilities. However, the output from the model can be calibrated so that either risk-neutral or real-world default probabilities are produced.

Real-world probabilities should be used for scenario analysis and the calculation of credit VaR. Risk-neutral probabilities should be used for valuing credit-sensitive instruments. Risk-neutral default probabilities are usually significantly higher than real-world probabilities.

FURTHER READING

Altman, E. I., "Measuring Corporate Bond Mortality and Performance," *Journal of Finance*, 44 (1989): 902–922.

Duffie, D., and K. Singleton, "Modeling Term Structures of Defaultable Bonds," *Review of Financial Studies*, 12 (1999): 687–720.

Hull, J., M. Predescu, and A. White, "Relationship between Credit Default Swap Spreads, Bond Yields, and Credit Rating Announcements," *Journal of Banking and Finance*, 28 (November 2004): 2789–2811.

Hull, J., M. Predescu, and A. White, "Bond Prices, Default Probabilities, and Risk Premiums," *Journal of Credit Risk*, 1, No. 2 (2004): 53–60.

Kealhofer, S., "Quantifying Default Risk I: Default Prediction," *Financial Analysts Journal*, 59, No. 1 (2003): 30–44.

Kealhofer, S., "Quantifying Default Risk II: Debt Valuation," *Financial Analysts Journal*, 59, No. 3 (2003), 78–92.

Litterman, R., and T. Iben, "Corporate Bond Valuation and the Term Structure of Credit Spreads," *Journal of Portfolio Management*, Spring 1991: 52–64.

Merton, R. C., "On the Pricing of Corporate Debt: The Risk Structure of Interest Rates," *Journal of Finance*, 29 (1974): 449–470.

Rodriguez, R. J., "Default Risk, Yield Spreads, and Time to Maturity," *Journal of Financial and Quantitative Analysis*, 23 (1988): 111–117.

QUESTIONS AND PROBLEMS (Answers at End of Book)

11.1. How many ratings does Moody's use for companies that have not defaulted? What are they?

11.2. How many ratings does S&P use for companies that have not defaulted? What are they?

11.3. Calculate the average default intensity for B-rated companies during the first year from the data in Table 11.1.

11.4. Calculate the average default intensity for Ba-rated companies during the third year from the data in Table 11.1.

11.5. The spread between the yield on a 3-year corporate bond and the yield on a similar risk-free bond is 50 basis points. The recovery rate is 30%. Estimate the average default intensity per year over the 3-year period.

11.6. The spread between the yield on a 5-year bond issued by a company and the yield on a similar risk-free bond is 80 basis points. Assume a recovery rate of 40%. Estimate the average default intensity per year over the 5-year period. If the spread is 70 basis points for a 3-year bond, what do your results indicate about the average default intensity in years 4 and 5?

11.7. Should researchers use real-world or risk-neutral default probabilities for (a) calculating credit value at risk and (b) adjusting the price of a derivative for defaults?

11.8. How are recovery rates usually defined?

11.9. Verify (a) that the numbers in the second column of Table 11.4 are consistent with the numbers in Table 11.1 and (b) that the numbers in the fourth column of Table 11.5 are consistent with the numbers in Table 11.4 and a recovery rate of 40%.

11.10. A 4-year corporate bond provides a coupon of 4% per year payable semiannually and has a yield of 5% expressed with continuous compounding. The risk-free yield curve is flat at 3% with continuous compounding. Assume that defaults can take place at the end of each year (immediately before a coupon or principal payment) and the recovery rate is 30%. Estimate the risk-neutral default probability on the assumption that it is the same each year.

11.11. A company has issued 3- and 5-year bonds with a coupon of 4% per annum payable annually. The yields on the bonds (expressed with continuous compounding) are 4.5% and 4.75%, respectively. Risk-free rates are 3.5% with continuous compounding for all maturities. The recovery rate is 40%. Defaults can take place halfway through each year. The risk-neutral default rates per year are Q_1 for years 1 to 3 and Q_2 for years 4 and 5. Estimate Q_1 and Q_2.

11.12. Suppose that in an asset swap B is the market price of the bond per dollar of principal, B^* is the default-free value of the bond per dollar of principal, and V is the present value of the asset swap spread per dollar of principal. Show that $V = B^* - B$.

11.13. Show that under Merton's model in Section 11.6 the credit spread on a T-year zero-coupon bond is
$$- \ln[N(d_2) + N(-d_1)/L]/T$$
where $L = De^{-rT}/V_0$.

11.14. The value of a company's equity is $2 million and the volatility of its equity is 50%. The debt that will have to be repaid in one year is $5 million. The risk-free interest rate is 4% per annum. Use Merton's model to estimate the probability of default. (*Hint*: The Solver function in Excel can be used for this question.)

11.15. Suppose that the LIBOR/swap curve is flat at 6% with continuous compounding and a 5-year bond with a coupon of 5% (paid semiannually) sells for 90.00. How would an asset swap on the bond be structured? What is the asset swap spread that would be calculated in this situation?

ASSIGNMENT QUESTIONS

11.16. Suppose a 3-year corporate bond provides a coupon of 7% per year payable semiannually and has a yield of 5% (expressed with semiannual compounding). The yields for all maturities on risk-free bonds is 4% per annum (expressed with semiannual compounding). Assume that defaults can take place every 6 months (immediately before a coupon payment) and the recovery rate is 45%. Estimate the default probabilities, assuming (a) that the unconditional default probabilities are the same on each possible default date and (b) that the default probabilities conditional on no earlier default are the same on each possible default date.

11.17. A company has 1- and 2-year bonds outstanding, each providing a coupon of 8% per year payable annually. The yields on the bonds (expressed with continuous compounding) are 6.0% and 6.6%, respectively. Risk-free rates are 4.5% for all maturities. The recovery rate is 35%. Defaults can take place halfway through each year. Estimate the risk-neutral default rate each year.

11.18. The value of a company's equity is $4 million and the volatility of its equity is 60%. The debt that will have to be repaid in 2 years is $15 million. The risk-free interest rate is 6% per annum. Use Merton's model to estimate the expected loss from default, the probability of default, and the recovery rate in the event of default. Explain why Merton's model gives a high recovery rate. (*Hint*: The Solver function in Excel can be used for this question.)

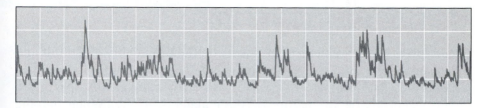

CHAPTER **12**

Credit Risk Losses and Credit VaR

This chapter starts by discussing the nature of the credit risk in derivatives transactions. It shows how expected credit losses can be calculated and looks at the various ways in which a financial institution can structure its contracts so as to reduce these expected credit losses.

The last part of the chapter covers the calculation of credit VaR. The 1986 amendment to Basel I allows banks to develop their own models for calculating VaR for market risk in the trading book. However, Basel II does not give banks quite the same freedom to calculate credit VaR for the banking book. The development of internal models for calculating credit VaR is nevertheless an important activity for banks. These models can be used to determine regulatory capital for credit risk in the trading book (the specific risk capital charge). They can also be used when economic capital is calculated, as we will explain in Chapter 16.

Chapter 11 covered the important difference between real-world and risk-neutral default probabilities (see Section 11.5). Real-world default probabilities can be estimated from historical data. Risk-neutral default probabilities can be estimated from bond prices. In the first part of this chapter, when calculating expected credit losses, we will use risk-neutral default probabilities. This is because we are calculating the present value of future cash flows. Later in the chapter, when calculating credit VaR, we will use real-world default probabilities. This is because we are looking at future scenarios and not calculating present values.

12.1 ESTIMATING CREDIT LOSSES

Credit losses on a loan depend primarily on the probability of default and the recovery rate. We covered estimates of the probability of default in Chapter 11. The estimate of recovery rate (or equivalently loss given default) depends on the nature of the collateral, if any. When making estimates, a financial institution is likely to use a mixture of its own experience and statistics published by rating agencies such as those in Table 11.2.

Derivatives Transactions

The credit exposure on a derivatives transaction is more complicated than that on a loan. This is because the claim that will be made in the event of a default is more uncertain than in the case of a loan. Consider a financial institution that has one derivatives contract outstanding with a counterparty. We can distinguish three possible situations:

1. The contract is always a liability to the financial institution.
2. The contract is always an asset to the financial institution.
3. The contract can become either an asset or a liability to the financial institution.

An example of a derivatives contract in the first category is a short option position; an example in the second category is a long option position; an example in the third category is a forward contract or a swap.

Derivatives in the first category have no credit risk to the financial institution. If the counterparty goes bankrupt, there will be no loss. The derivative is one of the counterparty's assets. It is likely to be retained, closed out, or sold to a third party. The result is no loss (or gain) to the financial institution.

Derivatives in the second category always have credit risk to the financial institution. If the counterparty goes bankrupt, a loss is likely to be experienced. The derivative is one of the counterparty's liabilities. The financial institution has to make a claim against the assets of the counterparty and may eventually realize some percentage of the value of the derivative.[1]

Derivatives in the third category may or may not have credit risk. If the counterparty defaults when the value of the derivative is positive to

---

[1] Counterparties to derivatives transactions usually rank equally with unsecured creditors in the event of a liquidation.

the financial institution, then a claim will be made against the assets of the counterparty and a loss is likely to be experienced. If the counterparty defaults when the value is negative to the financial institution, no loss is made because the derivative will be retained, closed out, or sold to a third party.[2]

Adjusting Derivatives Valuations for Counterparty Default Risk

How should a financial institution (or end-user of derivatives) adjust the value of a derivative to allow for counterparty credit risk? Consider a derivative that has a value of f_0 today assuming no defaults. Let us suppose that defaults can take place at times $t_1, t_2, \ldots, t_n$ and that the value of the derivative to the financial institution (assuming no defaults) at time t_i is f_i. Define the risk-neutral probability of default at time t_i as q_i and the expected recovery rate as R.[3]

The exposure at time t_i is the financial institution's potential loss. This is $\max(f_i, 0)$ as illustrated in Figure 12.1. Assume that the expected recovery in the event of a default is R times the exposure. Assume also that the recovery rate and the probability of default are independent of the value of the derivative. The risk-neutral expected loss from default at time t_i is

$$q_i(1 - R)\hat{E}[\max(f_i, 0)]$$

where $\hat{E}$ denotes expected value in a risk-neutral world. Taking present values leads to the cost of defaults being

$$\sum_{i=1}^{n} u_i v_i \tag{12.1}$$

where u_i equals $q_i(1 - R)$ and v_i is the value today of an instrument that pays off the exposure on the derivative under consideration at time t_i.

Consider again the three categories of derivatives mentioned earlier. The first category (where the derivative is always a liability to the financial institution) is easy to deal with. The value of f_i is always negative, and so the total expected loss from defaults given by equation (12.1) is always zero. The financial institution needs to make no adjustments for the cost

---

[2] A company usually defaults because of the total amount of its liabilities, not because of the value of any one transaction. At the time a company defaults it is likely that some of its contracts will have positive values.

[3] This probability of default can be calculated from bond prices in the way described in Section 11.4.

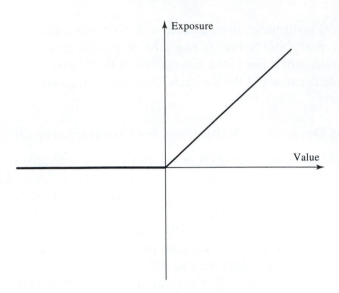

Figure 12.1   Exposure on a derivative as a function of
its no-default value.

of defaults. (Of course, the counterparty may want to take account of the
possibility of the financial institution defaulting in its own analysis.)

For the second category (where the derivative is always an asset to the
financial institution), the value of f_i is always positive. The expression
$\max(f_i, 0)$ is always equal to f_i. Since v_i is the present value of f_i, it
always equals f_0.[4] The expected loss from default is therefore f_0 times the
total probability of default during the life of the derivative times $1 - R$.

Example 12.1

Consider a two-year over-the-counter option with a value (assuming no
defaults) of \$3. Suppose that the company selling the option has a risk-
neutral probability of defaulting during the two-year period of 4% and the
recovery in the event of a default is 25%. The expected cost of defaults is
$3 \times 0.04 \times (1 - 0.25)$, or \$0.09. The buyer of the option should therefore be
prepared to pay only \$2.91.

For the third category of derivatives, the sign of f_i is uncertain. The
variable v_i is a call option on f_i with a strike price of zero. One way of
calculating all the v_i with a single analysis is to simulate the underlying
market variables over the life of the derivative. Sometimes approximate
analytic calculations are possible (see Problems 12.7, 12.8, and 12.14).

---

[4] This assumes no payoffs from the derivative prior to time t_i. The analysis can be
adjusted to cope with situations where there are intermediate payoffs.

Example 12.2

Consider an interest rate swap where a bank is receiving fixed and paying floating. The exposure on the swap at a particular future time t_i is

$$\max[V(t_i), 0]$$

where $V(t_i)$ is the value of the swap at time t_i. This is the payoff from a swap option. The variable v_i is therefore the value today of a type of European swap option exercisable at time t_i.

The analyses we have presented assume that the probability of default is independent of the value of the derivative. This is likely to be a reasonable approximation in circumstances when the derivative is a small part of the portfolio of the counterparty or when the counterparty is using the derivative for hedging purposes. When a counterparty wants to enter into a large derivatives transaction for speculative purposes, a financial institution should be wary. When the transaction has a large negative value for the counterparty (and a large positive value for the financial institution), the probability of the counterparty declaring bankruptcy may be much higher than when the situation is the other way round.

Interest Rate Swaps vs. Currency Swaps

The impact of default risk on interest rate swaps is considerably less than that on currency swaps. Figure 12.2 shows the reason for this. It compares the expected exposure for a bank on a pair of offsetting interest rate swaps

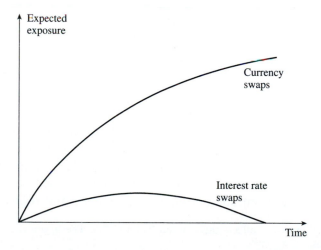

Figure 12.2 Expected exposure on a matched pair of interest rate swaps and a matched pair of currency swaps.

with different counterparties to the expected exposure on a pair of offsetting currency swaps with different counterparties. The expected exposure on the interest rate swaps starts at zero, increases, and then decreases to zero. By contrast, expected exposure on a the currency swaps increases steadily with the passage of time.[5] The reason for the difference is largely that principals are exchanged at the end of the life of a currency swap and there is uncertainty about the exchange rate at that time.[6]

Two-Sided Default Risk

One of the interesting aspects of contracts in the third category (i.e., contracts that can become assets or liabilities) is that there is two-sided default risk. For example, if Company X enters into a currency swap with Company Y, Company X may lose money if Company Y defaults and vice versa. Human nature being what it is, most financial and nonfinancial companies consider that there is no chance that they themselves will default but want to make an adjustment to contract terms for a possible default by their counterparty. In our example, Company X wants to be compensated for the possibility that Company Y will default and Company Y wants to be compensated for the possibility that Company X will default. This can make it very difficult for the two companies to agree on terms and explains why it is difficult for financial institutions that are not highly creditworthy to be active in the derivatives market.

In theory, the value of the currency swap to Company X should be

$$f - y + x$$

where f is the value if both sides were default-free, y is the adjustment necessary for the possibility of Company Y defaulting, and x is the adjustment necessary for Company X itself defaulting. Similarly, the value to Company Y should be

$$-f - x + y$$

In practice, Company X is likely to calculate a value of $f - y$ and Company Y is likely to calculate a value of $-f - x$. Unless x and y are small, it is unlikely that the companies will be able to agree on a price.

Continuing with our currency swap example, suppose that interest rates in the foreign and domestic currency are the same and that Company X

---

[5] The expected exposure affects the v_i in equation (12.1). The u_i are the same for both types of swaps.

[6] Currency swaps with no final exchange of principal have become more common in recent years. These have less credit risk and market risk than traditional currency swaps.

and Company Y are equally creditworthy. The swap is symmetrical in the sense that it has just as much chance of moving in the money for Company X as for Company Y. In this case, $x = y$ and neither side should in theory make any adjustment for credit risk.

12.2 CREDIT RISK MITIGATION

In many cases the analysis we have just presented overstates the credit risk in a derivatives transaction. This is because there are a number of clauses that derivatives dealers include in their contracts to mitigate credit risk.

Netting

We discussed netting in Section 7.5. A netting clause in a derivatives contract states that if a company defaults on one contract it has with a counterparty then it must default on all outstanding contracts with the counterparty. Netting has been successfully tested in the courts in most jurisdictions and can substantially reduce credit risk for a financial institution. We can extend the analysis presented in the previous section so that equation (12.1) gives the present value of the expected loss from all contracts with a counterparty when netting agreements are in place. This is achieved by redefining v_i in the equation as the present value of a derivative that pays off the exposure at time t_i on the portfolio of all contracts with a counterparty.

A challenging task for a financial institution when considering whether it should enter into a new derivatives contract with a counterparty is to calculate the incremental effect on expected credit losses. This can be done by using equation (12.1) in the way just described to calculate expected default costs with and without the contract. It is interesting to note that, because of netting, the incremental effect of a new contract on expected default losses can be negative. This tends to happen when the value of the new contract is highly negatively correlated with the value of existing contracts.

It might be thought that in well-functioning capital markets a company wanting to enter into a derivatives transaction will get the same quote from all dealers. Netting shows that this is not necessarily the case. The company is likely to get the most favorable quote from a financial institution it has done business with in the past—particularly if that business gives rise to exposures for the financial institution that are opposite to the exposure generated by the new transaction.

Collateralization

Another clause frequently used to mitigate credit risks is known as *collateralization*. Suppose that a company and a financial institution have entered into a number of derivatives contracts. A typical collateralization agreement specifies that the contracts be marked to market periodically using a pre-agreed formula. If the total value of the contracts to the financial institution is above a certain threshold level on a certain day, it can ask the company to post collateral. The amount of collateral posted, when added to collateral already posted, by the company is equal to the difference between the value of the contracts to the financial institution and the threshold level. When the contracts move in favor of the company, so that the difference between value of the contracts to the financial institution and the threshold level is less than the total margin already posted, the company can reclaim margin. In the event of a default by the company, the financial institution can seize the collateral. If the company does not post collateral as required, the financial institution can close out the contracts. Long-Term Capital Management made extensive use of collateralization agreements (see Business Snapshot 12.1).

Suppose, for example, that the threshold level for the company is $10 million and contract is marked to market daily for the purposes of collateralization. If on a particular day the value of the contract to the financial institution is $10.5 million, it can ask for $0.5 million of collateral. If on the next day the value of the contract rises to $11.4 million, it can ask for a further $0.9 million of collateral. If the value of the contract falls to $10.8 million on the following day, the company can ask for $0.6 million of the collateral to be returned. Note that the threshold ($10 million in this case) can be regarded as a line of credit that the financial institution is prepared to grant to the company.

Collateral must be deposited by the company with the financial institution in cash or in the form of acceptable securities such as bonds. Interest is normally paid on cash. The securities are subject to a discount known as a *haircut* applied to their market value for the purposes of collateral calculations.

If the collateralization agreement is a two-way agreement, a threshold will also be specified for the financial institution. The company can then ask the financial institution to post collateral when the marked-to-market value of the outstanding contracts to the company exceeds the threshold.

Collateralization agreements provide a great deal of protection against the possibility of default (just as the margin accounts discussed in

---

Business Snapshot 12.1   Long-Term Capital Management's Big Loss

Long-Term Capital Management (LTCM), a hedge fund formed in the mid-1990s, always collateralized its transactions. The hedge fund's investment strategy was known as convergence arbitrage. A very simple example of what it might do is the following. It would find two bonds, X and Y, issued by the same company, promising the same payoffs, with X being less liquid (i.e., less actively traded) than Y. The market always places a value on liquidity. As a result, the price of X would be less than the price of Y. LTCM would buy X and short Y, and wait, expecting the prices of the two bonds to converge at some future time.

When interest rates increased, the company expected both bonds to move down in price by about the same amount, so that the collateral it paid on bond X would be about the same as that which it received on bond Y. Similarly, when interest rates decreased, LTCM expected both bonds to move up in price by about the same amount, so that the collateral it received on bond X would be about the same as that which it paid on bond Y. It therefore expected no significant outflow of funds as a result of its collateralization agreements.

In August 1998, Russia defaulted on its debt and this led to what is termed a "flight to quality" in capital markets. One result was that investors valued liquid instruments more highly than usual and the spreads between the prices of the liquid and illiquid instruments in LTCM's portfolio increased dramatically. The prices of the bonds LTCM had bought went down and the prices of those it had shorted increased. It was required to post collateral on both. The company was highly leveraged and unable to make the payments required under the collateralization agreements. The result was that positions had to be closed out and there was a total loss of about $4 billion. If the company had been less highly leveraged, it would probably have been able to survive the flight to quality and could have waited for the prices of the liquid and illiquid bonds to become closer.

Chapter 2 provide protection for people who trade on an exchange). However, the threshold amount is not subject to protection. Furthermore, even when the threshold is zero, the protection is not total. When a company gets into financial difficulties it is likely to stop responding to requests to post collateral. By the time the counterparty exercises its right to close out contracts, their value may have moved further in its favor.

Downgrade Triggers

Another credit mitigation technique used by a financial institution is known as a *downgrade trigger*. This is a clause stating that if the credit

---

Business Snapshot 12.2   Downgrade Triggers and Enron's Bankruptcy

In December 2001, Enron, one of the largest companies in the United States, went bankrupt. Right up to the last few days, it had an investment-grade credit rating. The Moody's rating immediately prior to default was Baa3 and the S&P rating was BBB–. The default was, however, anticipated to some extent by the stock market because Enron's stock price fell sharply in the period leading up to the bankruptcy. The probability of default estimated by models such as the one described in Section 11.6 increased sharply during this period.

Enron had entered into a huge number of derivatives contracts with downgrade triggers. The downgrade triggers stated that, if its credit rating fell below investment grade (i.e., below Baa3/BBB–), its counterparties would have the option of closing out contracts. Suppose that Enron had been downgraded to below investment grade in, say, October 2001. The contracts that counterparties would choose to close out would be those with a negative values to Enron (and positive values to the counterparties). As a result Enron would have been required to make huge cash payments to its counterparties. It would not have been able to do this and immediate bankruptcy would result.

This example illustrates that downgrade triggers provide protection only when relatively little use is made of them. When a company enters into a huge number of contracts with downgrade triggers, they may actual cause a company to go bankrupt prematurely. In Enron's case we could argue that it was going to go bankrupt anyway and accelerating the event by two months would not have done any harm. In fact, Enron did have a chance of survival in October 2001. Attempts were being made to work out a deal with another energy company, Dynergy, and so forcing bankruptcy in October 2001 was not in the interests of either creditors or shareholders.

The credit rating companies found themselves in a difficult position. If they downgraded Enron to recognize its deteriorating financial position, they were signing its death warrant. If they did not do so, there was a chance of Enron surviving.

---

rating of the counterparty falls below a certain level, say Baa, then the financial institution has the option to close out a derivatives contract at its market value. (A procedure for determining the value of the contract must be agreed to in advance.)

Downgrade triggers do not provide protection from a big jump in a company's credit rating (e.g., from A to default). Also, downgrade triggers work well only when relatively little use is made of them. If a company has entered into downgrade triggers with many counterparties, they are liable to provide relatively little protection to the counterparties (see Business Snapshot 12.2).

12.3 CREDIT VaR

Credit value at risk can be defined in the same way as we defined market value at risk in Chapter 8. For example, a credit VaR with a confidence level of 99.9% and a one-year time horizon is the credit loss that we are 99.9% confident will not be exceeded over one year. Whereas the time horizon for market risk is usually between one day and one month that for credit risk is usually much longer—often one year.

For regulatory purposes banks using the internal ratings based approach must calculate credit VaR for items in the banking book using the methodology prescribed by the Basel Committee. Banks are given freedom in making their own estimates of probability of default, PD.[7] However, they must use the correlation model and correlation parameters specified by the Basel Committee.

When calculating credit VaR for specific risk, banks have more freedom. Specific risk is the risk in the trading book that is related to the credit quality of individual companies. Although standard rules for determining specific risk have been specified, banks can, with regulatory approval, use their own models. For a model to be approved, the bank supervisor must be satisfied that concentration risk, spread risk, downgrade risk, and default risk are appropriately captured. The capital charge for specific risk is the product of a multiplier and the ten-day 99% VaR, with the minimum level for the multiplier being 4.

12.4 VASICEK'S MODEL

Vasicek's model, which we discussed in Sections 6.5 and 7.8, provides an easy way to estimate credit VaR for a loan portfolio. From equation (6.12), there is a probability X that the percentage of defaults on a large portfolio by time T is, in a one-factor Gaussian copula model, less than

$$V(T, X) = N\left(\frac{N^{-1}[Q(T)] + \sqrt{\rho}\,N^{-1}(X)}{\sqrt{1 - \rho}}\right)$$

where $Q(T)$ is the cumulative probability of each loan defaulting by time T and ρ is the copula correlation. When multiplied by the average exposure per loan and by the average loss given default, this gives the T-year VaR for

[7] As mentioned earlier, the probability of default in credit VaR calculations should be a real-world probability of default, not a risk-neutral probability of default.

an $X\%$ confidence level. As explained in Chapter 7, the Basel Committee has based the capital it requires for credit risk in the banking book on this model. The time horizon T is one year, the confidence level X is 99.9%, and the value of ρ is determined by the Basel Committee. As we saw in Chapter 7, in some cases ρ depends on the one-year probability of default.

12.5 CREDIT RISK PLUS

In 1998 Credit Suisse Financial Products proposed a methodology for calculating VaR that it termed Credit Risk Plus.[8] It utilizes ideas that are well established in the insurance industry. We will present a simplified version of the approach.

Suppose that a financial institution has N counterparties of a certain type and the probability of default by each counterparty in time T is p. The expected number of defaults, μ, for the whole portfolio is given by $\mu = Np$. Assuming that default events are independent and that p is small, the probability of n defaults is given by the Poisson distribution as

$$\frac{e^{-\mu}\mu^n}{n!}$$

This can be combined with a probability distribution for the losses experienced on a single counterparty default (taking account of the impact of netting) to obtain a probability distribution for the total default losses from the counterparties. To estimate the probability distribution for losses from a single counterparty default, we can look at the current probability distribution of our exposures to counterparties and adjust this according to historical recovery rates.

In practice, it is likely to be necessary for the financial institution to consider several categories of counterparties. This means that the analysis just described must be done for each category and the results combined.

Another complication is that default rates vary significantly from year to year. Data provided by Moody's show that the default rate per year for all bonds during the 1970 to 1999 period ranged from 0.09% in 1979 to 3.52% in 2001. To account for this, we can assume a probability distribution for the overall default rate based on historical data such as that provided by

---

[8] See Credit Suisse Financial Products, "Credit Risk Management Framework," October, 1997.

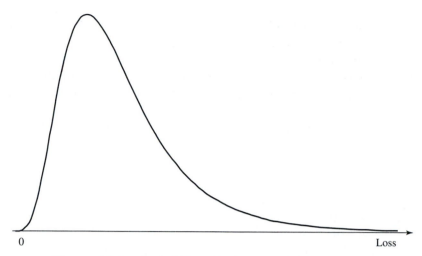

Figure 12.3 Probability distribution of default losses.

Moody's. The probability of default for each category of counterparty can then be assumed to be linearly dependent on the overall default rate.

Credit Suisse Financial Products show that, if certain assumptions are made, the total loss probability distribution can be calculated analytically. To accommodate more general assumptions, Monte Carlo simulation can be used. The procedure is as follows:

1. Sample an overall default rate.
2. Calculate a probability of default for each category.
3. Sample a number of defaults for each category.
4. Sample a loss for each default.
5. Calculate total loss.
6. Repeat Steps 1 to 5 many times.

The effect of assuming a probability distribution for default rates in the way just described is to build in default correlations. This makes the probability distribution of total default losses positively skewed, as indicated in Figure 12.3.

12.6 CREDITMETRICS

Credit Risk Plus estimates the probability distribution of losses arising from defaults. As indicated earlier, regulators like the internal models used for specific risk to reflect losses from downgrades and credit spread changes as well as defaults. This has led many banks to implement CreditMetrics for specific risk calculations.

CreditMetrics was proposed by J.P. Morgan in 1997. It is based on an analysis of credit migration. This is the probability of a company moving from one rating category to another during a certain period of time. A typical one-year *ratings transition matrix* is shown in Table 12.1. It indicates that the percentage probability of a bond moving from one rating category to another during a one-year period. For example, a bond that starts with an A credit rating has a 91.83% chance of still having an A rating at the end of one year. It has a 0.02% chance of defaulting during the year, a 0.13% chance of dropping to B, and so on.

Consider a bank with a portfolio of corporate bonds. Calculating a one-year VaR for the portfolio using CreditMetrics involves carrying out Monte Carlo simulation of ratings transitions for bonds in the portfolio over a one-year period. On each simulation trial the final credit rating of all bonds is calculated and the bonds are revalued to determine total credit losses for the year. The 99% worst result is the one-year 99% VaR for the portfolio.

It is interesting to note that if both the CreditMetrics and the Credit Risk Plus models are accurate, they should predict the same probability distribution for losses over the long term. It is the timing of losses that is different. Suppose, for example, that you hold a certain bond in your portfolio. In year 1 it gets downgraded from A to BBB; in year 2 it gets downgraded from BBB to B; in year 3 it defaults. You could assume that there are no losses in years 1 and 2 and calculate the loss in year 3 (the Credit Risk Plus approach). Alternatively, you can calculate separate

Table 12.1 One-year ratings transition matrix (probabilities expressed as percentages). From results reported by Moody's in 2004.

Initial rating	*Rating at year-end*							
	Aaa	*Aa*	*A*	*Baa*	*Ba*	*B*	*Caa*	*Default*
Aaa	92.18	7.06	0.73	0.00	0.02	0.00	0.00	0.00
Aa	1.17	90.85	7.63	0.26	0.07	0.01	0.00	0.02
A	0.05	2.39	91.83	5.07	0.50	0.13	0.01	0.02
Baa	0.05	0.24	5.20	88.48	4.88	0.80	0.16	0.18
Ba	0.01	0.05	0.50	5.45	85.13	7.05	0.55	1.27
B	0.01	0.03	0.13	0.43	6.52	83.20	3.04	6.64
Caa	0.00	0.00	0.00	0.58	1.74	4.18	67.99	25.50
Default	0.00	0.00	0.00	0.00	0.00	0.00	0.00	100.00

revaluation losses in years 1, 2, and 3 (the CreditMetrics approach). The losses under the second approach should in theory add up to the losses under the first approach.

There are two key issues in the implementation of CreditMetrics. One is handling correlations between bonds. The other is calculating credit spreads for valuing the bonds at the end of the year.

The CreditMetrics Correlation Model

In sampling to determine credit losses, the credit rating changes for different counterparties should not be assumed to be independent. A Gaussian copula model can be used to construct a joint probability distribution of rating changes (see Section 6.4 for a discussion of copula models). The copula correlation between the rating transitions for two companies is typically set equal to the correlation between their equity returns using a factor model similar to that in Section 6.3.

As an illustration of the CreditMetrics approach, suppose that we are simulating the rating change of an A-rated and a B-rated company over a one-year period using the transition matrix in Table 12.1. Suppose that the correlation between the equity returns of the two companies is 0.2. On each simulation trial we would sample two variables x_A and x_B from standard normal distributions, so that their correlation is 0.2. The variable x_A determines the new rating of the A-rated company and variable x_B determines the new rating of the B-rated company. Since

$$N^{-1}(0.0005) = -3.2905$$
$$N^{-1}(0.0005 + 0.0239) = -1.9703$$
$$N^{-1}(0.0005 + 0.0239 + 0.9183) = 1.5779$$

the A-rated company gets upgraded to Aaa if $x_A < -3.2905$, it becomes Aa if $-3.2905 < x_A < -1.9703$, it stays A if $-1.9703 < x_A < 1.5779$, and so on. Similarly, since

$$N^{-1}(0.0001) = -3.7190$$
$$N^{-1}(0.0001 + 0.0003) = -3.3528$$
$$N^{-1}(0.0001 + 0.0003 + 0.0013) = -2.9290$$

the B-rated company becomes Aaa if $x_B < -3.7190$, it becomes Aa if $-3.7190 < x_B < -3.3528$, it becomes A if $-3.3528 < x_B < -2.9290$, and so on. The A-rated company defaults if $x_A > N^{-1}(0.9998)$, that is, when

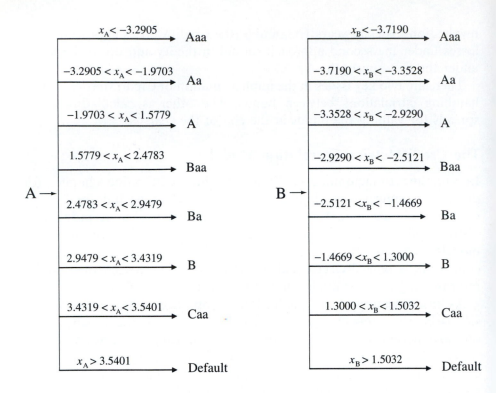

Figure 12.4   The CreditMetrics correlation model: transition of an A-rated and a B-rated company to a new rating after one year. Here x_A and x_B are sampled from standard normal distributions with the correlation equal to the correlation between the equity returns of A and B.

$x_A > 3.5401$. The B-rated company defaults when $x_B > N^{-1}(0.9336)$, that is, when $x_B > 1.5032$. This example is illustrated in Figure 12.4.

Spread Changes

In order to revalue the portfolio of bonds on each simulation trial, it is necessary to calculate spread changes. One way of proceeding is to use a one-factor regression model to divide the spread changes for each bond into a systematic component and an idiosyncratic component. The systematic component is the spread change that affects all bonds in the rating category being considered. The idiosyncratic component affects only one particular bond.

If the systematic component of spread changes is reflected in market risk VaR calculations, it is only necessary to take account of the idiosyncratic spread changes in specific risk VaR calculations. On each trial, therefore, we calculate not only what happens to the rating of each bond but also an idiosyncratic spread change for the bond. For each bond on each simulation trial, one of three things can happen:

1. The credit rating of the bond stays the same. In this case the bond is revalued in a way that reflects the idiosyncratic spread change for the bond.
2. The credit rating of the bond changes. In this case the bond is revalued using a spread corresponding to the new rating category.
3. The bond defaults. In this case a recovery rate is sampled. Often the recovery rate is assumed to have a beta distribution centered on the mean recovery rate published by rating agencies (see Table 11.2).

Time Horizon

Regulators require a bank's credit VaR for specific risk to be a ten-day 99% VaR. In practice, this means a bank has two choices. One is to calculate a one-year 99% VaR in the way we have just outlined and then use the square-root rule to scale it to a ten-day 99% VaR. If we assume 250 days in a year, this means that the calculated VaR is divided by 5. The other is to convert the transition matrix in Table 12.1 from a one-year transition matrix to a ten-day transition matrix and use the procedure we have just described to calculate a ten-day loss distribution directly. Assuming that ratings transitions in successive periods are independent, the second approach involves finding a matrix B such that

$$B^{25} = A$$

where A is the matrix in Table 12.1. A procedure for doing this is outlined in Appendix E at the end of the book.

12.7 INTERPRETING CREDIT CORRELATIONS

Care should be taken in interpreting credit correlations. Different ways of calculating a credit correlation can give quite different answers. We illustrate this by considering the *binomial correlation measure* that is sometimes used by rating agencies and comparing it with the Gaussian copula correlation measure that underlies Vasicek's model.

For two companies, A and B, the binomial correlation measure is the coefficient of correlation between:

1. A variable that equals 1 if Company A defaults between times 0 and T and zero otherwise; and
2. A variable that equals 1 if Company B defaults between times 0 and T and zero otherwise.

The measure is

$$\beta_{AB}(T) = \frac{P_{AB}(T) - Q_A(T)Q_B(T)}{\sqrt{[Q_A(T) - Q_A(T)^2][Q_B(T) - Q_B(T)^2]}} \tag{12.2}$$

where $P_{AB}(T)$ is the joint probability of A and B defaulting between time 0 and time T, $Q_A(T)$ is the cumulative probability that Company A will default by time T, and $Q_B(T)$ is the cumulative probability that Company B will default by time T. Typically $\beta_{AB}(T)$ depends on T, the length of the time period considered. Usually it increases as T increases.

In the Gaussian copula model, $P_{AB}(T) = M[x_A(T), x_B(T); \rho_{AB}]$, where $x_A(T) = N^{-1}(Q_A(T))$ and $x_B(T) = N^{-1}(Q_B(T))$ are the transformed times to default for companies A and B, and ρ_{AB} is the Gaussian copula correlation for the times to default for A and B. The quantity $M(a, b; \rho)$ is the probability that, in a bivariate normal distribution where the correlation between the variables is ρ, the first variable is less than a and the second variable is less than b.[9] It follows that

$$\beta_{AB}(T) = \frac{M[x_A(T), x_B(T); \rho_{AB}] - Q_A(T)Q_B(T)}{\sqrt{[Q_A(T) - Q_A(T)^2][Q_B(T) - Q_B(T)^2]}} \tag{12.3}$$

This shows that, if $Q_A(T)$ and $Q_B(T)$ are known, $\beta_{AB}(T)$ can be calculated from ρ_{AB} and vice versa. Usually ρ_{AB} is markedly greater than $\beta_{AB}(T)$, as is illustrated by the following example.

Example 12.3
Suppose that the probability of Company A defaulting in one-year period is 1% and the probability of Company B defaulting in a one-year period is also 1%. In this case, $x_A(1) = x_B(1) = N^{-1}(0.01) = -2.326$. If ρ_{AB} is 0.20, $M(x_A(1), x_B(1), \rho_{AB}) = 0.000337$, and equation (12.2) shows that $\beta_{AB}(T) = 0.024$ when $T = 1$.

---

[9] An Excel function for calculating $M(a, b; \rho)$ is on the author's website.

SUMMARY

The credit risk on a loan depends on the probability of default and the recovery rate (or equivalently the loss given default). The credit risk in a derivatives transaction is more complicated than that in a loan because the exposure at the time of default is uncertain. Some derivatives transactions (e.g., written options) are always liabilities and give rise to no credit risk. Some (e.g., long positions in options) are always assets and entail significant credit risks. The most difficult types of derivatives transactions to deal with from a credit risk perspective are those that may become either assets or liabilities during their life. Examples are forward contracts and swaps.

The over-the-counter market has developed a number of ways of mitigating credit risk. The most important of these is netting. This is a clause in most contracts written by a financial institution stating that, if a counterparty defaults on one contract it has with the financial institution, then it must default on all contracts it has with that financial institution. Another credit mitigation technique is collateralization. This requires a counterparty to post collateral. If the value of the contract moves against the counterparty, more collateral is required. In the event that collateral is not posted in a timely fashion the contract is closed out using a pre-agreed procedure for valuation. A third credit mitigation technique is downgrade trigger. This gives a company the option to close out a contract if the credit rating of the counterparty falls below a certain level.

Credit VaR can be defined similarly to the way VaR is defined for market risk. It is the credit loss that will not be exceeded over some time horizon with a specified confidence level. Basel II calculates credit VaR for the banking book using a one-factor Gaussian copula model of time to default that was originally developed by Vasicek. An approach for calculating credit VaR that is similar to procedures used in the insurance industry is Credit Risk Plus which was proposed by Credit Suisse Financial Products in 1997. For specific risk in the trading book most large banks use CreditMetrics which was proposed by J.P. Morgan in 1997. This involves simulating rating changes for companies. The correlation between different companies is handled using a Gaussian copula model for rating changes.

FURTHER READING

Credit Suisse Financial Products, "Credit Risk Management Framework," October, 1997.

Finger, C. C., "The One-Factor CreditMetrics Model in the New Basel Capital Accord," *RiskMetrics Journal*, Summer 2001.

J.P. Morgan, "CreditMetrics–Technical Document," April, 1997.

QUESTIONS AND PROBLEMS (Answers at End of Book)

12.1. A bank already has one transaction with a counterparty on its books. Explain why a new transaction by a bank with a counterparty can have the effect of increasing or reducing the bank's credit exposure to the counterparty.

12.2. Suppose that the measure $\beta_{AB}(T)$ in equation (12.2) is the same in the real world and the risk-neutral world. Is the same true of the Gaussian copula measure ρ_{AB}?

12.3. What is meant by a "haircut" in a collateralization agreement. A company offers to post its own equity as collateral. How would you respond?

12.4. Explain the difference between Vasicek's model, the Credit Risk Plus model, and CreditMetrics as far as the following are concerned: (a) when a credit loss is recognized, and (b) the way in which default correlation is modeled.

12.5. Suppose that the probability of Company A defaulting during a 2-year period is 0.2 and the probability of Company B defaulting during this period is 0.15. If the Gaussian copula measure of default correlation is 0.3, what is the binomial correlation measure?

12.6. Suppose that a financial institution has entered into a swap dependent on the sterling interest rate with counterparty X and an exactly offsetting swap with counterparty Y. Which of the following statements are true and which are false? (a) The total present value of the cost of defaults is the sum of the present value of the cost of defaults on the contract with X plus the present value of the cost of defaults on the contract with Y. (b) The expected exposure in 1 year on both contracts is the sum of the expected exposure on the contract with X and the expected exposure on the contract with Y. (c) The 95% upper confidence limit for the exposure in 1 year on both contracts is the sum of the 95% upper confidence limit for the exposure in 1 year on the contract with X and the 95% upper confidence limit for the exposure in 1 year on the contract with Y. Explain your answers.

12.7. A company enters into a 1-year forward contract to sell $100 for AUD 150. The contract is initially at the money. In other words, the forward exchange rate is 1.50. The 1-year dollar risk-free rate of interest is 5% per annum. The 1-year dollar rate of interest at which the counterparty can borrow is 6% per annum. The exchange rate volatility is 12% per annum. Estimate the present value of the cost of defaults on the contract. Assume that defaults are recognized only at the end of the life of the contract.

12.8. Suppose that in Problem 12.7 the 6-month forward rate is also 1.50 and the 6-month dollar risk-free interest rate is 5% per annum. Suppose further that the 6-month dollar rate of interest at which the counterparty can borrow is 5.5% per annum. Estimate the present value of the cost of defaults assuming that defaults can occur either at the 6-month point or at the 1-year point? (If a default occurs at the 1-month point, the company's potential loss is the market value of the contract.)

12.9. "A long forward contract subject to credit risk is a combination of a short position in a no-default put and a long position in a call subject to credit risk." Explain this statement.

12.10. Explain why the credit exposure on a pair of offsetting forward contracts with different counterparties resembles a straddle.

12.11. "When a bank is negotiating a pair of offsetting currency swaps, it should try to ensure that it is receiving the lower interest rate currency from a company with a low credit risk." Explain.

ASSIGNMENT QUESTIONS

12.12. Explain carefully the distinction between real-world and risk-neutral default probabilities. Which is higher? A bank enters into a credit derivative where it agrees to pay $100 at the end of 1 year if a certain company's credit rating falls from A to Baa or lower during the year. The 1-year risk-free rate is 5%. Using Table 12.1, estimate a value for the derivative. What assumptions are you making? Do they tend to overstate or understate the value of the derivative.

12.13. Suppose that a bank has a total of $10 million of exposures of a certain type. The one-year probability of default averages 1% and the recovery rate averages 40%. The copula correlation parameter is 0.2. Estimate the 1-year 99.5% credit VaR.

12.14. Consider an option on a non-dividend-paying stock where the stock price is $52, the strike price $50, the risk-free rate is 5%, the volatility is 30%, and the time to maturity is 1 year. (a) What is the value of the option assuming no possibility of a default? (b) What is the value of the option to the buyer if there is a 2% chance that the option seller will default at maturity? (c) Suppose that, instead of paying the option price up front, the option buyer agrees to pay the forward value of the option price at the end of the life of the contract. By how much does this reduce the cost of defaults to the option buyer in the case where there is a 2% chance of the option seller defaulting? (d) If in case (c) the option buyer has a 1% chance of defaulting at the end of the life of the contract, what is the default risk to the option seller? Discuss the two-sided nature of default risk in this case and the value of the option to each side.

12.15. Can the existence of downgrade triggers increase default risk? Explain your answer.

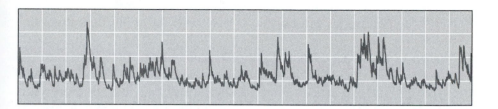

CHAPTER 13

Credit Derivatives

The credit derivatives market has seen huge growth in recent years. In 2000 the total notional principal for outstanding credit derivative contracts was about $800 billion. By 2005 this had risen to $12 trillion.

Credit derivatives are contracts where the payoff depends on the creditworthiness of one or more companies or countries. They allow companies to trade credit risks in much the same way that they trade market risks. Banks and other financial institutions, once they had assumed a credit risk, used to be in the position where they could do little except wait (and hope for the best). Now they can actively manage their portfolios of credit risks, keeping some and entering into credit derivative contracts to protect themselves from others.

13.1 CREDIT DEFAULT SWAPS

The most popular credit derivative is a *credit default swap* (CDS). This is a contract that provides insurance against the risk of a default by particular company. The company is known as the *reference entity* and a default by the company is known as a *credit event*. The buyer of the insurance obtains the right to sell bonds issued by the company for their face value when a credit event occurs and the seller of the insurance agrees to buy the bonds for their face value when a credit event occurs.[1] The total face

---

[1] The face value (or par value) of a bond is the principal amount that the issuer will repay at maturity if it does not default.

value of the bonds that can be sold is known as the credit default swap's *notional principal*.

The buyer of the CDS makes periodic payments to the seller until the end of the life of the CDS or until a credit event occurs. These payments are typically made in arrears every quarter, every half year, or every year. The settlement in the event of a default involves either physical delivery of the bonds or a cash payment.

An example will help to illustrate how a typical deal is structured. Suppose that two parties enter into a five-year credit default swap on March 1, 2006. Assume that the notional principal is $100 million and the buyer agrees to pay 90 basis points annually for protection against default by the reference entity.

The CDS is shown in Figure 13.1. If the reference entity does not default (i.e., there is no credit event), the buyer receives no payoff and pays $900,000 on March 1 of each of the years 2007, 2008, 2009, 2010, and 2011. If there is a credit event a substantial payoff is likely. Suppose that the buyer notifies the seller of a credit event on June 1, 2009 (a quarter of the way into the fourth year). If the contract specifies physical settlement, the buyer has the right to sell bonds issued by the reference entity with a face value of $100 million for $100 million. If the contract requires cash settlement, an independent calculation agent will conduct a poll of dealers at a predesignated number of days after the credit event to determine the mid-market value of the cheapest deliverable bond. Suppose this bond is worth $35 per $100 of face value. The cash payoff would be $65 million.

The regular quarterly, semiannual, or annual payments from the buyer of protection to the seller of protection cease when there is a credit event. However, because these payments are made in arrears, a final accrual payment by the buyer is usually required. In our example, the buyer would be required to pay to the seller the amount of the annual payment accrued between March 1, 2009, and June 1, 2009 (approximately $225,000), but no further payments would be required.

The total amount paid per year, as a percent of the notional principal, to buy protection is known as the *CDS spread*. Several large banks are

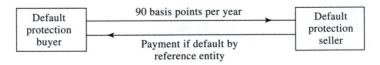

Figure 13.1   Credit default swap.

Business Snapshot 13.1   Who Bears the Credit Risk?

Traditionally banks have been in the business of making loans and then bearing the credit risk that the borrower will default. Since 1988 banks have been reluctant to keep loans to companies with good credit ratings on their balance sheets. This is because the capital required under Basel I is such that the expected return from the loans is less attractive than that from investments in other assets. During the 1990s banks created asset-backed securities to pass loans (and their credit risk) on to investors. In the late 1990s and early 2000s, banks have made extensive use of credit derivatives to shift the credit risk in their loans to other parts of the financial system. (Under Basel II the regulatory capital for loans to highly rated companies will decline and this may lead to banks being more willing to keep quality loans on their balance sheet.)

If banks have been net buyers of credit protection, who have been net sellers? The answer is insurance companies. Insurance companies have not been regulated in the same way as banks and as a result are sometimes more willing to bear credit risks than banks.

The result of all this is that the financial institution bearing the credit risk of a loan is often different from the financial institution that did the original credit checks. Whether this proves to be good for the overall health of the financial system remains to be seen.

---

market makers in the credit default swap market. When quoting on a new five-year credit default swap on Ford Motor Credit, a market maker might bid 250 basis points and offer 260 basis points. This means that the market maker is prepared to buy protection on Ford by paying 250 basis points per year (i.e., 2.5% of the principal per year) and to sell protection on Ford for 260 basis points per year (i.e., 2.6% of the principal per year).

As indicated in Business Snapshot 13.1, banks have been the largest buyers of CDS credit protection and insurance companies have been the largest sellers.

Credit Default Swaps and Bond Yields

A CDS can be used to hedge a position in a corporate bond. Suppose that an investor buys a five-year corporate bond yielding 7% per year for its face value and at the same time enters into a five-year CDS to buy protection against the issuer of the bond defaulting. Suppose that the CDS spread is 2% per annum. The effect of the CDS is to convert the corporate bond to a risk-free bond (at least approximately). If the bond issuer does not default the investor earns 5% per year (when the CDS spread is netted against the corporate bond yield). If the bond does default, the investor earns 5% up to the time of the default. Under the terms of the CDS, the investor is then able to exchange the bond for its face value. This face value can be invested at the risk-free rate for the remainder of the five years.

The n-year CDS spread should be approximately equal to the excess of the par yield on an n-year corporate bond over the par yield on an n-year risk-free bond.[2] If it is markedly less than this, an investor can earn more than the risk-free rate by buying the corporate bond and buying protection. If it is markedly greater than this, an investor can borrow at less than the risk-free rate by shorting the corporate bond and selling CDS protection. These are not perfect arbitrages, but they are sufficiently good that the CDS spread cannot depart very much from the excess of the corporate bond par yield over the risk-free par yield. As we discussed in Section 11.4, a good estimate of the risk-free rate is the LIBOR/swap rate minus 10 basis points.

The Cheapest-to-Deliver Bond

As explained in Section 11.3, the recovery rate on a bond is defined as the value of the bond immediately after default as a percent of face value. This means that the payoff from a CDS is $L(1 - R)$, where L is the notional principal and R is the recovery rate.

Usually a CDS specifies that a number of different bonds can be delivered in the event of a default. The bonds typically have the same seniority, but they may not sell for the same percentage of face value immediately after a default.[3] This gives the holder of a CDS a cheapest-to-deliver bond option. When a default happens, the buyer of protection (or the calculation agent in the event of cash settlement) will review alternative deliverable bonds and choose for delivery the one that can be purchased most cheaply. In the context of CDS valuation, R should therefore be the lowest recovery rate applicable to a deliverable bond.

---

[2] The par yield on an n-year bond is the coupon rate per year that causes the bond to sell for its par value (i.e., its face value).

[3] There are a number of reasons for this. The claim that is made in the event of a default is typically equal to the bond's face value plus accrued interest. Bonds with high accrued interest at the time of default therefore tend to have higher prices immediately after default. The market may also judge that in the event of a reorganization of the company some bondholders will fare better than others.

13.2 CREDIT INDICES

Participants in credit derivatives markets have developed indices to track credit default swap spreads. In 2004 there were agreements between different producers of indices. This led to some consolidation. Among the indices now used are:

1. The five- and ten-year CDX NA IG indices tracking the credit spread for 125 investment grade North American companies
2. The five- and ten-year iTraxx Europe indices tracking the credit spread for 125 investment grade European companies

In addition to monitoring credit spreads, indices provide a way market participants can easily buy or sell a portfolio of credit default swaps. For example, an investment bank, acting as market maker might quote the CDX NA IG five-year index as bid 65 basis points and offer 66 basis points. An investor could then buy $800,000 of five-year CDS protection on each of the 125 underlying companies for a total of $660,000 per year. The investor can sell $800,000 of five-year CDS protection on each of the 125 underlying names for a total of $650,000 per year. When a company defaults the annual payment is reduced by $660,000/125 = $5,280.[4]

13.3 VALUATION OF CREDIT DEFAULT SWAPS

Mid-market CDS spreads on individual reference entities (i.e., the average of the bid and offer CDS spreads quoted by brokers) can be calculated from default probability estimates. We will illustrate how this is done with a simple example.

Suppose that the probability of a reference entity defaulting during a year conditional on no earlier default is 2%.[5] Table 13.1 shows survival probabilities and unconditional default probabilities (i.e., default probabilities as seen at time zero) for each of the five years. The probability of a default during the first year is 0.02 and the probability the reference entity

---

[4] The index is slightly lower than the average of the credit default swap spreads for the companies in the portfolio. To understand the reason for this, consider two companies, one with a spread of 1,000 basis points and the other with a spread of 10 basis points. To buy protection on both companies would cost slightly less than 505 basis points per company. This is because the 1,000 basis points is not expected to be paid for as long as the 10 basis points and should therefore carry less weight.

[5] As mentioned in Section 11.2, conditional default probabilities are known as default intensities or hazard rates.

Table 13.1 Unconditional default probabilities and survival probabilities.

Time (years)	Default probability	Survival probability
1	0.0200	0.9800
2	0.0196	0.9604
3	0.0192	0.9412
4	0.0188	0.9224
5	0.0184	0.9039

will survive until the end of the first year is 0.98. The probability of a default during the second year is $0.02 \times 0.98 = 0.0196$ and the probability of survival until the end of the second year is $0.98 \times 0.98 = 0.9604$. The probability of default during the third year is $0.02 \times 0.9604 = 0.0192$, and so on.

We will assume that defaults always happen halfway through a year and that payments on the credit default swap are made once a year, at the end of each year. We also assume that the risk-free (LIBOR) interest rate is 5% per annum with continuous compounding and the recovery rate is 40%. There are three parts to the calculation. These are shown in Tables 13.2, 13.3, and 13.4.

Table 13.2 shows the calculation of the expected present value of the payments made on the CDS assuming that payments are made at the rate of s per year and the notional principal is $1. For example, there is a 0.9412 probability that the third payment of s is made. The expected payment is therefore $0.9412s$ and its present value is $0.9412se^{-0.05 \times 3} = 0.8101s$. The total present value of the expected payments is $4.0704s$.

Table 13.2 Calculation of the present value of expected payments. Payment $= s$ per annum.

Time (years)	Probability of survival	Expected payment	Discount factor	PV of expected payment
1	0.9800	0.9800s	0.9512	0.9322s
2	0.9604	0.9604s	0.9048	0.8690s
3	0.9412	0.9412s	0.8607	0.8101s
4	0.9224	0.9224s	0.8187	0.7552s
5	0.9039	0.9039s	0.7788	0.7040s
Total				4.0704s

Table 13.3 Calculation of the present value of expected payoff. Notional principal $= \$1$.

Time (years)	Probability of default	Recovery rate	Expected payoff ($)	Discount factor	PV of expected payoff ($)
0.5	0.0200	0.4	0.0120	0.9753	0.0117
1.5	0.0196	0.4	0.0118	0.9277	0.0109
2.5	0.0192	0.4	0.0115	0.8825	0.0102
3.5	0.0188	0.4	0.0113	0.8395	0.0095
4.5	0.0184	0.4	0.0111	0.7985	0.0088
Total					0.0511

Table 13.3 shows the calculation of the expected present value of the payoff assuming a notional principal of $1. As mentioned earlier, we are assuming that defaults always happen halfway through a year. For example, there is a 0.0192 probability of a payoff halfway through the third year. Given that the recovery rate is 40% the expected payoff at this time is $0.0192 \times 0.6 \times 1 = \$0.0115$. The present value of the expected payoff is $0.0115e^{-0.05 \times 2.5} = \$0.0102$. The total present value of the expected payoffs is $0.0511.

As a final step we evaluate in Table 13.4 the accrual payment made in the event of a default. For example, there is a 0.0192 probability that there will be a final accrual payment halfway through the third year. The accrual payment is $0.5s$. The expected accrual payment at this time is therefore $0.0192 \times 0.5s = 0.0096s$. Its present value is $0.0096se^{-0.05 \times 2.5} = 0.0085s$. The total present value of the expected accrual payments is $0.0426s$.

Table 13.4 Calculation of the present value of accrual payment.

Time (years)	Probability of default	Expected accrual payment	Discount factor	PV of expected accrual payment
0.5	0.0200	0.0100s	0.9753	0.0097s
1.5	0.0196	0.0098s	0.9277	0.0091s
2.5	0.0192	0.0096s	0.8825	0.0085s
3.5	0.0188	0.0094s	0.8395	0.0079s
4.5	0.0184	0.0092s	0.7985	0.0074s
Total				0.0426s

From Tables 13.2 and 13.4, we see that the present value of the expected payments is

$$4.0704s + 0.0426s = 4.1130s$$

From Table 13.3 the present value of the expected payoff is $0.0511. Equating the two, the CDS spread for a new CDS is given by

$$4.1130s = 0.0511$$

or $s = 0.0124$. The mid-market spread should be 0.0124 times the principal or 124 basis points per year. This example is designed to illustrate the calculation methodology. In practice, we are likely to find that calculations are more extensive than those in Tables 13.2 to 13.4 because (a) payments are often made more frequently than once a year and (b) we might want to assume that defaults can happen more frequently than once a year.

Marking to Market a CDS

At the time it is negotiated, a CDS like most other swaps is worth close to zero. At later times it may have a positive or negative value. Suppose, for example, that the credit default swap in our example had been negotiated some time ago for a spread of 150 basis points, the present value of the payments by the buyer would be $4.1130 \times 0.0150 = 0.0617$ and the present value of the payoff would be 0.0511 as above. The value of the swap to the seller would therefore be $0.0617 - 0.0511$, or 0.0106 times the principal. Similarly, the mark-to market value of the swap to the buyer of protection would be -0.0106 times the principal.

Estimating Default Probabilities

The default probabilities used to value a CDS should be risk-neutral default probabilities, not real-world default probabilities (see Section 11.5 for a discussion of the difference between the two). Risk-neutral default probabilities can be estimated from bond prices or asset swaps, as explained in Chapter 11. An alternative is to imply them from CDS quotes. The latter approach is similar to the practice in options markets of implying volatilities from the prices of actively traded options.

Suppose we change the example in Tables 13.2, 13.3, and 13.4 so that we do not know the default probabilities. Instead, we know that the mid-market CDS spread for a newly issued five-year CDS is 100 basis points per year. We can then reverse-engineer our calculations to conclude that the implied default probability (conditional on no earlier default) is 1.61% per year.[6]

Binary Credit Default Swaps

A binary credit default swap is structured similarly to a regular credit default swap except that the payoff is a fixed dollar amount. Suppose, in the example we have considered in Tables 13.1 to 13.4, that the payoff is $1 instead of $1 - R$ dollars and that the swap spread is s. Tables 13.1, 13.2, and 13.4 are the same. Table 13.3 is replaced by Table 13.5. The CDS spread for a new binary CDS is given by

$$4.1130s = 0.0852$$

so that the CDS spread s is 0.0207, or 207 basis points.

How Important is the Recovery Rate?

Whether we use CDS spreads or bond prices to estimate default probabilities, we need an estimate of the recovery rate. However, provided that we use the same recovery rate for (a) estimating risk-neutral default probabilities and (b) valuing a CDS, the value of the CDS (or the estimate of the CDS spread) is not very sensitive to the recovery rate. This is because the implied probabilities of default are approximately proportional to $1/(1 - R)$ and the payoffs from a CDS are proportional to $1 - R$.

Table 13.5 Calculation of the present value of expected payoff from a binary credit default swap. Principal $= \$1$.

Time (years)	Probability of default	Expected payoff ($)	Discount factor	PV of expected payoff ($)
0.5	0.0200	0.0200	0.9753	0.0195
1.5	0.0196	0.0196	0.9277	0.0182
2.5	0.0192	0.0192	0.8825	0.0170
3.5	0.0188	0.0188	0.8395	0.0158
4.5	0.0184	0.0184	0.7985	0.0147
Total				0.0852

---

[6] Ideally, we would like to estimate a different default probability for each year instead of a single default intensity. We could do this if we had spreads for 1-, 2-, 3-, 4-, and 5-year credit default swaps or bond prices.

This argument does not apply to the valuation of a binary CDS. The probabilities of default implied from a regular CDS are still proportional to $1/(1 - R)$. However, for a binary CDS, the payoffs from the CDS are independent of R. If we have CDS spreads for both a plain vanilla CDS and a binary CDS, we can estimate both the recovery rate and the default probability (see Problem 13.23).

The Future of the CDS Market

The market for credit default swaps has grown rapidly in the late 1990s and early 2000s. Credit default swaps have become important tools for managing credit risk. A financial institution can reduce its credit exposure to particular companies by buying protection. It can also use CDSs to diversify credit risk. For example, if a financial institution has too much credit exposure to a particular business sector, it can buy protection against defaults by companies in the sector and at the same time sell protection against default by companies in other unrelated sectors.

Some market participants believe that the growth of the CDS market will continue and that it will be as big as the interest rate swap market by 2010. Others are less optimistic. As pointed out in Business Snapshot 13.2, there is a potential asymmetric information problem in the CDS market that is not present in other over-the-counter derivatives markets.

13.4 CDS FORWARDS AND OPTIONS

Once the CDS market was well established, it was natural for derivatives dealers to trade forwards and options on credit default swap spreads.[7]

A forward credit default swap is the obligation to buy or sell a particular credit default swap on a particular reference entity at a particular future time T. If the reference entity defaults before time T the forward contract ceases to exist. Thus, a bank could enter into a forward contract to sell five-year protection on Ford Motor Credit for 280 basis points starting one year from now. If Ford defaults during the next year, the bank's obligation under the forward contract ceases to exist.

A credit default swap option is an option to buy or sell a particular credit default swap on a particular reference entity at a particular future time T. For example, an investor could negotiate the right to buy five-year

---

[7] The valuation of these instruments is discussed in J.C. Hull and A. White, "The Valuation of Credit Default Swap Options," *Journal of Derivatives*, 10, No. 5 (Spring 2003), 40–50.

Business Snapshot 13.2 Is the CDS Market a Fair Game?

There is one important difference between credit default swaps and the other over-the-counter derivatives that we have considered in this book. The other over-the-counter derivatives depend on interest rates, exchange rates, equity indices, commodity prices, and so on. There is no reason to assume that any one market participant has better information than other market participants about these variables.

Credit default swaps spreads depend on the probability that a particular company will default during a particular period of time. Arguably some market participants have more information to estimate this probability than others. A financial institution that works closely with a particular company by providing advice, making loans, and handling new issues of securities is likely to have more information about the creditworthiness of the company than another financial institution that has no dealings with the company. Economists refer to this as an *asymmetric information* problem.

Whether asymmetric information will curtail the expansion of the credit default swap market remains to be seen. Financial institutions emphasize that the decision to buy protection against the risk of default by a company is normally made by a risk manager and is not based on any special information that many exist elsewhere in the financial institution about the company.

---

protection on Ford Motor Credit starting in one year for 280 basis points. This is a call option. If the five-year CDS spread for Ford in one year turns out to be more than 280 basis points the option will be exercised; otherwise it will not be exercised. The cost of the option would be paid up front. Similarly, an investor might negotiate the right to sell five-year protection on Ford Motor Credit for 280 basis points starting in one year. This is a put option. If the five-year CDS spread for Ford in one year turns out to be less than 280 basis points the option will be exercised; otherwise it will not be exercised. Again the cost of the option would be paid up front. Like CDS forwards, CDS options are usually structured so that they will cease to exist if the reference entity defaults before option maturity.

An option contract that is sometimes traded in the credit derivatives market is a call option on a basket of reference entities. If there are m reference entities in the basket that have not defaulted by the option maturity, the option gives the holder the right to buy a portfolio of CDSs on the names for mK basis points, where K is the strike price. In addition, the holder gets the usual CDS payoff on any reference entities that do default during the life of the contract.

13.5 TOTAL RETURN SWAPS

A *total return swap* is a type of credit derivative. It is an agreement to exchange the total return on a bond (or any portfolio of assets) for LIBOR plus a spread. The total return includes coupons, interest, and the gain or loss on the asset over the life of the swap.

An example of a total return swap is a five-year agreement with a notional principal of $100 million to exchange the total return on a corporate bond for LIBOR plus 25 basis points. This is illustrated in Figure 13.2. On coupon payment dates the payer pays the coupons earned on an investment of $100 million in the bond. The receiver pays interest at a rate of LIBOR plus 25 basis points on a principal of $100 million. (LIBOR is set on one coupon date and paid on the next as in a plain vanilla interest rate swap.) At the end of the life of the swap there is a payment reflecting the change in value of the bond. For example, if the bond increases in value by 10% over the life of the swap, the payer is required to pay $10 million (= 10% of $100 million) at the end of the five years. Similarly, if the bond decreases in value by 15%, the receiver is required to pay $15 million at the end of the five years. If there is a default on the bond, the swap is usually terminated and the receiver makes a final payment equal to the excess of $100 million over the market value of the bond.

If we add the notional principal to both sides at the end of the life of the swap, we can characterize the total return swap as follows. The payer pays the cash flows on an investment of $100 million in the corporate bond. The receiver pays the cash flows on a $100 million bond paying LIBOR plus 25 basis points. If the payer owns the corporate bond, the total return swap allows it to pass the credit risk on the bond to the receiver. If it does not own the bond, the total return swap allows it to take a short position in the bond.

Total return swaps are often used as a financing tool. One scenario that could lead to the swap in Figure 13.2 is as follows. The receiver wants financing to invest $100 million in the reference bond. It approaches the payer (which is likely to be a financial institution) and agrees to the swap. The payer then invests $100 million in the bond. This leaves the receiver in the same position as it would have been if it had borrowed money at

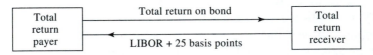

Figure 13.2   Total return swap.

LIBOR plus 25 basis points to buy the bond. The payer retains ownership of the bond for the life of the swap and faces less credit risk than it would have done if it had lent money to the receiver to finance the purchase of the bond, with the bond being used as collateral for the loan. If the receiver defaults, the payer does not have the legal problem of trying to realize on the collateral.[8]

The spread over LIBOR received by the payer is compensation for bearing the risk that the receiver will default. The payer will lose money if the receiver defaults at a time when the reference bond's price has declined. The spread therefore depends on the credit quality of the receiver and of the bond issuer, and on the default correlation between the two.

There are a number of variations on the standard deal we have described. Sometimes, instead of a cash payment for the change in the value of the bond, there is physical settlement where the payer exchanges the underlying asset for the notional principal at the end of the life of the swap. Sometimes the change-in-value payments are made periodically rather than all at the end of the life of the swap.

13.6 BASKET CREDIT DEFAULT SWAPS

In what is referred to as a *basket credit default swap* there are a number of reference entities. An *add-up basket* CDS provides a payoff when any of the reference entities default. A *first-to-default* CDS provides a payoff only when the first default occurs. A *second-to-default* CDS provides a payoff only when the second default occurs. More generally, an nth-to-default CDS provides a payoff only when the nth default occurs. Payoffs are calculated in the same way as for a regular CDS. After the relevant default has occurred, there is a settlement. The swap then terminates and there are no further payments by either party.

13.7 COLLATERALIZED DEBT OBLIGATIONS

A collateralized debt obligation (CDO) is a way of creating securities with widely different risk characteristics from a portfolio of debt instruments.

---

[8] Repos are structured to minimize credit risk in a similar way. A company requiring short-term funds sells securities to the lender and agrees to buy them back at a later time at a slightly higher price. The difference between the prices is the interest the lender earns. If the borrower defaults, the lender keeps the securities. If the lender defaults, the borrower keeps the funds.

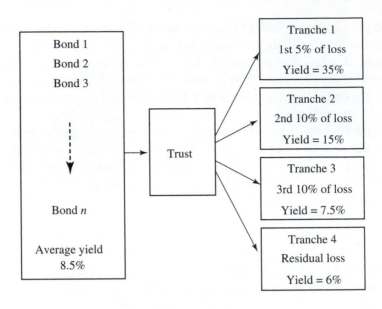

Figure 13.3 Collateralized debt obligation.

An example is shown in Figure 13.3, where four types of securities (or tranches) are created from a portfolio of bonds. The first tranche has 5% of the total bond principal and absorbs all credit losses from the portfolio during the life of the CDO until they have reached 5% of the total bond principal. The second tranche has 10% of the principal and absorbs all losses during the life of the CDO in excess of 5% of the principal up to a maximum of 15% of the principal. The third tranche has 10% of the principal and absorbs all losses in excess of 15% of the principal up to a maximum of 25% of the principal. The fourth tranche has 75% of the principal and absorbs all losses in excess of 25% of the principal. The yields in Figure 13.3 are the rates of interest paid to tranche holders. These rates are paid on the balance of the principal remaining in the tranche after losses have been paid. Consider the first tranche. Initially the return of 35% is paid on the whole amount invested by the tranche holders. But after losses equal to 1% of the total bond principal have been experienced, the tranche holders have lost 20% of their investment and the return is paid on only 80% of the original amount invested.[9] Tranche 1 is referred to as the

---

[9] When a bond with principal Q defaults and a recovery of QR is made, the usual arrangement is that a loss of $(1 - Q)R$ is sustained by the most junior tranche. An amount QR is paid to the most senior tranche and this tranche's principal is reduced by QR.

equity tranche. A default loss of 2.5% on the bond portfolio translates into a loss of 50% of the tranche's principal. Tranche 4 is usually given an Aaa rating. Defaults on the bond portfolio must exceed 25% before the holders of this tranche are responsible for any credit losses.

The creator of the CDO normally retains the equity tranche and sells the remaining tranches in the market. A CDO provides a way of creating high-quality debt from average-quality (or even low-quality) debt.

Synthetic CDOs

The CDO in Figure 13.3 is referred to as a *cash* CDO. An alternative structure which has become popular is a *synthetic* CDO, where the creator of the CDO sells a portfolio of credit default swaps to third parties. It then passes the default risk on to the synthetic CDO's tranche holders. Analogously to Figure 13.3, the first tranche might be responsible for the payoffs on the credit default swaps until they have reached 5% of the total notional principal; the second tranche might be responsible for the pay-offs between 5% and 15% of the total notional principal; and so on. The income from the credit default swaps is distributed to the tranches in a way that reflects the risk they are bearing. For example, the first tranche might get 3,000 basis points; the second tranche 1,000 basis points, and so on. As with a cash CDO, losses on defaults would be netted against the principal to determine the amount on which interest is paid.

Single-Tranche Trading

In Section 13.2 we discussed the portfolios of 125 companies that are used to generate CDX and iTraxx indices. The market uses these portfolios to define standard CDO tranches. The trading of these standard tranches is known as *single-tranche trading*. A single-tranche trade is an agreement where one side agrees to sell protection against losses on a tranche and the other side agrees to buy the protection. The tranche is not part of a synthetic CDO, but cash flows are calculated in the same way as if it were part of a synthetic CDO. The tranche is referred to as "unfunded" because it has not been created by selling credit default swaps or buying bonds.

In the case of the CDX NA IG index, the equity tranche covers losses between 0% and 3% of the principal. The second tranche, which is referred to as the *mezzanine tranche*, covers losses between 3% and 7%. The remaining tranches cover losses from 7% to 10%, 10% to 15%, and 15% to 30%. In the case of the iTraxx Europe index, the equity tranche covers losses between 0% and 3%. The mezzanine tranche covers losses

Table 13.6 Five-year CDX IG NA and iTraxx Europe tranches on August 30, 2005. Quotes are in basis points except for 0–3% tranche. *Source*: Reuters

CDX IG NA					
Tranche	0–3%	3–7%	7–10%	10–15%	15–30%
Quote	40%	127	35.5	20.5	9.5
iTraxx Europe					
Tranche	0–3%	3–6%	6–9%	9–12%	12–22%
Quote	24%	81	26.5	15	9

between 3% and 6%. The remaining tranches cover losses from 6% to 9%, 9% to 12%, and 12% to 22%.

Table 13.6 shows the mid-market quotes for the five-year CDX and iTraxx tranches on August 30, 2005. On that date the CDX index level was 50 basis points and the iTraxx index was 36.375 basis points. For example, the mid-market price of mezzanine protection for the CDX IG NA was 127 basis points per year, while that for iTraxx Europe was 81 basis points per year. Note that the equity tranche is quoted differently from the other tranches. The market quote of 40% for CDX means that the protection seller receives an initial payment of 40% of the principal plus a spread of 500 basis points per year. Similarly, the market quote of 24% for iTraxx means that the protection seller receives an initial payment of 24% of the principal plus a spread of 500 basis points per year.

13.8 VALUATION OF A BASKET CDS AND CDO

The spread for an nth-to-default CDS or the tranche of a CDO is critically dependent on default correlation. Suppose that a basket of 100 reference entities is used to define a five-year nth-to-default CDS and that each reference entity has a risk-neutral probability of defaulting during the five years equal to 2%. When the default correlation between the reference entities is zero, the binomial distribution shows that the probability of one or more defaults during the five years is 86.74% and the probability of ten or more defaults is 0.0034%. A first-to-default CDS is therefore quite valuable, whereas a tenth-to-default CDS is worth almost nothing.

As the default correlation increases the probability of one or more defaults declines and the probability of ten or more defaults increases. In the limit where the default correlation between the reference entities

> **Business Snapshot 13.3** Correlation Smiles
>
> Credit derivatives dealers imply default correlations from the spreads on tranches. The compound correlation is the correlation that prices a particular tranche correctly. The base correlation is the correlation that prices all tranches up to a certain level of seniority correctly. If all implied correlations were the same, we could deduce that market prices are consistent with the one-factor Gaussian copula model for time to default. In practice, we find that compound correlations exhibit a "smile" with the correlations for the most junior (equity) and senior tranches higher than those for intermediate tranches. The base correlations exhibit a "skew" where the correlation increases with the level of seniority considered.

is perfect, the probability of one or more defaults equals the probability of ten or more defaults and is 2%. This is because in this extreme situation the reference entities are essentially the same. Either they all default (with probability 2%) or none of them default (with probability 98%).

The valuation of a tranche of a CDO is similarly dependent on default correlation. If the correlation is low, the junior equity tranche is very risky and the senior tranches are very safe. As the default correlation increases, the junior tranches become less risky and the senior tranches become more risky. In the limit where the default correlation is perfect the tranches are equally risky.

Using the Gaussian Copula Model of Time to Default

The one-factor Gaussian copula model of time to default presented in Section 6.5 has become the standard market model for valuing an nth-to-default CDS or a tranche of a CDO.

Consider a portfolio of N companies, each having a probability $Q(T)$ of defaulting by time T. From equation (6.11), the probability of default, conditional on the level of the factor F, is

$$Q(T \mid F) = N\left(\frac{N^{-1}[Q(T)] - \sqrt{\rho}\,F}{\sqrt{1 - \rho}}\right) \tag{13.1}$$

The trick to valuing an nth-to-default CDS or a CDO is to calculate expected cash flows conditional on F and then integrate over F. The advantage of this is that, conditional on F, defaults are independent. The probability of exactly k defaults by time T, conditional on F, is

$$\frac{N!}{(N-k)!\,k!}\,Q(T \mid F)^k[1 - Q(T \mid F)]^{N-k}$$

Derivatives dealers calculate the implied copula correlation ρ in equation (13.1) from the spreads quoted in the market for tranches of CDOs and tend to quote these rather than the spreads themselves (see Business Snapshot 13.3). This is similar to the practice in options markets of quoting Black–Scholes implied volatilities rather than dollar prices.

SUMMARY

Financial institutions use credit derivatives to actively manage their credit risks. They use them to transfer credit risk from one company to another and to diversify credit risk by swapping one type of exposure for another.

The most common credit derivative is a credit default swap. This is a contract where one company buys insurance against another company defaulting on its obligations. The payoff is usually the difference between the face value of a bond issued by the second company and its value immediately after a default. Credit default swaps can be analyzed by calculating the present value of the expected payments and the present value of the expected payoff.

A forward credit default swap is an obligation to enter into a particular credit default swap on a particular date. A credit default swap option is the right to enter into a particular credit default swap on a particular date. Both cease to exist if the reference entity defaults before the date.

A total return swap is an instrument where the total return on a portfolio of credit-sensitive assets is exchanged for LIBOR plus a spread. Total return swaps are often used as financing vehicles. A company wanting to purchase a portfolio of bonds approaches a financial institution, who buys the bonds on its behalf. The financial institution then enters into a total return swap where it pays the return on the bonds to the company and receives LIBOR plus a spread. The advantage of this type of arrangement is that the financial institution reduces its exposure to defaults by the company.

An nth-to-default CDS is defined as a CDS that pays off when the nth default occurs in a portfolio of companies. In a collateralized debt obligation, a number of different securities are created from a portfolio of corporate bonds or commercial loans. There are rules for determining how credit losses are allocated to the securities. The result of the rules is that securities with both very high and very low credit ratings are created from the portfolio. A synthetic collateralized debt obligation creates a similar set of securities from credit default swaps. The standard market model for pricing both an nth-to-default CDS and tranches of a CDO is the one-factor Gaussian copula model for time to default.

FURTHER READING

Andersen, L., J. Sidenius, and S. Basu, "All Your Hedges in One Basket," *Risk*, November 2003.

Andersen, L., and J. Sidenius, "Extensions to the Gaussian Copula: Random Recovery and Random Factor Loadings," *Journal of Credit Risk*, 1, No. 1 (Winter 2004): 29–70.

Das, S., *Credit Derivatives: Trading & Management of Credit & Default Risk.* Singapore: Wiley, 1998.

Hull, J.C., and A. White, "Valuation of a CDO and nth to Default Swap without Monte Carlo Simulation," *Journal of Derivatives*, 12, No. 2 (Winter 2004): 8–23.

Hull, J.C., and A. White, "The Perfect Copula," Working Paper, University of Toronto.

Laurent, J.-P., and J. Gregory, "Basket Default Swaps, CDOs and Factor Copulas," Working Paper, ISFA Actuarial School, University of Lyon, 2003.

Li, D.X., "On Default Correlation: A Copula Approach," *Journal of Fixed Income*, March 2000: 43–54.

Tavakoli, J.M., *Credit Derivatives: A Guide to Instruments and Applications.* New York: Wiley, 1998.

Schonbucher, P.J., *Credit Derivatives Pricing Models.* Wiley, 2003.

QUESTIONS AND PROBLEMS (Answers at End of Book)

13.1. Explain the difference between a regular credit default swap and a binary credit default swap.

13.2. A credit default swap requires a semiannual payment at the rate of 60 basis points per year. The principal is $300 million and the credit default swap is settled in cash. A default occurs after 4 years and 2 months, and the calculation agent estimates that the price of the cheapest deliverable bond is 40% of its face value shortly after the default. List the cash flows and their timing for the seller of the credit default swap.

13.3. Explain the two ways a credit default swap can be settled.

13.4. Explain how a cash CDO and a synthetic CDO are created.

13.5. Explain what a first-to-default credit default swap is. Does its value increase or decrease as the default correlation between the companies in the basket increases? Explain your answer.

13.6. Explain the difference between risk-neutral and real-world default probabilities.

13.7. Explain why a total return swap can be useful as a financing tool.

13.8. Suppose that the risk-free zero curve is flat at 7% per annum with continuous compounding and that defaults can occur halfway through each year in a new 5-year credit default swap. Suppose that the recovery rate is 30% and the default probabilities each year conditional on no earlier default is 3%. Estimate the credit default swap spread. Assume payments are made annually.

13.9. What is the value of the swap in Problem 13.8 (per dollar of notional principal) to the protection buyer if the credit default swap spread is 150 basis points?

13.10. What is the credit default swap spread in Problem 13.8 if it is a binary CDS?

13.11. How does a 5-year nth-to-default credit default swap work? Consider a basket of 100 reference entities where each reference entity has a probability of defaulting in each year of 1%. As the default correlation between the reference entities increases, what would you expect to happen to the value of the swap when (a) $n = 1$ and (b) $n = 25$. Explain your answer.

13.12. How is the recovery rate of a bond usually defined?

13.13. Show that the spread for a new plain vanilla CDS should be $(1 - R)$ times the spread for a similar new binary CDS, where R is the recovery rate.

13.14. A company enters into a total return swap where it receives the return on a corporate bond paying a coupon of 5% and pays LIBOR. Explain the difference between this and a regular swap where 5% is exchanged for LIBOR.

13.15. Explain how forward contracts and options on credit default swaps are structured.

13.16. "The position of a buyer of a credit default swap is similar to the position of someone who is long a risk-free bond and short a corporate bond." Explain this statement.

13.17. Why is there a potential asymmetric information problem in credit default swaps?

13.18. Does valuing a CDS using real-world default probabilities rather than risk-neutral default probabilities overstate or understate the value of the protection? Explain your answer.

13.19. What is the difference between a total return swap and an asset swap?

13.20. Suppose that in a one-factor Gaussian copula model the 5-year probability of default for each of 125 names is 3% and the pairwise copula correlation is 0.2. Calculate, for factor values of −2, −1, 0, 1, and 2, (a) the default probability conditional on the factor value and (b) the probability of more than 10 defaults conditional on the factor value.

13.21. What is a CDO squared? How about a CDO cubed?

ASSIGNMENT QUESTIONS

13.22. Suppose that the risk-free zero curve is flat at 6% per annum with continuous compounding and that defaults can occur at times 0.25 years, 0.75 years, 1.25 years, and 1.75 years in a 2-year plain vanilla credit default swap with semiannual payments. Suppose that the recovery rate is 20% and the unconditional probabilities of default (as seen at time zero) are 1% at times 0.25 years and 0.75 years, and 1.5% at times 1.25 years and 1.75 years. What is the credit default swap spread? What would the credit default spread be if the instrument were a binary credit default swap?

13.23. Assume that the default probability for a company in a year, conditional on no earlier defaults is λ and the recovery rate is R. The risk-free interest rate is 5% per annum. Default always occurs halfway through a year. The spread for a 5-year plain vanilla CDS where payments are made annually is 120 basis points and the spread for a 5-year binary CDS where payments are made annually is 160 basis points. Estimate R and λ.

13.24. Explain how you would expect the yields offered on the various tranches in a CDO to change when the correlation between the bonds in the portfolio increases.

13.25. Suppose that (a) the yield on a 5-year risk-free bond is 7%, (b) the yield on a 5-year corporate bond issued by company X is 9.5%, and (c) a 5-year credit default swap providing insurance against company X defaulting costs 150 basis points per year. What arbitrage opportunity is there in this situation? What arbitrage opportunity would there be if the credit default spread were 300 basis points instead of 150 basis points? Give two reasons why arbitrage opportunities such as those you have identified are less than perfect.

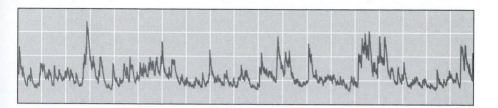

C H A P T E R **14**

Operational Risk

In 1999, bank supervisors announced plans to assign capital for operational risk in the new Basel II regulations. This met with some opposition from banks. The chairman and CEO of one major international bank described it as "the dopiest thing I have ever seen". However, bank supervisors persisted. They argued that operational risk was a major issue for banks. They pointed out that during a ten-year period more than 100 operational risk losses, each exceeding $100 million, had occurred. Some of these losses, listed by the categories used by the Bank for International Settlements, are:

Internal fraud: Allied Irish Bank, Barings, and Daiwa lost $700 million, $1 billion, and $1.4 billion, respectively, from fraudulent trading.

External fraud: Republic New York Corp. lost $611 million because of fraud committed by a custodial client.

Employment practices and workplace safety: Merrill Lynch lost $250 million in a legal settlement regarding gender discrimination.

Clients, products, & business practices: Household International lost $484 million from improper lending practices; Providian Financial Corporation lost $405 million from improper sales and billing practices.

Damage to physical assets: Bank of New York lost $140 million because of damage to its facilities related to the September 11, 2001, terrorist attack.

Business disruption and system failures: Solomon Brothers lost $303 million from a change in computing technology.

Execution, delivery and process management: Bank of America and Wells Fargo Bank lost $225 million and $150 million, respectively, from systems integration failures and transactions processing failures.

Most banks have always had some framework in place for managing operational risk. However, the prospect of new capital requirements has led them to greatly increase the resources they devote to measuring and monitoring operational risk.

It is much more difficult to quantify operational risk than credit or market risk. Operational risk is also more difficult to manage. Banks make a conscious decision to take a certain amount of credit and market risk, and there are many traded instruments that can be used to reduce these risks. Operational risk, by contrast, is a necessary part of doing business. An important part of operational risk management is identifying the types of risks that are being taken and which should be insured against. There is always a danger that a huge loss will be incurred from taking an operational risk that *ex ante* was not even recognized as a risk.

It might be thought that a loss such as that which brought down Barings Bank was a result of market risk because it was movements in market variables that led to it. However, it should be classified as operational risk because it involved fraud by one of its traders, Nick Leeson (see Business Snapshot 2.4). Suppose there was no fraud. If it was the bank's policy to let traders take huge risks, then the loss would be classified as market risk. But if this was not the bank's policy and there was a breakdown in its controls, then it would be classified as operational risk. Operational risk losses are often contingent on market movements. If the market had moved in Leeson's favor, there would have been no loss. The fraud and breakdown in the bank's control systems would probably never have come to light.

There are some parallels between the operational risk losses of banks and the losses of insurance companies. Insurance companies face a small probability of a large loss arising from a hurricane, earthquake, or other natural disaster. Similarly, banks face a small probability of a large operational risk loss. But there is one important difference. When insurance companies lose a large amount of money because of a natural disaster, all companies in the industry tend to be affected and premiums rise the next year to cover losses. Operational risk losses tend to affect only one bank. Since it operates in a competitive environment, the bank does not have the luxury of increasing prices for the services it offers during the following year.

14.1 WHAT IS OPERATIONAL RISK?

There are many different ways in which operational risk can be defined. It is tempting to consider operational risk as a residual risk and define it as any risk faced by a bank that is not market risk or credit risk. To produce an estimate of operational risk, we could then look at the bank's financial statements and remove from the income statement (a) the impact of credit losses and (b) the profits or losses from market risk exposure. The variation in the resulting income would then be attributed to operational risk.

Most people agree that this definition of operational risk is too broad. It includes the risks associated with entering new markets, developing new products, economic factors, and so on. Another possible definition is that operational risk, as its name implies, is the risk arising from operations. This includes the risk of mistakes in processing transactions, making payments, etc. This definition of risk is too narrow. It does not include major risks such as the "rogue trader" risk.

We can distinguish between internal risks and external risks. Internal risks are those over which the company has control. The company chooses whom it employs, what computer systems it develops, what controls are in place, and so on. Some people define operational risks as all internal risks. Operational risk then includes more than just the risk arising from operations. It includes risks arising from inadequate controls such as the rogue trader risk and the risks of other sorts of employee fraud.

Regulators favor including more than just internal risks in their definition of operational risk. They include the impact of external events, such as natural disasters (e.g., a fire or an earthquake that affects the bank's operations), political or regulatory risk (e.g., being prevented from operating in a foreign country by that country's government), security breaches, and so on. All of this is reflected in the following definition of operational risk produced by the Basel Committee on Banking Supervision in 2001:

> The risk of loss resulting from inadequate or failed internal processes, people, and systems or from external events.

Note that this definition includes legal risk, but does not include reputation risk or the risk resulting from strategic decisions.

Some operational risks result in increases in the bank's operating cost or decreases in its revenue. Other operational risks interact with credit and market risk. For example, when mistakes are made in a loan's documentation, it is usually the case that losses result if and only if the counterparty defaults. When a trader exceeds limits and misreports positions, losses result if and only if the market moves against the trader.

14.2 DETERMINATION OF REGULATORY CAPITAL

Banks have three alternatives for determining operational risk regulatory capital. The simplest approach is the *basic indicator approach*. Under this approach, operational risk capital is set equal to 15% of annual gross income over the previous three years. Gross income is defined as net interest income plus noninterest income.[1] A slightly more complicated approach is the *standardized approach*, in which a bank's activities are divided into eight business lines: corporate finance, trading and sales, retail banking, commercial banking, payment and settlement, agency services, asset management, and retail brokerage. The average gross income over the last three years for each business line is multiplied by a "beta factor" for that business line and the result summed to determine the total capital. The beta factors are shown in Table 14.1. The third alternative is the *advanced measurement approach* (AMA), in which the operational risk regulatory capital requirement is calculated by the bank internally using qualitative and quantitative criteria.

The Basel Committee has listed conditions that a bank must satisfy in order to use the standardized approach or the AMA approach. It expects large internationally active banks to move toward adopting the AMA

Table 14.1 Beta factors in standardized approach.

Business line	Beta factor
Corporate finance	18%
Trading and sales	18%
Retail banking	12%
Commercial banking	15%
Payment and settlement	18%
Agency services	15%
Asset management	12%
Retail brokerage	12%

---

[1] Net interest income is the excess of income earned on loans over interest paid on deposits and other instruments that are used to fund the loans (see Section 1.3).

approach through time. To use the standardized approach, a bank must satisfy the following conditions:

1. The bank must have an operational risk management function that is responsible for identifying, assessing, monitoring, and controlling operational risk.

2. The bank must keep track of relevant losses by business line and must create incentives for the improvement of operational risk.

3. There must be regular reporting of operational risk losses throughout the bank.

4. The bank's operational risk management system must be well documented.

5. The bank's operational risk management processes and assessment system must be subject to regular independent reviews by internal auditors. It must also be subject to regular review by external auditors or supervisors or both.

To use the AMA approach, the bank must satisfy additional requirements. It must be able to estimate unexpected losses based on an analysis of relevant internal and external data, and scenario analyses. The bank's system must be capable of allocating economic capital for operational risk

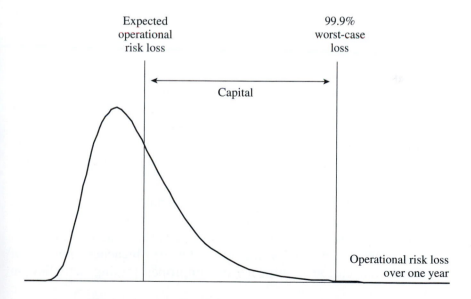

Figure 14.1   Calculation of VaR for operational risk.

across business lines in a way that creates incentives for the business lines to improve operational risk management.

The objective of banks using the AMA approach for operational risk is analogous to their objectives when they attempt to quantify credit risk. They would like to produce a probability distribution of losses such as that shown in Figure 14.1. Assuming that they can convince regulators that their expected operational risk cost is incorporated into their pricing of products, capital is assigned to cover unexpected costs. The confidence level is 99.9% and the time horizon is one year.

14.3 CATEGORIZATION OF OPERATIONAL RISKS

The Basel Committee on Bank Supervision has identified seven categories of operational risk.[2] These are:

1. *Internal fraud*: Acts of a type intended to defraud, misappropriate property or circumvent regulations, the law, or company policy (excluding diversity or discrimination events which involve at least one internal party). Examples include intentional misreporting of positions, employee theft, and insider trading on an employee's own account.

2. *External fraud*: Acts by third party of a type intended to defraud, misappropriate property or circumvent the law. Examples include robbery, forgery, check kiting, and damage from computer hacking.

3. *Employment practices and workplace safety*: Acts inconsistent with employment, health or safety laws or agreements, or which result in payment of personal injury claims, or claims relating to diversity or discrimination issues. Examples include workers compensation claims, violation of employee heath and safety rules, organized labor activities, discrimination claims, and general liability (e.g., a customer slipping and falling at a branch office).

4. *Clients, products, and business practices*: Unintentional or negligent failure to meet a professional obligation to specific clients (including fiduciary and suitability requirements), or from the nature or design of a product. Examples include fiduciary breaches, misuse of confidential customer information, improper trading activities on

---

[2] See Basel Committee on Bank Supervision, "Sound Practices for the Management and Supervision of Operational Risk," Bank for International Settlements, July 2002.

the bank's account, money laundering, and the sale of unauthorized products.

5. *Damage to physical assets*: Loss or damage to physical assets from natural disasters or other events. Examples include terrorism, vandalism, earthquakes, fires, and floods.

6. *Business disruption and system failures*: Disruption of business or system failures. Examples include hardware and software failures, telecommunication problems, and utility outages.

7. *Execution, delivery, and process management*: Failed transaction processing or process management, and relations with trade counter-parties and vendors. Examples include data entry errors, collateral management failures, incomplete legal documentation, unapproved access given to clients accounts, nonclient counterparty misperform-ance, and vendor disputes.

Banks must assess their exposure to each type of risk for each of the eight business lines listed in Table 14.1. Ideally this will lead to a result where VaR is estimated for each of $7 \times 8 = 56$ risk-type/business-line combinations.

14.4 LOSS SEVERITY AND LOSS FREQUENCY

There are two distributions that are important in estimating potential operational risk losses. One is the *loss frequency distribution* and the other is the *loss severity distribution*. The loss frequency distribution is the distribution of the number of losses observed during the time horizon (usually one year). The loss severity distribution is the distribution of the size of a loss, given that a loss occurs. It is usually assumed that loss severity and loss frequency are independent.

For loss frequency, the natural probability distribution to use is a Poisson distribution. This distribution assumes that losses happen randomly through time so that in any short period of time Δt there is a probability $\lambda \Delta t$ of a loss being sustained. The probability of n losses in time T is

$$e^{-\lambda T} \frac{(\lambda T)^n}{n!}$$

The parameter λ can be estimated as the average number of losses per unit time. For example, if during a 10-year period there were a total 12 losses, then λ is 1.2 per year or 0.1 per month. A Poisson distribution has the property that the mean frequency of losses equals the variance of the frequency of losses.[3]

For the loss severity probability distribution, a lognormal probability distribution is often used. The parameters of this probability distribution are the mean and standard deviation of the logarithm of the loss.

The loss frequency distribution must be combined with the loss severity distribution for each loss type and business line to determine a total loss distribution. Monte Carlo simulation can be used for this purpose.[4] As mentioned earlier, the usual assumption is that loss severity is independent of loss frequency. On each simulation trial, we proceed as follows:

1. We sample from the frequency distribution to determine the number of loss events ($= n$).

2. We sample n times from the loss severity distribution to determine the loss experienced for each loss event ($L_1, L_2, \ldots, L_n$).

3. We determine the total loss experienced ($= L_1 + L_2 + \cdots + L_n$).

When many simulation trials are used, we obtain a total loss distribution.

Figure 14.2 illustrates the procedure. In this example the expected loss frequency is 3 per year and the loss severity is drawn from a lognormal distribution. The logarithm of a loss ($ millions) is assumed to have a mean of 0 and a standard deviation of 0.4. The Excel worksheet used to produce Figure 14.2 is on the author's website.

Data Issues

Unfortunately there is usually relatively little historical data available within a bank to estimate loss severity and loss frequency distributions. Many banks have not kept records of losses arising from different types of operational risks for different business lines. As a result of regulatory pressure, they are starting to do so, but it may be some time before a reasonable amount of historical data is available. It is interesting to compare operational risk losses with credit risk losses in this respect.

---

[3] If the mean frequency is greater than the variance of the frequency, a binomial distribution may be more appropriate. If the mean frequency is less than the variance, a negative binomial distribution (mixed Poisson distribution) may be more appropriate.

[4] Combining the loss severity and loss frequency distribution is a very common problem in insurance. Apart from Monte Carlo simulation, two approaches that are used are Panjer's algorithm and fast Fourier transforms. See H. H. Panjer, "Recursive Evaluation of a Family of Compound Distributions," *ASTIN Bulletin*, 12 (1981), 22–29.

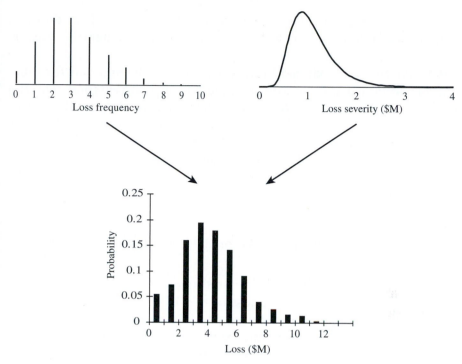

Figure 14.2 Calculation of loss distribution from loss frequency and loss severity.

Traditionally banks have done a much better job at documenting their credit risk losses than their operational risk losses. Moreover, in the case of credit risks, a bank can rely on a wealth of information published by credit-rating agencies to assess probabilities of default and expected losses given default. Similar data on operational risk has not in the past been collected in such a systematic way. It may also be a problem that banks sometimes conceal a large operational risk loss from the market because they feel it will damage their reputation.

As indicated above, the Poisson distribution is often used for loss frequency and the lognormal distribution is often used for loss severity. Available data is usually used to estimate the parameters of these distributions. The loss frequency distribution should be estimated from the bank's own data as far as possible. For the loss severity distribution, regulators encourage banks to use their own data in conjunction with external data. There are two sources of external data. The first is data obtained through sharing arrangements between banks. (The insurance industry has had mechanisms for sharing loss data for many years and banks are now beginning to do this as well.) The second is publicly available data that has been collected in a systematic way by data vendors.

Both internal and external historical data must be adjusted for inflation. In addition, a scale adjustment should be made to external data. If a bank with a revenue of $10 billion reports a loss of $8 million, how should the loss be scaled for a bank with a revenue of $5 billion? A natural assumption is that a similar loss for a bank with a revenue of $5 billion would be $4 million. This estimate is probably too small. For example, research by Shih *et al.* suggests that the effect of firm size on the size of a loss experience is relatively small.[5] Their estimate is

$$\text{Estimated loss for Bank A} = \text{Observed loss for Bank B} \times \left(\frac{\text{Bank A revenue}}{\text{Bank B revenue}}\right)^{\alpha}$$

where $\alpha = 0.23$. This means that in our example the bank with a revenue of $5 billion would experience a loss of $8 \times 0.5^{0.23} = 6.82$ million.

After the appropriate scale adjustment, data obtained through sharing arrangements with other banks can be merged with the bank's own data to obtain a larger sample for determining the loss severity distribution. Public data purchased from data vendors cannot be used in this way because it is subject to biases. For example:

1. Only large losses are publicly reported, and the larger the loss, the more likely it is to be reported.

2. Institutions with weak controls are more likely to be represented in the database because they suffer more losses. Moreover, their losses tend to be larger.

Public data is most useful for determining *relative* loss severity. Suppose that a bank has good information on the mean and standard deviation of its loss severity distribution for internal fraud in corporate finance, but not for external fraud in corporate finance or for internal fraud in trading and sales. Suppose that the mean and standard deviation of its internal loss severity distribution for internal fraud in corporate finance are $50,000 and $30,000. Suppose further that external data indicates that for external fraud in corporate finance the mean severity is twice that for internal fraud

---

[5] See J. Shih, A. Samad-Khan, and P. Medapa, "Is the Size of an Operational Loss Related to Firm Size," *Operational Risk*, January 2000. Whether Shih *et al.*'s results apply to legal risks is debatable. It often seems that the size of a settlement in a large lawsuit against a bank is governed by how much the bank can afford.

in corporate finance and the standard deviation of the severity is 1.5 times as great. In the absence of a better alternative, the bank might assume that its own severity for external fraud in corporate finance has a mean of $2 \times 50,000 = \$100,000$ and a standard deviation of severity equal to $1.5 \times 30,000 = \$45,000$. Similarly, if the external data indicates that the mean severity for internal fraud in trading and sales is 2.5 times that for internal fraud in corporate finance and the standard deviation is twice as great, the bank might assume that its own severity for internal fraud in trading and sales has a mean of $2.5 \times 50,000 = \$100,000$ and a standard deviation of $2 \times 30,000 = \$60,000$.

Scenario Analysis

Since historical data is relatively difficult to obtain, regulators encourage banks to use scenario analyses in addition to internal and external loss data. This involves using managerial judgement to generate scenarios where large losses occur. Managers estimate the loss frequency parameter λ associated with each scenario and the parameters of the loss severity distribution. The advantage of scenario analysis is that it can include losses that the financial institution has never experienced, but, in the judgement of senior management, could occur. It reflects the controls in place in the bank and the type of business it is currently doing.

One advantage of the scenario analysis approach is that it leads to management thinking actively and creatively about potential adverse events. This can have a number of benefits. In some cases strategies for responding to an event so as to minimize its severity are likely to be developed. In other cases, proposals may be made for reducing the probability of the event occurring at all.

The main drawback of scenario analysis is that it requires a great deal of senior management time. It seems likely that standard scenarios will be developed by consultants and by banks themselves to make the process less of a burden.

14.5 FORWARD LOOKING APPROACHES

Risk managers should try to be proactive in preventing losses from occurring. One approach is to monitor what is happening at other banks and try and learn from their mistakes. When a $700 million rogue trader loss happened at a Baltimore subsidiary of Allied Irish Bank in 2002, risk managers throughout the world studied the situation carefully and asked:

Business Snapshot 14.1 The Hammersmith and Fulham Story

Between 1987 to 1989 the London Borough of Hammersmith and Fulham in Great Britain entered into about 600 interest rate swaps and related instruments with a total notional principal of about 6 billion pounds. The transactions appear to have been entered into for speculative rather than hedging purposes. The two employees of Hammersmith and Fulham that were responsible for the trades had only a sketchy understanding of the risks they were taking and how the products they were trading worked.

By 1989, because of movements in sterling interest rates, Hammersmith and Fulham had lost several hundred million pounds on the swaps. To the banks on the other side of the transactions, the swaps were worth several hundred million pounds. The banks were concerned about credit risk. They had entered into offsetting swaps to hedge their interest rate risks. If Hammersmith and Fulham defaulted, they would still have to honor their obligations on the offsetting swaps and would take a huge loss.

What actually happened was not a default. Hammersmith and Fulham's auditor asked to have the transactions declared void because Hammersmith and Fulham did not have the authority to enter into the transactions. The British courts agreed. The case was appealed and went all the way to the House of Lords, Britain's highest court. The final decision was that Hammersmith and Fulham did not have the authority to enter into the swaps, but that they ought to have the authority to do so in the future for risk management purposes. Needless to say, banks were furious that their contracts were overturned in this way by the courts.

"Could this happen to us?" Business Snapshot 14.1 describes a situation concerning a British local authority in the late 1980s. It immediately led to all banks instituting procedures for checking that counterparties had the authority to enter into derivatives transactions.

Causal Relationships

Operational risk managers should try and establish causal relations between decisions taken and operational risk losses. Does increasing the average educational qualifications of employees reduce losses arising from mistakes in the way transactions are processed? Will a new computer system reduce the probabilities of losses from system failures? Are operational risk losses correlated with the employee turnover rate? If so, can they be reduced by measures taken to improve employee retention? Can the risk of a rogue trader be reduced by the way responsibilities are divided between different individuals and by the way traders are motivated?

One approach to establishing causal relationships is statistical. If we look at 12 different locations where a bank operates and find a high negative correlation between the education of back office employees and the cost of mistakes in processing transactions, it might well make sense to do a cost–benefit analysis of changing the educational requirements for a back-office job in some of the locations. In some cases, a detailed analysis of the cause of losses may provide insights. For example, if 40% of computer failures can be attributed to the fact that the current hardware is several years old and less reliable than newer versions, a cost–benefit analysis of upgrading is likely to be useful.

RCSA and KRIs

Risk and control self assessment (RCSA) is an important way in which banks try and achieve a better understanding of their operational risk exposures. This involves asking the managers of the business units themselves to identify their operational risks. Sometimes questionnaires designed by senior management are used.

A by-product of any program to measure and understand operational risk is likely to be the development of key risk indicators (KRIs). Risk indicators are key tools in the management of operational risk. The most important indicators are prospective. They provide an early-warning system to track the level of operational risk in the organization. Examples of key risk indicators are staff turnover and number of failed transactions. The hope is that key risk indicators can identify potential problems and allow remedial action to be taken before losses are incurred.

It is important for a bank to quantify operational risks, but it is even more important to take action to control and manage those risks.

14.6 ALLOCATION OF OPERATIONAL RISK CAPITAL

Operational risk capital should be allocated to business units in a way that encourages them to improve their operational risk management. If a business unit can show that it has taken steps to reduce the frequency or severity of a particular risk, it should be allocated less capital. This will have the effect of improving the business unit's return on capital (and possibly lead to the business unit manager receiving an increased bonus).

Note that it is not always optimal for a manager to reduce a particular operational risk. Sometimes the costs of reducing the risk outweigh the benefits of reduced capital, so that return on allocated capital decreases. A business unit should be encouraged to make appropriate calculations and determine the amount of operational risk that maximizes return on capital.

Scorecard Approaches

Some banks use scorecard approaches to allocate operational risk capital. Experts identify the key determinants of each type of risk and then formulate questions for managers of business units to enable risk levels to be quantified. The total number of different business units is likely to be greater than the eight listed in Table 14.1 because each region of the world in which the bank operates often has to be considered separately. Examples of the questions that might be used are:

- What is the number of sensitive positions filled by temps?
- What is the ratio of supervisors to staff?
- Does your business have confidential client information?
- What is the employee turnover rate per annum?
- How many open employee positions are there at any time?
- What percentage of your staff has a performance-based component to their remuneration?
- What percentage of your staff did not take ten consecutive days leave in the last 12 months?

Scores are assigned to the answers. The total score for a particular business unit indicates the amount of risk present in the business unit and can be used as a basis for allocating capital to the business unit. The scores given by a scorecard approach should be validated by comparing scores with actual loss experience whenever possible.

The overall result of operational risk assessment and operational risk capital allocation should be that business units become more sensitive to the need for managing operational risk. Hopefully operational risk management will be seen to be an important part of every manager's job. A key ingredient for the success of any operational risk program is the support of senior management. The Basel Committee on Banking Supervision is very much aware of this. It recommends that the bank's board of directors be involved in the approval of a risk management program and that it reviews the program on a regular basis.

14.7 USE OF THE POWER LAW

In Section 5.4 we introduced the power law. This states that for a wide range of variables

$$\text{Prob}(v > x) = Kx^{-\alpha}$$

where v is the value of the variable, x is a relatively large value of v, and K and α are constants. We covered the theoretical underpinnings of the power law and maximum-likelihood estimation procedures when we looked at extreme value theory in Section 9.4.

De Fountnouvelle *et al.,* using data on losses from external vendors, find that the power law holds well for the large losses experienced by banks.[6] This makes the calculation of VaR with high degrees of confidence such as 99.9% possible. Loss data (internal or external) is used to estimate the power law parameters using the maximum-likelihood approach in Chapter 9. The 99.9% quantile of the loss distribution is then estimated using equation (9.6).

When loss distributions are aggregated, the distribution with the heaviest tails tends to dominate. This means that the loss with the lowest α defines the extreme tails of the total loss distribution.[7] Therefore, if all we are interested in is calculating the extreme tail of the total operational risk loss distribution, it may only be necessary to consider one or two business-line/loss-type combinations.

14.8 INSURANCE

An important decision for operational risk managers is the extent to which operational risks should be insured against. Insurance policies are available on many different kinds of risk ranging from fire losses to rogue trader losses. Provided that the insurance company's balance sheet satisfies certain criteria, a bank using AMA can reduce the capital it is required to hold by entering into insurance contracts. In this section we review some of the key issues facing insurance companies in the design of their insurance contracts and show how these are likely to influence the type of contracts that banks can negotiate.

---

[6] See P. De Fountnouvelle, V. DeJesus-Rueff, J. Jordan, and E. Rosengren, "Capital and Risk: New Evidence on Implications of Large Operational Risk Losses," Federal Reserve Board of Boston, Working Paper, September 2003.

[7] In Chapter 9 the parameter ξ equals $1/\alpha$, so it is the loss distribution with the largest ξ that defines the extreme tails.

Moral Hazard

One of the risks facing an insurance company is moral hazard. This is the risk that the existence of the insurance contract will cause the bank to behave differently than it otherwise would. This changed behavior increases the risks to the insurance company. Consider, for example, a bank that insures itself against robberies. As a result of the insurance policy, it may be tempted to be lax in its implementation of security measures— making a robbery more likely than it would otherwise have been.

Insurance companies have traditionally dealt with moral hazard in a number of ways. Typically there is a *deductible* in any insurance policy. This means that the bank is responsible for bearing the first part of any loss. Sometimes there is a *coinsurance provision* in a policy. The insurance company then pays a predetermined percentage (less than 100%) of losses in excess of the deductible. In addition, there is nearly always a *policy limit*. This is a limit on the total liability of the insurer. Consider again a bank that has insured itself against robberies. The existence of deductibles, coinsurance provisions, and policy limits are likely to provide an incentive for a bank not to relax security measures in its branches. The moral hazard problem in rogue trader insurance in discussed in Business Snapshot 14.2.

Adverse Selection

The other major problem facing insurance companies is adverse selection. This is where an insurance company cannot distinguish between good and bad risks. It offers the same price to everyone and inadvertently attracts more of the bad risks. For example, banks without good internal controls are more likely to enter into rogue trader insurance contracts; banks without good internal controls are more likely to buy insurance policies to protect themselves against external fraud.

To overcome the adverse selection problem, an insurance company must try to understand the controls that exist within banks and the losses that have been experienced. As a result of its initial assessment of risks, it may not charge the same premium for the same contract to all banks. Over time it gains more information about the bank's operational risk losses and may increase or reduce the premium charged. This is much the same as the approach adopted by insurance companies when they sell automobile insurance to a driver. At the outset the insurance company obtains as much information on the driver as possible. As time goes by, it collects more information on the driver's risk (number of accidents, number of speeding tickets, etc.) and modifies the premium charged accordingly.

Business Snapshot 14.2   Rogue Trader Insurance

A rogue trader insurance policy presents particularly tricky moral hazard problems. An unscrupulous bank could enter into an insurance contract to protect itself against losses from rogue trader risk and then choose to be lax in its implementation of trading limits. If a trader exceeds the trading limit and makes a large profit, the bank is better off than it would be otherwise. If a large loss results, a claim can be made under the rogue trader insurance policy. Deductibles, coinsurance provisions, and policy limits may mean that the amount recovered is less than the loss incurred by the trader. However, potential net losses to the bank are likely to be far less than potential profits, making the lax trading limits strategy a good bet for the bank.

Given this problem, it is perhaps surprising that some insurance companies do offer rogue trader insurance policies. These companies tend to specify carefully how trading limits are implemented. They may also require that the existence of the insurance policy not be revealed to anyone on the trading floor. They are likely to want to retain the right to investigate the circumstances underlying any loss. It is also worth pointing out that, from the bank's point of view, the lax trading limits strategy we have outlined may be very shortsighted. The bank might well find that future insurance costs rise significantly as a result of a rogue trader claim. Furthermore, a large rogue trader loss (even if insured) would cause its reputation to suffer.

14.9 SARBANES–OXLEY

Largely as a result of the Enron bankruptcy the Sarbanes–Oxley Act was passed in the United States in 2002. This provides another dimension to operational risk management for financial and nonfinancial institutions in the United States. The Act requires boards of directors to become much more involved with day-to-day operations. They must monitor internal controls to ensure risks are being assessed and handled well.

The Act specifies rules concerning the composition of the board of directors of public companies and lists the responsibilities of the board. It gives the SEC the power to censure the board or give it additional responsibilities. A company's auditors are not allowed to carry out any significant nonauditing services for the company.[8] Audit partners must be rotated. The audit committee of the board must be made aware of alternative accounting treatments. The CEO and CFO must prepare a

---

[8] Enron's auditor, Arthur Andersen, provided a wide range of services in addition to auditing. It did not survive the litigation that followed the downfall of Enron.

statement to accompany the audit report to the effect that the financial statements are accurate. The CEO and CFO are required to return bonuses in the event that financial statements are restated. Other rules concern insider trading, disclosure, personal loans to executives, reporting of transactions by directors, and the monitoring of internal controls by directors.

SUMMARY

In 1999, bank supervisors indicated their intention to charge capital for operational risk. This has led banks to carefully consider how they should measure and manage operational risk. Bank supervisors have identified seven different types of operational risk and eight different business lines. They encourage banks to quantify risks for each of the 56 risk-type/business-line combinations.

One approach that has been developed is the statistical approach. This treats operational risk losses in much the same way as actuaries treat losses from insurance policies. A frequency of loss distribution and a severity of loss distribution is estimated and these are combined to form a total operational loss distribution. If possible, the frequency of loss distribution is estimated from internal data. The loss severity distribution is estimated from a combination of internal and external data.

There are two sources of external data. One is data obtained from other banks via sharing arrangements; the other is publicly available data on large losses collected by data vendors. Increasingly banks are augmenting loss data with scenario analyses where senior managers develop loss-event scenarios and estimate parameters describing loss frequency and severity.

Risk managers should try to be forward-looking in their approach to operational risk. They should try to understand what determines operational risk losses and develop key risk indicators to track the level of operational risk in different parts of the organization.

Once operational risk capital has been estimated, it is important to develop procedures for allocating it to business units. This should be done in a way that encourages business units to reduce operational risk when they can do so without incurring excessive costs. One approach to allocation is the use of scorecards.

The power law introduced in Chapter 5 seems to apply to operational risk losses. This makes it possible to use extreme value theory to estimate the tails of a loss distribution from empirical data. When several loss distributions are aggregated, it is the loss distribution with the heaviest tail that dominates. In principle, this makes the calculation of VaR for total operational risk easier.

Many operational risks can be insured against. However, most policies include deductibles, coinsurance provisions, and policy limits. As a result a bank is always left bearing part of any risk itself. Moreover, the way insurance premiums change as time passes is likely to depend on the claims made and other indicators that the insurance company has of how well operational risks are being managed.

The whole process of measuring, managing, and allocating operational risk is still in its infancy. As time goes by and data is accumulated, more precise procedures than those we have mentioned in this chapter are likely to emerge. One of the key problems is that there are two sorts of operational risk: high-frequency low-severity risks and low-frequency high-severity risks. The former are relatively easy to quantify, but operational risk VaR is largely driven by the latter.

Bank supervisors seem to be succeeding in their objective of making banks more sensitive to the importance of operational risk. In many ways the key benefit of an operational risk management program is not the numbers that are produced, but the process that banks go through in producing the numbers. If well handled, the process can sensitize managers to the importance of operational risk and perhaps lead to them thinking about it differently.

FURTHER READING

Bank for International Settlements, "Sound Practices for the Management and Supervision of Operational Risk," February 2003.

Baud, N., A. Frachot, and T. Roncalli, "Internal Data, External Data and Consortium Data for Operational Risk Management: How to Pool Data Properly," Working Paper, Groupe de Recherche Operationelle, Credit Lyonnais, 2002.

Chorafas, D. N., *Operational Risk Control with Basel II: Basic Principles and Capital Requirements*. Elsevier, 2003.

De Fountnouvelle, P., V. DeJesus-Rueff, J. Jordan, and E. Rosengren, "Capital and Risk: New Evidence on Implications of Large Operational Risk Losses," Federal Reserve Board of Boston, Working Paper, September 2003.

Netter, J., and A. Poulsen, "Operational Risk in Financial Service Providers and the Proposed Basel Accord: An Overview," Working Paper, Terry College of Business, University of Georgia.

Van Den Brink, G.J., *Operational Risk: The New Challenge for Banks.* Basingstoke, UK: Palgrave, 2001.

QUESTIONS AND PROBLEMS (Answers at End of Book)

14.1. What risks are included by regulators in their definition of operational risks? What risks are not included?

14.2. Suppose that external data shows that a loss of $100 million occurred at a bank with annual revenues of $1 billion. Your bank has annual revenues of $3 billion. What is the implication of the external data for losses that could occur at your bank.

14.3. Suppose that there is a 90% probability that operational risk losses of a certain type will not exceed $20 million. The power law parameter α is 0.8. What is the probability of losses exceeding (a) $40 million, (b) $80 million, and (c) $200 million.

14.4. Discuss how moral hazard and adverse selection are handled in car insurance.

14.5. Give two ways Sarbanes–Oxley affects the CEOs of public companies.

14.6. When is a trading loss classified as a market risk and when is it classified as an operational risk?

14.7. Discuss whether there is (a) moral hazard and (b) adverse selection in life insurance contracts.

14.8. What is external loss data? How is it obtained? How is it used in determining operational risk loss distributions for a bank?

14.9. What distributions are commonly used for loss frequency and loss severity?

14.10. Give examples of key risk indicators that might be monitored by a central operational risk management group within a bank.

14.11. The worksheet used to produce Figure 14.2 is on the author's website. What is the mean and standard deviation of the loss distribution. Modify the inputs to the simulation to test the effect of changing the loss frequency from 3 to 4.

ASSIGNMENT QUESTIONS

14.12. Suppose that there is a 95% probability that operational risk losses of a certain type exceed $10 million. Use the power law to estimate the 99.97% worst-case operational risk loss when the α parameter equals (a) 0.25, (b) 0.5, (c) 0.9, and (d) 1.0.

14.13. Consider the following two events: (a) a bank loses \$1 billion from an unexpected lawsuit relating to its transactions with a counterparty and (b) an insurance company loses \$1 billion because of an unexpected hurricane in Texas. Suppose you own shares in both the bank and the insurance company. Which loss are you more concerned about? Why?

14.14. The worksheet used to produce Figure 14.2 is on the author's website. How does the loss distribution change when the loss severity has a beta distribution with an upper bound of 5, a lower bound of 0, and the other parameters both 1?

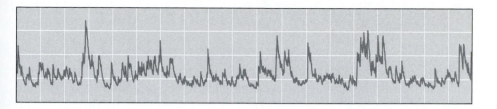

CHAPTER **15**

Model Risk and Liquidity Risk

In this chapter we discuss two additional types of risk faced by financial institutions: model risk and liquidity risk. Model risk is the risk related to the models a financial institution uses to value derivatives. Liquidity risk is the risk that there may not be enough buyers (or sellers) in the market for a financial institution to execute the trades it desires. The two risks are related. Sophisticated models are only necessary to price products that are relatively illiquid. When there is an active market for a product, prices can be observed in the market and models play a less important role.

There are two main types of model risk. One is the risk that the model will give the wrong price at the time a product is bought or sold. This can result in a company buying a product for a price that is too high or selling it for a price that is too low. The other risk concerns hedging. If a company uses the wrong model, the Greek letters it calculates—and the hedges it sets up based on those Greek letters—are liable to be wrong.

Liquidity risk is the risk that, even if a financial institution's theoretical price is in line with the market price and the price of its competitors, it cannot trade in the volume required at the price. Suppose that the offer price for a particular option is $40. The financial institution could probably buy 10,000 options at this price. But it is likely to be quite difficult to buy 10 million options at or close to the price. If the financial institution went into the market and started buying large numbers of options from different market makers, then the price of the option would probably go up, making the rest of its trades more expensive.

15.1 THE NATURE OF MODELS IN FINANCE

Many physicists work in the front and middle office of banks and many of the models they use are similar to those encountered in physics. For example, the differential equation that leads to the famous Black–Scholes model is the heat-exchange equation that has been used by physicists for many years. However, as Derman has pointed out, there is an important difference between the models of physics and those of finance.[1] The models of physics describe physical processes and are highly accurate. By contrast, the models of finance describe the behavior of market variables. This behavior depends on the actions of human beings. As a result the models are at best approximate descriptions of the market variables. This is why the use of models in finance entails what is referred to as "model risk".

One important difference between the models of physics and the models of finance concerns model parameters. The parameters of models in the physical sciences are usually constants that do not change. The parameters in finance models are often assumed to be constant for the whole life of the model when the model is used to calculate an option price on any particular day. But the parameters are changed from day to day so that market prices are matched. The process of choosing model parameters is known as *calibration*.

An example of calibration is the choice of the volatility parameter in the Black–Scholes model. This model assumes that volatility remains constant for the life of the model. However, the volatility parameter that is used in the model changes daily. For a particular option maturing in three months, the volatility parameter might be 20% when the option is valued today, 22% when valued tomorrow, and 19% when valued on the next day. For some models in finance, the calibration process is quite involved. For example, calibrating an interest rate model on a particular day involves (a) fitting the zero-coupon yield curve observed on that day and (b) fitting the market prices of actively traded interest rate options such as caps and swap options.

Sometimes parameters in finance models have to be calibrated to historical data rather than to market prices. Consider a model involving both an exchange rate and an equity index. It is likely that the correlation between the exchange rate movements and the equity price movements would be estimated from historical data because there are no actively traded instruments from which the correlation can be implied.

---

[1] See E. Derman, *My Life as a Quant: Reflections on Physics and Finance*, Wiley, 2004

Business Snapshot 15.1 Kidder Peabody's Embarrassing Mistake

Investment banks have developed a way of creating a zero-coupon bond, called a *strip*, from a coupon-bearing Treasury bond by selling each of the cash flows underlying the coupon-bearing bond as a separate security. Joseph Jett, a trader working for Kidder Peabody, had a relatively simple trading strategy. He would buy strips and sell them in the forward market. The forward price of the strip was always greater than the spot price and so it appeared that he had found a money machine! In fact the difference between the forward price and the spot price represents nothing more than the cost of funding the purchase of the strip. Suppose, for example, that the three-month interest rate is 4% per annum and the spot price of a strip is $70. The three-month forward price of the strip is $70e^{0.04 \times 3/12} = \$70.70$.

Kidder Peabody's computer system reported a profit on each of Jett's trades equal to the excess of the forward price over the spot price ($0.70 in our example). By rolling his contracts forward, Jett was able to prevent the funding cost from accruing to him. The result was that the system reported a profit of $100 million on Jett's trading (and Jett received a big bonus) when in fact there was a loss in the region of $350 million. This shows that even large financial institutions can get relatively simple things wrong!

15.2 MODELS FOR LINEAR PRODUCTS

Pricing linear products such as forward contracts and swaps is straightforward and relies on little more than present value arithmetic. There is usually very little disagreement in the market on the correct pricing models for these products and very little model risk. However, this does not mean that there is no model risk. As indicated in Business Snapshot 15.1, Kidder Peabody's computer system did not account correctly for funding costs when a linear product was traded. As a result the system indicated that one of the company's traders was making a large profit when in fact he was making a huge loss.

Another type of model risk arises when a financial institution assumes a product is simpler than it actually is. Consider the interest rate swap market. A plain vanilla interest rate swap such as that described in Section 2.3 can be valued by assuming that forward interest rates will be realized as described in Appendix B. For example, if the forward interest rate for the period between 2 and 2.5 years is 4.3%, we value the swap on the assumption that the floating rate that is exchanged for fixed at the 2.5-year point is 4.3%.

> **Business Snapshot 15.2**   Exploiting the Weaknesses of a
> Competitor's Model
>
> A LIBOR-in-arrears swap is an interest rate swap where the floating interest rate is paid on the day it is observed, not one accrual period later. Whereas a plain vanilla swap is correctly valued by assuming that future rates will be today's forward rates, a LIBOR-in-arrears swap should be valued on the assumption that the future rate is today's forward interest rate plus a "convexity adjustment".
>
> In the mid-1990s sophisticated financial institutions understood the correct approach for valuing a LIBOR-in-arrears swap. Less sophisticated financial institutions used the naive "assume forward rates will be realized" approach. The result was that by choosing trades judiciously sophisticated financial institutions were able to make substantial profits at the expense of their less sophisticated counterparts.
>
> The derivatives business is one where traders do not hesitate to exploit the weaknesses of their competitor's models!

It is tempting to generalize from this and argue that any agreement to exchange cash flows can be valued on the assumption that forward rates are realized. This is not so. Consider, for example, what is known as a *LIBOR-in-arrears swap*. In this instrument the floating rate that is observed on a particular date is paid on that date (not one accrual period later as is the case for a plain vanilla swap). A LIBOR-in-arrears swap should be valued on the assumption that the realized interest rate equals the forward interest rate plus a "convexity adjustment". As indicated in Business Snapshot 15.2, financial institutions that did not understand this lost money in the mid-1990s.

15.3 MODELS FOR ACTIVELY TRADED PRODUCTS

When a product trades actively in the market, we do not need a model to know what its price is. The market tells us this. Suppose, for example, that a certain option on a stock index trades actively and is quoted by market makers as bid $30 and offer $31. Our best estimate of its current value is the mid-market price of $30.50.

A model is often used as a communication tool in these circumstances. Traders like to use models where only one of the variables necessary to determine the price of a product is not directly observable in the market. The model then provides a one-to-one mapping of the product's price to the variable and vice versa. The Black–Scholes model (see Appendix C) is a case in point. The only unobservable variable in the model is the volatility of the underlying asset. The model therefore provides a one-to-one mapping of option prices to volatilities and vice versa. As explained in Chapter 5, the volatility calculated from the market price is known as the implied volatility. Traders frequently quote implied volatilities rather than the dollar prices. The reason is that the implied volatility is more stable than the price. For example, when the underlying asset price or the interest rate changes, there is likely to be a much bigger percentage jump in the dollar price of an option than in its implied volatility.

Consider again the index option that has a mid-market price of $30.50. Suppose it is a one-year European call option where the strike price is 1,000, the one-year forward price of the index is 1,100, and the one-year risk-free interest rate is 3%. The mid-market implied volatility would be quoted as 15.37%.[2] The bid–offer spread might be "bid 15.24%, offer 15.50%".

Volatility Smiles

The volatility implied by Black–Scholes (or by a binomial tree calculation such as that in Appendix D) as a function of the strike price for a particular option maturity is known as a *volatility smile*.[3] If traders really believed the assumptions underlying the Black–Scholes model, the

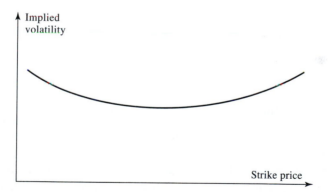

Figure 15.1   Volatility smile for foreign currency options.

[2] Implied volatility calculations can be done with the DerivaGem software available on the author's website.

[3] It can be shown that the relationship between strike price and implied volatility should be exactly the same for calls and puts in the case of European options and approximately the same in the case of American options.

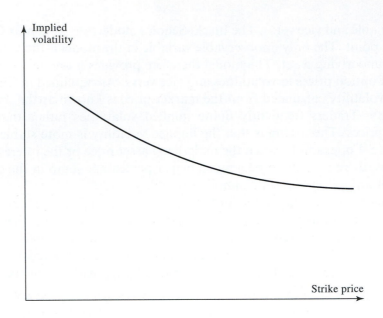

Figure 15.2   Volatility smile for equity options.

implied volatility would be the same for all options and the volatility smile would be flat. In fact, this is rarely the case.

The volatility smile used by traders to price foreign currency options has the general form shown in Figure 15.1. The volatility is relatively low for at-the-money options. It becomes progressively higher as an option moves either in the money or out of the money. The reason for the volatility smile is that Black–Scholes assumes

1. The volatility of the asset is constant.

2. The price of the asset changes smoothly with no jumps.

In practice, neither of these conditions is satisfied for an exchange rate. The volatility of an exchange rate is far from constant, and exchange rates frequently exhibit jumps.[4] It turns out that the effect of both a nonconstant volatility and jumps is that extreme outcomes become more likely. This leads to the volatility smile in Figure 15.1.

The volatility smile used by traders to price equity options (both those on individual stocks and those on stock indices) has the general form shown in Figure 15.2. This is sometimes referred to as a *volatility skew*. The

---

[4] Often the jumps are in response to the actions of central banks.

Business Snapshot 15.3 Crashophobia

It is interesting that the pattern in Figure 15.2 for equities has existed only since the stock market crash of October 1987. Prior to October 1987 implied volatilities were much less dependent on strike price. This has led Mark Rubinstein to suggest that one reason for the equity volatility smile may be "crashophobia". Traders are concerned about the possibility of another crash similar to October 1987 and assign relatively high prices (and therefore relatively high implied volatilities) for deep-out-of-the-money puts.

There is some empirical support for this explanation. Declines in the S&P 500 tend to be accompanied by a steepening of the volatility skew, perhaps because traders become more nervous about the possibility of a crash. When the S&P increases, the skew tends to become less steep.

---

volatility decreases as the strike price increases. The volatility used to price a low-strike-price option (i.e., a deep-out-of-the-money put or a deep-in-the-money call) is significantly higher than that used to price a high-strike-price option (i.e., a deep-in-the-money put or a deep-out-of-the-money call). One possible explanation for the smile in equity options concerns leverage. As a company's equity declines in value, the company's leverage increases. This means that the equity becomes more risky and its volatility increases. As a company's equity increases in value, leverage decreases. The equity then becomes less risky and its volatility decreases. This argument shows that we can expect the volatility of equity to be a decreasing function of price and is consistent with Figure 15.2. Another explanation is crashophobia (see Business Snapshot 15.3).

Volatility smiles and skews such as those shown in Figures 15.1 and 15.2 are liable to change on a daily basis. This means that the volatilities traders use change from day to day as well as from option to option. Why does the market continue to use Black–Scholes (and its extensions) when it provides such a poor fit to market prices? The answer is that traders like the model. They find it easy to use and easy to understand.

Volatility Surfaces

Figures 15.1 and 15.2 are for options with a particular maturity. Traders like to combine the volatility smiles for different maturities into a *volatility surface*. This shows implied volatility as a function of both strike price and time to maturity. Table 15.1 gives a typical volatility surface for currency options. The table indicates that the volatility smile becomes less

Table 15.1   Volatility surface.

Time to maturity	Strike price				
	0.90	0.95	1.00	1.05	1.10
1 month	14.2	13.0	12.0	13.1	14.5
3 month	14.0	13.0	12.0	13.1	14.2
6 month	14.1	13.3	12.5	13.4	14.3
1 year	14.7	14.0	13.5	14.0	14.8
2 year	15.0	14.4	14.0	14.5	15.1
5 year	14.8	14.6	14.4	14.7	15.0

pronounced as the time to maturity increases. This is what is usually observed in practice.[5]

The volatility surface is produced primarily from information provided by brokers. Brokers are in the business of bringing buyers and sellers together in the over-the-counter market and have more information on the implied volatilities at which transactions are being done on any given day than individual derivatives dealers. Over time an options trader develops an understanding of what the volatility surface for a particular underlying asset should look like.

To value a new option, traders look up the appropriate volatility in the table using interpolation. For example, to value a 9-month option with a strike price of 1.05, a trader would interpolate between 13.4 and 14.0 in Table 15.1 to obtain a volatility of 13.7%. This is the volatility that would be used in a Black–Scholes formula or a binomial tree calculation. When valuing a 1.5-year option with a strike price of 0.925, a two-dimensional interpolation would be used to give an implied volatility of 14.525%.

Hedging

It should be clear from the above discussion that models play a relatively minor role in the pricing of actively traded products. Dealers interpolate between prices observed in the market. A model such as Black–Scholes is nothing more than a tool to facilitate the interpolation. It is easier to interpolate between implied volatilities than between dollar prices.

---

[5] If T is the time to maturity and F_0 is the forward price of the asset, some traders choose to define the volatility smile as the relationship between implied volatility and

$$\frac{1}{\sqrt{T}}\ln\frac{K}{F_0}$$

rather than as the relationship between the implied volatility and K. The smile is then usually much less dependent on the time to maturity.

Models are used in a more significant way when it comes to hedging. Traders must manage their exposure to delta, gamma, vega, etc. (see Chapter 3). We can distinguish between *within-model hedging* and *outside-model hedging*. Within-model hedging is designed to deal with the risk of changes in variables that are assumed to be uncertain by the model. Outside-model hedging deals with the risk of changes in variables that are assumed to be constant (or deterministic) by the model. When Black–Scholes is used, hedging against movements in the underlying stock price (delta and gamma hedging) is within-model hedging because the model assumes that stock price changes are uncertain. However, hedging against volatility (vega hedging) is outside-model hedging because the model assumes that volatility is constant.

In practice, traders almost invariably do outside-model hedging as well as within-model hedging. This is because, as we have explained, the calibration process causes parameters such as volatilities to change daily. A natural assumption is that if hedging is implemented for all the variables that could change in a day (both those that are assumed to be constant by the model and those that are assumed to be stochastic) the value of hedger's position will not change. In fact, this is not necessarily the case. If the model used to calculate the hedge is wrong, then there may be an unexpected gain or loss. The good news here is that on average the gain or loss from hedging using the wrong model is approximately zero. The risk of imperfect hedging is likely to be largely diversified away across the portfolio of a large financial institution.

Many financial institutions carefully evaluate the effectiveness of their hedging. They find it revealing to decompose the day-to-day change in a portfolio's value into the following:

1. A change resulting from risks that were unhedged
2. A change resulting from the hedging model being imperfect
3. A change resulting from new trades done during the day

This is sometimes referred to as a *P&L decomposition*.

15.4 MODELS FOR STRUCTURED PRODUCTS

Exotic options and other nonstandard products that are tailored to the needs of clients are referred to as *structured products*. Usually they do not trade actively and a financial institution must rely on a model to determine the price it charges the client. Note the important difference between structured products and actively traded products. When a product trades actively, there is very little uncertainty about its price and the model affects only hedge performance. In the case of structured products, model risk is much greater because there is the potential for both pricing and hedging being incorrect.

A financial institution should not rely on a single model for pricing structured products. Instead it should, whenever possible, use several different models. This leads to a price range for the instrument and a better understanding of the model risks being taken.

Suppose that three different models give prices of $6 million, $7.5 million, and $8.5 million for a particular product that a financial institution is planning to sell to a client. Even if the financial institution believes that the first model is the best one and plans to use that model as its standard model for daily repricing and hedging, it should ensure that the price it charges the client is at least $8.5 million. Moreover, it should be conservative about recognizing profits. If the product is sold for $9 million, it is tempting to recognize an immediate profit of $3 million ($9 million less the believed-to-be-accurate price of $6 million). However, this is overly aggressive. A better, more conservative, practice is to put the $3 million into a reserve account and transfer it to profits slowly during the life of the product.[6]

Most large financial institutions have model audit groups as part of their risk management teams. These groups are responsible for vetting new models proposed by traders for particular products. A model cannot usually be used until the model audit group has approved it. Vetting typically includes (a) checking that a model has been correctly implemented, (b) examining whether there is a sound rationale for the model, (c) comparing the model with other models that can accomplish the same task, (d) specifying the limitations of the model, and (e) assessing uncertainties in the prices and hedge parameters given by the model.

15.5 DANGERS IN MODEL BUILDING

The art of model building is to capture what is important for valuing and hedging an instrument without making the model more complex than it needs to be. Sometimes models have to be quite complex to capture the important features of a product, but this is not always the case.

---

[6] This is also likely to have sensible implications for the way bonuses are paid.

One danger in model building is *overfitting*. Consider the problem posed by the volatility surface in Table 15.1. We can exactly match the volatility surface with a single model by extending Black–Scholes so that volatility is a complex function of the underlying asset price and time.[7] But when we do this, we may find that other properties of the model are less reasonable than those of simpler models. In particular, the joint probability of the asset prices at two or more times may be unrealistic.[8]

Another danger in model building is *overparameterization*. The Black–Scholes model can be extended to include features such as a stochastic volatility or jumps in the asset price. This invariably introduces extra parameters that have to be estimated. It is usually claimed that the parameters in complex models are more stable those in simpler models and do not have to be adjusted as much from day to day. This may be true, but we should remember that we are not dealing with physical processes. The parameters in a complex model may remain relatively constant for a period of time and then change, perhaps because there has been what economists refer to as a *regime shift*. A financial institution may find that a complicated model is an improvement over a simple model until the parameters change. At that time it may not have the flexibility to cope with changing market conditions.

As we have mentioned, traders like simple models that have just one unobservable parameter. They are skeptical of more complex models because they are "black boxes" and it is very difficult to develop intuition about them. In some situations their skepticism is well founded for the reasons we have just mentioned.

15.6 DETECTING MODEL PROBLEMS

The risk management function within a financial institution should carefully monitor the financial institution's trading patterns. In particular it

---

[7] This is the implied volatility function model proposed by B. Dupire, "Pricing with a Smile," *Risk*, 7 (February 1994), 18–20; E. Derman and I. Kani, "Riding on a Smile," *Risk*, 7 (February 1994), 32–39; M. Rubinstein, "Implied Binomial Trees," *Journal of Finance*, 49, 3 (July 1994), 771–818.

[8] Instruments such as barrier options and compound options depend on the joint probability distribution of the asset price at different times. Hull and Suo find that the implied volatility function model works reasonably well for compound options, but sometimes gives serious errors for barrier options. See J.C. Hull and W. Suo, "A Methodology for the Assessment of Model Risk and its Application to the Implied Volatility Function Model," *Journal of Financial and Quantitative Analysis*, 37, 2 (June 2002), 297–318.

should keep track of the following:

1. The type of trading the financial institution is doing with other financial institutions
2. How competitive it is in bidding for different types of structured transactions
3. The profits being recorded from the trading of different products

Getting too much of a certain type of business or making huge profits from relatively simple trading strategies can be a warning sign. Another clear indication that something is wrong is when the financial institution is unable to unwind trades at close to the prices given by its computer models.

The high profits being recorded for Joseph Jett's trading at Kidder Peabody (see Business Snapshot 15.1) should have been a warning sign.[9] Furthermore, if in the mid-1990s a financial institution's risk management team discovered that traders were entering into a large number of LIBOR-in-arrears swaps with other financial institutions (see Business Snapshot 15.2) where they were receiving fixed and paying floating, they could have alerted modelers to a potential problem and directed that trading in the product be temporarily stopped.

There are other ways in which a derivatives dealer might find that one of its models is out of line with that used by other market participants. Dealers often subscribe to services that are designed to provide market quotes for representative trades. Typically the company providing this service periodically asks its dealer clients for quotes on specific hypothetical transactions. It then averages the quotes (possibly after eliminating the highest and lowest) and feeds the results back to the dealers.

15.7 TRADITIONAL VIEW OF LIQUIDITY RISK

Liquidity is liable to affect both the funding and trading activities of a financial institution. We start by considering trading activities and move on to consider funding activities in Section 15.10.

The traditional view of liquidity risk in trading is that there is a relationship between price and quantity. This relationship is shown in Figure 15.3. When the quantity of an asset that is traded is relatively

---

[9] Barry Finer, risk manager for the government bond desk at Kidder Peabody, did point out the difficulty of making large arbitrage profits from a market as efficient as the US government bond market, but his concerns were dismissed out of hand.

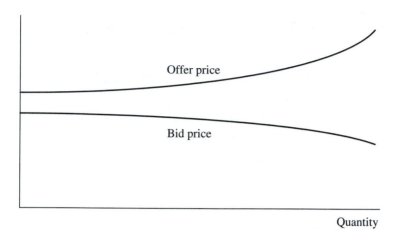

Figure 15.3   Bid and offer prices as a function of quantity transacted.

small, bid–offer spreads are low. As the quantity increases, the price paid by the buyer of the asset increases and the price received by the seller of the asset decreases.

How can a financial institution manage liquidity in the trading book? One way is by using position limits. If the size of the financial institution's position is limited, the size of a trade it has to do to unwind a position is also limited. It is often argued that the time horizon in a VaR calculation should reflect the time necessary to unwind a position. If a position can be unwound very quickly, a one-day time horizon is appropriate; in other circumstances, time horizons as long as one month may be needed.

Liquidity-Adjusted VaR

The percentage bid–offer spread for an asset can be defined as

$$s = \frac{\text{offer price} - \text{bid price}}{\text{mid-price}}$$

where the mid-price is halfway between the bid and the offer. In liquidating a position in the asset, a financial institution incurs a cost equal to $s\alpha/2$, where α is the dollar value of the position. This reflects the fact that trades are not done at the mid-market price. A buy trade is done at a proportional amount $s/2$ above the market price and a sell trade is done at a proportional amount $s/2$ below the market price.

Risk managers sometimes calculate a *liquidity-adjusted VaR* by adding

$s\alpha/2$ for each position in the book. Formally, we have

$$\text{Liquidity-adjusted VaR} = \text{VaR} + \sum_{i=1}^{n} s_i \alpha_i / 2$$

where n is the number of positions, s_i is the percentage bid–offer spread for the ith position and α_i is the amount of money invested in the ith position. As the number of positions, n, grows, VaR benefits from diversification but the liquidity adjustment does not. Consequently, the percentage difference between VaR and liquidity-adjusted VaR grows as n grows.

A variation on this calculation that takes account of uncertainty in the spread has been suggested by Bangia et al.[10] This involves estimating the mean μ_i and standard deviation σ_i of s_i, and defining

$$\text{Liquidity-adjusted VaR} = \text{VaR} + \sum_{i=1}^{n} (\mu_i + \lambda \sigma_i) \alpha_i / 2$$

The parameter λ gives the required confidence level for the spread on the assumption that spreads are normally distributed. For example, if a 95% confidence level is required, then $\lambda = 1.64$. Bangia et al.'s equation assumes (conservatively) that spreads in all instruments are perfectly correlated.

15.8 LIQUIDITY BLACK HOLES

The liquidity risk we have just described is real. Banks cannot trade at mid-market prices and the bigger the size of their transaction the higher the bid–offer spread that they face. However, there is a more serious liquidity risk. This is the risk that liquidity in a particular market will dry up completely because everyone wants to buy and no-one wants to sell, or vice versa.

It is sometimes argued that technological and other developments have led to a steady improvement in the liquidity of financial markets. This is questionable. It is true that bid–offer spreads have on average declined. However, there has been an increasing tendency toward "herd behavior" where almost everyone wants to do the same type of trade at particular

---

[10] See A. Bangia, F. Diebold, T. Schuermann, and J. Stroughair, "Liquidity on the Outside," *Risk*, 12 (June), 68–73.

times. The result has been what Persaud refers to as "liquidity black holes" occurring with increasing frequency.[11]

In a well-functioning market, the market may change its opinion about the price of an asset because of new information. However, the price does not overreact. If a price decrease is too great, traders will quickly move in and buy the asset and a new equilibrium price will be established. A liquidity black hole is created when a price decline causes more market participants to want to sell, driving prices well below where they will eventually settle. During the sell-off, liquidity dries up and the asset can be sold only at a fire-sale price.[12]

Among the reasons for herd behavior and the creation of liquidity black holes are:

1. The computer models used by different traders are similar.
2. All financial institutions are regulated in the same way and respond in the same way to changes in volatilities and correlations.
3. There is a natural tendency to feel that if other people are doing a certain type of trade then they must know something that you do not.

Computer Models

A classic example of computer models causing a liquidity black hole is the stock market crash of October 1987. In the period leading up to the crash, the stock market had performed very well. Increasing numbers of portfolio managers were using commercially available programs to synthetically create put options on their portfolios. These programs told them to sell part of their portfolio immediately after a price decline and buy it back immediately after a price increase. The result, as indicated in Business Snapshot 15.4, was prices plunging well below their long-run equilibrium levels on October 19, 1987.

As another example of computer models leading to liquidity black holes, consider the situation where financial institutions are on one side of the market for a derivative and their clients are on the other side. When the price of the underlying asset moves, all financial institutions execute the same trades to maintain a delta-neutral position. This causes the price of the asset to move further in the same direction. An example of this is outlined in Business Snapshot 15.5.

---

[11] See A. D. Persaud (ed.), *Liquidity Black Holes: Understanding, Quantifying and Managing Financial Liquidity Risk*, Risk Books, 1999.

[12] Liquidity black holes tend to be associated with price decreases, but it is possible for them to occur when there are price increases.

Business Snapshot 15.4   The Crash of 1987

On Monday, October 19, 1987, the Dow Jones Industrial Average dropped by more than 20%. Portfolio insurance played a major role in this crash. In October 1987 between $60 billion and $90 billion of equity assets were subject to portfolio insurance schemes where put options were created synthetically using a type of "stop–loss" trading strategy.

During the period Wednesday, October 14, 1987, to Friday, October 16, 1987, the market declined by about 10%, with much of this decline taking place on Friday afternoon. The portfolio insurance schemes should have generated at least $12 billion of equity or index futures sales as a result of this decline. In fact, portfolio insurers had time to sell only $4 billion and they approached the following week with huge amounts of selling already dictated by their models. It is estimated that, on Monday, October 19, sell programs by three portfolio insurers accounted for almost 10% of the sales on the New York Stock Exchange, and that portfolio insurance sales amounted to 21.3% of all sales in index futures markets. It is likely that the decline in equity prices was exacerbated by investors other than portfolio insurers selling heavily in anticipation of the actions of portfolio insurers.

As the market declined so fast and the stock exchange systems were overloaded, many portfolio insurers were unable to execute the trades generated by their models and failed to obtain the protection they required. Needless to say, the popularity of portfolio insurance schemes has declined significantly since 1987. One of the morals of this story is that it is dangerous to follow a particular trading strategy—even a hedging strategy—when many other market participants are doing the same thing.

The Impact of Regulation

In many ways it is a laudable goal on the part of regulators to seek to ensure that banks and other financial institutions throughout the world are regulated in the same way. As we explained in Chapter 7, capital requirements and the extent to which they were enforced varied from country to country prior to Basel I. Banks were competing globally and as a result a bank subject to low capital requirements, or capital requirements that were not strictly enforced, had a competitive edge.

However, a uniform regulatory environment comes with costs. All banks tend to respond in the same way to external events. Consider, for example, market risk. When volatilities and correlations increase, market VaR and the capital required for market risks increase. As a result, banks tend to take steps to reduce their exposures. Since banks

---

Business Snapshot 15.5 British Insurance Companies

In the late 1990s, British insurance companies had entered into many contracts promising that the rate of interest applicable to an annuity received by an individual on retirement would be the greater of the market rate and a guaranteed rate. At about the same time, largely because of regulatory pressures, all insurance companies decided to hedge part of their risks on these contracts by buying long-dated swap options from financial institutions. The financial institutions they dealt with hedged their risks by buying large numbers of long-dated sterling bonds. As a result, bond prices rose and sterling long-term interest rates declined. More bonds had to be bought to maintain the dynamic hedge, long-term sterling interest rates declined further, and so on. Financial institutions lost money and, because long-term interest rates declined, insurance companies found themselves in a worse position on the risks that they had chosen not to hedge.

---

often have similar positions to each other, they try to do similar trades. A liquidity black hole can then develop.

Consider next credit risk. During the low point of the economic cycle, default probabilities are relatively high and capital requirements for loans under the Basel II internal ratings based models tend to be high. As a result banks may be less willing to make loans, creating a liquidity black hole for small and medium-sized businesses. The Basel Committee has recognized this as a problem and has dealt with it by asserting that the probability of default should be an average of the probability of default through the economic or credit cycle, rather than an estimate applicable to one particular point in time.

The Importance of Diversity

Economic models usually assume that market participants act independently. We have argued that this is often not the case. It is this lack of independence that causes liquidity black holes. To solve the problem of liquidity black holes, we need more diversity in financial markets.

One conclusion from the arguments we have put forward is that a contrarian investment strategy has some merit. If markets overreact an investor can do quite well by buying when everyone else is selling and there is very little liquidity. However, it can be quite difficult for a fund to follow such a strategy if it is subject to the VaR-based risk management measures that have become standard.

Volatilities and correlations tend to be "mean reverting". They sometimes increase but over time they get pulled back to long-run average levels. One way of creating diversity is to recognize in regulation and in risk management practices that not all market participants should be concerned about short-term changes in volatilities and correlations. Asset managers, for example, should base their decisions on long-term average volatilities and correlations. They should not join the herd when liquidity holes develop.

Hedge Funds

Hedge funds have become important participants in financial markets in recent years. A hedge fund is similar to a mutual fund in that it invests money on behalf of clients. However, unlike mutual funds hedge funds are not required to register under US federal securities law. This is because they accept funds only from financially sophisticated individuals and do not publicly offer their securities. Mutual funds are subject to regulations requiring that shares in the funds be fairly priced, that the shares be redeemable at any time, that investment policies be disclosed, that the use of leverage be limited, that no short positions be taken, and so on. Hedge funds are relatively free of these regulations. This gives them a great deal of freedom to develop sophisticated, unconventional, and proprietary investment strategies. The fees charged by hedge fund managers are dependent on the fund's performance and are relatively high— typically 1 to 2% of the amount invested plus 20% of the profits.

Hedge funds have grown in popularity with about $1 trillion being invested throughout the world for clients in 2004. "Funds of funds" have been set up to invest in a portfolio of other hedge funds. At the time of writing, hedge funds are still largely unregulated. This means that they do not have to assess risk in the same way as other financial institutions. As a result, hedge funds are in an ideal position to provide liquidity when black holes show signs of developing. If hedge funds are regulated in the future, it is to be hoped that the regulations will not be the same as those applying to other financial institutions.

15.9 LONG-TERM CAPITAL MANAGEMENT

Hedge funds themselves can run into liquidity problems and create or exacerbate liquidity black holes. The most famous example here is Long-

Term Capital Management (LTCM) which was discussed in Business Snapshot 12.1.

LTCM's problems were exacerbated by the fact that its leverage was huge. It had about $125 billion of assets (plus large numbers of off-balance-sheet derivatives transactions such as swaps) and only $5 billion of capital. It was unable to make the payments required under its collateralization agreements. There was a great deal of concern about the ability of the financial system to cope with a potential failure of LTCM. What actually happened was a cash injection by a group of banks and an orderly liquidation that led to a total loss of about $4 billion. If the fund had been less highly leveraged, it would probably have been able to survive the flight to quality and could have waited for the previous relationship between the prices of the liquid and illiquid securities to resume.

Why was the flight to quality so large? One reason is that there were rumors in the market that LTCM was experiencing financial difficulties. These rumors led people to anticipate the sort of trades LTCM would have to do to close out its positions and the likely effect of those trades on market prices. When everyone anticipates that something will happen in financial markets it tends to happen. Another reason is that LTCM had been highly successful during the 1995 to 1997 period. As a result there were many other hedge funds trying to imitate its strategy. These hedge funds also experienced financial difficulties and tried to close out their positions. This accentuated market movements.

15.10 LIQUIDITY vs. PROFITABILITY

Finally it should be noted that there can be liquidity problems without profitability problems. For example, a profitable bank can experience a run on deposits and run into liquidity problems. Banking is to a large extent about confidence. A bank relies on the withdrawal of deposits being roughly balanced by new deposits so that funding from liabilities remains roughly constant (see Section 1.3). If there is a temporary shortfall, it is handled by interbank borrowing.[13] However, if there is a loss of confidence in the bank—however unjustified this might be—the bank is liable to experience catastrophic liquidity problems.

Liquidity funding problems can be experienced by all sorts of companies. We have all heard stories about profitable companies that for

---

[13] Across the whole banking system the funds on deposit should remain roughly constant as a withdrawal from one bank usually becomes a deposit with another bank.

Business Snapshot 15.6   Metallgesellschaft

In the early 1990s, Metallgesellschaft (MG) sold a large volume of five- to ten-year heating oil and gasoline fixed-price supply contracts to its customers at 6 to 8 cents above market prices. It hedged its exposure with long positions in short-dated futures contracts that were rolled forward. As it turned out, the price of oil fell and there were margin calls on the futures positions. Considerable short-term cash-flow pressures were placed on MG. Those at MG who devised the hedging strategy argued that these short-term cash outflows were offset by positive cash flows that would ultimately be realized on the long-term fixed-price contracts. However, the company's senior management and its bankers became concerned about the huge cash drain. As a result, the company closed out all the hedge positions and agreed with its customers that the fixed-price contracts would be abandoned. The outcome was a loss to MG of $1.33 billion.

---

some reason "fell through the cracks" when trying to arrange venture capital funding or bank loans. An extreme example of a liquidity funding problem is provided by a German company, Metallgesellschaft, that entered into profitable fixed-price oil and gas contracts with its customers (see Business Snapshot 15.6).

Liquidity funding problems can in part be avoided by carrying out scenario analyses and taking steps to avoid the possibility of outcomes where short-term cash drains are difficult to fund.

SUMMARY

Since the publication of the Black–Scholes model in 1973 a huge amount of effort has been devoted to the development of improved models for the behavior of asset prices. It might be thought that it is just a matter of time before the perfect model is produced. Unfortunately, this is not the case. Models in finance are different from those in the physical sciences because they are ultimately models of human behavior. They are always likely to be at best approximations to the way market variables behave. Furthermore, from time to time there are regime shifts where there are fundamental changes in the behavior of market variables.

For products that trade actively, models are used primarily for communicating prices, interpolating between market prices, and hedging. When hedging, traders use both within-model hedging and outside-model hedging. This means that they hedge against movements in variables that the model assumes to be constant (or deterministic) as well movements in variables that are assumed to be stochastic. This type of hedging is imperfect, but hopefully the unhedged risks are largely diversified in a large portfolio.

For products that are highly structured or do not trade actively models are used for pricing. In this case choosing the right model is often more of an art than a science. It is a good practice to use several models and assumptions about the underlying parameters in order to obtain a realistic range for pricing and understand the accompanying model risk.

Liquidity risk is the risk that the market will not be able to absorb the trades a financial institution wants to do at the time it wants to do them. In normal market conditions liquidity is characterized by a bid–offer spread. This spread widens as the size of a transaction increases.

The most serious liquidity risks arise from what are sometimes termed liquidity black holes. These occur when all traders want to be on the same side of the market at the same time. This may be because they are using similar models or are subject to similar regulations, or because of a herd mentality that sometimes develops among traders. Traders that have long-term objectives should avoid allowing themselves to be influenced by the short-term overreaction of markets.

FURTHER READING

Derman, E., *My Life as a Quant: Reflections on Physics and Finance*. New York: Wiley, 2004.

Persaud, A. D., (ed.), *Liquidity Black Holes: Understanding, Quantifying and Managing Financial Liquidity Risk*. London: Risk Books, 1999.

QUESTIONS AND PROBLEMS (Answers at End of Book)

15.1. Give two explanations for the volatility skew observed for options on equities.

15.2. Give two explanations for the volatility smile observed for options on a foreign currency.

15.3. "The Black–Scholes model is nothing more than a sophisticated interpolation tool." Discuss this viewpoint.

15.4. Using Table 15.1, calculate the volatility a trader would use for an 8-month option with a strike price of 1.04.

15.5. What is the key difference between the models of physics and the models of finance.

15.6. How is a financial institution liable to find that it is using a model different from its competitors for a particular type of derivatives product.

15.7. What is a liquidity-adjusted VaR designed to measure?

15.8. Explain how liquidity black holes occur. How can regulation lead to liquidity black holes?

15.9. Distinguish between within-model and outside-model hedging.

15.10. A stock price is currently $20. Tomorrow, news is expected to be announced that will either increase the price by $5 or decrease the price by $5. What are the problems in using Black–Scholes to value 1-month options on the stock?

15.11. Suppose that a central bank's policy is to allow an exchange rate to fluctuate between 0.97 and 1.03. What pattern of implied volatilities for options on the exchange rate would you expect to see?

15.12. "For actively traded products traders can mark to market. For structured products they mark to model." Explain this remark.

15.13. "Hedge funds can either be the solution to black holes or the cause of black holes." Explain this remark.

ASSIGNMENT QUESTIONS

15.14. Suppose that all options traders decide to switch from Black–Scholes to another model that makes different assumptions about the behavior of asset prices. What effect do you think this would have on (a) the pricing of standard options and (b) the hedging of standard options?

15.15. Using Table 15.1, calculate the volatility a trader would use for an 11-month option with a strike price of 0.98.

15.16. A futures price is currently $40. The risk-free interest rate is 5%. Some news is expected tomorrow that will cause the volatility over the next 3 months to be either 10% or 30%. There is a 60% chance of the first outcome and a 40% chance of the second outcome. Use the DerivaGem software (available on the author's website) to calculate a volatility smile for 3-month options.

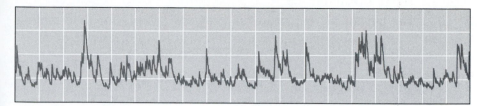

CHAPTER 16

Economic Capital and RAROC

As we saw in Chapter 1, the role of capital in a bank is to protect depositors against losses. The capital of a bank consists of common shareholder's equity, preferred shareholder's equity, subordinated debt, and other similar items.

In Chapter 7 we discussed the rules that the Basel Committee uses to determine regulatory capital. These rules are the same for all banks and, however carefully they have been chosen, it is inevitable that they will not be exactly appropriate for any particular bank. This has led banks to calculate *economic capital* (sometimes also referred to as *risk capital*). Economic capital is a bank's own internal estimate of the capital it needs for the risks it is taking. Economic capital can be regarded as a "currency" for risk-taking within a bank. A business unit can take a certain risk only when it is allocated the appropriate economic capital for that risk. The profitability of a business unit is measured relative to the economic capital allocated to the unit.

In this chapter we discuss the approaches a bank uses to arrive at estimates of economic capital for particular risk types and particular business units and how these estimates are aggregated to produce a single economic capital estimate for the whole bank. We also discuss risk-adjusted return on capital or RAROC. This is the return earned by a business unit on the capital assigned to it. RAROC can be used to assess the past performance of business units. It can also be used to forecast future performance of the units and decide on the most appropriate way of allocating capital in the future. It provides a basis for determining whether some activities should be discontinued and others expanded.

16.1 DEFINITION OF ECONOMIC CAPITAL

Economic capital is defined as the amount of capital a bank needs to absorb losses over a certain time horizon with a certain confidence level. The time horizon is usually chosen as one year. The confidence level depends on the bank's objectives. A common objective for a large international bank is to maintain an AA credit rating. Corporations rated AA have a one-year probability of default of about 0.03%. This suggests that the confidence level should be 99.97%. For a bank wanting to maintain a BBB credit rating the confidence level is lower. A BBB-rated corporation has a probability of about 0.2% of defaulting in one year so that the confidence level is 99.80%.

Capital is required to cover unexpected loss. This is defined as the difference between the actual loss and the expected loss. The idea here is that expected losses should be taken account of in the way a bank prices its products so that only unexpected losses require capital. As indicated in Figure 16.1, the economic capital for a bank that wants to maintain an

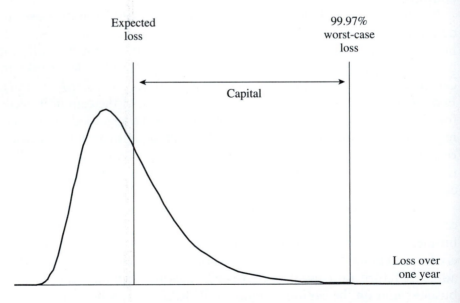

Figure 16.1 Calculation of economic capital from one-year loss distribution for a AA-rated bank.

AA rating is the difference between expected losses and the 99.97 percentile point on the probability distribution of losses.

Example 16.1
When lending in a certain region of the world an AA-rated bank estimates its losses as 1% of outstanding loans per year on average. The 99.97% worst-case loss (i.e., the loss exceeded only 0.03% of the time) is estimated as 5% of outstanding loans. The economic capital required per $100 of loans is therefore $4.0 (the difference between the 99.97% worst-case loss and the expected loss).

Approaches to Measurement

There are two broad approaches to measuring economic capital: the "top–down" and "bottom–up" approaches. In the top–down approach the volatility of the bank's assets is estimated and then used to calculate the probability that the value of the assets will fall below the value of the liabilities by the end of the time horizon. A theoretical framework that can be used for the top–down approach is Merton's model, which was discussed in Section 11.6.

The approach most often used is the bottom–up approach, where loss distributions are estimated for different types of risk and different business units and then aggregated. The first step in the aggregation can be to calculate probability distributions for total losses by risk type or total losses by business unit. A final aggregation gives a probability distribution of total losses for the whole financial institution.

The various risks facing a bank are summarized in Figure 16.2. As we saw in Chapter 14, regulators have chosen to define operational risk as "the risk of loss resulting from inadequate or failed internal processes,

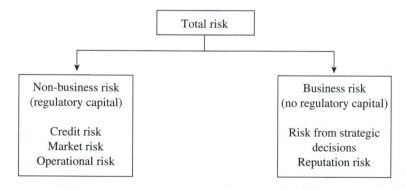

Figure 16.2   Categorization of risks faced by a bank in the Basel II regulatory environment.

people, and systems or from external events." Operational risk includes model risk and legal risk, but not risks arising from strategic decisions or business reputation. We will refer to the latter risks collectively as *business risk*. Regulatory capital is not required for business risk under Basel II, but some banks do assess economic capital for business risk.

16.2 COMPONENTS OF ECONOMIC CAPITAL

In earlier chapters we covered approaches used to calculate loss distributions for different types of risks. Here we review some of the key points.

Market Risk Economic Capital

In Chapters 9 and 10 we discussed the historical simulation and model-building approaches for estimating the probability distribution of the loss or gain from market risk. As explained, this distribution is usually calculated in the first instance with a one-day time horizon. Regulatory capital for market risk is calculated as a multiple (at least 3.0) of the ten-day 99% VaR and bank supervisors have indicated that they are comfortable calculating the ten-day 99% VaR as $\sqrt{10}$ times the one-day 99% VaR.

When calculating economic capital, we want to use the same time horizon and confidence level for all risks. The time horizon is usually one year and, as explained, the confidence level is often chosen as 99.97% for an AA-rated bank. The simplest assumptions are (a) that the probability distribution of gains and losses for each day during the next year will be the same as that estimated for the first day and (b) that the distributions are independent. We can then use the central limit theorem to argue that the one-year loss/gain distribution is normal. Assuming 252 business days in the year, the standard deviation of the one-year loss/gain equals the standard deviation of the daily loss/gain multiplied by $\sqrt{252}$. The mean loss/gain is much more difficult to estimate than the standard deviation. A reasonable, if somewhat conservative, assumption is that the mean loss/gain is zero. The 99.97% worst-case loss is then 3.43 times the standard deviation of the one-year loss/gain. The 99.8% worst-case loss is 2.88 times the standard deviation of the one-year loss/gain.

Example 16.2

Suppose that the one-day standard deviation of market risk losses/gains for a bank is $5 million. The one-year 99.8% worst-case loss is $2.88 \times \sqrt{252} \times 5 = 228.6$, or $228.6 million.

Note that we are not assuming that the daily losses/gains are normal. All we are assuming is that they are independent and identically distributed. The central limit theorem of statistics tells us that the sum of many independent identically distributed variables is approximately normal. If losses on successive days are correlated, we can assume first-order autocorrelation, estimate the correlation parameter from historical data, and use the results in Section 8.4. When the autocorrelation is not too high, it is still reasonable to assume that the one-year loss distribution is normal. If a more complicated model for the relationship between losses on successive days is considered appropriate, then the one-year loss distribution can be calculated using Monte Carlo simulation.

Credit Risk Economic Capital

Although Basel II gives banks that use the internal ratings based approach for regulatory capital a great deal of freedom, it does not allow them to choose their own credit correlation model and correlation parameters. When calculating economic capital, banks are free to make the assumptions they consider most appropriate for their situation. As explained in Section 12.6, CreditMetrics is often used to calculate the specific risk capital charge for credit risk in the trading book. It is also sometimes used when economic capital is calculated for the banking book. A bank's own internal rating system can be used instead of that of Moody's or S&P when this method is used.

Another approach that is sometimes used is Credit Risk Plus, which is described in Section 12.5. This approach borrows a number of ideas from actuarial science to calculate a probability distribution for losses from defaults. Whereas CreditMetrics calculates the loss from downgrades and defaults, Credit Risk Plus calculates losses from defaults only.

In calculating credit risk economic capital, a bank can choose to adopt a conditional or unconditional model. In a conditional (cycle-specific) model, the expected and unexpected losses take account of current economic conditions. In an unconditional (cycle-neutral) model, they are calculated by assuming economic conditions that are in some sense an average of those experienced through the cycle. Rating agencies aim to produce ratings that are unconditional. Moreover, when regulatory capital is calculated using the internal ratings based approach, the PD and LGD estimates should be unconditional. Obviously it is important to be consistent when economic capital is calculated. If expected losses are conditional, unexpected losses should also be conditional. If expected losses are unconditional, the same should be true of unexpected losses.

A particularly challenging task is to take counterparty risk on derivatives into account when credit risk loss distributions are calculated. In practice, banks often use approximations to the approach outlined in Section 12.1. For example, they might develop look-up tables for expected exposure during the life of an instrument and assume that exposure remains constant at this level. When a bank has several different exposures with the same counterparty and there are netting agreements, algorithms for calculating expected exposure can be developed. Other features of derivative contracts such as collateralization and downgrade triggers can be incorporated.

Operational Risk Economic Capital

Banks are given a great deal of freedom in the assessment of regulatory capital for operational risk under the advanced measurement approach. It is therefore likely that most banks using this approach will calculate operational risk economic capital and operational risk regulatory capital in the same way. As noted in Chapter 14, methods for calculating operational risk capital are still evolving. Some approaches are statistical and others are more subjective.

Business Risk Economic Capital

As mentioned earlier, business risk includes strategic risk (relating to a bank's decision to enter new markets and develop new products) and reputational risk. Business risk is even more difficult to quantify than operational risk and estimates are likely to be largely subjective. It is important that senior risk managers within a financial institution have a good understanding of the portfolio of business risks being taken. This should enable them to assess the capital required for the risks and, more importantly, the marginal impact on total risk of new strategic initiatives that are being contemplated.

16.3 SHAPES OF THE LOSS DISTRIBUTIONS

The loss probability distributions for market, credit, and operational risk are very different. Rosenberg and Schuermann used data from a variety of

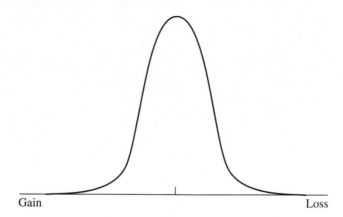

Gain   Loss

Figure 16.3   Loss density distribution for market risk.

different sources to estimate typical shapes for these distributions.[1] These are shown in Figures 16.3, 16.4, and 16.5. The market risk loss distribution (see Figure 16.3) is symmetrical, but not perfectly normally distributed. A t-distribution with 11 degrees of freedom provides a good fit. The credit risk loss distribution in Figure 16.4 is quite skewed, as one would expect. The operational risk distribution in Figure 16.5 has a quite extreme shape. Most of the time losses are modest, but occasionally they are very large.

We can characterize a distribution by its second, third, and fourth moments. Loosely speaking, the second moment measures standard deviation (or variance), the third skewness, and the fourth kurtosis

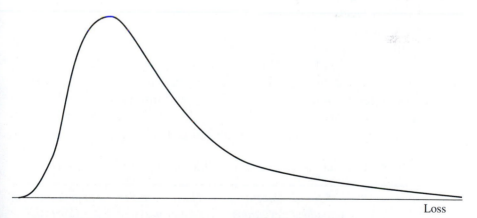

Loss

Figure 16.4   Loss density distribution for credit risk.

[1] See J. V. Rosenberg and T. Schuermann, "A General Approach to Integrated Risk Management with Skewed, Fat-Tailed Risks," Federal Reserve Bank of New York, Staff Report No. 185, May 2004.

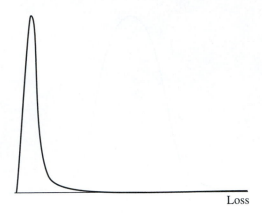

Loss

Figure 16.5   Loss density distribution for
operational risk.

(i.e., the heaviness of tails). Table 16.1 summarizes the properties of typical loss distributions for market, credit, and operational risk.

16.4 RELATIVE IMPORTANCE OF RISKS

The relative importance of different types of risks depends on the business mix. For a bank whose prime business is taking deposits and making loans, credit risk is of paramount importance. For an investment bank, credit risk and market risk are both important. For an asset manager, the greatest risk is operational risk. If rules on the ways funds are to be invested are not followed, there are liable to be expensive investor law suits. Business Snapshot 16.1 gives one example of this. Another high-profile example is provided by the Unilever's pension plan. Mercury Asset Management, owned by Merrill Lynch, pledged not to underperform a benchmark index by more than 3%. Between January 1997 and March 1998 it underperformed the index by 10.5%. Unilever sued Merrill Lynch for $185 million and the matter was settled out of court.

Table 16.1   Characteristics of loss distributions for different risk types.

	Second moment (*standard deviation*)	*Third moment* (*skewness*)	*Fourth moment* (*kurtosis*)
Market risk	High	Zero	Low
Credit risk	Moderate	Moderate	Moderate
Operational risk	Low	High	High

Business Snapshot 16.1 The EGT Fund

In 1996 Peter Young was fund manager at Deutsche Morgan Grenfell, a subsidiary of Deutsche Bank. He was responsible for managing a fund called the European Growth Trust (EGT). It had grown very large and Young had responsibilities for managing over one billion pounds of investors' money.

Certain rules applied to EGT. One of these was that no more than 10% of the fund could be invested in unlisted securities. Peter Young violated this rule in a way, it can be argued, that benefited him personally. When the facts were uncovered, he was fired and Deutsche bank had to compensate investors. The total cost to Deutsche Bank was over 200 million pounds.

Interactions between Risks

There are interactions between the different types of risk. For example, when a derivative such as a swap is traded, there are interactions between credit and market risk. If the counterparty defaults, credit risk exists only if market variables have moved so that the value of the derivative to the financial institution is positive. Another interaction is that the probability of default by a counterparty may depend on the value of a financial institution's contract (or contracts) with the counterparty.[2] If the counterparty has entered into the contract for hedging purposes, this is not likely to be the case. However, if the contract has been entered into for speculative purposes and the contract is large in relation to the size of the counterparty, there is likely to be some dependence.

As the Long-Term Capital Management saga clearly shows there can be interactions between liquidity risks and market risks (see Section 15.9). There are also interactions between operational risks and market risks. It is unlikely that we would know about the activities of Nick Leeson at Barings Bank if he had guessed right about the Nikkei index (see Business Snapshot 2.3). It is also unlikely that we would hear about a violation of the rules for a fund (such as the one in Business Snapshot 16.1) if it had led to a gain rather than a loss.

16.5 AGGREGATING ECONOMIC CAPITAL

Typically a financial institution calculates market, credit, operational, and (possibly) business risk loss distributions for a number of different business

---

[2] When calculating the expected cost of counterparty default risk in Section 12.1, we assumed no dependence.

units. It is then faced with the problem of aggregating the loss distributions to calculate a total economic capital for the whole enterprise.

The simplest approach is to assume that the total economic capital for a set of n different risks is the sum of the economic capital amounts for each risk considered separately so that

$$E_{\text{total}} = \sum_{i-1}^{n} E_i \qquad (16.1)$$

where E_{total} is the total economic capital for the financial institution facing n different risks and E_i is the economic capital for the ith risk considered on its own. This is what the Basel Committee does for regulatory capital. The total regulatory capital a bank is required to keep under Basel II is the sum of the regulatory capital amounts for credit, market, and operational risks.

Equation (16.1) is clearly a very conservative assumption. It assumes perfect correlation. In the context of economic capital calculations where the confidence level is 99.97%, it would mean that, if a financial institution experiences the 99.97% worst-case loss for market risk, it also experiences the 99.97% worst-case loss for credit risk and operational risk. Rosenberg and Schuermann estimate the correlation between market risk and credit risk to be approximately 50% and the correlation between each of these risks and operational risk to be approximately 20%. They estimate that equation (16.1), when used as a way of aggregating market, credit, and operational risk, overstates the total capital required by about 40%.

Assuming Normal Distributions

A simple assumption when aggregating loss distributions is that they are normally distributed. The standard deviation of the total loss from n sources of risk is then

$$\sigma_{\text{total}} = \sqrt{\sum_{i=1}^{n} \sum_{j=1}^{n} \sigma_i \sigma_j \rho_{ij}} \qquad (16.2)$$

where σ_i is the standard deviation of the loss from the ith source of risk and ρ_{ij} is the correlation between risk i and risk j. The capital requirement can be calculated from this. For example, the excess of the 99.97% worst-case loss over the expected loss is 3.44 times the number calculated in equation (16.2).

This approach tends to underestimate the capital requirement because it takes no account of the skewness and kurtosis of the loss distributions.

Rosenberg and Schuermann estimate that, when the approach is applied to aggregating market, credit, and operational risk, the total capital is underestimated by about 40%.

Using Copulas

A more sophisticated approach to aggregating loss distributions is by using copulas. Copulas were discussed in Chapter 6. Each loss distribution is mapped on a percentile-to-percentile basis to a standard well-behaved distribution. A correlation structure between the standard distributions is defined and this indirectly defines a correlation structure between the original distributions.

Many different copulas can be defined. In the Gaussian copula the standard distributions are assumed to be multivariate normal. An alternative is to assume that they are multivariate *t*. This leads to the joint probability of extreme values of two variables being higher than in the Gaussian copula. This is discussed further in Section 6.4.

The Hybrid Approach

A simple approach that seems to work well is known as the *hybrid approach*. This involves calculating the economic capital for a portfolio of risks from the economic capital for the individual risks using

$$E_{total} = \sqrt{\sum_{i=1}^{n} \sum_{j=1}^{n} E_i E_j \rho_{ij}} \qquad (16.3)$$

When the distributions are normal, this approach is exactly correct. When they are nonnormal, the hybrid approach gives an approximate answer—but one that reflects any heaviness in the tails of the individual loss distributions. Rosenberg and Schuermann find that the answers given by the hybrid approach are reasonably close to those given by copula models.

Example 16.3

Suppose that the estimates for economic capital for market, credit, and operational risk for two business units are as shown in Table 16.2. The correlations between the losses are shown in Table 16.3. The correlation between credit risk and market risk within the same business unit is 0.5, and the correlation between operational risk and either credit or market risk within the same business unit is 0.2. (These correspond to the estimates of Rosenberg and Schuermann mentioned above.) The correlation between two different risk types in two different business units is zero. The correlation between market risks across business units is 0.4. The correlation between

Table 16.2   Economic capital estimates for
Example 16.3.

	Business unit	
	1	2
Market risk	30	40
Credit risk	70	80
Operational risk	30	90

credit risk across business units is 0.6. The correlation between operational risk across business units is zero.

We can aggregate the economic capital in a number of ways. The total market risk economic capital is

$$\sqrt{30^2 + 40^2 + 2 \times 0.4 \times 30 \times 40} = 58.8$$

The total credit risk economic capital is

$$\sqrt{70^2 + 80^2 + 2 \times 0.6 \times 70 \times 80} = 134.2$$

The total operational risk economic capital is

$$\sqrt{30^2 + 90^2} = 94.9$$

The total economic capital for Business Unit 1 is

$$\sqrt{\begin{array}{c} 30^2 + 70^2 + 30^2 + 2 \times 0.5 \times 30 \times 70 \\ + 2 \times 0.2 \times 30 \times 30 + 2 \times 0.2 \times 70 \times 30 \end{array}} = 100.0$$

The total economic capital for Business Unit 2 is

$$\sqrt{\begin{array}{c} 40^2 + 80^2 + 90^2 + 2 \times 0.5 \times 40 \times 80 \\ + 2 \times 0.2 \times 40 \times 90 + 2 \times 0.2 \times 80 \times 90 \end{array}} = 153.7$$

Table 16.3   Correlations between losses in Example 16.3. MR, CR, and OR refer to market risk, credit risk, and operational risk; 1 and 2 refer to business units.

	MR-1	CR-1	OR-1	MR-2	CR-2	OR-2
MR-1	1.0	0.5	0.2	0.4	0.0	0.0
CR-1	0.5	1.0	0.2	0.0	0.6	0.0
OR-1	0.2	0.2	1.0	0.0	0.0	0.0
MR-2	0.4	0.0	0.0	1.0	0.5	0.2
CR-2	0.0	0.6	0.0	0.5	1.0	0.2
OR-2	0.0	0.0	0.0	0.2	0.2	1.0

The total enterprise-wide economic capital is the square root of

$$30^2 + 40^2 + 70^2 + 80^2 + 30^2 + 90^2 + 2 \times 0.4 \times 30 \times 40 + 2 \times 0.5 \times 30 \times 70$$
$$+ 2 \times 0.2 \times 30 \times 30 + 2 \times 0.5 \times 40 \times 80 + 2 \times 0.2 \times 40 \times 90$$
$$+ 2 \times 0.6 \times 70 \times 80 + 2 \times 0.2 \times 70 \times 30 + 2 \times 0.2 \times 80 \times 90$$

or 203.224.

There are significant diversification benefits. The sum of the economic capital estimates for market, credit, and operational risk is $58.8 + 134.2 + 94.9 = 287.9$ and the sum of the economic capital estimates for two business units is $100 + 153.7 = 253.7$. Both of these are greater than the total economic capital estimate of 203.2.

16.6 ALLOCATION OF THE DIVERSIFICATION BENEFIT

Suppose that the sum of the economic capital for each business unit, $\sum_{i=1}^{n} E_i$, is \$2 billion and the total economic capital for the whole bank, after taking less-than-perfect correlations into account, is \$1.3 billion ($= 65\%$ of the sum of the E's). The \$0.7 billion is a diversification gain to the bank. How should it be allocated to the business units?

A simple approach is to reduce the economic capital of each business unit by 35%. However, this is probably not the best approach. Suppose there are 50 business units and that two particular business units both have an economic capital of \$100 million. Suppose that when the first business unit is excluded from the calculations the bank's economic capital reduces by \$60 million and that when the second business unit is excluded from the calculation the bank's economic capital reduces by \$10 million. Arguably the first business unit should have more economic capital than the second business unit because its incremental impact on the bank's total economic capital is greater.

The issues here are analogous to the issues we discussed in Section 8.5 concerned with allocating VaR. The theoretically best allocation scheme is to allocate an amount

$$x_i \frac{\partial E}{\partial x_i}$$

to the ith business unit, where E is the total economic capital and x_i is the investment in the ith business unit. As we pointed out in Section 8.5, a result known as Euler's theorem ensures that the total of the allocated capital is E.

Define ΔE_i as the increase in the total economic capital when we increase x_i by Δx_i. A discrete approximation for the amount allocated to business unit i is

$$\frac{\Delta E_i}{\Delta y_i} \qquad (16.4)$$

where $y_i = \Delta x_i / x_i$.

Example 16.4

Consider again Example 16.3. The total economic capital is 203.2. The economic capital calculated for Business Unit 1 is 100 and that calculated for Business Unit 2 is 153.7.

A naive procedure would allocate 100/253.7 of the total economic capital to Business Unit 1 and 153.7/253.7 of the economic capital to Business Unit 2. This would result in 80.1 for Business Unit 1 and 123.1 for Business Unit 2.

The incremental effect of Business Unit 1 on the total economic capital is $203.2 - 153.7 = 49.5$. Similarly, the incremental effect of Business Unit 2 is $203.2 - 100 = 103.2$. The two incremental capitals do not add up to the total capital (as is usually the case). We could use them as a basis for allocating the total capital. We would then allocate $49.5/(49.5 + 103.2)$ of the capital to Business Unit 1 and $103.2/(49.5 + 103.2)$ of it to Business Unit 2. This would result in 65.9 for Business Unit 1 and 137.3 for Business Unit 2.

To apply equation (16.4), we could calculate the partial derivative analytically. Alternatively, we can use a numerical approximation. When we increase the size of Business Unit 1 by 1%, its economic capital amounts for market, credit, and operational risk in Table 16.2 increase to 30.3, 70.7, and 30.3, respectively. The total economic capital becomes 203.906, so that $\Delta E_1 = 203.906 - 203.224 = 0.682$.

When we increase the size of Business Unit 2 by 1%, its economic capital amounts for market, credit, and operational risk in Table 16.2 increase to 40.4, 80.8, and 90.9, respectively. The total economic capital becomes 204.577, so that $\Delta E_2 = 204.577 - 203.224 = 1.353$.

In this case, because we are considering 1% increases in the size of each unit, $\Delta x_1 / x_1 = \Delta x_2 / x_2 = 0.01$. From equation (16.4) the economic capital allocations to the two business units are 68.2 and 135.2. (These do not quite add up to the total economic capital of 203.2 because we approximated the partial derivative.)

16.7 DEUTSCHE BANK'S ECONOMIC CAPITAL

Deutsche Bank publishes the result of its economic capital calculation in its annual financial statements. Table 16.4 summarizes the economic capital and regulatory capital for 2004. Deutsche Bank calculated a

Table 16.4 Deutsche Bank's economic capital and regulatory capital (millions of euros).

Credit risk	5,971
Market risk	5,476
Diversification benefit across credit and market risk	(870)
Operational risk	2,243
Business risk	381
Total economic capital	13,201
Total risk-weighted assets	216,787
Tier 1 capital held (% of risk-weighted assets)	8.6%
Tier 2 capital held (% of risk-weighted assets)	4.6%
Total capital held (% of risk-weighted assets)	13.2%

diversification benefit for credit and market risk, but not for other risk-type combinations. The total economic capital is about 13.2 billion euros. This is considerably less than the total regulatory capital which is 8% of 216.8, or about 17.3 billion euros. The actual capital held is about 18.6 billion euros of Tier 1 capital and 10.0 billion euros of Tier 2 capital. It would appear that Deutsche Bank is very well capitalized relative to the risks it is taking.

16.8 RAROC

Risk-adjusted performance measurement (RAPM) has become an important part of how business units are assessed. There are many different approaches, but all have one thing in common. They compare return with capital employed in a way that incorporates an adjustment for risk.

The most common approach is to compare expected return with economic capital. This is usually referred to as RAROC (risk-adjusted return on capital). The formula is

$$\text{RAROC} = \frac{\text{Revenues} - \text{Costs} - \text{Expected losses}}{\text{Economic capital}} \qquad (16.5)$$

The numerator may be calculated on a pre-tax or post-tax basis. Very often, a risk-free rate of return on the economic capital is calculated and added to the numerator.

Example 16.5

When lending in a certain region of the world, an AA-rated bank estimates its losses as 1% of outstanding loans per year on average. The 99.97% worst-case loss (i.e., the loss exceeded only 0.03% of the time) is 5% of outstanding loans. As shown in Example 16.1, the economic capital required per $100 of loans is $4, which is the difference between the 99.97% worst-case loss and the expected loss. (This ignores diversification benefits that would in practice be allocated to the lending.) The spread between the cost of funds and the interest charged is 2.5%. Subtracting from this the expected loan loss of 1%, the expected profit per $100 of loans is $1.50. Assume that the lending department's administrative costs total 0.7% of the amount loan, the expected profit is reduced to $0.80 per $100 in the loan portfolio. RAROC is therefore

$$\frac{0.80}{4} = 20\%$$

An alternative calculation would add the interest on the economic capital to the numerator. Suppose the risk-free interest rate is 2%. Then $0.02 \times 4 = 0.08$ is added to the numerator, so that RAROC becomes

$$\frac{0.88}{4} = 22\%$$

As pointed out by Matten, it is more accurate to refer to the approach in equation (16.5) as RORAC (return on risk-adjusted capital) rather than RAROC.[3] In theory, RAROC should involve adjusting the return (i.e., the numerator) for risk. In equation (16.5) it is the capital (i.e., the denominator) that is adjusted for risk.

There are two ways in which RAROC is used. One is as a tool to compare the past performance of different business units, decide on end-of-the-year bonuses, etc. The other is as a tool to decide whether a particular business unit should be expanded or contracted. The latter involves predicting an average RAROC for the unit and comparing it with the bank's threshold return on capital.

When RAROC is used for the second purpose, it should be noted that it could be low simply because the business unit had a bad year. Perhaps credit losses were much larger than average or there was an unexpectedly large operational risk loss. This is not necessarily an indication that the business unit should be shut down. When RAROC is used as a forward-looking measure, the calculation should reflect average losses. The aim is to assess the long-term viability of the business unit, whether it should be expanded or scaled back, and so on.

---

[3] See C. Matten, *Managing Bank Capital: Capital Allocation and Performance Measurement*, 2nd edn., Chichester, UK: Wiley, 2000.

SUMMARY

Economic capital is the capital that a bank or other financial institution deems necessary for the risks it is bearing. When calculating economic capital, a financial institution is free to adopt any approach it likes. It does not have to use the one proposed by regulators. Typically, it estimates economic capital for credit risk, market risk, operational risk, and (possibly) business risk for its business units and then aggregates these estimates to produce an estimate of the economic capital for the whole enterprise. The one-year loss distributions for market risk, credit risk and operational risk are quite different. The loss distribution for market risk is symmetrical. For credit risk, it is skewed and for operational risk it is highly skewed with very heavy tails.

The total economic capital for a financial institution is allocated to business units so that a return on capital can be calculated. There are a number of allocation schemes. The best are those that reflect the incremental impact of the business unit on the total economic capital. The amount of capital allocated to a business unit is generally less than the capital estimated for the business unit as a stand-alone entity because of diversification benefits.

FURTHER READING

Dev, A., *Economic Capital: A Practitioner's Guide*. London: Risk Books, 2004.

Matten, C., *Managing Bank Capital: Capital Allocation and Performance Measurement*, 2nd edn. Chichester, UK: Wiley, 2000.

Rosenberg, J. V., and T. Schuermann, "A General Approach to Integrated Risk Management with Skewed, Fat-Tailed Risks," Federal Reserve Bank of New York, Staff Report No. 185, May 2004.

QUESTIONS AND PROBLEMS (Answers at End of Book)

16.1. What is the difference between economic capital and regulatory capital?

16.2. Why do AA-rated banks use a confidence level of 99.97% when calculating economic capital for a one-year time horizon?

16.3. What is included in business risk?

16.4. In what respects are the models used to calculate economic capital for market risk, credit risk, and operational risk likely to be different from those used to calculate regulatory capital?

16.5. Suppose the credit loss in a year has a lognormal distribution. The logarithm of the loss is normal with mean 0.5 and standard deviation 4. What is the economic capital requirement if a confidence level of 99.97% is used?

16.6. Suppose that the economic capital estimates for two business units are as follows:

	Business unit	
	1	2
Market risk	20	40
Credit risk	40	30
Operational risk	70	10

The correlations are as in Table 16.3. Calculate the total economic capital for each business unit and the two business units together.

16.7. In Problem 16.6, what is the incremental effect of each business unit on the total economic capital? Use this to allocate economic capital to business units. What is the impact on the economic capital of each business unit increasing by 0.5%? Show that your results are consistent with Euler's theorem.

16.8. A bank is considering expanding its asset management operations. The main risk is operational risk. It estimates that the expected operational risk loss from the new venture in one year is $2 million and the 99.97% worst-case loss (arising from a large investor law suit) is $40 million. The expected fees it will receive from investors for the funds under administration are $12 million per year and administrative costs are expected to be $5 million per year. Estimate the before-tax RAROC?

16.9. RAROC can be used in two different ways. What are they?

ASSIGNMENT QUESTIONS

16.10. Suppose that daily gains and losses are normally distributed with a standard deviation of σ_{day}. (a) Estimate the minimum regulatory capital the bank is required to hold for market risk. (Assume a multiplicative factor of 3.0.) (b) Estimate the economic capital for market risk using a one-year time horizon and a 99.97% confidence limit. (c) Why is the ratio of your answer in (a) to your answer in (b) not a good indication of the ratio of regulatory market risk capital to economic market risk capital in practice?

16.11. Suppose that a bank's sole business is to lend in two regions of the world. The lending in each region has the same characteristics as in Example 16.5 of Section 16.8. Lending to Region A is three times as great as lending to

Region B. The correlation between loan losses in the two regions is 0.4. Estimate the total RAROC.

16.12. Suppose that the economic capital estimates for two business units are as follows:

	Business unit	
	1	2
Market risk	10	50
Credit risk	30	30
Operational risk	50	10

The correlation between market risk and credit risk in the same business unit is 0.3. The correlation between credit risk in one business unit and credit risk in another is 0.7. The correlation between market risk in one business unit and market risk in the other is 0.2. All other correlations are zero. Calculate the total economic capital. How much should be allocated to each business unit?

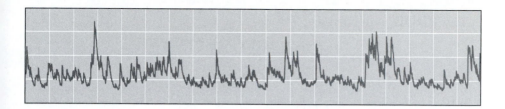

Weather, Energy, and Insurance Derivatives

Products to manage equity risks, interest rate risks, and foreign currency risks are well established and were covered in Chapter 2. This chapter examines the products that have been developed to manage risk in less traditional markets. Specifically, it considers weather risk, energy price risk, and insurance risks. The markets that we will talk about are in some cases in the early stages of their development. As they evolve, we may well see significant changes in both the products that are offered and the ways in which they are used.

17.1 WEATHER DERIVATIVES

Many companies are in the position where their performance is liable to be adversely affected by the weather.[1] It makes sense for these companies to consider hedging their weather risk in much the same way as they hedge foreign exchange or interest rate risks.

The first over-the-counter weather derivatives were introduced in 1997. To understand how they work, we explain two variables:

HDD: Heating degree days

CDD: Cooling degree days

---

[1] The US Department of Energy has estimated that one-seventh of the US economy is subject to weather risk.

A day's HDD is defined as

$$HDD = \max(0, \, 65 - A)$$

and a day's CDD is defined as

$$CDD = \max(0, \, A - 65)$$

where A is the average of the highest and lowest temperature during the day at a specified weather station, measured in degrees Fahrenheit. For example, if the maximum temperature during a day (midnight to midnight) is 68° Fahrenheit and the minimum temperature is 44° Fahrenheit, $A = 56$. The daily HDD is then 9 and the daily CDD is 0.

A typical over-the-counter product is a forward or option contract providing a payoff dependent on the cumulative HDD or CDD during a month (i.e., the total of the HDDs or CDDs for every day in the month). For example, a dealer could in January 2007 sell a client a call option on the cumulative HDD during February 2008 at the Chicago O'Hare Airport weather station with a strike price of 700 and a payment rate of $10,000 per degree day. If the actual cumulative HDD is 820, the payoff is $1.2 million. Often contracts include a payment cap. If the cap in our example is $1.5 million, the client's position is equivalent to a long call option on cumulative HDD with a strike price of 700 and a short call option with a strike price of 850.

A day's HDD is a measure of the volume of energy required for heating during the day. A day's CDD is a measure of the volume of energy required for cooling during the day. Most weather derivative contracts are entered into by energy producers and energy consumers. But retailers, supermarket chains, food and drink manufacturers, health service companies, agriculture companies, and companies in the leisure industry are also potential users of weather derivatives. The Weather Risk Management Association (www.wrma.org) has been formed to serve the interests of the weather risk management industry.

In September 1999, the Chicago Mercantile Exchange began trading weather futures and European options on weather futures. The contracts are on the cumulative HDD and CDD for a month observed at a weather station.[2] The contracts are settled in cash just after the end of the month once the HDD and CDD are known. One futures contract is on $100 times

---

[2] The CME has introduced contracts for ten different weather stations (Atlanta, Chicago, Cincinnati, Dallas, Des Moines, Las Vegas, New York, Philadelphia, Portland, and Tucson).

the cumulative HDD or CDD. The HDD and CDD are calculated by a company, Earth Satellite Corporation, using automated data collection equipment.

17.2 ENERGY DERIVATIVES

Energy companies are among the most active and sophisticated users of derivatives. Many energy products trade in both the over-the-counter market and on exchanges. In this section we will examine the trading in crude oil, natural gas, and electricity derivatives.

Crude Oil

Crude oil is one of the most important commodities in the world with global demand amounting to about 80 million barrels daily. Ten-year fixed-price supply contracts have been commonplace in the over-the-counter market for many years. These are swaps where oil at a fixed price is exchanged for oil at a floating price.

In the 1970s the price of oil was highly volatile. The 1973 war in the Middle East led to a tripling of oil prices. The fall of the Shah of Iran in the late 1970s again increased prices. These events led oil producers and users to a realization that they needed more sophisticated tools for managing oil price risk. In the 1980s both the over-the-counter market and the exchange-traded market developed products to meet this need.

In the over-the-counter market, virtually any derivative that is available on common stocks or stock indices is now available with oil as the underlying asset. Swaps, forward contracts, and options are popular. Contracts sometimes require settlement in cash and sometimes require settlement by physical delivery (i.e., by delivery of the oil).

Exchange-traded contracts are also popular. The New York Mercantile Exchange (NYMEX) and the International Petroleum Exchange (IPE) trade a number of oil futures and futures options contracts. Some of the futures contracts are settled in cash; others are settled by physical delivery. For example, the Brent crude oil futures traded on the IPE has cash settlement based on the Brent index price; the light sweet crude oil futures traded on NYMEX requires physical delivery. In both cases the amount of oil underlying one contract is 1,000 barrels. NYMEX also trades popular contracts on two refined products: heating oil and gasoline. In both cases one contract is for the delivery of 42,000 gallons.

Natural Gas

The natural gas industry throughout the world has been going through a period of deregulation and the elimination of government monopolies. The supplier of natural gas is now not necessarily the same company as the producer of the gas. Suppliers are faced with the problem of meeting daily demand.

A typical over-the-counter contract is for the delivery of a specified amount of natural gas at a roughly uniform rate over a one-month period. Forward contracts, options, and swaps are available in the over-the-counter market. The seller of gas is usually responsible for moving the gas through pipelines to the specified location.

NYMEX trades a contract for the delivery of 10,000 million British thermal units of natural gas. The contract, if not closed out, requires physical delivery to be made during the delivery month at a roughly uniform rate to a particular hub in Louisiana. The IPE trades a similar contract in London.

Electricity

Electricity is an unusual commodity because it cannot easily be stored.[3] The maximum supply of electricity in a region at any moment is determined by the maximum capacity of all the electricity-producing plants in the region. In the United States there are 140 regions known as *control areas*. Demand and supply are first matched within a control area, and any excess power is sold to other control areas. It is this excess power that constitutes the wholesale market for electricity. The ability of one control area to sell power to another control area depends on the transmission capacity of the lines between the two areas. Transmission from one area to another involves a transmission cost, charged by the owner of the line, and there are generally some energy transmission losses.

A major use of electricity is for air-conditioning systems. As a result the demand for electricity, and therefore its price, is much greater in the summer months than in the winter months. The nonstorability of electricity causes occasional very large movements in the spot price. Heat waves have been known to increase the spot price by as much as 1000% for short periods of time.

Like natural gas, electricity has been going through a period of

---

[3] Electricity producers with spare capacity sometimes use it to pump water to the top of their hydroelectric plants so that it can be used to produce electricity at a later time. This is the closest they can get to storing this commodity.

deregulation and the elimination of government monopolies. This has been accompanied by the development of an electricity derivatives market. NYMEX now trades a futures contract on the price of electricity, and there is an active over-the-counter market in forward contracts, options, and swaps. A typical contract (exchange-traded or over-the-counter) allows one side to receive a specified number of megawatt hours for a specified price at a specified location during a particular month. In a 5×8 contract, power is received for five days a week (Monday to Friday) during the off-peak period (11 p.m. to 7 a.m.) for the specified month. In a 5×16 contract, power is received five days a week during the on-peak period (7 a.m. to 11 p.m.) for the specified month. In a 7×24 contract, it is received around the clock every day during the month. Option contracts have either daily exercise or monthly exercise. In the case of daily exercise, the option holder can choose on each day of the month (by giving one day's notice) to receive the specified amount of power at the specified strike price. When there is monthly exercise a single decision on whether to receive power for the whole month at the specified strike price is made at the beginning of the month.

An interesting contract in electricity and natural gas markets is what is known as a *swing option* or *take-and-pay option*. In this contract a minimum and maximum for the amount of power that must be purchased at a certain price by the option holder is specified for each day during a month and for the month in total. The option holder can change (or swing) the rate at which the power is purchased during the month, but usually there is a limit on the total number of changes that can be made.

How an Energy Producer Can Hedge Risks

There are two components to the risks facing an energy producer. One is the price risk; the other is the volume risk. Although prices do adjust to reflect volumes, there is a less-than-perfect relationship between the two, and energy producers have to take both into account when developing a hedging strategy. The price risk can be hedged using the energy derivative contracts discussed in this section. The volume risks can be hedged using the weather derivatives discussed in the previous section.

Define:

Y: Profit for a month
P: Average energy prices for the month
T: Relevant temperature variable (HDD or CDD) for the month

An energy producer can use historical data to obtain a best-fit linear regression relationship of the form

$$Y = a + bP + cT + \epsilon$$

where ϵ is the error term. The energy producer can then hedge risks for the month by taking a position of $-b$ in energy forwards or futures and a position of $-c$ in weather forwards or futures. The relationship can also be used to analyze the effectiveness of alternative option strategies.

17.3 INSURANCE DERIVATIVES

When derivative contracts are used for hedging purposes, they have many of the same characteristics as insurance contracts. Both types of contracts are designed to provide protection against adverse events. It is therefore not surprising that many insurance companies have subsidiaries that trade derivatives and that many of the activities of insurance companies are becoming very similar to those of investment banks.

Traditionally the insurance industry has hedged its exposure to catastrophic (CAT) risks such as hurricanes and earthquakes using a practice known as reinsurance. Reinsurance contracts can take a number of forms. Suppose that an insurance company has an exposure of $100 million to earthquakes in California and wants to limit this to $30 million. One alternative is to enter into annual reinsurance contracts that cover on a pro rata basis 70% of its exposure. If California earthquake claims in a particular year total $50 million, the costs to the company would then be only $0.3 \times \$50$ or $15 million. Another more popular alternative, involving lower reinsurance premiums, is to buy a series of reinsurance contracts covering what are known as *excess cost layers*. The first layer might provide indemnification for losses between $30 million and $40 million; the next layer might cover losses between $40 million and $50 million; and so on. Each reinsurance contract is known as an *excess-of-loss* reinsurance contract. The insurance company is long a call option with a strike price equal to the lower end of the layer and short a call option with a strike price equal to the upper end of the layer.

The principal providers of CAT reinsurance have traditionally been reinsurance companies and Lloyds syndicates (unlimited liability syndicates of wealthy individuals). In recent years the industry has come to the conclusion that its reinsurance needs have outstripped what can be provided from these traditional sources. It has searched for new ways in which capital markets can provide reinsurance. One of the events that caused the industry to rethink its practices was Hurricane Andrew in 1992. This caused about $15 billion of insurance costs in Florida, which exceeded the total of relevant insurance premiums received there during the previous seven years. If the hurricane had hit Miami, it is estimated that insured losses would have exceeded $40 billion. Hurricane Andrew and other catastrophes have led to increases in insurance/reinsurance premiums.

Exchange-traded insurance futures contracts have been developed by the CBOT, but have not been highly successful. The over-the-counter market has come up with a number of products that are alternatives to traditional reinsurance. The most popular is a *CAT bond*. This is a bond issued by a subsidiary of an insurance company that pays a higher-than-normal interest rate. In exchange for the extra interest, the holder of the bond agrees to provide an excess-of-cost reinsurance contract. Depending on the terms of the CAT bond, the interest or principal (or both) can be used to meet claims. In the example considered above where an insurance company wants protection for California earthquake losses between $30 million and $40 million, the insurance company could issue CAT bonds with a total principal of $10 million. In the event that the insurance company's California earthquake losses exceed $30 million, bondholders will lose some or all of their principal. As an alternative, the insurance company could cover this excess cost layer by making a much bigger bond issue where only the bondholders' interest is at risk.

CAT bonds typically give a high probability of an above-normal rate of interest and a low-probability of a high loss. Why would investors be interested in such instruments? The answer is that there are no statistically significant correlations between CAT risks and market returns.[4] CAT bonds are therefore an attractive addition to an investor's portfolio. They have no systematic risk, so that their total risk can be completely diversified away in a large portfolio. If a CAT bond's expected return is greater than the risk-free interest rate (and typically it is), it has the potential to improve risk–return trade-offs.

SUMMARY

When there are risks to be managed, markets have been very innovative in developing products to meet the needs of market participants.

---

[4] See R. H. Litzenberger, D. R. Beaglehole, and C. E. Reynolds, "Assessing Catastrophe Reinsurance-Linked Securities as a New Asset Class," *Journal of Portfolio Management*, Winter 1996, 76–86.

In the weather derivatives market, two measures, HDD and CDD, have been developed to describe the temperature during a month. These are used to define the payoffs on both exchange-traded and over-the-counter derivatives. As the weather derivatives market develops, we will see contracts on rainfall, snow, and similar variables become more commonplace.

In energy markets, oil derivatives have been important for some time and play a key role in helping oil producers and oil consumers manage their price risk. Natural gas and electricity derivatives are relatively new. They became important for risk management when these markets were deregulated and government monopolies discontinued.

Insurance derivatives are beginning to become an alternative to traditional reinsurance as a way for insurance companies to manage the risks of a catastrophic event such as a hurricane or an earthquake. No doubt we will see other sorts of insurance (e.g., life insurance and automobile insurance) being securitized in a similar way as this market develops.

FURTHER READING

On Weather Derivatives

Arditti, F., L. Cai, M. Cao, and R. McDonald, "Whether to Hedge," *Risk*, Supplement on Weather Risk, 1999: 9–12.

Cao, M., and J. Wei, "Weather Derivatives Valuation and the Market Price of Weather Risk," *Journal of Futures Markets*, 24, 11 (November 2004), 1065–1089.

Hunter, R., "Managing Mother Nature," *Derivatives Strategy*, February 1999.

On Energy Derivatives

Clewlow, L., and C. Strickland, *Energy Derivatives: Pricing and Risk Management*. Lacima Group, 2000.

Eydeland, A., and H. Geman, "Pricing Power Derivatives." *Risk*, October 1998: 71–73.

Joskow, P., "Electricity Sectors in Transition," *The Energy Journal*, 19 (1998): 25–52.

Kendall, R., "Crude Oil: Price Shocking," *Risk*, Supplement on Commodity Risk, May 1999.

On Insurance Derivatives

Canter, M. S., J. B. Cole, and R. L. Sandor, "Insurance Derivatives: A New Asset Class for the Capital Markets and a New Hedging Tool for the Insurance Industry," *Journal of Applied Corporate Finance*, Autumn 1997: 69–83.

Froot, K. A., "The Market for Catastrophe Risk: A Clinical Examination," *Journal of Financial Economics*, 60 (2001): 529–571.

Froot, K. A., *The Financing of Catastrophe Risk*. University of Chicago Press, 1999.

Geman, H., "CAT Calls," *Risk*, September 1994: 86–89.

Hanley, M., "A Catastrophe Too Far," *Risk*, Supplement on Insurance, July 1998.

Litzenberger, R. H., D. R. Beaglehole, and C. E. Reynolds, "Assessing Catastrophe Reinsurance-Linked Securities as a New Asset Class," *Journal of Portfolio Management*, Winter 1996: 76–86.

QUESTIONS AND PROBLEMS (Answers at End of Book)

17.1. What is meant by HDD and CDD?

17.2. How is a typical natural gas forward contract structured?

17.3. Suppose that each day during July the minimum temperature is 68° Fahrenheit and the maximum temperature is 82° Fahrenheit. What is the payoff from a call option on the cumulative CDD during July with a strike of 250 and a payment rate of $5,000 per degree day?

17.4. Why is the price of electricity more volatile than that of other energy sources?

17.5. "HDD and CDD can be regarded as payoffs from options on temperature." Explain.

17.6. Suppose that you have 50 years of temperature data at your disposal. Explain carefully the analyses you would carry out to value a forward contract on the cumulative CDD for a particular month.

17.7. Would you expect the volatility of the one-year forward price of oil to be greater than or less than the volatility of the spot price. Explain.

17.8. How can an energy producer use derivative markets to hedge risks?

17.9. Explain how a 5 × 8 option contract on electricity for May 2006 with daily exercise works. Explain how a 5 × 8 option contract on electricity for May 2006 with monthly exercise works. Which is worth more?

17.10. Explain how CAT bonds work.

17.11. Consider two bonds that have the same coupon, time to maturity, and price. One is a B-rated corporate bond. The other is a CAT bond. An analysis based on historical data shows that the expected losses on the two bonds in each year of their life is the same. Which bond would you advise a portfolio manager to buy and why?

17.12. "Oil, gas, and electricity exhibit mean reversion." What is meant by this statement? Which product has the highest mean-reversion rate? Which has the lowest?

ASSIGNMENT QUESTION

17.13. An insurance company's losses of a particular type are to a reasonable approximation normally distributed with a mean of $150 million and a standard deviation of $50 million. (Assume no difference between losses in a risk-neutral world and losses in the real world.) The one-year risk-free rate is 5%. Estimate the cost of the following: (a) a contract that will pay in one-year's time 60% of the insurance company's costs on a pro rata basis, and (b) a contract that pays $100 million in one-year's time if losses exceed $200 million.

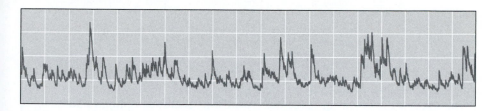

Big Losses and What We Can Learn from Them

Since the mid-1980s there have been some spectacular losses in financial markets. This chapter explores the lessons we can learn from them and emphasizes some of the key points made in earlier chapters. The losses that we will consider are listed in Business Snapshot 18.1.

One remarkable aspect of the list in Business Snapshot 18.1 is the number of times huge losses were caused by the activities of a single employee. In 1995, Nick Leeson's trading brought a 200-year-old British bank, Barings, to its knees; in 1994, Robert Citron's trading led to Orange County, a municipality in California, losing about $2 billion. Joseph Jett's trading for Kidder Peabody caused losses of $350 million. John Rusnak's losses of $700 million at Allied Irish Bank came to light in 2002.

Some of the losses involve derivatives, but they should not be viewed as an indictment of the whole derivatives industry. The derivatives market is a vast multitrillion-dollar market that by most measures has been outstandingly successful and has served the needs of its users well. Derivatives trades involving unacceptable risks represent a tiny proportion of total trades (both in number and in value). To quote Alan Greenspan, who was Chairman of the Federal Reserve, in May 2003:

> The use of a growing array of derivatives and the related application of more-sophisticated methods for measuring and managing risk are key factors underpinning the enhanced resilience of our largest financial intermediaries.

Business Snapshot 18.1 Big Losses

Allied Irish Bank
This bank lost about $700 million from the unauthorized speculative activities of one of its foreign exchange traders, John Rusnak, that lasted a number of years. Rusnak covered up his losses by creating fictitious options trades.

Barings (See Business Snapshot 2.4)
This 200-year-old British bank was wiped out in 1995 by the activities of one trader, Nick Leeson, in Singapore. The trader's mandate was to arbitrage between Nikkei 225 futures quotes in Singapore and Osaka. Instead he made big bets on the future direction of the Nikkei 225 using futures and options. The total loss was close to $1 billion.

Enron's Counterparties
Enron managed to conceal its true situation from its shareholders with some creative contracts. Several financial institutions that allegedly helped Enron do this have had to settle shareholder lawsuits for over $1 billion.

Hammersmith and Fulham (See Business Snapshot 14.1)
This British Local Authority lost about $600 million on sterling interest rate swaps and options in 1988. The two traders responsible for the loss knew surprisingly little about the products they were trading.

Kidder Peabody (See Business Snapshot 15.1)
The activities of a single trader, Joseph Jett, led to this New York investment dealer losing $350 million trading US government securities. The loss arose because of a mistake in the way the company's computer system calculated profits.

Long-Term Capital Management (See Business Snapshot 12.1)
This hedge fund lost about $4 billion in 1998 carrying out convergence arbitrage strategies. The loss was caused by a flight to quality after Russia defaulted on its debt.

National Westminster Bank
This British bank lost about $130 million from using an inappropriate model to value swap options in 1997.

Orange County (See Business Snapshot 4.1)
The activities of the treasurer, Robert Citron, led to this California municipality losing about $2 billion in 1994. The treasurer was using derivatives to speculate that interest rates would not rise.

Procter and Gamble (See Business Snapshot 2.2)
The treasury department of this large US company lost about $90 million in 1994 trading highly exotic interest rate derivatives contracts with Bankers Trust. It later sued Bankers Trust and settled out of court.

18.1 RISK LIMITS

The first and most important lesson from the losses concerns risk limits. It is essential that all companies (financial and nonfinancial) define in a clear and unambiguous way limits to the financial risks that can be taken. They should then set up procedures for ensuring that the limits are obeyed. Ideally, overall risk limits should be set at board level. These should then be converted to limits applicable to the individuals responsible for managing particular risks. Daily reports should indicate the gain or loss that will be experienced for particular movements in market variables. These should be checked against the actual gains and losses that are experienced to ensure that the valuation procedures underlying the reports are accurate.

It is particularly important that companies monitor risks carefully when derivatives are used. This is because derivatives can be used for hedging or speculation or arbitrage. Without close monitoring, it is impossible to know whether a derivatives trader has switched from being a hedger to a speculator or from being an arbitrageur to a speculator. Barings is a classic example of what can go wrong. Nick Leeson's mandate was to carry out low-risk arbitrage between the Singapore and Osaka markets on Nikkei 225 futures. Unknown to his superiors in London, Leeson switched from being an arbitrageur to taking huge bets on the future direction of the Nikkei 225. Systems within Barings were so inadequate that nobody knew what he was doing.

The argument here is not that no risks should be taken. A treasurer working for a corporation or a trader in a financial institution or a fund manager should be allowed to take positions on the future direction of relevant market variables. What we are arguing is that the sizes of the positions that can be taken should be limited and the systems in place should accurately report the risks being taken.

A Difficult Situation

What happens if an individual exceeds risk limits and makes a profit? This is a tricky issue for senior management. It is tempting to ignore violations of risk limits when profits result. However, this is shortsighted. It leads to a culture where risk limits are not taken seriously, and it paves the way for a disaster. The classic example here is Orange County. Robert Citron's activities in 1991–1993 had been very profitable for Orange County, and the municipality had come to rely on his trading for additional funding. People chose to ignore the risks he was taking because he had produced profits. Unfortunately, the losses made in 1994 far exceeded the profits from previous years.

The penalties for exceeding risk limits should be just as great when profits result as when losses result. Otherwise, traders that make losses are liable to keep increasing their bets in the hope that eventually a profit will result and all will be forgiven.

Do Not Assume You Can Outguess the Market

Some traders are quite possibly better than others. But no trader gets it right all the time. A trader who correctly predicts the direction in which market variables will move 60% of the time is doing well. If a trader has an outstanding track record (as Robert Citron did in the early 1990s), it is likely to be a result of luck rather than superior trading skill.

Suppose that a financial institution employs 16 traders and one of those traders makes profits in every quarter of a year. Should the trader receive a good bonus? Should the trader's risk limits be increased? The answer to the first question is that inevitably the trader will receive a good bonus. The answer to the second question should be no. The chance of making a profit in four consecutive quarters from random trading is 0.5^4 or one in 16. This means that just by chance one of the 16 traders will "get it right" every single quarter of the year. We should not assume that the trader's luck will continue and we should not increase the trader's risk limits.

Do Not Underestimate the Benefits of Diversification

When a trader appears good at predicting a particular market variable, there is a tendency to increase the trader's risk limits. We have just argued that this is a bad idea because it is quite likely that the trader has been lucky rather than clever. However, let us suppose that we are really convinced that the trader has special talents. How undiversified should we allow ourselves to become in order to take advantage of the trader's special skills? The answer, as indicated in Section 1.1, is that the benefits from diversification are huge, and it is unlikely that any trader is so good that it is worth foregoing these benefits to speculate heavily on just one market variable.

An example will illustrate the point here. Suppose that there are 20 stocks, each of which have an expected return of 10% per annum and a standard deviation of returns of 30%. The correlation between the returns from any two of the stocks is 0.2. By dividing an investment equally among the 20 stocks, an investor has an expected return of 10% per annum and standard deviation of returns of 14.7%. Diversification enables the investor to reduce risks by over half. Another way of expressing this is that diversification enables an investor to double the expected return per unit of risk taken. The investor would have to be extremely good at stock picking to get a better risk–return trade-off by investing in just one stock.

Carry out Scenario Analyses and Stress Tests

The calculation of risk measures such as VaR should always be accompanied by scenario analyses and stress testing to obtain an understanding of what can go wrong. These techniques were mentioned in Section 8.7. They are very important. Human beings have an unfortunate tendency to anchor on one or two scenarios when evaluating decisions. In 1993 and 1994, for example, Procter and Gamble was so convinced that interest rates would remain low that, in their decision-making, they ignored the possibility of a 100 basis point rate increase.

It is important to be creative in the way scenarios are generated. One approach is to look at ten or twenty years of data and choose the most extreme events as scenarios. Sometimes there is a shortage of data on a key variable. It is then sensible to choose a similar variable for which much more data is available and use historical daily percentage changes in that variable as a proxy for possible daily percentage changes in the key variable. For example, if there is little data on the prices of bonds issued by a particular country, we can look at historical data on prices of bonds issued by other similar countries to develop possible scenarios.

18.2 MANAGING THE TRADING ROOM

In trading rooms there is a tendency to regard high-performing traders as "untouchable" and to not subject their activities to the same scrutiny as other traders. Apparently Joseph Jett, Kidder Peabody's star trader of Treasury instruments, was often "too busy" to answer questions and discuss his positions with the company's risk managers.

It is important that all traders—particularly those making high profits—be fully accountable. It is important for the financial institution to know whether the high profits are being made by taking unreasonably high risks. It is also important to check that the financial institution's computer systems and pricing models are correct and are not being manipulated in some way.

Separate the Front, Middle, and Back Office

The *front office* in a financial institution consists of the traders who are executing trades, taking positions, etc. The *middle office* consists of risk managers who are monitoring the risks being taken. The *back office* is where the record-keeping and accounting takes place. Some of the worst derivatives disasters have occurred because these functions were not kept separate. Nick Leeson controlled both the front and back office for Barings in Singapore and was, as a result, able to conceal the disastrous nature of his trades from his superiors in London for some time.

Do Not Blindly Trust Models

We discussed model risk in Chapter 15. Some of the large losses experienced by financial institutions arose because of the models and computer systems being used. Kidder Peabody was misled by its own systems. Another example of an incorrect model leading to losses is provided by National Westminster Bank. This bank had an incorrect model for valuing swap options that led to significant losses.

If large profits are reported when relatively simple trading strategies are followed, there is a good chance that the models underlying the calculation of the profits are wrong. Similarly, if a financial institution appears to be particularly competitive on its quotes for a particular type of deal, there is a good chance that it is using a different model from other market participants, and it should analyze what is going on carefully. To the head of a trading room, getting too much business of a certain type can be just as worrisome as getting too little business of that type.

Be Conservative in Recognizing Inception Profits

When a financial institution sells a highly exotic instrument to a non-financial corporation, the valuation can be highly dependent on the underlying model. For example, instruments with long-dated embedded interest rate options can be highly dependent on the interest rate model used. In these circumstances, a phrase used to describe the daily marking to market of the deal is *marking to model*. This is because there are no market prices for similar deals that can be used as a benchmark.

Suppose that a financial institution manages to sell an instrument to a client for $10 million more than it is worth—or at least $10 million more than its model says it is worth. The $10 million is known as an *inception profit*. When should it be recognized? There appears to be a lot of variation in what different investment banks do. Some recognize the $10 million immediately, whereas others are much more conservative and recognize it slowly over the life of the deal.

Recognizing inception profits immediately is very dangerous. It encourages traders to use aggressive models, take their bonuses, and leave before the model and the value of the deal come under close scrutiny. It is much better to recognize inception profits slowly so that traders are motivated to investigate the impact of several different models and several different sets of assumptions before committing themselves to a deal.

Do Not Sell Clients Inappropriate Products

It is tempting to sell corporate clients inappropriate products, particularly when they appear to have an appetite for the underlying risks. But this is shortsighted. The most dramatic example of this is provided by the activities of Bankers Trust (BT) in the period leading up to the spring of 1994. Many of BT's clients were persuaded to buy high-risk and totally inappropriate products. A typical product would give the client a good chance of saving a few basis points on its borrowings and a small chance of costing a large amount of money. The products worked well for BT's clients in 1992 and 1993, but blew up in 1994 when interest rates rose sharply. The bad publicity that followed hurt BT greatly. The years it had spent building up trust among corporate clients and developing an enviable reputation for innovation in derivatives were largely lost as a result of the activities of a few overly aggressive salesmen. BT was forced to pay large amounts of money to its clients to settle lawsuits out of court. It was taken over by Deutsche Bank in 1999.

Enron provides another example of how overly aggressive deal makers cost their banks billions of dollars. One lesson from Enron is: "The fact that many banks are pushing hard to get a certain type of business should not be taken as an indication that the business will be ultimately profitable." Businesses where high profits seem easy to achieve should be looked at closely for potential operational, credit, or market risks. A number of banks have had to settle lawsuits with Enron shareholders for over $1 billion.

18.3 LIQUIDITY RISK

We discussed liquidity risk in Chapter 15. Financial engineers usually base the pricing of exotic instruments and other instruments that trade relatively infrequently on the prices of actively traded instruments. For example:

1. A financial engineer often calculates a zero curve from actively traded government bonds (known as on-the-run bonds) and uses it to price bonds that trade less frequently (off-the-run bonds).

2. A financial engineer often implies the volatility of an asset from actively traded options and uses it to price less actively traded options.

3. A financial engineer often implies information about the behavior of interest rates from actively traded interest rate caps and swap options and uses it to price products that are highly structured.

These practices are not unreasonable. However, it is dangerous to assume that less actively traded instruments can always be traded at close to their theoretical price. When financial markets experience a shock of one sort or another, liquidity black holes may develop (see Section 15.8). Liquidity then becomes very important to investors, and illiquid instruments often sell at a big discount to their theoretical values. Trading strategies that assume large volumes of relatively illiquid instruments can be sold at short notice at close to their theoretical values are dangerous.

An example of liquidity risk is provided by Long-Term Capital Management (LTCM), which we discussed in Business Snapshot 12.1. This hedge fund followed a strategy known as *convergence arbitrage*. It attempted to identify two securities (or portfolios of securities) that should in theory sell for the same price. If the market price of one security was less that of the other, it would buy that security and sell the other. The strategy is based on the idea that if two securities have the same theoretical price their market prices should eventually be the same.

In the summer of 1998 LTCM made a huge loss. This was largely because a default by Russia on its debt caused a flight to quality. LTCM tended to be long illiquid instruments and short the corresponding liquid instruments. (For example, it was long off-the-run bonds and short on-the-run bonds.) The spreads between the prices of illiquid instruments and the corresponding liquid instruments widened sharply after the Russian default. LTCM was highly leveraged. It experienced huge losses and there were margin calls on its positions that it was unable to meet.

The LTCM story reinforces the importance of carrying out scenario analyses and stress testing to look at what can happen in the worst of all worlds. LTCM could have tried to examine other times in history when there have been extreme flights to quality to quantify the liquidity risks it was facing.

Beware When Everyone Is Following the Same Trading Strategy

It sometimes happens that many market participants are following essentially the same trading strategy. This creates a dangerous environment where there are liable to be big market moves, liquidity black holes, and large losses for the market participants.

We gave one example of this in Business Snapshot 15.4 when discussing portfolio insurance and the market crash of October 1987. In the months leading up to the crash, increasing numbers of portfolio managers were attempting to insure their portfolios by creating synthetic put options. They bought stocks or stock index futures after a rise in the market and sold them after a fall. This created an unstable market. A relatively small decline in stock prices could lead to a wave of selling by portfolio insurers. The latter would lead to a further decline in the market, which could give rise to another wave of selling, and so on. There is little doubt that without portfolio insurance the crash of October 1987 would have been much less severe.

Another example is provided by LTCM in 1998. Its position was made more difficult by the fact that many other hedge funds were following similar convergence arbitrage strategies. After the Russian default and the flight to quality, LTCM tried to liquidate part of its portfolio to meet margin calls. Unfortunately, other hedge funds were facing similar problems to LTCM and trying to do similar trades. This exacerbated the situation, causing liquidity spreads to be even higher than they would otherwise have been and reinforcing the flight to quality. Consider, for example, LTCM's position in US Treasury bonds. It was long the illiquid off-the-run bonds and short the liquid on-the-run bonds. When a flight to quality caused spreads between yields on the two types of bonds to widen, LTCM had to liquidate its positions by selling off-the-run bonds and buying on-the-run bonds. Other large hedge funds were doing the same. As a result, the price of on-the-run bonds rose relative to off-the-run bonds and the spread between the two yields widened even more than it had already.

A further example is provided by British insurance companies in the late 1990s. This is discussed in Business Snapshot 15.5. All insurance companies decided to hedge their exposure to a fall in long-term rates at about the same time. The result was a fall in long-term rates!

The chief lesson to be learned from these stories is that it is important to see the big picture of what is going on in financial markets and to understand the risks inherent in situations where many market participants are following the same trading strategy.

18.4 LESSONS FOR NONFINANCIAL CORPORATIONS

We conclude with some lessons applicable primarily to nonfinancial corporations.

Make Sure You Fully Understand the Trades You Are Doing

Corporations should never undertake a trade or a trading strategy that they do not fully understand. This is a somewhat obvious point, but it is surprising how often a trader working for a nonfinancial corporation will, after a big loss, admit to not really understanding what was going on and claim to have been misled by investment bankers. Robert Citron, the treasurer of Orange County, did this. So did the traders working for Hammersmith and Fulham, who in spite of their huge positions were surprisingly uninformed about how the swaps and other interest rate derivatives they traded really worked.

If a senior manager in a corporation does not understand a trade proposed by a subordinate, the trade should not be approved. A simple rule of thumb is that if a trade and the rationale for entering into it are so complicated that they cannot be understood by the manager, it is almost certainly inappropriate for the corporation. The trades undertaken by Procter and Gamble would have been vetoed using this criterion.

One way of ensuring that you fully understand a financial instrument is to value it. If a corporation does not have the in-house capability to value an instrument, it should not trade it. In practice, corporations often rely on their investment bankers for valuation advice. This is dangerous, as Procter and Gamble found out. When it wanted to unwind its transactions, it found it was facing prices produced by Bankers Trust's proprietary models, which it had no way of checking.

Make Sure a Hedger Does Not Become a Speculator

One of the unfortunate facts of life is that hedging is relatively dull, whereas speculation is exciting. When a company hires a trader to manage foreign exchange, commodity price, or interest rate risk there is a danger that the following happens. At first the trader does the job diligently and earns the confidence of top management. He or she assesses the company's exposures and hedges them. As time goes by, the trader becomes convinced that he or she can outguess the market. Slowly the trader becomes a speculator. At first things go well, but then a loss is made. To recover the loss, the trader doubles up the bets. Further losses are made, and so on. The result is likely to be a disaster.

As mentioned earlier, clear limits to the risks that can be taken should be set by senior management. Controls should be put in place to ensure that the limits are obeyed. The trading strategy for a corporation should start with an analysis of the risks facing the corporation in foreign exchange, interest rate, commodity markets, and so on. A decision should then be taken on how the risks are to be reduced to acceptable levels. It is a clear sign that something is wrong within a corporation if the trading strategy is not derived in a very direct way from the company's exposures.

Be Cautious about Making the Treasury Department a Profit Center

In the last 20 years there has been a tendency to make the treasury department within a corporation a profit center. This seems to have much to recommend it. The treasurer is motivated to reduce financing costs and manage risks as profitably as possible. The problem is that the potential for the treasurer to make profits is limited. When raising funds and investing surplus cash, the treasurer is facing an efficient market. The treasurer can usually improve the bottom line only by taking additional risks. The company's hedging program gives the treasurer some scope for making shrewd decisions that increase profits, but it should be remembered that the goal of a hedging program is to reduce risks, not to increase expected profits. The decision to hedge will lead to a worse outcome than the decision not to hedge roughly 50% of the time. The danger of making the treasury department a profit center is that the treasurer is motivated to become a speculator. An outcome like that of Orange County or Procter and Gamble is then liable to occur.

SUMMARY

The key lesson to be learned from the losses is the importance of *internal controls*. The risks taken by traders, the models used, and the amount of different types of business done should all be controlled. It is important to "think outside the box" about what could go wrong. LTCM, Enron's bank counterparties, and many other financial institutions have failed to do this, with huge adverse financial consequences.

FURTHER READING

Dunbar, N., *Inventing Money: The Story of Long-Term Capital Management and the Legends Behind It*. Chichester, UK: Wiley, 2000.

Jorion, P., *Big Bets Gone Bad: Derivatives and Bankruptcy in Orange County*. New York: Academic Press, 1995.

Jorion, P., "How Long-Term Lost Its Capital," *Risk*, September 1999: 31–36.

Ju, X., and N. Pearson, "Using Value at Risk to Control Risk Taking: How Wrong Can You Be?" *Journal of Risk*, 1 (1999): 5–36.

Thomson, R., *Apocalypse Roulette: The Lethal World of Derivatives*. London: Macmillan, 1998.

Zhang, P. G., *Barings Bankruptcy and Financial Derivatives*. Singapore: World Scientific Publishing, 1995.

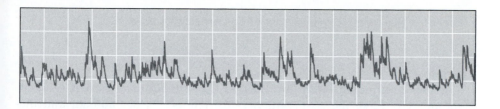

Valuing Forward and Futures Contracts

The forward or futures price of an investment asset that provides no income is given by

$$S_0 e^{rT}$$

where S_0 is the spot price of the asset today, T is the time to maturity of the forward or futures contract, and r is the continuously compounded risk-free rate for maturity T. When the asset provides income during the life of the contract that has a present value I, this becomes

$$(S_0 - I)e^{rT}$$

When it provides a yield at rate q, it becomes

$$S_0 e^{(r-q)T}$$

A foreign currency can be regarded as an investment asset that provides a yield equal to the foreign risk-free rate.

The value of a forward contract where the holder has the right to buy the asset for a price of K is in all cases

$$(F - K)e^{-rT}$$

where F is the forward price. The value of a forward contract where the holder has the right to sell the asset for a price of K is similarly

$$(K - F)e^{-rT}$$

Example A.1

Consider a six-month futures contract on the S&P 500. The current value of the index is 1200, the six-month risk-free rate is 5% per annum, and the average dividend yield on the S&P 500 over the next six months is expected to be 2% per annum (both rates continuously compounded). The futures price is $1200e^{(0.05-0.02)\times0.5}$, or 1,218.14.

Example A.2

The current forward price of gold for a contract maturing in nine months is $550. A company has a forward contract to buy 1,000 ounces of gold for a delivery price of $530 in nine months. The nine-month risk-free rate is 4% per annum continuously compounded. The value of the forward contract is $1,000 \times (550 - 530)e^{-0.04\times9/12}$, or $19,409.

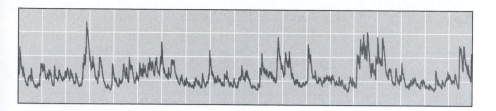

Valuing Swaps

An interest rate swap can be valued by assuming that the interest rates that are realized in the future equal today's forward interest rates. As an example, consider an interest rate swap has 14 months remaining and a notional principal of $100 million. A fixed rate of 5% per annum is received and LIBOR is paid, with exchanges taking place every six months. Assume that (a) four months ago the six-month LIBOR rate was 4%, (b) the forward LIBOR interest rate for a six-month period starting in two months is 4.6%, and (c) the forward LIBOR for a six-month period starting in eight months is 5.2%. All rates are expressed with semiannual compounding. Assuming that forward rates are realized, the cash flows on the swap are as shown in Table B.1. (For example, in eight months the fixed-rate cash flow received is $0.5 \times 0.05 \times 100$, or $2.5 million; the floating-rate cash flow paid is $0.5 \times 0.046 \times 100$, or

Table B.1   Valuing an interest rate swap by assuming forward rates are realized.

Time	Fixed cash flow ($ million)	Floating cash flow ($ million)	Net cash flow ($ million)
2 months	2.5	−2.0	0.5
8 months	2.5	−2.3	0.2
14 months	2.5	−2.6	−0.1

Table B.2   Valuing a currency swap by assuming forward exchange rates are realized (all cash flows in millions).

Time	USD cash flow	GBP cash flow	Forward exchange rate	USD value of GBP cash flow	Net cash flow in USD
1	−0.6	0.2	1.8000	0.360	−0.240
2	−0.6	0.2	1.8400	0.368	−0.232
3	−0.6	0.2	1.8800	0.376	−0.224
3	−10.0	5.0	1.8800	9.400	−0.600

$2.3 million.) The value of the swap is the present value of the net cash flows in the final column.[1]

An alternative approach (which gives the same valuation) is to assume that the swap principal of $100 million is paid and received at the end of the life of the swap. This makes no difference to the value of the swap but allows it to be regarded as the exchange of interest and principal on a fixed-rate bond for interest and principal on a floating-rate bond. The fixed-rate bond's cash flows can be valued in the usual way. A general rule is that the floating-rate bond is always worth an amount equal to the principal immediately after an interest payment. In our example, the value of the floating rate bond is worth $100 million immediately after the payment in two months. This payment (determined four months ago) is $2 million. The value of the floating-rate bond is therefore $102 million immediately before the payment at the two-month point. The value of the swap is therefore the present value of the fixed-rate bond less the present value of a cash flow of $102 million in two months.

Currency Swaps

A currency swap can be valued by assuming that exchange rates in the future equal today's forward exchange rates. As an example consider a currency swap in which 4% will be received in GBP and 6% will be paid in USD once a year. The principals in the two currencies are 10 million USD and 5 million GBP. The swap will last for another three years. The swap cash flows are shown in the second and third columns of Table B.2. The forward exchange rates are (we assume) those shown in the fourth column. These are used to convert the GBP cash flows to USD. The final

---

[1] Note that this is not perfectly accurate because it does not take account of day count conventions and holiday calendars.

column shows the net cash flows. The value of the swap is the present value of these cash flows.

An alternative approach (which gives the same valuation) is to regard the swap as a long position in a GBP bond and a short position in a USD bond. Each bond can be valued in its own currency in the usual way and the current exchange rate can be used to convert the value of the GBP bond from GBP to USD.

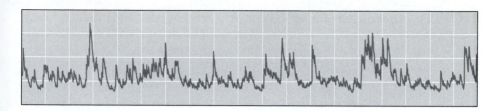

Valuing European Options

The Black–Scholes–Merton formulas for valuing European call and put options on an investment asset that provides no income are

$$c = S_0 N(d_1) - Ke^{-rT} N(d_2)$$

and

$$p = Ke^{-rT} N(-d_2) - S_0 N(-d_1)$$

where

$$d_1 = \frac{\ln(S_0/K) + (r + \sigma^2/2)T}{\sigma\sqrt{T}}$$

$$d_2 = \frac{\ln(S_0/K) + (r - \sigma^2/2)T}{\sigma\sqrt{T}} = d_1 - \sigma\sqrt{T}$$

The function $N(x)$ is the cumulative probability distribution function for a standardized normal distribution (see tables at the end of the book). The variables c and p are the European call and European put price, S_0 is the stock price at time zero, K is the strike price, r is the continuously compounded risk-free rate, σ is the stock price volatility, and T is the time to maturity of the option.

When the underlying asset provides a cash income, the present value of the income during the life of the option should be subtracted from S_0. When the underlying asset provides a yield at rate q, the formulas become

$$c = S_0 e^{-qT} N(d_1) - Ke^{-rT} N(d_2)$$

Table C.1 Greek letters for options on an asset that provides a yield at rate q.

Greek letter	Call option	Put option
Delta	$e^{-qT}N(d_1)$	$e^{-qT}[N(d_1) - 1]$
Gamma	$\dfrac{N'(d_1)e^{-qT}}{S_0\sigma\sqrt{T}}$	$\dfrac{N'(d_1)e^{-qT}}{S_0\sigma\sqrt{T}}$
Theta (per year)	$\begin{aligned} &-S_0N'(d_1)\sigma e^{-qT}/(2\sqrt{T}) \\ &+qS_0N(d_1)e^{-qT} \\ &-rKe^{-rT}N(d_2) \end{aligned}$	$\begin{aligned} &-S_0N'(d_1)\sigma e^{-qT}/(2\sqrt{T}) \\ &-qS_0N(-d_1)e^{-qT} \\ &+rKe^{-rT}N(-d_2) \end{aligned}$
Vega (per %)	$\dfrac{S_0\sqrt{T}\,N'(d_1)e^{-qT}}{100}$	$\dfrac{S_0\sqrt{T}\,N'(d_1)e^{-qT}}{100}$
Rho (per %)	$\dfrac{KTe^{-rT}N(d_2)}{100}$	$-\dfrac{KTe^{-rT}N(-d_2)}{100}$

and

$$p = Ke^{-rT}N(-d_2) - S_0e^{-qT}N(-d_1)$$

where

$$d_1 = \frac{\ln(S_0/K) + (r - q + \sigma^2/2)T}{\sigma\sqrt{T}}$$

$$d_2 = \frac{\ln(S_0/K) + (r - q - \sigma^2/2)T}{\sigma\sqrt{T}} = d_1 - \sigma\sqrt{T}$$

Options on a foreign currency can be valued by setting q equal to the foreign risk-free rate.

Table C.1 gives formulas for the Greek letters. $N'(x)$ is the standard normal density function, given by

$$N'(x) = \frac{1}{\sqrt{2\pi}}e^{-x^2/2}$$

Example C.1

Consider a six-month European option on a stock index. The current value of the index is 1200, the strike price is 1250, the risk-free rate is 5%, the dividend yield on the index is 2%, and the index volatility is 20%. In this case, $S_0 = 1200$, $K = 1250$, $r = 0.05$, $q = 0.02$, $\sigma = 0.2$, and $T = 0.5$. The value of the option is 53.44, the delta of the option is 0.45, the gamma is 0.0023, the theta is −0.22, the vega is 3.33, and rho is 2.44. Note that the formula in Table C.1 gives theta per year. The theta quoted here is per calendar day.

The calculations in this appendix can be done with the DerivaGem software on the author's website by selecting Analytic European for the Option Type. Option valuation is described more fully in Hull (2006).[1]

---

[1] See J. C. Hull, *Options, Futures, and Other Derivatives*, 6th edn., Prentice Hall, 2006.

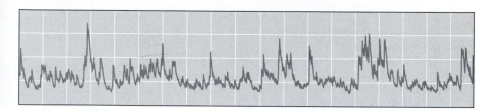

Valuing
American Options

To value American-style options, we divide the life of the option into n time steps of length Δt. Suppose that the asset price at the beginning of a step is S. At the end of the time step it moves up to Su with probability p and down to Sd with probability $1 - p$. For an investment asset that provides no income, the values of u, d and p are given by

$$u = e^{\sigma\sqrt{\Delta t}}, \qquad d = \frac{1}{u}$$

$$p = \frac{a - d}{u - d}, \qquad a = e^{r\Delta t}$$

Figure D.1 shows the tree constructed for valuing a five-month American put option on a non-dividend-paying stock where the initial stock price is 50, the strike price is 50, the risk-free rate is 10%, and the volatility is 40%. In this case, there are five steps, so that $\Delta t = 0.08333$, $u = 1.1224$, $d = 0.8909$, $a = 1.0084$, and $p = 0.5073$. The upper number at each node is the stock price and the lower number is the value of the option.

At the final nodes of the tree the option price is its intrinsic value. For example, at node G the option price is $50 - 35.36 = 14.64$. At earlier nodes we first calculate a value assuming that the option is held for a further time period of length Δt and then check to see whether early exercise is optimal. Consider first node E. If the option is held for a further time period it will be worth 0.00 if there is an up move (probability: p) and 5.45 if there is a

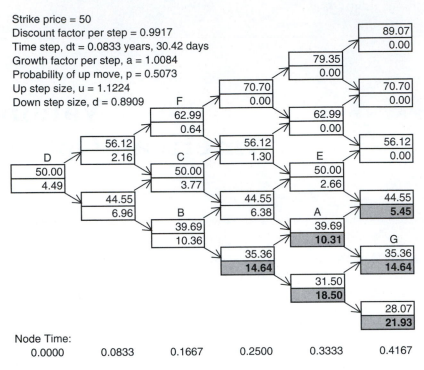

At each node:
Upper value = Underlying Asset Price
Lower value = Option Price
Shading indicates where option is exercised

Strike price = 50
Discount factor per step = 0.9917
Time step, dt = 0.0833 years, 30.42 days
Growth factor per step, a = 1.0084
Probability of up move, p = 0.5073
Up step size, u = 1.1224
Down step size, d = 0.8909

Node Time:
0.0000   0.0833   0.1667   0.2500   0.3333   0.4167

Figure D.1   Binomial tree from DerivaGem for an American put on a non-dividend-paying stock.

down move (probability: $1 - p$). The expected value in time Δt is therefore $0.5073 \times 0 + 0.4927 \times 5.45$, or 2.686, and the 2.66 value at node E is calculated by discounting this at the risk-free rate of 10% for one month. The option should not be exercised at node E as the payoff from early exercise would be zero. Consider next node A. A similar calculation to that just given shows that, assuming it is held for a further time period, the option's value at node A is 9.90. If exercised, its value is $50 - 39.69 = 10.31$. In this case, it should be exercised and the value of being at node A is 10.31.

Continuing to work back from the end of the tree to the beginning, the value of the option at the initial node D is found to be 4.49. As the number of steps on the tree is increased, the accuracy of the option price increases.

With 30, 50, and 100 time steps, we get values for the option of 4.263, 4.272, and 4.278.

To calculate delta, we consider the two nodes at time Δt. In our example, as we move from the lower node to the upper node the option price changes from 6.96 to 2.16 and the stock price changes from 44.55 to 56.12. The estimate of delta is the change in the option price divided by the change in the stock price:

$$\text{Delta} = \frac{2.16 - 6.96}{56.12 - 44.55} = -0.41$$

To calculate gamma, we consider the three nodes at time $2\Delta t$. The delta calculated from the upper two nodes (C and F) is -0.241. This can be regarded as the delta for a stock price of $(62.99 + 50)/2 = 56.49$. The delta calculated from the lower two nodes (B and C) is -0.639. This can be regarded as the delta for a stock price of $(50 + 39.69)/2 = 44.84$. The estimate of gamma is the change in delta divided by the change in the stock price:

$$\text{Gamma} = \frac{-0.241 - (-0.639)}{56.49 - 44.84} = 0.034$$

We estimate theta from nodes D and C as

$$\text{Theta} = \frac{3.77 - 4.49}{2 \times 0.08333}$$

or -4.30 per year. This is -0.0118 per calendar day. Vega is estimated by increasing the volatility, constructing a new tree, and observing the effect of the increased volatility on the option price. Rho is calculated similarly.

When the asset underlying the option provides a yield at rate q the procedure is exactly the same except that $a = e^{(r-q)\Delta t}$ instead of $e^{r\Delta t}$ in the equation for p. The calculations we have described can be done using the DerivaGem software by selecting Binomial American for the Option Type. Binomial trees and other numerical procedures are described more fully in Hull (2006).[1]

---

[1] See J. C. Hull, *Options, Futures, and Other Derivatives*, 6th edn., Prentice Hall, 2006.

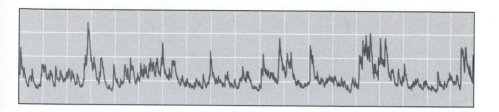

The Manipulation of Credit Transition Matrices

Suppose that A is an $N \times N$ matrix of credit rating changes in one year. This is a matrix such as the one shown in Table 12.1. The matrix of credit rating changes in m years is A^m. This can be readily calculated using the normal rules for matrix multiplication.

The matrix corresponding to a shorter period than one year, say six months or one month, is more difficult to compute. We first use standard routines to calculate eigenvectors $x_1, x_2, \ldots, x_N$ and the corresponding eigenvalues $\lambda_1, \lambda_2, \ldots, \lambda_N$. These have the property that

$$A x_i = \lambda x_i$$

Define X as a matrix whose ith row is x_i and Λ as a diagonal matrix where the ith diagonal element is λ_i. A standard result in matrix algebra shows that

$$A = X^{-1} \Lambda X$$

From this it is easy to see that the nth root of A is

$$X^{-1} \Lambda^* X$$

where Λ^* is a diagonal matrix where the ith diagonal element is $\lambda_i^{1/n}$.

Some authors, such as Jarrow, Lando, and Turnbull,[1] prefer to handle

---

[1] See R. A. Jarrow, D. Lando, and S. M. Turnbull, "A Markov Model for the Term Structure of Credit Spreads," *Review of Financial Studies*, 10 (1997), 481–523.

this problem in terms of what is termed a *generator matrix*. This is a matrix Γ such that the transition matrix for a short period of time Δt is $I + \Gamma \Delta t$, where I is the identity matrix, and the transition matrix for a longer period of time t is

$$\exp(t\Gamma) = \sum_{k=0}^{\infty} \frac{(t\Gamma)^k}{k!}$$

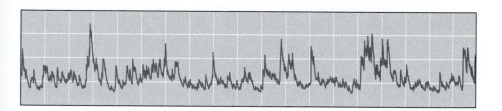

Answers to Questions and Problems

CHAPTER 1

1.1. Expected return is 12.5%. SD of return is 17.07%.

1.2. From equations (1.1) and 1.2), expected return is 12.5%. SD of return is

$$\sqrt{0.5^2 \times 0.1707^2 + 0.5^2 \times 0.1707^2 + 2 \times 0.15 \times 0.5^2 \times 0.1707} = 0.1294$$

or 12.94%.

1.3.

w_1	w_2	μ_P	σ_P ($\rho = 0.3$)	σ_P ($\rho = 1$)	σ_P ($\rho = -1$)
0.0	1.0	15%	24.00%	24.00%	24.00%
0.2	0.8	14%	20.39%	22.40%	16.00%
0.4	0.6	13%	17.42%	20.80%	8.00%
0.6	0.4	12%	15.48%	19.20%	0.00%
0.8	0.2	11%	14.96%	17.60%	8.00%
1.0	0.0	10%	16.00%	16.00%	16.00%

1.4. Nonsystematic risk can be diversified; systematic risk cannot. Systematic risk is most important to an equity investor. Either type of risk can lead to the bankruptcy of a corporation.

1.5. We assume that investors trade off mean return and standard deviation of return. For a given mean return, they want to minimize standard deviation of returns. All make the same estimates of means, standard deviations, and coefficients of correlation for returns on individual investments. Furthermore they can borrow or lend at the risk-free rate. The result is that they all want to be on the "new efficient frontier" in Figure 1.4. They choose the same portfolio of risky investments combined with borrowing or lending at the risk-free rate.

1.6. (a) 7.2%, (b) 9%, (c) 14.4%.

1.7. The capital asset pricing theory assumes that there is one factor driving returns. Arbitrage pricing theory assumes multiple factors.

1.8. In many jurisdictions, interest on debt is deductible to the corporation whereas dividends are not deductible. It can therefore be more tax efficient for a company to fund itself with debt. However, as debt increases, the probability of bankruptcy increases.

1.9. When potential losses are large, we cannot aggregate them and assume they will be diversified away. It is necessary to consider them one by one and handle them with insurance contracts, tighter internal controls, etc.

1.10. This is the probability that profit is no worse than −4% of assets. This profit level is $4.6/1.5 = 3.067$ standard deviations from the mean. The probability that the bank will have a positive equity is therefore $N(3.067)$, where N is the cumulative normal distribution function. This is 99.89%.

1.11. Banks have the privilege of being allowed to take money from depositors. Companies in retailing and manufacturing do not.

1.12. There was an interest rate mismatch at Continental Illinois. About $5.5 billion of loans with maturities more than a year were financed by deposits with maturities less than a year. If interest rates rose 1%, the deposits would be rolled over at higher rates while the loans would continue to earn the same rate. The cost to Continental Illinois would be $55 million.

1.13. S&Ls financed long-term fixed-rate mortgages with short-term deposits creating a serious interest rate mismatch. As a result, they lost money when interest rates rose.

1.14. In this case, the interest rate mismatch is $10 billion. The bank's net interest income declines $100 million each year for the next three years.

1.15. Professional fees ($5 million per month), lost sales (people are reluctant to do business with a company that is being reorganized), and key senior executives left (lack of continuity).

CHAPTER 2

2.1. When a trader enters into a long forward contract, she is agreeing to *buy* the underlying asset for a certain price at a certain time in the future. When a trader enters into a short forward contract, she is agreeing to *sell* the underlying asset for a certain price at a certain time in the future.

2.2. A trader is hedging when she has an exposure to the price of an asset and takes a position in a derivative to offset the exposure. In a *speculation* the trader has no exposure to offset. She is betting on the future movements in the price of the asset. *Arbitrage* involves taking a position in two or more different markets to lock in a profit.

2.3. In the first case, the trader is obligated to buy the asset for $50 (she does not have a choice). In the second case, the trader has an option to buy the asset for $50 (she does not have to exercise the option).

2.4. Selling a call option involves giving someone else the right to buy an asset from you for a certain price. Buying a put option gives you the right to sell the asset to someone else.

2.5. (a) The investor is obligated to sell pounds for 1.5000 when they are worth 1.4900. The gain is $(1.5000 - 1.4900) \times 100,000 = \$1,000$. (b) The investor is obligated to sell pounds for 1.5000 when they are worth 1.5200. The loss is $(1.5200 - 1.5000) \times 100,000 = \$2,000$.

2.6. (a) The trader sells for 50 cents per pound something that is worth 48.20 cents per pound. Gain $= (\$0.5000 - \$0.4820) \times 50,000 = \$900$. (b) The trader sells for 50 cents per pound something that is worth 51.30 cents per pound. Loss $= (\$0.5130 - \$0.5000) \times 50,000 = \$650$.

2.7. You have sold a put option. You have agreed to buy 100 shares for $40 per share if the party on the other side of the contract chooses to exercise the right to sell for this price. The option will be exercised only when the price of stock is below $40. Suppose, for example, that the option is exercised when the price is $30. You have to buy at $40 shares that are worth $30; you lose $10 per share, or $1,000 in total. If the option is exercised when the price is $20, you lose $20 per share, or $2,000 in total. The worst that can happen is that the price of the stock declines to almost zero during the three-month period. This highly unlikely event would cost you $4,000. In return for the possible future losses, you receive the price of the option from the purchaser.

2.8. The over-the-counter (OTC) market is a telephone- and computer-linked network of financial institutions, fund managers, and corporate treasurers where two participants can enter into any mutually acceptable contract. An exchange-traded market is a market organized by an exchange where traders either meet physically or communicate electronically and the contracts that can be traded have been defined by the exchange. (a) OTC, (b) exchange, (c) both, (d) OTC, (e) OTC.

2.9. One strategy would be to buy 200 shares. Another would be to buy 2,000 options. If the share price does well, the second strategy will give rise to greater gains. For example, if the share price goes up to $40, you gain $[2,000 \times (\$40 - \$30)] - \$5,800 = \$14,200$ from the second strategy and only $200 \times (\$40 - \$29) = \$2,200$ from the first. However, if the share price does badly, the second strategy gives greater losses. For example, if the share price goes down to $25, the first strategy leads to a loss of $200 \times (\$29 - \$25) = \$800$, whereas the second strategy leads to a loss of the whole $5,800 investment. This example shows that options contain built in leverage.

2.10. You could buy 5,000 put options (or 50 contracts) with a strike price of $25 and an expiration date in 4 months. This provides a type of insurance. If at the end of 4 months the stock price proves to be less than $25, you can exercise the options and sell the shares for $25 each. The cost of this strategy is the price you pay for the put options.

2.11. A stock option provides no funds for the company. It is a security sold by one trader to another. The company is not involved. By contrast, a stock when it is first issued is a claim sold by the company to investors and does provide funds for the company.

2.12. Ignoring the time value of money, the holder of the option will make a profit if the stock price in March is greater than $52.50. This is because the payoff to the holder of the option is, in these circumstances, greater than the $2.50 paid for the option. The option will be exercised if the stock price at maturity is greater than $50.00. Note that if the stock price is between $50.00 and $52.50 the option is exercised, but the holder of the option takes a loss overall.

2.13. Ignoring the time value of money, the seller of the option will make a profit if the stock price in June is greater than $56.00. This is because the cost to the seller of the option is in these circumstances less than the price received for the option. The option will be exercised if the stock price at maturity is less than $60.00. Note that if the stock price is between $56.00 and $60.00 then the seller of the option makes a profit even though the option is exercised.

2.14. A long position in a four-month put option can provide insurance against the exchange rate falling below the strike price. It ensures that the foreign currency can be sold for at least the strike price.

2.15. The company could enter into a long forward contract to buy 1 million Canadian dollars in six months. This would have the effect of locking in an exchange rate equal to the current forward exchange rate. Alternatively the company could buy a call option giving it the right (but not the obligation) to purchase 1 million Canadian dollars at a certain exchange rate in six months. This would provide insurance against a strong Canadian dollar in six months while still allowing the company to benefit from a weak Canadian dollar at that time.

2.16. The payoff from an ICON is the payoff from (a) a regular bond, (b) a short position in call options to buy 169,000 yen with an exercise price of $1/169$, (c) a long position in call options to buy 169,000 yen with an exercise price of $1/84.5$. This is demonstrated by the following table:

	Terminal value of regular bond	*Terminal value of short calls*	*Terminal value of long calls*	*Terminal value of whole position*
$S_T > 169$	1000	0	0	1000
$84.5 \leqslant S_T \leqslant 169$	1000	$-169{,}000 \times (1/S_T - 1/169)$	0	$2000 - 169{,}000/S_T$
$S_T < 84.5$	1000	$-169{,}000 \times (1/S_T - 1/169)$	$-169{,}000 \times (1/S_T - 1/84.5)$	0

2.17. (a) The trader buys a 180-day call option and takes a short position in a 180-day forward contract. (b) The trader buys 90-day put options and takes a long position in a 90-day forward contract.

2.18. It enters into a 5-year swap where it pays 6.51% and receives LIBOR. Its investment is then at LIBOR minus 1.51%.

2.19. It enters into a 5-year swap where it receives 6.47% and pays LIBOR. Its net cost of borrowing is LIBOR +0.53%.

2.20. It enters into a three-year swap where it receives LIBOR and pays 6.24%. Its net borrowing cost for the three years is then 7.24% per annum.

2.21. Suppose that the weather is bad and the farmer's production is lower than expected. Other farmers are likely to have been affected similarly. Corn production overall will be low and as a consequence the price of corn will be relatively high. The farmer is likely to be overhedged relative to actual production. The farmer's problems arising from the bad harvest will be made worse by losses on the short futures position. This problem emphasizes the importance of looking at the big picture when hedging. The farmer is correct to question whether hedging price risk while ignoring other risks is a good strategy.

2.22. It may well be true that there is just as much chance that the company will lose as that it will gain. This means that the use of a futures contract for speculation would be like betting on whether a coin comes up heads or tails. But it might make sense for the airline to use futures for hedging rather than speculation. The futures contract then has the effect of reducing risks. It can be argued that an airline should not expose its shareholders to risks associated with the future price of oil when there are contracts available to hedge the risks.

2.23. The optimal hedge ratio is

$$0.7 \times \frac{1.2}{1.4} = 0.6$$

The beef producer requires a long position in $200,000 \times 0.6 = 120,000$ lbs of cattle. The beef producer should therefore take a long position in three December contracts closing out the position on November 15.

2.24. Microsoft is choosing an option on a portfolio of assets instead of the corresponding portfolio of options. The former is always less expensive because there is the potential for an increase in the price of one asset to be netted off against a decrease in the price of another. Compare (a) an option with a strike price of $20 on a portfolio of two assets each worth $10 and (b) a portfolio of two options with a strike price of $10, one on each of assets. If both assets increase in price or both assets decrease in price, the payoffs are the same. But if one decreases and the other increases, the payoff from (a) is less than that from (b). Both the Asian feature and the basket feature in Microsoft's options help to reduce the cost of the options because of the possibility of gains and loss being netted.

CHAPTER 3

3.1. The value of the portfolio decreases by $10,500.

3.2. The value of the portfolio increases by $400.

3.3. In both cases it increases by $0.5 \times 30 \times 2^2$, or \$60.

3.4. A delta of 0.7 means that, when the price of the stock increases by a small amount, the price of the option increases by 70% of this amount. Similarly, when the price of the stock decreases by a small amount, the price of the option decreases by 70% of this amount. A short position in 1,000 options has a delta of -700 and can be made delta neutral with the purchase of 700 shares.

3.5. A theta of -100 per day means that if one day passes with no change in either the stock price or its volatility, the value of the option position declines by \$100. If a trader feels that neither the stock price nor its implied volatility will change, she should write an option with as high a theta as possible. Relatively short-life at-the-money options have the highest theta.

3.6. The gamma of an option position is the rate of change of the delta of the position with respect to the asset price. For example, a gamma of 0.1 would indicate that, when the asset price increases by a certain small amount, delta increases by 0.1 of this amount. When the gamma of an option-writer's position is large and negative and the delta is zero, the option writer will lose significant amounts of money if there is a large movement (either an increase or a decrease) in the asset price.

3.7. To hedge an option position, it is necessary to create the opposite option position synthetically. For example, to hedge a long position in a put, it is necessary to create a short position in a put synthetically. It follows that the procedure for creating an option position synthetically is the reverse of the procedure for hedging the option position.

3.8. A long position in either a put or a call option has a positive gamma. From Figure 15.8, when gamma is positive the hedger gains from a large change in the stock price and loses from a small change in the stock price. Hence the hedger will fare better in case (b). When the portfolio contains short option position, the hedger will similarly fare better in (a).

3.9. The delta indicates that, when the value of the euro exchange rate increases by \$0.01, the value of the bank's position increases by $0.01 \times 30,000 = \$300$. The gamma indicates that, when the euro exchange rate increases by \$0.01, the delta of the portfolio decreases by $0.01 \times 80,000 = 800$. For delta neutrality, 30,000 euros should be shorted. When the exchange rate moves up to 0.93, we expect the delta of the portfolio to decrease by $(0.93 - 0.90) \times 80,000 = 2,400$, so that it becomes 27,600. To maintain delta neutrality, it is therefore necessary for the bank to unwind its short position 2,400 euros so that a net 27,600 have been shorted. When a portfolio is delta neutral and has a negative gamma, a loss is experienced when there is a large movement in the underlying asset price. We can conclude that the bank is likely to have lost money.

3.10. When used in the way described in the text, it does assume volatility is constant. In theory, we could implement a static options replication scheme where there are three dimensions: time, the stock price, and volatility. Prices are then matched on a surface in the three-dimensional space.

3.11. Ten regular options are likely to be needed. This is because there are ten equations to be satisfied, one for each point on the boundary.

3.12. The payoff from an Asian option becomes more certain with the passage of time. As a result, the amount of uncertainty that needs to be hedged decreases with the passage of time.

3.13. Consider a portfolio of options dependent on a single market variable. A single trade is all that is necessary to make the position delta neutral, regardless of the size of the position.

3.14. The price, delta, gamma, vega, theta, and rho are 0.0217, −0.396, 5.415, 0.00203, −0.0000625, and −0.00119. Delta predicts that the option price should decrease by approximately 0.000396 when the exchange rate increases by 0.001. This is what we find. When the exchange rate is increased to 0.751, the option price decreases to 0.0213.

CHAPTER 4

4.1. (a) 13.76% per annum, (b) 14.75% per annum.

4.2. (a) 10% per annum, (b) 9.76% per annum, (c) 9.57% per annum, (d) 9.53% per annum.

4.3. The equivalent rate of interest with quarterly compounding is 12.18%. The amount of interest paid each quarter is therefore

$$10,000 \times \frac{0.1218}{4} = 304.55$$

or $304.55.

4.4. The rate of interest is 14.91% per annum.

4.5. The forward rates with continuous compounding for the 2nd, 3rd, 4th, and 5th years are 4.0%, 5.1%, 5.7%, and 5.7%, respectively.

4.6. The forward rates with continuous compounding for the 2nd, 3rd, 4th, 5th, and 6th quarters are 8.4%, 8.8%, 8.8%, 9.0%, and 9.2%, respectively.

4.7. When the term structure is upward sloping, $c > a > b$. When it is downward sloping, $b > a > c$.

4.8. Suppose the bond has a face value of $100. Its price is obtained by discounting the cash flows at 10.4%. The price is

$$\frac{4}{1.052} + \frac{4}{1.052^2} + \frac{104}{1.052^3} = 96.74$$

If the 18-month zero rate is R, we must have

$$\frac{4}{1.05} + \frac{4}{1.05^2} + \frac{104}{(1 + R/2)^3} = 96.74$$

which gives $R = 10.42\%$.

4.9. The bond pays $2 in 6, 12, 18, and 24 months, and $102 in 30 months. The cash price is

$$2e^{0.04 \times 0.5} + 2e^{0.042 \times 1.0} + 2e^{0.044 \times 1.5} + 2e^{0.046 \times 2} + 102e^{0.048 \times 2.5} = 98.04$$

4.10. The bond pays $4 in 6, 12, 18, 24, and 30 months, and $104 in 36 months. The bond yield is the value of y that solves

$$4e^{-0.5y} + 4e^{-1.0y} + 4e^{-1.5y} + 4e^{-2.0y} + 4e^{-2.5y} + 104e^{-3.0y} = 104$$

Using the *Goal Seek* tool in Excel, we get $y = 0.06407$, or 6.407%.

4.11. There are three reasons: (i) Treasury bills and Treasury bonds must be purchased by financial institutions to fulfill a variety of regulatory requirements. This increases demand for these Treasury instruments driving the price up and the yield down. (ii) The amount of capital a bank is required to hold to support an investment in Treasury bills and bonds is substantially smaller than the capital required to support a similar investment in other very-low-risk instruments. (iii) In the United States, Treasury instruments are given a favorable tax treatment compared with most other fixed-income investments because they are not taxed at the state level.

4.12. Duration provides information about the effect of a small parallel shift in the yield curve on the value of a bond portfolio. The percentage decrease in the value of the portfolio equals the duration of the portfolio multiplied by the amount by which interest rates are increased in the small parallel shift. Its limitation is that it applies only to parallel shifts in the yield curve that are small.

4.13. (a) The bond's price is 86.80, (b) the bond's duration is 4.256 years, (c) the duration formula shows that when the yield decreases by 0.2% the bond's price increases by 0.74, (d) recomputing the bond's price with a yield of 10.8% gives a price of 87.54, which is approximately consistent with (a) and (c).

4.14. (a) The bond's price is 88.91, (b) the bond's modified duration is 3.843 years, (c) the duration formula estimates that when the yield decreases by 0.2% the bond's price increases by 0.68, (d) recomputing the bond's price with a yield of 10.8% (annually compounded) gives a price of 89.60 which is approximately consistent with (a) and (c).

4.15. The bond price is 104.80. The duration of the bond is 5.35. The convexity is 30.60. The effect of a 1% increase in the yield is estimated by equation (4.14) as

$$104.80(-0.01 \times 5.35 + 0.5 \times 30.60 \times 0.0001) = -5.44$$

The bond price actually changes to 99.36, which is consistent with the estimate.

4.16. We can (a) perturb points on the yield curve (see Figure 4.4), (b) perturb sections of the yield curve (see Figure 4.6), and (c) perturb the market quotes used to create the yield curve.

4.17. The deltas are 10.7 and -190.1.

CHAPTER 5

5.1. 4.16%.

5.2. The standard deviation of the percentage price change in one day is 1.57%. The 95% confidence limits are from -3.09% to $+3.09\%$.

5.3. Volatility is much higher when markets are open than when they are closed. Traders therefore measure time in trading days rather than calendar days when applying volatility.

5.4. Implied volatility is the volatility that leads to the option price equaling the market price when Black–Scholes assumptions are used. It is found by "trial and error". Because different options have different implied volatilities, traders are not using the same assumptions as Black–Scholes. (See Chapter 15 for a further discussion of this.)

5.5. The approach in Section 5.3 gives 0.547% per day. The simplified approach in equation 5.4 gives 0.530% per day.

5.6. (a) 0.25%, (b) 0.0625%.

5.7. The variance rate estimated at the end of day n equals λ times the variance rate estimated at the end of day $n - 1$ plus $1 - \lambda$ times the squared return on day n.

5.8. GARCH(1, 1) adapts the EWMA model by giving some weight to a long-run average variance rate. Whereas the EWMA has no mean reversion, GARCH(1, 1) is consistent with a mean-reverting variance rate model.

5.9. In this case, $\sigma_{n-1} = 0.015$ and $u_n = 0.5/30 = 0.01667$, so that equation (19.7) gives

$$\sigma_n^2 = 0.94 \times 0.015^2 + 0.06 \times 0.01667^2 = 0.0002281$$

The volatility estimate on day n is therefore $\sqrt{0.0002281} = 0.015103$, or 1.5103%.

5.10. Reducing λ from 0.95 to 0.85 means that more weight is put on recent observations of u_i^2 and less weight is given to older observations. Volatilities calculated with $\lambda = 0.85$ will react more quickly to new information and will "bounce around" much more than volatilities calculated with $\lambda = 0.95$.

5.11. With the usual notation, $u_{n-1} = 20/1040 = 0.01923$, so that

$$\sigma_n^2 = 0.000002 + 0.06 \times 0.01923^2 + 0.92 \times 0.01^2 = 0.0001162$$

This gives $\sigma_n = 0.01078$. The new volatility estimate is therefore 1.078% per day.

5.12. The proportional daily change is $-0.005/1.5000 = -0.003333$. The current daily variance estimate is $0.006^2 = 0.000036$. The new daily variance estimate is

$$0.9 \times 0.000036 + 0.1 \times 0.003333^2 = 0.000033511$$

The new daily volatility is the square root of this. It is 0.00579, or 0.579%.

5.13. The weight given to the long-run average variance rate is $1 - \alpha - \beta$ and the long-run average variance rate is $\omega/(1 - \alpha - \beta)$. Increasing ω increases the long-run average variance rate; increasing α increases the weight given to the most recent data item, reduces the weight given to the long-run average variance rate, and increases the level of the long-run average variance rate. Increasing β increases the weight given to the previous variance estimate, reduces the weight given to the long-run average variance rate, and increases the level of the long-run average variance rate.

5.14. The long-run average variance rate is $\omega/(1 - \alpha - \beta)$, or $0.000004/0.03 = 0.0001333$. The long-run average volatility is $\sqrt{0.0001333}$, or 1.155%. The equation describing the way the variance rate reverts to its long-run average is

$$E[\sigma_{n+k}^2] = V_L + (\alpha + \beta)^k(\sigma_n^2 - V_L)$$

In this case,

$$E[\sigma_{n+k}^2] = 0.0001333 + 0.97^k(\sigma_n^2 - 0.0001333)$$

If the current volatility is 20% per year, $\sigma_n = 0.2/\sqrt{252} = 0.0126$. The expected variance rate in 20 days is

$$0.0001333 + 0.97^{20}(0.0126^2 - 0.0001333) = 0.0001471$$

The expected volatility in 20 days is therefore $\sqrt{0.0001471} = 0.0121$, or 1.21% per day.

5.15. The FTSE expressed in dollars is XY where X is the FTSE expressed in sterling and Y is the exchange rate (value of one pound in dollars). Define x_i as the proportional change in X on day i and y_i as the proportional change in Y on day i. The proportional change in XY is approximately $x_i + y_i$. The standard deviation of x_i is 0.018 and the standard deviation of y_i is 0.009. The correlation between the two is 0.4. The variance of $x_i + y_i$ is therefore

$$0.018^2 + 0.009^2 + 2 \times 0.018 \times 0.009 \times 0.4 = 0.0005346$$

so that the volatility of $x_i + y_i$ is 0.0231, or 2.31%. This is the volatility of the FTSE expressed in dollars. Note that it is greater than the volatility of the FTSE expressed in sterling. This is the impact of the positive correlation. When the FTSE increases, the value of sterling measured in dollars also tends to increase. This creates an even bigger increase in the value of FTSE measured in dollars. Similarly for a decrease in the FTSE.

5.16. In this case, $V_L = 0.00015$ and the expected variance rate in 30 days is 0.000123. The volatility is 1.11% per day.

5.17. In equation (5.15), $V_L = 0.0001$, $a = 0.0202$, $T = 20$, and $V(0) = 0.000169$, so that the volatility is 19.88%.

CHAPTER 6

6.1. You need the standard deviations of the two variables.

6.2. Loosely speaking correlation measures the extent of linear dependence. It does not measure other types of dependence. When $y = x^2$ there is perfect dependence between x and y. However $E(xy) = E(x^3)$. This is zero for a symmetrical distribution such as the normal showing that the coefficient of correlation between x and y is zero.

6.3. In a factor model the correlation between two variables arises entirely because of their correlation with one or more other variables. The latter are known as factors. A factor model reduces the number of estimates that have to be made when correlations between large numbers of variables are being produced.

6.4. A positive-semidefinite matrix is a matrix that satisfies equation (6.4) for all vectors w. If a correlation matrix is not positive semidefinite, the correlations are internally inconsistent.

6.5. (a) The volatilities and correlation imply that the current estimate of the covariance is $0.25 \times 0.016 \times 0.025 = 0.0001$. (b) If the prices of the assets at close of trading are \$20.5 and \$40.5, the proportional changes are $0.5/20 = 0.025$ and $0.5/40 = 0.0125$. The new covariance estimate is

$$0.95 \times 0.0001 + 0.05 \times 0.025 \times 0.0125 = 0.0001106$$

The new variance estimate for asset A is

$$0.95 \times 0.016^2 + 0.05 \times 0.025^2 = 0.00027445$$

so that the new volatility is 0.0166. The new variance estimate for asset B is

$$0.95 \times 0.025^2 + 0.05 \times 0.0125^2 = 0.000601562$$

so that the new volatility is 0.0245. The new correlation estimate is

$$\frac{0.0001106}{0.0166 \times 0.0245} = 0.272$$

6.6. Using the notation in the text, $\sigma_{u,n-1} = 0.01$ and $\sigma_{v,n-1} = 0.012$ and the most recent estimate of the covariance between the asset returns is

$$\text{cov}_{n-1} = 0.01 \times 0.012 \times 0.50 = 0.00006$$

The variable $u_{n-1} = 1/30 = 0.03333$ and the variable $v_{n-1} = 1/50 = 0.02$. The new estimate of the covariance, cov_n, is

$$0.000001 + 0.04 \times 0.03333 \times 0.02 + 0.94 \times 0.00006 = 0.0000841$$

The new estimate of the variance of the first asset, $\sigma_{u,n}^2$, is

$$0.000003 + 0.04 \times 0.03333^2 + 0.94 \times 0.01^2 = 0.0001414$$

so that $\sigma_{u,n} = \sqrt{0.0001414} = 0.01189$, or 1.189%. The new estimate of the variance of the second asset, $\sigma_{v,n}^2$ is

$$0.000003 + 0.04 \times 0.02^2 + 0.94 \times 0.012^2 = 0.0001544$$

so that $\sigma_{v,n} = \sqrt{0.0001544} = 0.01242$, or 1.242%. The new estimate of the correlation between the assets is therefore

$$0.0000841/(0.01189 \times 0.01242) = 0.569$$

6.7. Continuing with the notation in Problem 5.15, define z_i as the proportional change in the value of the S&P 500 on day i. The covariance between x_i and z_i is $0.7 \times 0.018 \times 0.016 = 0.0002016$. The covariance between y_i and z_i is $0.3 \times 0.009 \times 0.016 = 0.0000432$. The covariance between $x_i + y_i$ and z_i equals the covariance between x_i and z_i plus the covariance between y_i and z_i. It is

$$0.0002016 + 0.0000432 = 0.0002448$$

The correlation between $x_i + y_i$ and z_i is

$$\frac{0.0002448}{0.016 \times 0.0231} = 0.662$$

Note that the volatility of the S&P 500 drops out in this calculation.

6.8.

V_1	V_2		
	0.25	0.5	0.75
0.25	0.095	0.163	0.216
0.5	0.163	0.298	0.413
0.75	0.216	0.413	0.595

6.9. Suppose x_1, x_2, and x_3 are random samples from three independent normal distributions. Random samples with the required correlation structure are ϵ_1, ϵ_2, ϵ_3, where

$$\epsilon_1 = z_1, \qquad \epsilon_2 = \rho_{12}z_1 + z_2\sqrt{1 - \rho_{12}^2}, \qquad \epsilon_3 = \alpha_1 z_1 + \alpha_2 z_2 + \alpha_3 z_3$$

where

$$\alpha_1 = \rho_{13}, \qquad \alpha_1\rho_{12} + \alpha_2\sqrt{1 - \rho_{12}^2} = \rho_{23}, \qquad \alpha_1^2 + \alpha_2^2 + \alpha_3^2 = 1$$

This means that

$$\alpha_1 = \rho_{13}, \qquad \alpha_2 = \frac{\rho_{23} - \rho_{13}\rho_{12}}{\sqrt{1 - \rho_{12}^2}}, \qquad \alpha_3 = \sqrt{1 - \alpha_1^2 - \alpha_2^2}$$

6.10. Tail dependence is the tendency for extreme values for two or more variables to occur together. The choice of copula affects tail dependence.

For example, the Student *t*-copula gives more tail dependence than the Gaussian copula.

6.11. Sample from a bivariate Student *t*-distribution as in Figure 6.5. Convert each sample to a normal distribution on a "percentile-to-percentile" basis.

6.12. The probability that $V_1 < 0.1$ is 0.05. The conditional probability that $V_2 < 0.1$ is $0.006/0.05 = 0.12$. The conditional probability that $V_2 < 0.2$ is $0.017/0.05 = 0.34$, etc.

6.13. When $V_1 = 0.2$, we have $U_1 = -0.84$. From the properties of the bivariate normal distribution, the median of U_2 is $-0.5 \times 0.84 = -0.42$. This translates into a median value for V_2 of 0.458.

6.14. In this case,

$$V(T, X) = N\left(\frac{N^{-1}(0.015) + \sqrt{0.2}\,N^{-1}(0.995)}{\sqrt{1 - 0.2}}\right) = 0.127$$

The "99.5% worst case" is that there is a loss of $500 \times 0.7 \times 0.127 = 44.62$, or \$44.62 million.

CHAPTER 7

7.1. The removal of a competitor may be beneficial. However, banks enter into many contracts with each other. When one bank goes bankrupt, other banks are liable to lose money on the contracts they have with the bank. Also, other banks will be adversely affected if the bankruptcy reduces the public's overall level of confidence in the banking system.

7.2. Deposit insurance means that depositors are safe regardless of the risks taken by their financial institution. It is liable to lead to financial institutions taking more risks than they otherwise would because they can do so without the risk of losing deposits. This in turn leads to more bank failures and more claims under the deposit insurance system. Regulation requiring the capital held by a bank to be related to the risks taken is necessary to avoid this happening.

7.3. The credit risk on the swap is the risk that the counterparty defaults at some future time when the swap has a positive value to the bank.

7.4. The value of a currency swap is liable to deviate further from zero than the value of an interest rate swap because of the final exchange of principal. As a result the potential loss from a counterparty default is higher.

7.5. There is some exposure. If the counterparty defaulted now there would be no loss. However, interest rates could change so that at a future time the swap has a positive value to the financial institution. If the counterparty defaulted at that time there would be a loss to the financial institution.

7.6. The risk-weighted assets for the three transactions are (a) $1.875 million, (b) $2 million, and (c) $3 million, for a total of $6.875 million. Capital is 0.08×6.875, or $0.55 million.

7.7. The NRR is $2.5/4.5 = 0.556$. The credit equivalent amount is $2.5 + (0.4 + 0.6 \times 0.556) \times 9.25$, or $9.28 million. The risk-weighted assets is $4.64 million and the capital required is $0.371 million.

7.8. In this case there is no value to the netting provisions.

7.9. This converts the estimated capital requirement to an estimated risk-weighted assets. Capital required equals 8% of risk-weighted assets.

7.10. The trading book consists of instruments that are actively traded and marked to market daily. The banking book consists primarily of loans and is not market to market daily. Prior to the change the bank keeps credit risk capital calculated according to Basel I or Basel II. The effect of the change is to move the clients borrowings from the banking book to the trading book. The bank will be required to hold specific risk capital for the securities reflecting the credit exposure, as well as market risk capital reflecting the market risk exposure. The previous credit risk capital is no longer required.

7.11. Under Basel I the capital charged for lending to a corporation is the same regardless of the credit rating of the corporation. This leads to a bank's return on capital being relatively low for lending to highly credit-worthy corporations. Under Basel II the capital requirements of a loan are tied much more carefully to the creditworthiness of the borrower. As a result lending to highly creditworthy companies may become attractive again.

7.12. Regulatory arbitrage involves entering into a transaction or series of transactions solely to reduce regulatory capital requirements.

7.13. EAD is the estimated exposure at default. LGD is the loss given default, that is, the proportion of the exposure that will be lost if a default occurs. WCDR is the one-year probability of default in a bad year that occurs only one time in 1,000. PD is the probability of default in an average year. MA is the maturity adjustment. The latter allows for the fact that in the case of instruments lasting longer than a year there may be losses arising from a decline in the creditworthiness of the counterparty during the year as well as from a default during the year.

7.14. Under the simple approach, the risk weight of the counterparty is replaced by the risk weight of the collateral for the part of the exposure covered by the collateral. Under the comprehensive approach, the exposure is adjusted for possible increases and the collateral is adjusted for possible decreases in value. The counterparty's risk weight is applied to the excess of the adjusted exposure over the adjusted collateral.

7.15. The standardized approach uses external ratings to determine capital requirements (but in a more sophisticated way than in Basel I). In the IRB approach the Basel II correlation model is used with PD being determined by the bank. In the advanced IRB approach, the Basel II correlation model is used with PD, LGD, EAD, and MA being determined by the bank.

7.16. In the basic indicator approach total capital is 15% of the average total annual gross income. In the standardized approach, gross income is calculated for different business lines and capital as a percentage of gross income is different for different business lines. In the advanced measurement approach, the bank uses internal models to determine the 1-year 99.9% VaR.

7.17. $\rho = 0.1216$, WCDR $= 0.0914$, and the capital requirement is $200 \times 0.7 \times 0.0814$, or \$11.39 million. At least half of this must be Tier I.

CHAPTER 8

8.1. VaR is the loss that is not expected to be exceeded with a certain confidence level. Expected shortfall is the expected loss conditional that the loss is worse than the VaR level. Expected shortfall has the advantage that it always satisfies the subadditivity (diversification is good) condition.

8.2. A spectral risk measure is a risk measure that assigns weights to the quantiles of the loss distribution. For the subadditivity condition to be satisfied the weight assigned to the qth quantile must be a nondecreasing function of q.

8.3. There is a 5% chance that you will lose \$6,000 or more during a one-month period.

8.4. Your expected loss during a "bad month" is \$6,000. Bad months are defined as the worst 5% of months.

8.5. (a) \$1 million, (b) \$9.1 million, (c) \$11 million, (d) \$11.07 million, (e) $1 + 1 < 11$ but $9.2 + 9.2 > 11.07$.

8.6. (a) \$3.92 million, (b) \$8.77 million, (c) \$10.40 million.

8.7. (b) becomes \$9.96 million and (c) becomes \$11.82 million.

8.8. Marginal VaR is the rate of change of VaR with the amount invested in the ith asset. Incremental VaR is the incremental effect of the ith asset on VaR (i.e., the difference between VaR with and without the asset). Component VaR is the part of VaR that can be attributed the ith asset (the sum of component VaRs equals the total VaR).

8.9. The probability of 17 or more exceptions is

$$1 - \text{BINOMDIST}(16,1000,0.01,\text{TRUE})$$

or 2.64%. The model should be rejected at the 5% confidence level.

8.10. Bunching is the tendency for exceptions to be bunched rather than occurring randomly throughout the time period considered.

8.11. Either historical data or brainstorming by senior management can be used to develop extreme scenarios.

8.12. We are interested in the standard deviation of $R_1 + R_2 + \cdots + R_n$, where R_i is the return on day i. This is $\sum_{i=1}^{n} \sigma_i^2 + 2\sum_{i>j} \rho_{ij}\sigma_i\sigma_j$, where σ_i is the standard deviation of R_i and ρ_{ij} is the correlation between R_i and R_j. In this case, $\sigma_i = \sigma$ for all i, and $\rho_{ij} = \rho^{i-j}$ when $i > j$. After further algebraic manipulations this leads directly to equation (8.3).

8.13. The probability of 5 or more exceptions is

$$1 - \text{BINOMDIST}(4,250,0.01,\text{TRUE})$$

or 10.8%.

CHAPTER 9

9.1. The assumption is that the statistical process driving changes in market variables over the next day is the same as that over the last 500 days.

9.2.

$$\frac{\lambda^{i-1}(1-\lambda)}{(1-\lambda^n)} = \frac{\lambda^{i-1}}{1 + \lambda + \lambda^2 + \cdots + \lambda^{n-1}}$$

This shows that, as λ approaches 1, the weights approach $1/n$.

9.3. The tenth-worst outcome is a return of -3.78%. The estimate of the 1-day 99% VaR is therefore \$3.78 million.

9.4. The 1-day 99% VaR is estimated as $1.36 million. This is much less than that given in Problem 9.3 because most of the really bad returns were more than 500 days ago and carry relatively little weight.

9.5. The volatility is initially 1.14% per day. It varies from 0.428% per day to 2.97% per day. After adjustment, the tenth-worst outcome is 1.77%. The VaR estimate is therefore $1.77 million.

9.6. The VaR estimates given by u equal to 0.005, 0.01, and 0.015 are 3.34, 3.34, and 3.30, respectively.

9.7. The standard error of the VaR estimate is

$$\frac{1}{0.01}\sqrt{\frac{0.05 \times 0.95}{1,000}} = 0.69$$

or $0.69 million.

CHAPTER 10

10.1. The standard deviation of the daily change in the investment in each asset is $1,000. The variance of the portfolio's daily change is

$$1,000^2 + 1,000^2 + 2 \times 0.3 \times 1,000 \times 1,000 = 2,600,000$$

The standard deviation of the portfolio's daily change is the square root of this, or $1,612.45. The 5-day 99% VaR is therefore

$$2.33 \times \sqrt{5} \times 1,612.45 = \$8,401$$

10.2. The three alternative procedures mentioned in the chapter for handling interest rates when the model-building approach is used to calculate VaR involve (a) the use of the duration model, (b) the use of cash-flow mapping, and (c) the use of principal components analysis.

10.3. When a final exchange of principal is added in, the floating side is equivalent to a zero-coupon bond with a maturity date equal to the date of the next payment. The fixed side is a coupon-bearing bond, which is equivalent to a portfolio of zero-coupon bonds. The swap can therefore be mapped into a portfolio of zero-coupon bonds with maturity dates corresponding to the payment dates. Each of the zero-coupon bonds can then be mapped into positions in the adjacent standard-maturity zero-coupon bonds.

10.4. $\Delta P = 56 \times 1.5\Delta x$. The standard deviation of ΔP is $56 \times 1.5 \times 0.007 = 0.588$. It follows that the 10-day 99% VaR for the portfolio is

$$0.588 \times 2.33 \times \sqrt{10} = 4.33$$

10.5. The relationship is $\Delta P = 56 \times 1.5\Delta x + 0.5 \times 1.5^2 \times 16.2 \times \Delta x^2$, or $\Delta P = 84\Delta x + 18.225\Delta x^2$.

10.6. The 6.5-year cash flow is equivalent to a position of $48.56 in a 5-year zero-coupon bond and a position of $605.49 in a 7-year zero-coupon bond. The equivalent 5-year and 7-year cash flows are $48.56 \times 1.06^5 = 64.98$ and $605.49 \times 1.07^7 = 972.28$.

10.7. A similar calculation to that in the text shows that $37,397 of the value is allocated to the 3-month bond worth and $11,793 of the value is allocated to the 6-month bond.

10.8. The daily variance of the portfolio is

$$6^2 \times 20^2 + 4^2 \times 8^2 = 15,424$$

and the daily standard deviation is $\sqrt{15,424} = \$124.19$. Since $N(-1.282) = 0.9$, the 5-day 90% VaR is

$$124.19 \times \sqrt{5} \times 1.282 = \$356.01$$

10.9. (a) 3.26, (b) 63.87.

10.10. The delta of the options is the rate of change of the value of the options with respect to the price of the asset. When the asset price increases by a small amount, the value of the options decreases by 30 times this amount. The gamma of the options is the rate of change of their delta with respect to the price of the asset. When the asset price increases by a small amount, the delta of the portfolio decreases by five times this amount.

In this case, $E(\Delta P) = -0.10$, $E(\Delta P^2) = 36.03$, and $E(\Delta P^3) = -32.415$. The mean change in the portfolio value in 1 day is -0.1 and the standard deviation of the change in 1 day is $\sqrt{36.03 - 0.1^2} = 6.002$. The skewness is

$$\frac{-32.415 - 3 \times 36.03 \times (-0.1) + 2 \times (-0.1)^3}{6.002^3} = -21.608 = -0.10$$

Using only the first two moments, we find that the 1-day 99% VaR is $14.08. When three moments are considered in conjunction with a Cornish–Fisher expansion, it is $14.53.

10.11. Define σ as the volatility per year, $\Delta\sigma$ as the change in σ in 1 day, and Δw as the proportional change in σ in 1 day. We measure in σ as a multiple of 1% so that the current value of σ is $1 \times \sqrt{252} = 15.87$. The delta–gamma–vega model is

$$\Delta P = -30\Delta S - 0.5 \times 5 \times (\Delta S)^2 - 2\Delta\sigma$$

or

$$\Delta P = -30 \times 20\Delta x - 0.5 \times 5 \times 20^2(\Delta x)^2 - 2 \times 15.87\Delta w$$

where $\Delta x = \Delta S/S$, which simplifies to

$$\Delta P = -600\Delta x - 1,000(\Delta x)^2 - 31.74\Delta w$$

The change in the portfolio value now depends on two market variables. Once the daily volatility of σ and the correlation between σ and S have been estimated, we can estimate moments of ΔP and use a Cornish–Fisher expansion.

10.12. The change in the value of an option is not linearly related to the change in the value of the underlying variables. When the change in the values of underlying variables is normal, the change in the value of the option is not normal. The linear model assumes that it is normal and is, therefore, only an approximation.

10.13. The contract is a long position in a sterling bond combined with a short position in a dollar bond. The value of the sterling bond is $1.53e^{-0.05\times0.5}$, or \$1.492 million. The value of the dollar bond is $1.5e^{-0.05\times0.5}$, or \$1.463 million. The variance of the change in the value of the contract in 1 day is

$$1.492^2 \times 0.0006^2 + 1.463^2 \times 0.0005^2$$
$$-2 \times 0.8 \times 1.492 \times 0.0006 \times 1.463 \times 0.0005 = 0.000000288$$

The standard deviation is therefore \$0.000537 million. The 10-day 99% VaR is $0.000537 \times \sqrt{10} \times 2.33 = \$0.00396$ million.

CHAPTER 11

11.1 Moody's has 19 ratings (excluding the "in default" rating): Aaa, Aa1, Aa2, Aa3, A1, A2, A3, Baa1, Baa2, Baa3, Ba1, Ba2, Ba3, B1, B2, B3, Caa1, Caa2, Caa3.

11.2. S&P has 19 ratings (excluding the "in default" rating): AAA, AA+, AA, AA−, A+, A, A−, BBB+, BBB, BBB−, BB+, BB, B−, B+, B, B−, CCC+, CCC, CCC−.

11.3. Average default intensity is λ where $e^{-\lambda \times 1} = 0.9379$. It is 6.41% per year.

11.4. Conditional on no default by year 2, the probability of no default by year 3 is $0.8926/0.9526 = 0.9370$. Average default intensity for the third year is $\bar{\lambda}$, where $e^{-\bar{\lambda} \times 1} = 0.9370$. It is 6.51% per year.

11.5. From equation (11.3) the average default intensity over the 3 years is $0.0050/(1 - 0.3) = 0.0071$, or 0.71% per year.

11.6. From equation (11.3) the average default intensity over 5 years is $0.0080/(1 - 0.4)$, or 1.333% per year. Similarly the average default intensity over 3 years is 1.1667% per year. This means that the average default intensity for years 4 and 5 is 1.58%.

11.7. Real-world probabilities of default should be used for calculating credit value at risk. Risk-neutral probabilities of default should be used for adjusting the price of a derivative for default.

11.8. The recovery rate for a bond is the value of the bond immediately after the issuer defaults as a percentage of its face value.

11.9. The first number in the second column of Table 11.4 is calculated as

$$-\tfrac{1}{7}\ln(1 - 0.0029) = 0.0004$$

or 0.04% per year. Other numbers in the column are calculated similarly. The numbers in the fourth column of Table 11.5 are the numbers in the second column of Table 11.4 multiplied by one minus the expected recovery rate. In this case, the expected recovery rate is 0.4.

11.10. The bond's market value is 96.19. Its risk-free value is 103.66. If Q is the default probability per year, the loss from defaults is $272.69Q$. The implied probability of default is therefore 2.74% per year.

11.11. The market price of the first bond is 98.35 and its risk-free value is 101.23. If Q_1 is the default probability at times 0.5, 1.5, and 2.5 years the loss from defaults for the first bond is $178.31Q_1$. It follows that $Q_1 = 0.0161$. If Q_2 is the probability of default at times 3.5 and 4.5, the loss from default from the second bond is $180.56Q_1 + 108.53Q_2$. The market price for the second bond is 96.24 and its risk-free value is 101.97. It follows that $180.56Q_1 + 108.53Q_2 = 5.73$ and $Q_2 = 0.0260$.

11.12. We can assume that the principal is paid and received at the end of the life of the swap without changing the swap's value. If the spread were zero, then the present value of the floating payments per dollar of principal would be 1. The payment of LIBOR plus the spread therefore has a present value of $1 + V$. The payment of the bond cash flows has a present value per dollar of principal of B^*. The initial payment required from the payer of the bond cash flows per dollar of principal is $1 - B$. (This may be negative; an initial amount of $B - 1$ is then paid by the payer of the floating rate.) Because the asset swap is initially worth zero, we have

$$1 + V = B^* + 1 - B$$

so that

$$V = B^* - B$$

11.13. The value of the debt in Merton's model is $V_0 - E_0$, or

$$V_0 - V_0 N(d_1) + De^{-rT} N(d_2) = De^{-rT} N(d_2) + V_0 N(-d_1)$$

If the credit spread is s, this should equal $De^{-(r+s)T}$, so that

$$De^{-(r+s)T} = De^{-rT} N(d_2) + V_0 N(-d_1)$$

Substituting $De^{-rT} = LV_0$, we get

$$Le^{-sT} = LN(d_2) + N(-d_1)$$

so that

$$s = -\ln[N(d_2) + N(-d_1)/L]/T$$

11.14. In this case, $E_0 = 2$, $\sigma_E = 0.50$, $D = 5$, $r = 0.04$, and $T = 1$. Solving the simultaneous equations gives $V_0 = 6.80$ and $\sigma_V = 14.82$. The probability of default is $N(-d_2)$, or 1.15%.

11.15. Suppose that the principal is $100. The asset swap is structured so that the $10 is paid initially. After that, $2.50 is paid every 6 months. In return, LIBOR plus a spread is received on the principal of $100. The present value of the fixed payments is

$$10 + 2.5e^{-0.06 \times 0.5} + 2.5e^{-0.06 \times 1} + \cdots$$

$$\cdots + 2.5e^{-0.06 \times 5} + 100e^{-0.06 \times 5} = 105.3579$$

The spread over LIBOR must therefore have a present value of 5.3579. The present value of $1 received every 6 months for 5 years is 8.5105. The spread received every 6 months must therefore be

$$5.3579/8.5105 = \$0.6296$$

The asset swap spread is therefore $2 \times 0.6296 = 1.2592\%$ per annum.

CHAPTER 12

12.1. The new transaction will increase the bank's exposure to the counterparty if it tends to have a positive value whenever the existing contract has a positive value and a negative value whenever the existing contract has a negative value. However, if the new transaction tends to offset the existing transaction, it is likely to have the incremental effect of reducing credit risk.

12.2. Equation (12.3) gives the relationship between $\beta_{AB}(T)$ and ρ_{AB}. This involves $Q_A(T)$ and $Q_B(T)$. These change as we move from the real world to the risk-neutral world. It follows that the relationship between $\beta_{AB}(T)$ and ρ_{AB} in the real world is not the same as in the risk-neutral world. If $\beta_{AB}(T)$ is the same in the two worlds, then ρ_{AB} is not, and vice versa.

12.3. When securities are pledged as collateral, the haircut is the discount applied to their market value for margin calculations. A company's own equity would not be good collateral. When the company defaults on its contracts, its equity is likely to be worth very little.

12.4. In Vasicek's model and Credit Risk Plus, a credit loss recognized when a default occurs. In CreditMetrics, both downgrades and defaults lead to credit losses. In Vasicek's model, a Gaussian copula model of time to default is used. In Credit Risk Plus, a probability distribution is assumed for the default rate per year. In CreditMetrics, a Gaussian copula model is used to define rating transitions.

12.5. The binomial correlation measure is 0.156.

12.6. The statements in (a) and (b) are true. The statement in (c) is not. Suppose that v_X and v_Y are the exposures to X and Y. The expected value of $v_X + v_Y$ is the expected value of v_X plus the expected value of v_Y. The same is not true of 95% confidence limits.

12.7. The cost of defaults is uv, where u is percentage loss from defaults during the life of the contract and v is the value of an option that pays off $\max(150S_T - 100, 0)$, where S_T is the AUD/USD exchange rate in 1 year (USD per AUD). The value of u is

$$u = 1 - e^{-(0.06-0.05)\times1} = 0.009950$$

The variable v is 150 times the value of a call option to buy 1 AUD for 0.6667. This is 4.545. It follows that the cost of defaults is 4.545×0.009950, or 0.04522.

12.8. In this case, the cost of defaults is $u_1v_1 + u_2v_2$, where

$$u_1 = 1 - e^{-(0.055-0.05)\times0.5} = 0.002497$$
$$u_2 = e^{-(0.055-0.05)\times0.5} - e^{-(0.06-0.05)\times1} = 0.007453$$

v_1 is the value of a 6-month call option on 150 AUD with a strike price of $100, and v_2 is the value of a similar 1-year option. $v_1 = 3.300$ and $v_2 = 4.545$. The cost of defaults is 0.04211.

12.9. Assume that defaults happen only at the end of the life of the forward contract. In a default-free world, the forward contract is the combination of a long European call and a short European put where the strike price of the options equals the delivery price and the maturity of the options equals the maturity of the forward contract. If the no-default value of the contract is positive at maturity, the call has a positive value and the put is worth zero. The impact of defaults on the forward contract is the same as that on the call. If the no-default value of the contract is negative at maturity, the call has a zero value and the put has a positive value. In this case, defaults have no effect. Again the impact of defaults on the forward contract is the same as that on the call. It follows that the contract has a value equal to a long position in a call that is subject to default risk and short position in a default-free put.

12.10. Suppose that the forward contract provides a payoff at time T. With our usual notation, the value of a long forward contract is $S_T - Ke^{-rT}$ (see Appendix A). The credit exposure on a long forward contract is therefore $\max(S_T - Ke^{-rT}, 0)$; that is, it is a call on the asset price with strike price Ke^{-rT}. Similarly, the credit exposure on a short forward contract is $\max(Ke^{-rT} - S_T, 0)$; that is, it is a put on the asset price with strike price Ke^{-rT}. The total credit exposure is therefore a straddle with strike price Ke^{-rT}.

12.11. As time passes, there is a tendency for the currency which has the lower interest rate to strengthen. This means that a swap where we are receiving this currency will tend to move in the money (i.e., have a positive value). Similarly, a swap where we are paying the currency will tend to move out of the money (i.e., have a negative value). From this it follows that our expected exposure on the swap where we are receiving the low-interest currency is much greater than our expected exposure on the swap where we are receiving the high-interest currency. We should therefore look for counterparties with a low credit risk on the side of the swap where we are receiving the low-interest currency. On the other side of the swap, we are far less concerned about the creditworthiness of the counterparty.

CHAPTER 13

13.1. Both provide insurance against a particular company defaulting during a period of time. In a credit default swap, the payoff is the notional principal amount multiplied by one minus the recovery rate. In a binary swap the payoff is the notional principal.

13.2. The seller receives $300,000,000 \times 0.0060 \times 0.5 = \$900,000$ at times 0.5, 1.0, 1.5, 2.0, 2.5, 3.0, 3.5, 4.0 years. The seller also receives a final accrual payment of about \$300,000 ($= \$300,000,000 \times 0.060 \times 2/12$) at the time of the default (4 years and 2 months). The seller pays $300,000,000 \times 0.6 = \$180,000,000$ at the time of the default.

13.3. Sometimes there is physical settlement and sometimes there is cash settlement. In the event of a default when there is physical settlement, the buyer of protection sells bonds issued by the reference entity for their face value. Bonds with a total face value equal to the notional principal can be sold. In the event of a default when there is cash settlement, a calculation agent estimates the value of the cheapest-to-deliver bond issued by the reference entity a specified number of days after the default event. The cash payoff is then based on the excess of the face value of these bonds over the estimated value.

13.4. A cash CDO is created from a bond portfolio. The returns from the bond portfolio flow to a number of tranches (i.e., different categories of investors). The tranches differ as far as the credit risk they assume. The first tranche might have an investment in 5% of the bond portfolio and be responsible for the first 5% of losses. The next tranche might have an investment in 10% of the portfolio and be responsible for the next 10% of the losses, and so on. In a synthetic CDO there is no bond portfolio. Instead, a portfolio of credit default swaps is sold and the resulting credit risks are allocated to tranches in a similar way to that just described.

13.5. In a first-to-default basket CDS, there are a number of reference entities. When the first one defaults, there is a payoff (calculated in the usual way for a CDS) and the basket CDS terminates. The value of the protection given by the first-to-default basket CDS decreases as the correlation between the reference entities in the basket increases. This is because the probability of a default decreases as the correlation increases. In the limit when the correlation is 1, there is in effect only one company and the probability of a default is quite low.

13.6. Risk-neutral default probabilities are backed out from credit default swaps or bond prices. Real-world default probabilities are calculated from historical data.

13.7. Suppose a company wants to buy some assets. If a total return swap is used, a financial institution buys the assets and enters into a swap with the company where it pays the company the return on the assets and receives from the company LIBOR plus a spread. The financial institution has less risk than it would have if it lent the company money and used the assets as collateral. This is because, in the event of a default by the company, it owns the assets.

13.8. An analysis similar to that in Tables 13.1 to 13.4 gives the PV of expected payments as $3.7364s$, the PV of the expected payoff as 0.0838, and the PV of the expected accrual payment as $0.0598s$. The credit default swap spread is 221 basis points.

13.9. If the credit default swap spread is 150 basis points, the value of the swap to the buyer of protection is

$$0.0838 - (3.7364 + 0.0598) \times 0.0150 = 0.0269$$

per dollar of notional principal.

13.10. If the swap is a binary CDS, the present value of expected payoffs is 0.1197 and the credit default swap spread is 315 basis points.

13.11. A 5-year nth-to-default credit default swap works in the same way as a regular credit default swap except that there is a basket of companies. The payoff occurs when the nth default from the companies in the basket occurs. After the nth default has occurred, the swap ceases to exist. When $n = 1$ (so that the swap is a "first to default"), an increase in the default correlation lowers the value of the swap to the protection buyer. When $n = 25$ (so that the swap is a 25th to default), an increase in the default correlation increases the value of the swap to the protection buyer.

13.12. The recovery rate of a bond is usually defined as the value of the bond a few days after a default occurs as a percentage of the bond's face value.

13.13. The payoff from a plain vanilla CDS is $1 - R$ times the payoff from a binary CDS with the same principal. The payoff always occurs at the same time on the two instruments. It follows that the regular payments on a new plain vanilla CDS must be $1 - R$ times the payments on a new binary CDS. Otherwise there would be an arbitrage opportunity.

13.14. In the case of a total return swap, a company receives (pays) the increase (decrease) in the value of the bond. In a regular swap this does not happen.

13.15. When a company enters into a long (short) forward contract it is obligated to buy (sell) the protection given by a specified credit default swap with a specified spread at a specified future time. When a company buys a call (put) option contract, it has the option to buy (sell) the protection given by a specified credit default swap with a specified spread at a specified future time. Both contracts are normally structured so that they cease to exist if a default occurs during the life of the contract.

13.16. A credit default swap insures a corporate bond issued by the reference entity against default. Its approximate effect is to convert the corporate bond into a risk-free bond. The buyer of a credit default swap has therefore chosen to exchange a corporate bond for a risk-free bond. This means that the buyer is long a risk-free bond and short a similar corporate bond.

13.17. Payoffs from credit default swaps depend on whether a particular company defaults. Arguably some market participants have more information about this that others (see Business Snapshot 13.2).

13.18. Real-world default probabilities are less than risk-neutral default probabilities. It follows that the use of real-world default probabilities will tend to understate the value of the protection.

13.19. In an asset swap the bond's promised payments are swapped for LIBOR plus a spread. In a total return swap the bond's actual payments are swapped for LIBOR plus a spread.

13.20. Using equation (13.2), we find that the probability of default conditional on a factor value of M is

$$N\left(\frac{N^{-1}(0.03) - \sqrt{0.2}\,M}{\sqrt{1 - 0.2}}\right)$$

For M equal to $-2, -1, 0, 1, 2$, the probabilities of default are 0.135, 0.054, 0.018, 0.005, 0.001, respectively. To six decimal places, the probability of more that 10 defaults for these values of M can be calculated using the BINOMDIST function in Excel. They are 0.959284, 0.79851, 0.000016, 0, 0, respectively.

13.21. For a CDO squared we form a portfolio of CDO tranches and tranche the default losses in a similar way to Figure 13.3. For a CDO cubed we form a portfolio of CDO squared tranches and tranche the default losses in a similar way to Figure 13.3.

CHAPTER 14

14.1. The definition includes all internal risks and external risks except reputational risk and risks resulting from strategic decisions.

14.2. Based on the results reported in Section 14.4, the loss would be $100 \times 3^{0.23}$, or \$127.8 million.

14.3. $\text{Prob}(v > x) = Kx^{-0.8}$. When $x = 20$, the probability is 0.1. This means that $K = 1.0986$. The probability of the specified losses being exceeded are (a) 5.74%, (b) 3.30%, and (c) 1.58%.

14.4. Moral hazard is handled by deductibles and by making premiums dependent on past claims. Adverse selection is handled by finding out as much as possible about a driver before insurance is granted and then modifying premiums as more information on the driver becomes available.

14.5. CEOs must prepare a statement asserting that the financial statements are accurate. They must return bonuses in the event that there is a restatement of financial statements.

14.6. If a trader operates within established risk limits and takes a loss, it is part of market risk. If risk limits are violated, the loss becomes classified as an operational risk.

14.7. (a) It is unlikely that an individual would not look after his or her health because of the existence of a life insurance contract. But it has been known for the beneficiary of a life insurance contract to commit murder to receive the payoff from the contract! (b) Individuals with short life expectancies are more likely to buy life insurance than individuals with long life expectancies.

14.8. External loss data is data relating to the losses of other banks. It is data obtained from sharing agreements with other banks or from data vendors. External data is used to determine relative loss severity. It can be a useful indicator of the ratio of mean losses in Business Unit A to mean losses in Business Unit B or the ratio of the standard deviation of losses in Business Unit A to the standard deviation of losses in Business Unit B.

14.9. The Poisson distribution is commonly used for loss frequency. The lognormal distribution is commonly used for loss severity.

14.10. Two examples of key risk indicators are staff turnover and number of failed transactions.

14.11. When the loss frequency is 3, the mean total loss is about 3.3 and the standard deviation is about 2.0. When the loss frequency is increased to 4, the mean loss is about 4.4 and the standard deviation is about 2.4.

CHAPTER 15

15.1. Leverage and crashophobia.

15.2. Uncertain volatility and jumps.

15.3. When plain vanilla call and put options are being priced, traders do use the Black–Scholes model as an interpolation tool. They calculate implied volatilities for the options that are actively traded. By interpolating between strike prices and between times to maturity, they estimate implied volatilities for other options. These implied volatilities are then substituted into Black–Scholes to calculate prices for these options. Black–Scholes is more than an interpolation tool when used for hedging.

15.4. 13.45%. We get the same answer by (a) interpolating between strike prices of 1.00 and 1.05 and then between maturities of 6 months and 1 year and (b) interpolating between maturities of 6 months and 1 year and then between strike prices of 1.00 and 1.05.

15.5. The models of physics describe the behavior of physical processes. The models of finance ultimately describe the behavior of human beings.

15.6. It might notice that it is getting a large amount of business of a certain type because it is quoting prices different from its competitors. The pricing differences may also become apparent if it decides to unwind transactions and approaches competitors for quotes. Also, it might subscribe to a service where it obtains the average price quotes by dealers for particular transactions.

15.7. A loss equal to half the bid–offer spread is recognized when positions are liquidated. Liquidity VaR takes this loss into account.

15.8. Liquidity black holes occur when most market participants want to be on one side of a market. Regulation is liable to lead to liquidity black holes. This is because when all financial institutions are regulated in the same way they tend to want to respond to external economic events in the same way.

15.9. Within-model hedging involves hedging against changes in variables that the model assumes to be stochastic. Outside-model hedging involves hedging against parameters that the model assumes to be constant.

15.10. The Black–Scholes model assumes that the probability distribution of the stock price in 1 month is lognormal. In this case it is clearly not lognormal. Possibly it consists of two lognormal distributions superimposed upon each other and is bimodal. Black–Scholes is clearly inappropriate.

15.11. In this case the probability distribution of the exchange rate has a thin left tail and a thin right tail relative to the lognormal distribution. Deep-out-of-the-money calls and puts will have relatively low prices.

15.12. The term "marking to market" refers to the practice of revaluing instruments (usually daily) so that they are consistent with the market. The prices calculated for actively traded products do reflect market prices. The model is used merely as an interpolation tool. The term "marking to market" is therefore accurate for these products. The prices for structured products depend on the model being used. Hence the term "marking to model".

15.13. Hedge funds are not regulated in the same way as other financial institutions and can therefore be contrarian investors buying whenever everyone else is selling and selling whenever everyone else is buying. However, black holes can be created when large numbers of hedge funds follow similar trading strategies.

CHAPTER 16

16.1. Economic capital is a bank's own estimate of the capital it requires. Regulatory capital is the capital it is required to keep by bank supervisors.

16.2. A company with an AA rating has a 0.03% chance of defaulting in 1 year.

16.3. Business risk includes risks relating to strategic decisions and reputation.

16.4. The models used for economic capital are likely to be broadly similar to those used to calculate regulatory capital in the case of market risk and operational risk. When calculating credit risk economic capital, a bank may consider it appropriate to use a different credit correlation model and different correlation parameters from those used in regulatory capital calculations.

16.5. The 99.97% worst-case value of the logarithm of the loss is $0.5 + 4 \times 3.43 = 14.23$. The 99.97% worst-case loss is therefore $1.510 million. From the properties of the lognormal distribution, the expected loss is $\exp(0.5 + 4^2/2)$, or $4,915. The capital requirement is therefore $1.505 million.

16.6. The economic capital for Business Unit 1 is 96.85. The economic capital for Business Unit 2 is 63.87. The total capital is 124.66.

16.7. The incremental effect of Business Unit 1 on total economic capital is 60.78. The incremental effect of Business Unit 2 on total economic capital is 27.81. This suggests that $60.78/(60.78 + 27.81)$, or 68.61%, of economic capital should be allocated to Business Unit 1 and $27.81/(60.78 + 27.81)$, or 31.39%, to Business Unit 2. The marginal effect of increasing the size of Business Unit 1 by 0.5% is 0.4182. The marginal effect of increasing the size of Business Unit 2 by 0.5% is 0.2056. Euler's theorem is satisfied because the total economic capital is approximately equal to the sum of 0.4182/0.005 and 0.2056/0.005.

16.8. The capital is $40 - 2 = \$38$ million and the return before tax is $12 - 5 - 2 = \$5$ million. The before-tax RAROC is therefore 13.2%. In practice, the allocation of diversification benefits to this venture might reduce capital and increase RAROC.

16.9. RAROC can be used to compare the past performance of different business units or to project the expected future performance of business units.

CHAPTER 17

17.1. A day's HDD is $\max(0, 65 - A)$ and a day's CDD is $\max(0, A - 65)$, where A is the average of the highest and lowest temperature during the day at a specified weather station, measured in degrees Fahrenheit.

17.2. It is an agreement by one side to deliver a specified amount of gas at a roughly uniform rate during a month to a particular hub for a specified price.

17.3. The average temperature each day is $75°$ Fahrenheit. The CDD each day is therefore 10 and the cumulative CDD for the month is $10 \times 31 = 310$. The payoff from the call option is therefore

$$(310 - 250) \times 5{,}000 = \$300{,}000$$

17.4. Unlike most commodities electricity cannot be stored easily. If the demand for electricity exceeds the supply, as it sometimes does during the air-conditioning season, the price of electricity in a deregulated environment will skyrocket. When supply and demand become matched again, the price will return to former levels.

17.5. HDD is $\max(65 - A, 0)$, where A is the average of the maximum and minimum temperature during the day. This is the payoff from a put option on A with a strike price of 65. CDD is $\max(A - 65, 0)$. This is the payoff from call option on A with a strike price of 65.

17.6. It would be useful to calculate the cumulative CDD for July of each year of the last 50 years. A linear regression relationship

$$CDD = a + bt + e$$

could then be estimated, where a and b are constants, t is the time in years measured from the start of the 50 years, and e is the error. This relationship allows for linear trends in temperature through time. The expected CDD for next year (year 51) is then $a + 51b$. This could be used as an estimate of the forward CDD.

17.7. The volatility of the one-year forward price will be less than the volatility of the spot price. This is because, when the spot price changes by a certain amount, mean reversion will cause the forward price will change by a lesser amount.

17.8. The energy producer faces quantity risks and price risks. It can use weather derivatives to hedge the quantity risks and energy derivatives to hedge against the price risks.

17.9. A 5×8 contract for May 2006 is a contract to provide electricity for 5 days per week during the off-peak period (11 p.m. to 7 a.m.). When daily exercise is specified, the holder of the option is able to choose each weekday whether he or she will buy electricity at the strike price at the agreed rate. When there is monthly exercise, he or she chooses once at the beginning of the month whether electricity is to be bought at the strike price at the agreed rate for the whole month. The option with daily exercise is worth more.

17.10. CAT bonds (catastrophe bonds) are an alternative to reinsurance for an insurance company that has taken on a certain catastrophic risk (e.g., the risk of a hurricane or an earthquake) and wants to get rid of it. CAT bonds are issued by the insurance company. They provide a higher rate of interest than government bonds. However, the bondholders agree to forego interest, and possibly principal, to meet any claims against the insurance company that are within a prespecified range.

17.11. The CAT bond has very little systematic risk. Whether a particular type of catastrophe occurs is independent of the return on the market. The risks in the CAT bond are likely to be largely "diversified away" by the other investments in the portfolio. A B-rated bond does have systematic risk that cannot be diversified away. It is likely therefore that the CAT bond is a better addition to the portfolio.

17.12. It means that the price of the energy source will be pulled back to a long-run average level. Electricity has the highest mean-reversion rate; oil has the lowest.

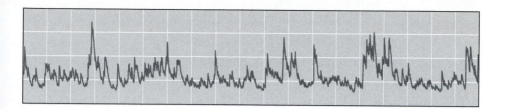

Glossary of Terms

Accrued Interest The interest earned on a bond since the last coupon payment date.

Add-on Factor When the credit equivalent amount for a derivatives transaction is being calculated, this is the percentage of principal added to the current exposure to allow for possible future changes in the value of the derivative.

Advanced Measurement Approach The way in which the most sophisticated banks will be allowed to calculate regulatory capital for operational risk under Basel II.

Adverse Selection The phenomenon that, if an insurance company offers the same premiums to everyone, it tends to end up providing coverage for the worst risks.

American Option An option that can be exercised at any time during its life.

Analytic Result Result where answer is in the form of an equation.

Arbitrage A trading strategy that takes advantage of two or more securities being mispriced relative to each other.

Arbitrage Pricing Theory A theory where the return from an investment is assumed to depend on several factors.

Arbitrageur An individual engaging in arbitrage.

Asian Option An option with a payoff dependent on the average price of the underlying asset during a specified period.

Ask Price The price that a dealer is offering to sell an asset. (Also called the *offer price*.)

Asked Price *See* Ask Price.

Asset Swap Exchanges the promised coupon on a bond for LIBOR plus a spread.

At-the-money Option An option in which the strike price equals the price of the underlying asset.

Autocorrelation The correlation between the value of a variable and the value of the same variable k days later (where k is referred to as the time lag).

Average Price Call Option An option giving a payoff equal to the greater of zero and the amount by which the average price of the asset exceeds the strike price.

Average Price Put Option An option giving a payoff equal to the greater of zero and the amount by which the strike price exceeds the average price of the asset.

Back Testing Testing a value-at-risk or other model using historical data.

Backwards Induction A procedure for working from the end of a tree to its beginning in order to value an option.

Bankruptcy Costs Costs such as lost sales, loss of key managers, and professional fees arising from a declaration of bankruptcy. These costs are not associated with the adverse events leading to bankruptcy.

Barrier Option An option whose payoff depends on whether the path of the underlying asset has reached a barrier (i.e., a certain predetermined level).

Basel I The first international agreement on the regulation of banks in 1988.

Basel II New international regulations for calculating bank capital expected to come into effect in 2007.

Basic Indicator Approach The simplest way of calculating regulatory capital for operational risk under Basel II.

Basis The difference between the spot price and the futures price of a commodity.

Basis Point When used to describe an interest rate, a basis point is one hundredth of one percent (= 0.01%).

Basis Risk The risk to a hedger arising from uncertainty about the basis at a future time.

Basket Credit Default Swap Credit default swap where there are several reference entities.

Basket Option Option on a portfolio of assets.

Beta A measure of the systematic risk of an asset.

Bid–Ask Spread *See* Bid–Offer Spread.

Bid–Offer Spread The amount by which the offer (or ask) price exceeds the bid price.

Bid Price The price that a dealer is prepared to pay for an asset.

Binary Credit Default Swap Instrument where there is a fixed dollar payoff in the event of a default by a particular company.

Binary Option Option with a discontinuous payoff, for example, a cash-or-nothing option or an asset-or-nothing option.

Binomial Model A model where the price of an asset is monitored over successive short periods of time. In each short period, it is assumed that only two price movements are possible.

Binomial Tree A tree that represents how an asset price can evolve under the binomial model.

Bivariate Normal Distribution A distribution for two correlated variables, each of which is normal.

Black's Model An extension of the Black–Scholes model for valuing European options on futures contracts. It is used extensively in practice to value European options when the distribution of the asset price at maturity is assumed to be lognormal.

Black–Scholes Model A model for pricing European options on stocks, developed by Fischer Black, Myron Scholes, and Robert Merton.

Bond Option An option where a bond is the underlying asset.

Bond Yield Discount rate which, when applied to all the cash flows of a bond, causes the present value of the cash flows to equal the bond's market price.

Bootstrap Method A procedure for calculating the zero-coupon yield curve from market data. Also a statistical procedure for calculating confidence levels when distributions are determined empirically.

Bunching A tendency for days when the loss is greater than the value at risk to be bunched close together.

Business Risk When used for a bank, this refers to strategic risk (related to a bank's decision to enter new markets and develop new products) and reputation risk.

Calendar Days Includes every day.

Calibration Method for implying a model's parameters from the prices of actively traded options.

Callable bond A bond containing provisions that allow the issuer to buy it back at a predetermined price at certain times during its life.

Call Option An option to buy an asset at a certain price by a certain date.

Cancelable Swap Swap that can be canceled by one side on prespecified dates.

Cap *See* Interest Rate Cap.

Capital Asset Pricing Model A model relating the expected return on an asset to its beta.

Caplet One component of an interest rate cap.

Cap Rate The rate determining payoffs in an interest rate cap.

Cash Flow Mapping A procedure for representing an instrument as a portfolio of zero-coupon bonds for the purpose of calculating value at risk.

Cash Settlement Procedure for settling a contract in cash rather than by delivering the underlying asset.

CAT Bond Bond where the interest and, possibly, the principal paid are reduced if a particular category of "catastrophic" insurance claims exceed a certain amount.

CDD Cooling degree days. The maximum of zero and the amount by which the daily average temperature is greater than 65° Fahrenheit. The average temperature is the average of the highest and lowest temperatures (midnight to midnight).

CDO *See* Collateralized Debt Obligation.

CDO Squared An instrument in which the default risks in a portfolio of CDO tranches are allocated to new securities.

CDX An index of the credit quality of 125 North American investment-grade companies.

Cholesky Decomposition Method of sampling from a multivariate normal distribution.

Clean Price of Bond The quoted price of a bond. The cash price paid for the bond (or dirty price) is calculated by adding the accrued interest to the clean price.

Clearinghouse A firm that guarantees the performance of the parties in an exchange-traded derivatives transaction. (Also referred to as a clearing corporation.)

Clearing margin A margin posted by a member of a clearinghouse.

Coherent Risk Measure A risk measure that satisfies a number of conditions.

Collar *See* Interest Rate Collar.

Collateralization A system for posting collateral by one or both parties in a derivatives transaction.

Collateralized Debt Obligation A way of packaging credit risk. Several classes of securities (known as tranches) are created from a portfolio of bonds and there are rules for determining how the cost of defaults are allocated to classes.

Component VaR VaR corresponding to a component of a portfolio. Defined so that the sum of the component VaRs for the components of a portfolio equals the VaR for the whole portfolio.

Compounding Frequency This defines how an interest rate is measured.

Compound Option An option on an option.

Compounding Swap Swap where interest compounds instead of being paid.

Conditional Value at Risk (C-VaR) *See* Expected Shortfall.

Confirmation Contract confirming verbal agreement between two parties to a trade in the over-the-counter market.

Consumption Asset An asset held for consumption rather than investment.

Continuous Compounding A way of quoting interest rates. It is the limit as the assumed compounding interval is made smaller and smaller.

Convenience Yield A measure of the benefits from ownership of an asset that are not obtained by the holder of a long futures contract on the asset.

Conversion Factor   Factor multiplied by principal to convert an off-balance-sheet item to its credit equivalent amount.

Convertible Bond   A corporate bond that can be converted into a predetermined amount of the company's equity at certain times during its life.

Convexity   A measure of the curvature in the relationship between bond prices and bond yields.

Convexity Adjustment   An overworked term. For example, it can refer to the adjustment necessary to convert a futures interest rate to a forward interest rate. It can also refer to the adjustment to a forward rate that is sometimes necessary when instruments are valued.

Cooke Ratio   Ratio of capital to risk-weighted assets under Basel I.

Copula   A way of defining the correlation between variables with known distributions.

Cornish–Fisher Expansion   An approximate relationship between the fractiles of a probability distribution and its moments.

Cost of Carry   The storage costs plus the cost of financing an asset minus the income earned on the asset.

Counterparty   The opposite side in a financial transaction.

Coupon   Interest payment made on a bond.

Covariance   Measure of the linear relationship between two variables (equals the correlation between the variables times the product of their standard deviations).

Covered Call   A short position in a call option on an asset combined with a long position in the asset.

Crashophobia   The fear of a stock market crash similar to that in 1987 that some people claim causes market participants to increase the value of deep-out-of-the-money put options.

Credit Default Swap   An instrument that gives the holder the right to sell a bond for its face value in the event of a default by the issuer.

Credit Derivative   A derivative whose payoff depends on the credit-worthiness of one or more companies or countries.

Credit Equivalent Amount   Size of loan that is considered equivalent to an off-balance-sheet transaction in Basel I.

Credit Rating   A measure of the creditworthiness of a bond issue.

Credit Ratings Transition Matrix   A table showing the probability that a company will move from one credit rating to another during a certain period of time.

Credit Risk   The risk that a loss will be experienced because of a default by the counterparty in a derivatives transaction.

Credit Risk Migration   Movement of a company from one rating category to another.

Credit Risk Plus   A procedure for calculating credit value at risk.

Credit Value at Risk   The credit loss that will not be exceeded at some specified confidence level.

CreditMetrics   A procedure for calculating credit value at risk.

Cumulative Distribution Function   The probability that a variable will be less than x as a function of x.

Currency Swap   A swap where interest and principal in one currency are exchanged for interest and principal in another currency.

Day Count   A convention for quoting interest rates.

Day Trade   A trade that is entered into and closed out on the same day.

Default Correlation   Measures the tendency of two companies to default at about the same time.

Default Intensity   *See* Hazard Rate.

Delivery Price   Price that will be paid or received in a forward contract.

Delta   The rate of change of the price of a derivative with the price of the underlying asset.

Delta Hedging   A hedging scheme that is designed to make the price of a portfolio of derivatives insensitive to small changes in the price of the underlying asset.

Delta-neutral Portfolio   A portfolio with a delta of zero so that there is no sensitivity to small changes in the price of the underlying asset.

DerivaGem   Software for valuing options, available on the author's website.

Derivative   An instrument whose price depends on, or is derived from, the price of another asset.

Deterministic Variable   A variable whose future value is known.

Dirty Price of Bond   Cash price of bond.

Discount Bond   *See* Zero-coupon Bond.

Discount Instrument An instrument, such as a Treasury bill, that provides no coupons.

Discount Rate The annualized dollar return on a Treasury bill or similar instrument expressed as a percentage of the final face value.

Distance to Default The number of standard deviations that the value of a company's assets must move for a default to be triggered.

Dividend A cash payment made to the owner of a stock.

Dividend Yield The dividend as a percentage of the stock price.

Down-and-in Option An option that comes into existence when the price of the underlying asset declines to a prespecified level.

Down-and-out Option An option that ceases to exist when the price of the underlying asset declines to a prespecified level.

Downgrade Trigger A clause in a contract that states that the contract can be terminated by one side if the credit rating of the other side falls below a certain level.

Duration A measure of the average life a bond. It is also an approximation to the ratio of the proportional change in the bond price to the absolute change in its yield.

Duration Matching A procedure for matching the durations of assets and liabilities.

Dynamic Hedging A procedure for hedging an option position by periodically changing the position held in the underlying asset. The objective is usually to maintain a delta-neutral position.

EAD *See* Exposure at Default.

Early Exercise Exercise prior to the maturity date.

Economic Capital The capital that a bank's own calculation indicates it needs.

Efficient Frontier The optimal trade-offs for an investor between expected return and standard deviation of return.

Efficient Market Hypothesis A hypothesis that asset prices reflect relevant information.

Electronic Trading System of trading where a computer is used to match buyers and sellers.

Embedded Option An option that is an inseparable part of another instrument.

Empirical Research Research based on historical market data.

Equity Swap A swap where the return on an equity portfolio is exchanged for either a fixed or a floating rate of interest.

Eurocurrency A currency that is outside the formal control of the issuing country's monetary authorities.

Eurodollar A dollar held in a bank outside the United States.

Eurodollar Futures Contract A futures contract written on a Eurodollar deposit.

Eurodollar Interest Rate The interest rate on a Eurodollar deposit.

European Option An option that can be exercised only at the end of its life.

EWMA Exponentially weighted moving average.

Exchange-traded Market Market organized by an exchange such as the New York Stock Exchange or Chicago Board Options Exchange.

Ex-dividend Date When a dividend is declared, an ex-dividend date is specified. Investors who own shares of the stock just before the ex-dividend date receive the dividend.

Exercise Price The price at which the underlying asset may be bought or sold in an option contract. (Also called the *strike price*.)

Exotic Option A nonstandard option.

Expectations Theory The theory that forward interest rates equal expected future spot interest rates.

Expected Shortfall Expected loss during N days conditional on being in the $(100 - X)\%$ tail of the distribution of profits/losses. The variable N is the time horizon and $X\%$ is the confidence level.

Expected Value of a Variable The average value of the variable obtained by weighting the alternative values by their probabilities.

Expiration Date The end of life of a contract.

Exponentially Weighted Moving Average Model A model where exponential weighting is used to provide forecasts for a variable from historical data. It is sometimes applied to variances and covariances in value-at-risk calculations.

Exponential Weighting A weighting scheme where the weight given to an observation depends on how recent it is. The weight given to an observation t time periods ago is λ times the weight given to an observation $t - 1$ time periods ago, where $\lambda < 1$.

Exposure at Default   The maximum amount that could be lost (assuming no recovery) when a default occurs.

Extreme Value Theory   A theory enabling the shape of the tails of a distribution to be estimated from data.

Factor   Source of uncertainty.

Factor Analysis   An analysis aimed at finding a small number of factors that describe most of the variation in a large number of correlated variables. (Similar to a *principal components analysis*.)

Factor Loadings   The values of variables in a factor model when we have one unit of a particular factor and no units of other factors.

Factor Model   Model where a set of correlated variables are assumed to depend linearly on a number of uncorrelated factors.

Factor Scores   In a factor model this is the amount of different factors present in a particular observation on the variables.

Financial Intermediary   A bank or other financial institution that facilitates the flow of funds between different entities in the economy.

Floor   *See* Interest Rate Floor.

Floor–Ceiling Agreement   *See* Collar.

Floorlet   One component of a floor.

Floor Rate   The rate in an interest rate floor agreement.

Foreign Currency Option   An option on a foreign exchange rate.

Forward Contract   A contract that obligates the holder to buy or sell an asset for a predetermined delivery price at a predetermined future time.

Forward Exchange Rate   The forward price of one unit of a foreign currency.

Forward Interest Rate   The interest rate for a future period of time implied by the rates prevailing in the market today.

Forward Price   The delivery price in a forward contract that causes the contract to be worth zero.

Forward Rate   Can refer to a forward interest rate or a forward exchange rate.

Forward Rate Agreement (FRA)   Agreement that a certain interest rate will apply to a certain principal amount for a certain time period in the future.

Futures Contract   A contract that obligates the holder to buy or sell an asset at a predetermined delivery price during a specified future time period. The contract is settled daily.

Futures Option   An option on a futures contract.

Futures Price   The delivery price currently applicable to a futures contract.

G-30 Policy Recommendations   A set of recommendations concerning derivatives issued by nonregulators in 1993.

Gamma   The rate of change of delta with respect to the asset price.

Gamma-neutral portfolio   A portfolio with a gamma of zero.

GARCH Model   A model for forecasting volatility where the variance rate follows a mean-reverting process.

Gaussian Copula Model   A copula model based on the multivariate normal distribution.

Glass–Steagall Act   An act passed in the United States separating commercial and investment banks.

Greeks   Hedge parameters such as delta, gamma, vega, theta, and rho.

Haircut   Discount applied to the value of an asset when it is used as collateral.

Hazard Rate   Measures probability of default in a short period of time conditional on no earlier default.

HDD   Heating degree days. The maximum of zero and the amount by which the daily average temperature is less than $65°$ Fahrenheit. The average temperature is the average of the highest and lowest temperatures (midnight to midnight).

Hedge   A trade designed to reduce risk.

Hedge Funds   Funds that are subject to less restrictions and less regulation than mutual funds. They can take short positions and use derivatives, but they cannot publicly offer their securities.

Hedger   An individual who enters into hedging trades.

Hedge Ratio   The ratio of the size of a position in a hedging instrument to the size of the position being hedged.

Historical Simulation   A simulation based on historical data.

Historic Volatility   A volatility estimated from historical data.

Holiday Calendar Calendar defining which days are holidays for the purposes of determining payment dates in a financial transaction.

Hybrid Approach Approach to aggregating different types of economic capital.

Implied Volatility Volatility implied from an option price using the Black–Scholes or a similar model.

Inception Profit Profit created by selling a derivative for more than its theoretical value.

Incremental Value at Risk The difference between the value at risk with and without a particular component of the portfolio.

Initial Margin The cash required from a futures trader at the time of the trade.

Instantaneous Forward Rate Forward rate for a very short period of time in the future.

Interest Rate Cap An option that provides a payoff when a specified interest rate is above a certain level. The interest rate is a floating rate that is reset periodically.

Interest Rate Collar A combination of an interest rate cap and an interest rate floor.

Interest Rate Derivative A derivative whose payoffs are dependent on future interest rates.

Interest Rate Floor An option that provides a payoff when an interest rate is below a certain level. The interest rate is a floating rate that is reset periodically.

Interest Rate Option An option where the payoff is dependent on the level of interest rates.

Interest Rate Swap An exchange of a fixed rate of interest on a certain notional principal for a floating rate of interest on the same notional principal.

In-the-money Option Either (a) a call option where the asset price is greater than the strike price or (b) a put option where the asset price is less than the strike price.

Intrinsic Value For a call option, this is the greater of the excess of the asset price over the strike price and zero. For a put option, it is the greater of the excess of the strike price over the asset price and zero.

Investment Asset   An asset held by significant numbers of individuals for investment purposes.

iTraxx   An index of the credit quality of 125 European investment grade companies.

IRB Approach   Internal ratings based approach for assessing credit risk capital in Basel II.

Key Risk Indicators   Indicators to track the level of operational risk.

Kurtosis   A measure of the fatness of the tails of a distribution.

LGD   *See* Loss Given Default.

LIBID   London interbank bid rate. The rate bid by banks on Eurocurrency deposits (i.e., the rate at which a bank is willing to borrow from other banks).

LIBOR   London interbank offered rate. The rate offered by banks on Eurocurrency deposits (i.e., the rate at which a bank is willing to lend to other banks).

LIBOR-in-arrears Swap   Swap where the interest paid on a date is determined by the interest rate observed on that date (not by the interest rate observed on the previous payment date).

LIBOR/Swap Zero Curve   Zero rates as a function of maturity that are calculated from LIBOR rates, eurodollar futures, and swap rates.

LIBOR Zero Curve   *See* LIBOR/Swap Zero Curve.

Linear Product   Derivative product whose price depends linearly on one or more underlying variables.

Liquidity-adjusted VaR   A value-at-risk calculation that takes account of the impact of the bid–offer spread when positions are unwound.

Liquidity Black Holes   The risk that liquidity will dry up because everyone wants to be on the same side of the market.

Liquidity Preference Theory   A theory leading to the conclusion that forward interest rates are above expected future spot interest rates.

Liquidity Premium   The amount that forward interest rates exceed expected future spot interest rates.

Liquidity Risk   Risk that it will not be possible to sell a holding of a particular instrument at its theoretical price.

Lognormal Distribution   A variable has a lognormal distribution when the logarithm of the variable has a normal distribution.

Long Position   A position involving the purchase of an asset.

Lookback Option   An option whose payoff is dependent on the maximum or minimum of the asset price achieved during a certain period.

Loss Given Default   The percentage of the exposure to a counterparty that is lost when a default by the counterparty occurs.

Maintenance Margin   When the balance in a trader's margin account falls below the maintenance margin level, the trader receives a margin call requiring the account to be topped up to the initial margin level.

Margin   The cash balance (or security deposit) required from a futures or options trader.

Margin Call   A request for extra margin when the balance in the margin account falls below the maintenance margin level.

Marginal Value at Risk   The rate of change of the value at risk with the size of one component of the portfolio.

Market Maker   A trader who is willing to quote both bid and offer prices for an asset.

Market Model   A model most commonly used by traders.

Market Portfolio   A portfolio consisting of the universe of all possible investments.

Market Risk   Risk relating to movements in market variables.

Marking to Market   The practice of revaluing an instrument to reflect the current values of the relevant market variables.

Maturity Date   The end of the life of a contract.

Maximum-likelihood Method   A method for choosing the values of parameters by maximizing the probability of a set of observations occurring.

Mean Reversion   The tendency of a market variable (such as a volatility or an interest rate) to revert back to some long-run average level.

Merton's Model   Model using equity prices to estimate default probabilities. (Other models developed by Merton are also sometimes referred to as Merton's model.)

Model-building Approach   The use of a model to estimate value at risk.

Model Risk   The risk relating to the use of models to price derivative products.

Modified Duration   A modification to the standard duration measure so that it more accurately describes the relationship between proportional changes in a bond price and actual changes in its yield. The modification takes account of the compounding frequency with which the yield is quoted.

Monte Carlo Simulation   A procedure for randomly sampling changes in market variables.

Moral Hazard   The possibility that the behavior of an insured entity will change because of the existence of an insurance contract.

Multivariate Normal Distribution   The joint distribution of many variables, each of which is normal.

Naked Position   A short position in a call option that is not combined with a long position in the underlying asset.

Net Interest Income   The excess of interest earned over interest paid for a bank.

Net Replacement Ratio   The ratio of current exposure with netting to current exposure without netting.

Netting   The ability to offset contracts with positive and negative values in the event of a default by a counterparty.

Nonlinear product   Derivative product that is not linearly dependent on the underlying variables.

Nonsystematic risk   Risk that can be diversified away.

Normal Distribution   The standard bell-shaped distribution of statistics.

Normal Market   A market where futures prices increase with maturity.

Notional Principal   The principal used to calculate payments in an interest rate swap. The principal is "notional" because it is neither paid nor received.

Numerical Procedure   A method of calculation when no formula is available.

Offer Price   The price that a dealer is offering to sell an asset. (Also called the *ask price*.)

Open Interest   The total number of long positions outstanding in a futures contract (equals the total number of short positions).

Open Outcry   System of trading where traders meet on the floor of the exchange.

Operational Risk   The risk of loss arising from inadequate or failed internal processes, people, and systems, or from external events.

Option   The right to buy or sell an asset.

Out-of-the-money Option Either (a) a call option where the asset price is less than the strike price or (b) a put option where the asset price is greater than the strike price.

Over-the-counter Market A market where traders deal by phone. The traders are usually financial institutions, corporations, and fund managers.

Par Value The principal amount of a bond.

Par Yield The coupon on a bond that makes its price equal the principal.

Parallel Shift A movement in the yield curve where each point on the curve changes by the same amount.

Partial Duration Percentage change in value of a portfolio for a small change in one point on the zero-coupon yield curve.

Payoff The cash realized by the holder of an option or other derivative at the end of its life.

PD Probability of default.

Plain Vanilla A term used to describe a standard deal.

Poisson Distribution Distribution for number of events in a certain time period in a Poisson process.

Poisson Process A process describing a situation where events happen at random. The probability of an event in time Δt is $\lambda \Delta t$, where λ is the intensity of the process.

Portfolio Immunization Making a portfolio relatively insensitive to interest rates.

Portfolio Insurance Entering into trades to ensure that the value of a portfolio will not fall below a certain level.

Positive SemiDefinite Condition that must be satisfied by a variance–covariance matrix for it to be valid.

Power Law Law describing the tails of many probability distributions that are encountered in practice.

Premium The price of an option.

Principal The par or face value of a debt instrument.

Principal Components Analysis An analysis aimed at finding a small number of factors that describe most of the variation in a large number of correlated variables. (Similar to a *factor analysis*.)

Put–Call Parity The relationship between the price of a European call option and the price of a European put option when they have the same strike price and maturity date.

Put Option An option to sell an asset for a certain price by a certain date.

Puttable Bond A bond where the holder has the right to sell it back to the issuer at certain predetermined times for a predetermined price.

Puttable Swap A swap where one side has the right to terminate early.

Quadratic Model Quadratic relationship between change in portfolio value and percentage changes in market variables.

Quantitative Impact Studies Studies by the Basel Committee of the effect of proposed new regulations on capital of banks.

RAROC Risk-adjusted return on capital.

Rebalancing The process of adjusting a trading position periodically. Usually the purpose is to maintain delta neutrality.

Recovery Rate Amount recovered in the event of a default as a percentage of the face value.

Regulatory arbitrage Transactions designed to reduce the total regulatory capital of the financial institutions involved.

Regulatory capital Capital a financial institution is required by regulators to keep.

Repo Repurchase agreement. A procedure for borrowing money by selling securities to a counterparty and agreeing to buy them back later at a slightly higher price.

Repo Rate The rate of interest in a repo transaction.

Reset Date The date in a swap or cap or floor when the floating rate for the next period is set.

Reversion Level The level that the value of a market variable (e.g., a volatility) tends to revert.

Rho Rate of change of the price of a derivative with the interest rate.

Risk-free Rate The rate of interest that can be earned without assuming any risks.

Risk-neutral Valuation The valuation of an option or other derivative assuming the world is risk neutral. Risk-neutral valuation gives the correct price for a derivative in all worlds, not just in a risk-neutral world.

Risk-neutral World   A world where investors are assumed to require no extra return on average for bearing risks.

Risk-weighted Amount   *See* Risk-weighted Assets.

Risk-weighted Assets   Quantity calculated in Basel I and Basel II. Total capital must be at least 8% of risk-weighted assets.

Roll Back   *See* Backwards Induction.

Sarbanes–Oxley   Act passed in the United States in 2002 increasing the responsibilities of directors, CEOs, and CFOs of public companies.

Scenario Analysis   An analysis of the effects of possible alternative future movements in market variables on the value of a portfolio. Also used to generate scenarios leading to operational risk losses.

Scorecard Approach   A self-assessment procedure used for operational risk.

SEC   Securities and Exchange Commission.

Short Position   A position assumed when traders sell shares they do not own.

Short Selling   Selling in the market shares that have been borrowed from another investor.

Simulation   *See* Monte Carlo Simulation.

Solvency II   A new regulatory framework for insurance companies proposed by the European Union.

Specific Risk Charge   Capital requirement for idiosyncratic risks in the trading book.

Spectral Risk Measure   Risk measure that assigns weights to the quantiles of the loss distribution.

Speculator   An individual who is taking a position in the market. Usually the individual is betting that the price of an asset will go up or that the price of an asset will go down.

Spot Interest Rate   *See* Zero-coupon Interest Rate.

Spot Price   The price for immediate delivery.

Spot Volatilities   The volatilities used to price a cap when a different volatility is used for each caplet.

Static Hedge   A hedge that does not have to be changed once it is initiated.

Static Options Replication A procedure for hedging a portfolio that involves finding another portfolio of approximately equal value on some boundary.

Stochastic Variable Variable whose future value is uncertain.

Stock Index An index monitoring the value of a portfolio of stocks.

Stock Index Futures Futures on a stock index.

Stock Index Option An option on a stock index.

Stock Option Option on a stock.

Storage Costs The costs of storing a commodity.

Stress Testing Testing of the impact of extreme market moves on the value of a portfolio.

Strike Price The price at which the asset may be bought or sold in an option contract. (Also called the *exercise price*.)

Structured Product Derivative designed by a financial institution to meet the needs of a client.

Student *t*-Copula Copula based on the multivariate Student *t*-distribution.

Student *t*-Distribution Distribution with heavier tails than the normal distribution.

Swap An agreement to exchange cash flows in the future according to a prearranged formula.

Swap Rate The fixed rate in an interest rate swap that causes the swap to have a value of zero.

Swap Zero Curve *See* LIBOR/Swap Zero Curve.

Swaption An option to enter into an interest rate swap where a specified fixed rate is exchanged for floating.

Synthetic CDO A CDO created by selling credit default swaps.

Synthetic Option An option created by trading the underlying asset.

Systematic Risk Risk that cannot be diversified away.

Systemic Risk Risk that a default by one financial institution will lead to defaults by other financial institutions.

Tail Correlation Correlation between the tails of two distributions. Measures the extent to which extreme values tend to occur together.

Tail Loss *See* Expected Shortfall.

Taylor Series Expansion For a function of several variables, this relates changes in the value of the function to changes in the values of the variables when the changes are small.

Term Structure of Interest Rates The relationship between interest rates and their maturities.

Terminal Value The value at maturity.

Theta The rate of change of the price of an option or other derivative with the passage of time.

Tier 1 Capital Equity and similar sources of capital.

Tier 2 Capital Subordinated debt (life greater than five years) and similar sources of capital.

Tier 3 Capital Short-term subordinated debt (life between two and five years).

Time Decay *See* Theta.

Time Value The value of an option arising from the time left to maturity (equals an option's price minus its intrinsic value).

Total Return Swap A swap where the return on an asset such as a bond is exchanged for LIBOR plus a spread. The return on the asset includes income such as coupons and the change in value of the asset.

Trading Days Days when markets are open for trading.

Tranche One of several securities that have different risk attributes. Examples are the tranches of a CDO.

Transaction Costs The cost of carrying out a trade (commissions plus the difference between the price obtained and the midpoint of the bid–offer spread).

Treasury Bill A short-term non-coupon-bearing instrument issued by the government to finance its debt.

Treasury Bond A long-term coupon-bearing instrument issued by the government to finance it debt.

Treasury Note Treasury bond lasting less than 10 years.

Treasury Note Futures A futures contract on Treasury notes.

Tree Representation of the evolution of the value of a market variable for the purposes of valuing an option or other derivative.

Underlying Variable A variable that the price of an option or other derivative depends on.

Unsystematic risk   *See* Nonsystematic Risk.

Up-and-in Option   An option that comes into existence when the price of the underlying asset increases to a prespecified level.

Up-and-out Option   An option that ceases to exist when the price of the underlying asset increases to a prespecified level.

Value at Risk   A loss that will not be exceeded at some specified confidence level.

Variance–covariance matrix   A matrix showing variances of, and covariances between, a number of different market variables.

Variance Rate   The square of volatility.

Vasicek's Model   Model of default correlation based on the Gaussian copula. (Other models developed by Vasicek are also sometimes referred to as Vasicek's model.)

Vega   The rate of change in the price of an option or other derivative with volatility.

Vega-neutral Portfolio   A portfolio with a vega of zero.

Volatility   A measure of the uncertainty of the return realized on an asset.

Volatility Skew   A term used to describe the volatility smile when it is nonsymmetrical.

Volatility Smile   The variation of implied volatility with strike price.

Volatility Surface   A table showing the variation of implied volatilities with strike price and time to maturity.

Volatility Term Structure   The variation of implied volatility with time to maturity.

Weather Derivative   Derivative where the payoff depends on the weather.

Writing an Option   Selling an option.

Yield   A return provided by an instrument.

Yield Curve   *See* Term Structure.

Zero-coupon Bond   A bond that provides no coupons.

Zero-coupon Interest Rate   The interest rate that would be earned on a bond that provides no coupons.

Zero-coupon Yield Curve   A plot of the zero-coupon interest rate against time to maturity.

Zero Curve   *See* Zero-coupon Yield Curve.

Zero Rate   *See* Zero-coupon Interest Rate.

Z-Score   A number indicating how likely a company is to default.

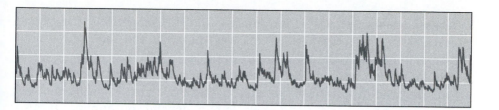

DerivaGem Software

You can download the DerivaGem option calculator from the author's website:

http://www.rotman.utoronto.ca/~hull

The software requires Microsoft Windows 98 or later and Microsoft Excel 2000 or later. It consists of two files: DG151.dll and DG151.xls. To install the software, you should create a folder with the name DerivaGem (or some other name of your own choosing) and load the files into the folder. You MUST then move DG151.dll into the Windows\System folder or the Windows\System 32 folder.[1]

Users should ensure that Security for Macros in Excel is set at *Medium* or *Low*. Check *Tools* followed by *Macros* followed by *Security* in Excel to change this. While using the software, you may be asked whether you want to enable macros. You should click *Enable Macros*.

THE OPTIONS CALCULATOR

DG151.xls is a user-friendly option calculator. It consists of three worksheets. The first worksheet is used to carry out computations for stock

---

[1] Note that it is not uncommon for Windows Explorer to be set up so that *.dll files are not displayed. To change the setting so that the *.dll file can be seen proceed as follows. In Windows 98 and ME, click *View*, followed by *File Options*, followed by *View*, followed by *Show All Files*. In Windows 2000, XP, and NT, click *Tools*, followed by *Folder Options*, followed by *View*, followed by *Show Hidden Files and Folders*.

options, currency options, index options, and futures options; the second is used for European and American bond options; and the third is used for caps, floors, and European swap options.

The software produces prices, Greek letters, and implied volatilities for a wide range of different instruments. It displays charts showing the way that option prices and the Greek letters depend on inputs. It also displays binomial and trinomial trees showing how the computations are carried out.

General Operation

To use the option calculator, you should choose a worksheet and click on the appropriate buttons to select Option Type, Underlying Type, and so on. You should then enter the parameters for the option you are considering, hit *Enter* on your keyboard, and click on *Calculate*. DerivaGem will then display the price or implied volatility for the option you are considering together with Greek letters. If the price has been calculated from a tree, and you are using the first or second worksheet, you can then click on *Display Tree* to see the tree. If a tree is to be displayed, there must be no more than ten time steps. An example of the tree that is displayed is shown in Appendix D. Many different charts can be displayed in all three worksheets. To display a chart, you must first choose the variable you require on the vertical axis, the variable you require on the horizontal axis, and the range of values to be considered on the horizontal axis. Following that you should hit *Enter* on your keyboard and click on *Draw Graph*. Whenever the values in one or more cells are changed, it is necessary to hit *Enter* on your keyboard before clicking on one of the buttons.

You may be asked whether you want to update to the new version when you first save the software. You should choose the *Yes* button.

Options on Stocks, Currencies, Indices, and Futures

The first worksheet (Equity_FX_Index_Futures) is used for options on stocks, currencies, indices, and futures. To use it, you should first select the Underlying Type (Equity, Currency, Index, or Futures). You should then select the Option Type. The alternatives are: Analytic European (i.e., Black–Scholes for a European option), Binomial European (i.e., European option using a binomial tree), Binomial American (i.e., American option using a binomial tree), Asian, Barrier Up and In, Barrier Up and Out, Barrier Down and In, Barrier Down and Out, Binary Cash or

Nothing, Binary Asset or Nothing, Chooser, Compound Option on Call, Compound Option on Put, or Lookback. You should then enter the data on the underlying asset and the data on the option. Note that all interest rates are expressed with continuous compounding.

In the case of European and American equity options, a table pops up allowing you to enter dividends. Enter the time of each ex-dividend date (measured in years from today) in the first column and the amount of the dividend in the second column. Dividends must be entered in chronological order.

You must click on buttons to choose whether the option is a call or a put and whether you wish to calculate an implied volatility. If you do wish to calculate an implied volatility, the option price should be entered in the cell labeled Price.

Once all the data has been entered you should hit *Enter* on your keyboard and click on *Calculate*. If Implied Volatility was selected, DerivaGem displays the implied volatility in the Volatility (% per year) cell. If Implied Volatility was not selected, it uses the volatility you entered in this cell and displays the option price in the Price cell.

Once the calculations have been completed, the tree (if used) can be inspected and charts can be displayed.

When Analytic European is selected, DerivaGem uses the equations in Appendix C to calculate prices and Greek letters. When Binomial European or Binomial American is selected, a binomial tree is constructed as described in Appendix D. Up to 500 time steps can be used.

The input data are largely self-explanatory. In the case of an Asian option, the Current Average is the average price since inception. If the Asian option is new (Time since Inception equals zero), then the Current Average cell is irrelevant and can be left blank. In the case of a Lookback Option, the Minimum to Date is used when a Call is valued and the Maximum to Date is used when a Put is valued. For a new deal, these should be set equal to the current price of the underlying asset.

Bond Options

The second worksheet (Bond_Options) is used for European and American options on bonds. You should first select a pricing model (Black-European, Normal-Analytic European, Normal-Tree European, Normal-American, Lognormal-European, or Lognormal-American; these models are explained in John Hull's book *Options, Futures, and Other Derivatives*). You should then enter the Bond Data and the Option

Data. The coupon is the rate paid per year and the frequency of payments can be selected as Quarterly, Semi-Annual, or Annual. The zero-coupon yield curve is entered in the table labeled Term Structure. Enter maturities (measured in years) in the first column and the corresponding continuously compounded rates in the second column. The maturities should be entered in chronological order. DerivaGem assumes a piecewise linear zero curve similar to that in Figure 4.1. Note that, when valuing interest rate derivatives, DerivaGem rounds all times to the nearest whole number of days.

When all data have been entered, hit *Enter* on your keyboard. The quoted bond price per $100 of principal, calculated from the zero curve, is displayed when the calculations are complete. You should indicate whether the option is a call or a put and whether the strike price is a quoted (clean) strike price or a cash (dirty) strike price. (The cash price is the quoted price plus accrued interest.) Note that the strike price is entered as the price per $100 of principal. You should indicate whether you are considering a call or a put option and whether you wish to calculate an implied volatility. If you select implied volatility and the normal model or lognormal model is used, DerivaGem implies the short-rate volatility keeping the reversion rate fixed.

Once all the inputs are complete, you should hit *Enter* on your keyboard and click *Calculate*. After that, the tree (if used) can be inspected and charts can be displayed. Note that the tree displayed lasts until the end of the life of the option. DerivaGem uses a much larger tree in its computations to value the underlying bond.

Note that Black's model is similar to Black–Scholes and assumes that the bond price is lognormal at option maturity. The approximate duration relationship in Chapter 4 is used to convert bond yield volatilities to bond price volatilities. This is the usual market practice.

Caps and Swap Options

The third worksheet (Caps_and_Swap_Options) is used for caps and swap options. You should first select the Option Type (Swap Option or Cap/Floor) and Pricing Model (Black-European, Normal-European, or Lognormal-European; these products and the alternative models are explained in John Hull's book *Options, Futures, and Other Derivatives*). You should then enter data on the option you are considering. The Settlement Frequency indicates the frequency of payments and can be Annual, Semi-Annual, Quarterly, or Monthly. The software calculates payment dates by working backward from the end of the life of the cap or swap option. The initial accrual period may be a nonstandard length between 0.5 and 1.5 times a normal accrual period. The software can be used to imply either a volatility or a cap rate/swap rate from the price. When a normal model or a lognormal model is used, DerivaGem implies the short-rate volatility keeping the reversion rate fixed. The zero-coupon yield curve is entered in the table labeled Term Structure. Enter maturities (measured in years) in the first column and the corresponding continuously compounded rates in the second column. The maturities should be entered in chronological order. DerivaGem assumes a piecewise linear zero curve similar to that in Figure 4.1.

Once all the inputs are complete, you should click *Calculate*. After that, charts can be displayed. Note that when Black's model is used, DerivaGem assumes (a) that future interest rates are lognormal when caps are valued and (b) that future swap rates are lognormal when swap options are valued.

Greek Letters

In the Equity_FX_Index_Futures worksheet, the Greek letters are calculated as follows.

Delta: Change in option price per dollar increase in underlying asset.

Gamma: Change in delta per dollar increase in underlying asset.

Vega: Change in option price per 1% increase in volatility (e.g., volatility increases from 20% to 21%).

Rho: Change in option price per 1% increase in interest rate (e.g., interest increases from 5% to 6%).

Theta: Change in option price per calendar day passing.

In the Bond_Options and Caps_and_Swap_Options worksheets, the Greek letters are calculated as follows:

DV01: Change in option price per one basis point upward parallel shift in the zero curve.

Gamma01: Change in DV01 per one basis point upward parallel shift in the zero curve, multiplied by 100.

Vega: Change in option price when volatility parameter increases by 1% (e.g., volatility increases from 20% to 21%)

Table for $N(x)$ When $x \leqslant 0$

This table shows values of $N(x)$ for $x \leqslant 0$. The table should be used with interpolation. For example,

$$N(-0.1234) = N(-0.12) - 0.34[N(-0.12) - N(-0.13)]$$
$$= 0.4522 - 0.34 \times (0.4522 - 0.4483)$$
$$= 0.4509$$

x	.00	.01	.02	.03	.04	.05	.06	.07	.08	.09
−0.0	0.5000	0.4960	0.4920	0.4880	0.4840	0.4801	0.4761	0.4721	0.4681	0.4641
−0.1	0.4602	0.4562	0.4522	0.4483	0.4443	0.4404	0.4364	0.4325	0.4286	0.4247
−0.2	0.4207	0.4168	0.4129	0.4090	0.4052	0.4013	0.3974	0.3936	0.3897	0.3859
−0.3	0.3821	0.3783	0.3745	0.3707	0.3669	0.3632	0.3594	0.3557	0.3520	0.3483
−0.4	0.3446	0.3409	0.3372	0.3336	0.3300	0.3264	0.3228	0.3192	0.3156	0.3121
−0.5	0.3085	0.3050	0.3015	0.2981	0.2946	0.2912	0.2877	0.2843	0.2810	0.2776
−0.6	0.2743	0.2709	0.2676	0.2643	0.2611	0.2578	0.2546	0.2514	0.2483	0.2451
−0.7	0.2420	0.2389	0.2358	0.2327	0.2296	0.2266	0.2236	0.2206	0.2177	0.2148
−0.8	0.2119	0.2090	0.2061	0.2033	0.2005	0.1977	0.1949	0.1922	0.1894	0.1867
−0.9	0.1841	0.1814	0.1788	0.1762	0.1736	0.1711	0.1685	0.1660	0.1635	0.1611
−1.0	0.1587	0.1562	0.1539	0.1515	0.1492	0.1469	0.1446	0.1423	0.1401	0.1379
−1.1	0.1357	0.1335	0.1314	0.1292	0.1271	0.1251	0.1230	0.1210	0.1190	0.1170
−1.2	0.1151	0.1131	0.1112	0.1093	0.1075	0.1056	0.1038	0.1020	0.1003	0.0985
−1.3	0.0968	0.0951	0.0934	0.0918	0.0901	0.0885	0.0869	0.0853	0.0838	0.0823
−1.4	0.0808	0.0793	0.0778	0.0764	0.0749	0.0735	0.0721	0.0708	0.0694	0.0681
−1.5	0.0668	0.0655	0.0643	0.0630	0.0618	0.0606	0.0594	0.0582	0.0571	0.0559
−1.6	0.0548	0.0537	0.0526	0.0516	0.0505	0.0495	0.0485	0.0475	0.0465	0.0455
−1.7	0.0446	0.0436	0.0427	0.0418	0.0409	0.0401	0.0392	0.0384	0.0375	0.0367
−1.8	0.0359	0.0351	0.0344	0.0336	0.0329	0.0322	0.0314	0.0307	0.0301	0.0294
−1.9	0.0287	0.0281	0.0274	0.0268	0.0262	0.0256	0.0250	0.0244	0.0239	0.0233
−2.0	0.0228	0.0222	0.0217	0.0212	0.0207	0.0202	0.0197	0.0192	0.0188	0.0183
−2.1	0.0179	0.0174	0.0170	0.0166	0.0162	0.0158	0.0154	0.0150	0.0146	0.0143
−2.2	0.0139	0.0136	0.0132	0.0129	0.0125	0.0122	0.0119	0.0116	0.0113	0.0110
−2.3	0.0107	0.0104	0.0102	0.0099	0.0096	0.0094	0.0091	0.0089	0.0087	0.0084
−2.4	0.0082	0.0080	0.0078	0.0075	0.0073	0.0071	0.0069	0.0068	0.0066	0.0064
−2.5	0.0062	0.0060	0.0059	0.0057	0.0055	0.0054	0.0052	0.0051	0.0049	0.0048
−2.6	0.0047	0.0045	0.0044	0.0043	0.0041	0.0040	0.0039	0.0038	0.0037	0.0036
−2.7	0.0035	0.0034	0.0033	0.0032	0.0031	0.0030	0.0029	0.0028	0.0027	0.0026
−2.8	0.0026	0.0025	0.0024	0.0024	0.0023	0.0023	0.0022	0.0021	0.0021	0.0020	0.0019
−2.9	0.0019	0.0018	0.0018	0.0017	0.0016	0.0016	0.0015	0.0015	0.0014	0.0014
−3.0	0.0014	0.0013	0.0013	0.0012	0.0012	0.0011	0.0011	0.0011	0.0010	0.0010
−3.1	0.0010	0.0009	0.0009	0.0009	0.0008	0.0008	0.0008	0.0008	0.0007	0.0007
−3.2	0.0007	0.0007	0.0006	0.0006	0.0006	0.0006	0.0006	0.0005	0.0005	0.0005
−3.3	0.0005	0.0005	0.0005	0.0004	0.0004	0.0004	0.0004	0.0004	0.0004	0.0003
−3.4	0.0003	0.0003	0.0003	0.0003	0.0003	0.0003	0.0003	0.0003	0.0003	0.0002
−3.5	0.0002	0.0002	0.0002	0.0002	0.0002	0.0002	0.0002	0.0002	0.0002	0.0002
−3.6	0.0002	0.0002	0.0001	0.0001	0.0001	0.0001	0.0001	0.0001	0.0001	0.0001
−3.7	0.0001	0.0001	0.0001	0.0001	0.0001	0.0001	0.0001	0.0001	0.0001	0.0001
−3.8	0.0001	0.0001	0.0001	0.0001	0.0001	0.0001	0.0001	0.0001	0.0001	0.0001
−3.9	0.0000	0.0000	0.0000	0.0000	0.0000	0.0000	0.0000	0.0000	0.0000	0.0000
−4.0	0.0000	0.0000	0.0000	0.0000	0.0000	0.0000	0.0000	0.0000	0.0000	0.0000

Table for $N(x)$ When $x \geqslant 0$

This table shows values of $N(x)$ for $x \geqslant 0$. The table should be used with interpolation. For example,

$$N(0.6278) = N(0.62) + 0.78[N(0.63) - N(0.62)]$$
$$= 0.7324 + 0.78 \times (0.7357 - 0.7324)$$
$$= 0.7350$$

x	.00	.01	.02	.03	.04	.05	.06	.07	.08	.09
0.0	0.5000	0.5040	0.5080	0.5120	0.5160	0.5199	0.5239	0.5279	0.5319	0.5359
0.1	0.5398	0.5438	0.5478	0.5517	0.5557	0.5596	0.5636	0.5675	0.5714	0.5753
0.2	0.5793	0.5832	0.5871	0.5910	0.5948	0.5987	0.6026	0.6064	0.6103	0.6141
0.3	0.6179	0.6217	0.6255	0.6293	0.6331	0.6368	0.6406	0.6443	0.6480	0.6517
0.4	0.6554	0.6591	0.6628	0.6664	0.6700	0.6736	0.6772	0.6808	0.6844	0.6879
0.5	0.6915	0.6950	0.6985	0.7019	0.7054	0.7088	0.7123	0.7157	0.7190	0.7224
0.6	0.7257	0.7291	0.7324	0.7357	0.7389	0.7422	0.7454	0.7486	0.7517	0.7549
0.7	0.7580	0.7611	0.7642	0.7673	0.7704	0.7734	0.7764	0.7794	0.7823	0.7852
0.8	0.7881	0.7910	0.7939	0.7967	0.7995	0.8023	0.8051	0.8078	0.8106	0.8133
0.9	0.8159	0.8186	0.8212	0.8238	0.8264	0.8289	0.8315	0.8340	0.8365	0.8389
1.0	0.8413	0.8438	0.8461	0.8485	0.8508	0.8531	0.8554	0.8577	0.8599	0.8621
1.1	0.8643	0.8665	0.8686	0.8708	0.8729	0.8749	0.8770	0.8790	0.8810	0.8830
1.2	0.8849	0.8869	0.8888	0.8907	0.8925	0.8944	0.8962	0.8980	0.8997	0.9015
1.3	0.9032	0.9049	0.9066	0.9082	0.9099	0.9115	0.9131	0.9147	0.9162	0.9177
1.4	0.9192	0.9207	0.9222	0.9236	0.9251	0.9265	0.9279	0.9292	0.9306	0.9319
1.5	0.9332	0.9345	0.9357	0.9370	0.9382	0.9394	0.9406	0.9418	0.9429	0.9441
1.6	0.9452	0.9463	0.9474	0.9484	0.9495	0.9505	0.9515	0.9525	0.9535	0.9545
1.7	0.9554	0.9564	0.9573	0.9582	0.9591	0.9599	0.9608	0.9616	0.9625	0.9633
1.8	0.9641	0.9649	0.9656	0.9664	0.9671	0.9678	0.9686	0.9693	0.9699	0.9706
1.9	0.9713	0.9719	0.9726	0.9732	0.9738	0.9744	0.9750	0.9756	0.9761	0.9767
2.0	0.9772	0.9778	0.9783	0.9788	0.9793	0.9798	0.9803	0.9808	0.9812	0.9817
2.1	0.9821	0.9826	0.9830	0.9834	0.9838	0.9842	0.9846	0.9850	0.9854	0.9857
2.2	0.9861	0.9864	0.9868	0.9871	0.9875	0.9878	0.9881	0.9884	0.9887	0.9890
2.3	0.9893	0.9896	0.9898	0.9901	0.9904	0.9906	0.9909	0.9911	0.9913	0.9916
2.4	0.9918	0.9920	0.9922	0.9925	0.9927	0.9929	0.9931	0.9932	0.9934	0.9936
2.5	0.9938	0.9940	0.9941	0.9943	0.9945	0.9946	0.9948	0.9949	0.9951	0.9952
2.6	0.9953	0.9955	0.9956	0.9957	0.9959	0.9960	0.9961	0.9962	0.9963	0.9964
2.7	0.9965	0.9966	0.9967	0.9968	0.9969	0.9970	0.9971	0.9972	0.9973	0.9974
2.8	0.9974	0.9975	0.9976	0.9977	0.9977	0.9978	0.9979	0.9979	0.9980	0.9981
2.9	0.9981	0.9982	0.9982	0.9983	0.9984	0.9984	0.9985	0.9985	0.9986	0.9986
3.0	0.9986	0.9987	0.9987	0.9988	0.9988	0.9989	0.9989	0.9989	0.9990	0.9990
3.1	0.9990	0.9991	0.9991	0.9991	0.9992	0.9992	0.9992	0.9992	0.9993	0.9993
3.2	0.9993	0.9993	0.9994	0.9994	0.9994	0.9994	0.9994	0.9995	0.9995	0.9995
3.3	0.9995	0.9995	0.9995	0.9996	0.9996	0.9996	0.9996	0.9996	0.9996	0.9997
3.4	0.9997	0.9997	0.9997	0.9997	0.9997	0.9997	0.9997	0.9997	0.9997	0.9998
3.5	0.9998	0.9998	0.9998	0.9998	0.9998	0.9998	0.9998	0.9998	0.9998	0.9998
3.6	0.9998	0.9998	0.9999	0.9999	0.9999	0.9999	0.9999	0.9999	0.9999	0.9999
3.7	0.9999	0.9999	0.9999	0.9999	0.9999	0.9999	0.9999	0.9999	0.9999	0.9999
3.8	0.9999	0.9999	0.9999	0.9999	0.9999	0.9999	0.9999	0.9999	0.9999	0.9999
3.9	1.0000	1.0000	1.0000	1.0000	1.0000	1.0000	1.0000	1.0000	1.0000	1.0000
4.0	1.0000	1.0000	1.0000	1.0000	1.0000	1.0000	1.0000	1.0000	1.0000	1.0000

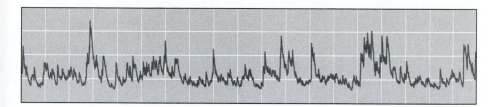

Index

Page numbers in **bold** refer to the Glossary of Terms